**Adobe® Acrobat® Official
JavaScript Reference**

Contents

Preface

Acrobat JavaScript is the cross-platform scripting language of the Adobe®
Acrobat® family of products that includes Acrobat Professional, Acrobat
Standard, and Adobe Reader®. Through JavaScript extensions, the viewer
application and its plug-ins expose much of their functionality to document
authors, form designers, and plug-in developers. This functionality includes
the following features, among others:

- Processing forms within the document
- Batch processing collections of PDF documents
- Developing and maintaining online collaboration schemes
- Communicating with local databases
- Controlling multimedia events

The chapter "JavaScript Scripting Reference" on page 7 describes in detail all
objects, properties and methods in Acrobat JavaScript and gives code
examples. The chapter "New Features and Changes" on page 659
summarizes the new features and changes introduced in this version of
Acrobat and in earlier versions.

Acrobat JavaScript objects, properties, and methods can also be accessed
through Microsoft® Visual Basic® to automate the processing of PDF
documents.

Note: Certain properties and methods that may be discoverable through
JavaScript's introspection facilities are not documented here.
Undocumented properties and methods should not be used. They
are entirely unsupported and subject to change without notice at any
time.

Audience

This document is intended for users familiar with core JavaScript 1.5. The
intended audience includes, but is not limited to, authors of interactive PDF
documents, form designers of intelligent documents, and Acrobat plug-in
developers.

A knowledge of the Acrobat user interface (UI) is essential. Familiarity with
the PDF file format is helpful.

Using Acrobat JavaScript to control additional Acrobat features such as
ADBC, multimedia, SOAP, XML, and various security protocols requires
knowledge of the corresponding technologies.

Resources

The web offers a great many resources to help you with JavaScript in general, as well as JavaScript for PDF.

References

Complete documentation for JavaScript 1.5, the version used by Acrobat 7.0, is available through http://partners.adobe.com/NSjscript/.

The following documents from Adobe are available at the Adobe Solutions Network website at http://partners.adobe.com/asn/acrobat/:

- *Acrobat JavaScript Scripting Reference.* This document, available in online format. On the website, it is accompanied by a spreadsheet (JavaScript_APIs.pdf) that summarizes the methods and properties.
- *PDF Reference, Fifth Edition, Version 1.6.* Provides a description of the PDF file format and is intended primarily for application developers wishing to develop PDF producer applications that create PDF files directly.
- *Acrobat JavaScript Scripting Guide.* Gives an overview and tutorial of Acrobat JavaScript.
- *Acrobat 3D JavaScript Reference.* Describes the JavaScript APIs specific to adding interactivity to 3D annotations within PDF.
- *Acrobat and PDF Library API Overview.* Gives an overview of the objects and methods provided by the plug-in API of the Acrobat viewer.
- *Acrobat and PDF Library API Reference.* Describes in detail the objects and methods provided by the Acrobat viewer's plug-in API.
- *Adobe Dialog Manager Programmer's Guide and Reference.* Describes the Adobe Dialog Manager (ADM), which is a collection of APIs for displaying and controlling dialog boxes in a platform-independent way.
- *Programming Acrobat JavaScript using Visual Basic.* Gives you the information you need to get started using the extended functionality of JavaScript from a Visual Basic programming environment.
- *Developing for Adobe Reader®.* Provides an introduction to those portions of the Adobe Acrobat Software Development Kit (SDK) that pertain to your development efforts for Adobe Reader.

These documents and others related to XML forms are available at http://partners.adobe.com/asn/tech/pdf/xmlformspec.jsp:

- *XFA-Picture Clause 2.0 Specification.* Describes the specific language for describing patterns utilized for formatting or parsing data.
- *XFA-Picture Clause Version 2.2 – CCJK Addendum.* Extends numeric, date, and time picture symbols to allow the parsing and formatting of the

various Chinese, Chinese (Taiwan), Japanese, and Korean numeric, date and time values.

- *XML Form Data Format Specification.* This document is the XFDF specification.

Online Help

The website http://partners.adobe.com/asn/acrobat/ provides Acrobat resources for developers. This listing includes the following sites:

- http://www.adobe.com/support/forums/main.html—Adobe Systems Incorporated provides dedicated online support forums for all Adobe products, including Acrobat and Adobe Reader.
- http://www.adobe.com/support/products/acrobat.html—In addition to the forums, Adobe maintains a searchable support database with answers to commonly asked questions.

Document Conventions

This document uses font conventions common to all Acrobat reference documents and also uses a *quick bar* for many methods and properties to summarize their availability and usage restrictions.

Font Conventions Used in This Book

The Acrobat documentation uses text styles according to the following conventions.

Font	Used for	Examples
monospaced	Paths and file names	`C:\templates\mytmpl.fm`
	Code examples set off from plain text	These are variable declarations: `AVMenu commandMenu,helpMenu;`
	Code items within plain text	The `GetExtensionID` method ...
	Parameter names and literal values in reference documents	The enumeration terminates if `proc` returns `false`.
monospaced italic	Pseudocode	`ACCB1 void ACCB2 ExeProc(void)` `{ do something }`
	Placeholders in code examples	`AFSimple_Calculate(cFunction, cFields)`

Font	Used for	Examples
bold	PostScript language and PDF operators, keywords, dictionary key names	The **setpagedevice** operator
	User interface names	The **File** menu
italic	Document titles that are not live links	*Acrobat Core API Overview*
	New terms	*User space* specifies coordinates for...
	PostScript variables	*filename* **deletefile**

Quick Bars

At the beginning of most property and method descriptions, a small table or *quick bar* provides a summary of the item's availability and usage recommendations.

The quick bar shown here has descriptive column headings that are not shown in the reference.

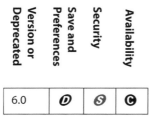

Note: Beginning with Acrobat 7.0, each icon within a quick bar has a link to the description of its meaning.

The following tables show the symbols that can appear in each column and their meanings.

Column 1: Version or Deprecated	

#.#	A number indicates the version of the software in which a property or method became available. If the number is specified, the property or method is available only in versions of the Acrobat software greater than or equal to that number.
	
	For Acrobat 7.0, there are some compatibility issues with older versions. Before accessing this property or method, the script should check that the forms version is greater than or equal to that number to ensure backward compatibility. For example:
	
	`if (typeof app.formsVersion != "undefined" && app.formsVersion >= 7.0)`
	`{`
	`        // Perform version specific operations.`
	`}`
	
	If the first column is blank, no compatibility checking is necessary.
	
	Historical Note: Acrobat JavaScript dates back to Adobe Exchange 3.01. JavaScript functionality was added to this version by means of the "Acrobat Forms Author Plug-in 3.5 Update".

⊘	As the Acrobat JavaScript extensions have evolved, some properties and methods have been superseded by other more flexible or appropriate properties and methods. The use of these older methods is discouraged.

Column 2: Save and Preferences	
Ⓓ	Writing to this property or method dirties (modifies) the PDF document. If the document is subsequently saved, the effects of this method are saved as well. (In Adobe Reader, the document requires specific rights to be saved.)
Ⓟ	Even though this property does not change the document, it can permanently change a user's application preferences.

Column 3: Security	
Ⓢ	This property or method may be available only during certain events for security reasons. These events include batch processing, application start, or execution within the console. (See the event Object , page 314, for details of the Acrobat events.) Beginning with Acrobat 7.0, to execute a security-restricted method (Ⓢ) through a menu event, one of the following must be true: • The JavaScript user preferences item "Enable menu items JavaScript execution privileges" is checked. • The method is executed through a trusted function. For details and examples, see the app.trustedFunction (page 107) method. See "Privileged versus Non-privileged Context" on page 8 for more information. **Note:** (Acrobat 6.0 or later) If the document has been certified by an author who is trusted for embedded JavaScript, methods marked with Ⓢ will execute without restriction, provided other limitations in the quick bar fields are met.

Column 4: Availability	
	If the column is blank, the property or method is allowed in Adobe Reader or Acrobat Professional or Standard.
ⓧ	The property or method is not allowed in Adobe Reader but is available in Acrobat Professional or Standard.
Ⓕ **Ⓒ** **Ⓢ** **Ⓓ** **Ⓖ**	The property or method is allowed in Acrobat Professional or Standard. It can be accessed in Adobe Reader (version 5.1 or later) depending on additional usage rights that have been applied to the document: • **Ⓕ** Requires forms rights • **Ⓒ** Requires the right to manipulate comments • **Ⓢ** Requires the document save right • **Ⓓ** Requires file attachment rights • **Ⓖ** Requires digital signature rights
Ⓟ	The property or method is available only in Acrobat Professional.

Note: The previous edition of this document contained two columns that have been removed. The fifth column referred to the Acrobat Approval product, which has been discontinued. The sixth column was Availability in Adobe Acrobat, which has been combined with column 4.

1 | JavaScript Scripting Reference

Introduction

This chapter is a complete reference to Acrobat JavaScript objects, methods, and properties. It is organized alphabetically by object type.

See "Quick Bars" on page 4 for a description of the symbols that appear at the beginning of property and method descriptions.

Syntax

Some JavaScript objects are *static* objects that can be used as is and must be spelled as indicated. For example, the `app` Object (page 49) represents the JavaScript application. There is only one such object and it must be spelled `app` (case-sensitive).

Other objects are dynamic objects that can be assigned to a variable. For example, a Document Object (page 188) may be obtained and assigned to a variable:

```
var myDoc = app.newDoc();
```

In this example, `myDoc` can access all methods and properties of the Document Object (page 188). For example:

```
myDoc.closeDoc();
```

Method Arguments

Many of the JavaScript methods provided by Acrobat accept either a list of arguments, as is customary in JavaScript, or a single object argument with properties that contain the arguments. For example, these two calls are equivalent:

```
app.alert( "Acrobat Multimedia", 3);

app.alert({ cMsg: "Acrobat Multimedia", nIcon: 3});
```

Note: The JavaScript methods defined in support of multimedia do not accept these two argument formats interchangeably. Use the exact argument format described for each method.

Parameter Help

When using Acrobat Professional, if you give an Acrobat JavaScript method an argument of `acrohelp` and execute that method in the JavaScript Debugger console (or any internal JavaScript editor), the method returns a list of its own arguments.

For example, enter the following code in the console window:

```
app.response(acrohelp)
```

While the cursor is still on the line just entered, press either Ctrl-Enter or the Enter key on the numeric pad. The output to the console is seen to be

```
HelpError: Help.
app.response:1:Console undefined:Exec
====> [cQuestion: string]
====> [cTitle: string]
====> [cDefault: string]
====> [bPassword: boolean]
====> [cLabel: string]
```

Parameters listed in square brackets indicate optional parameters.

Note: Parameter help is not implemented for every Acrobat JavaScript method. For example, it is not implemented for methods defined in the App JavaScript folder.

Pathnames

Several methods take *device-independent pathnames* as arguments. See Section 3.10.1, "File Specification Strings," in the PDF Reference for details about the device-independent pathname format.

Safe Path

Acrobat 6.0 introduced the concept of a *safe path* for JavaScript methods that write data to the local hard drive based on a path passed to it by one of its parameters.

A path cannot point to a system critical folder, for example, a root, windows or system directory. A path is also subject to other unspecified tests.

For many methods, the file name must have an extension appropriate to the type of data that is to be saved. Some methods may have a no-overwrite restriction. These additional restrictions are noted in the documentation.

Generally, when a path is judged to be not safe, a `NotAllowedError` exception is thrown (see "Error Object" on page 311) and the method fails.

Privileged versus Non-privileged Context

Some Acrobat JavaScript methods, marked by ✪ in the third column of the quick bar, have security restrictions. These methods can be executed only in a *privileged context*, which includes console, batch, menu, and application initialization events. All other events (for example, page open and mouse-up events) are considered *non-privileged*.

The description of each security-restricted method indicates the events during which the method can be executed.

Beginning with Acrobat 6.0, security-restricted methods can execute in a non-privileged context if the document is *certified* by the document author for embedded JavaScript.

In Acrobat versions earlier than 7.0, menu events were considered privileged contexts. Beginning with Acrobat 7.0, execution of JavaScript through a menu event is no longer privileged. You can execute security-restricted methods through menu events in one of the following ways:

- By checking the item named **Enable menu items JavaScript execution privileges**.
- By executing a specific method through a *trusted function* (introduced in Acrobat 7.0). Trusted functions allow privileged code—code that normally requires a privileged context to execute—to execute in a non-privileged context. For details and examples, see `app.trustedFunction` (page 107).

User Preferences

There are many references in this document to the Acrobat user preferences. The user preferences dialog box is accessed through the following menu commands, depending on platform:

- Macintosh®: **Acrobat > Preferences**
- Microsoft Windows®: **Edit > Preferences**

The preferences dialog box contains several panels that have relevant commands, including Forms, General, and JavaScript.

ADBC Object

5.0			Ⓧ

The Acrobat Database Connectivity (ADBC) plug-in allows JavaScripts in PDF documents to access databases through a consistent object model. ADBC is a Windows-only feature and requires Open Database Connectivity from Microsoft Corporation (ODBC) to be installed on the client machine.

The object model is based on general principles used in the object models for the ODBC and Java Database Connectivity (JDBC) APIs. Like ODBC and JDBC, ADBC is a means of communicating with a database through Structured Query Language (SQL).

Note: (Security Ⓢ): ADBC provides no security for any of the databases it is programmed to access. It is the responsibility of the database administrator to keep all data secure.

The ADBC object is a global object whose methods allow a JavaScript to create database connection contexts or connections. Related objects used in database access are described separately:

Object	Brief Description
ADBC Object (page 10)	An object through which a list of accessible databases can be obtained and a connection made to one of them.
Connection Object (page 161)	An object through which a list of tables in the connected database can be obtained.
Statement Object (page 619)	An object through which SQL statements can be executed and rows retrieved based on the query.

ADBC Properties

SQL Types

5.0			Ⓧ

The ADBC object has the following constant properties representing various SQL Types:

Constant property name	value	version
SQLT_BIGINT	0	
SQLT_BINARY	1	
SQLT_BIT	2	
SQLT_CHAR	3	

Constant property name	value	version
SQLT_DATE	4	
SQLT_DECIMAL	5	
SQLT_DOUBLE	6	
SQLT_FLOAT	7	
SQLT_INTEGER	8	
SQLT_LONGVARBINARY	9	
SQLT_LONGVARCHAR	10	
SQLT_NUMERIC	11	
SQLT_REAL	12	
SQLT_SMALLINT	13	
SQLT_TIME	14	
SQLT_TIMESTAMP	15	
SQLT_TINYINT	16	
SQLT_VARBINARY	17	
SQLT_VARCHAR	18	
SQLT_NCHAR	19	6.0
SQLT_NVARCHAR	20	6.0
SQLT_NTEXT	21	6.0

The `type` properties of the Column Object (page 159) and ColumnInfo Object (page 160) use these properties.

JavaScript Types

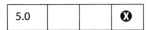

| 5.0 | | | **X** |

The ADBC object has the following constant properties representing various JavaScript data types.

Constant Property Name	value
Numeric	0
String	1
Binary	2
Boolean	3

Constant Property Name	value
Time	4
Date	5
TimeStamp	6

The Statement Object (page 619) methods getColumn (page 620) and getColumnArray (page 620) use these types.

ADBC Methods

getDataSourceList

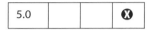

Obtains information about the databases accessible from a given system.

Parameters

None

Returns

An array containing a DataSourceInfo Object (page 169) for each accessible database on the system. The method never fails but may return a zero-length array.

Example

See ADBC.newConnection (page 12).

newConnection

Creates a Connection Object (page 161) associated with the specified database. Optionally, you can supply a user ID and a password.

Note: (Security ⊘, Acrobat 6.0) It is possible to connect to a database using a connection string with no Data Source Name (DSN), but this is only permitted, beginning with Acrobat 6.0, during a console, batch, or menu event. See also "Privileged versus Non-privileged Context" on page 8.

Parameters

cDSN	The data source name (DSN) of the database.
cUID	(optional) User ID.
cPWD	(optional) Password.

Returns

A Connection Object (page 161), or `null` on failure.

Example

```
/* First, get the array of DataSourceInfo objects available on
the system */
var aList = ADBC.getDataSourceList();
console.show(); console.clear();

try {
    /* now display them, while searching for the one named
        "q32000data". */
    var DB = "", msg = "";
    if (aList != null) {
        for (var i=0; i < aList.length; i++) {
            console.println("Name: "+aList[i].name);
            console.println("Description:
"+aList[i].description);
            // and choose one of interest
            if (aList[i].name=="q32000data")
                DB = aList[i].name;
        }
    }

    // did we find the database?
    if (DB != "") {
        // yes, establish a connection.
        console.println("The requested database has been
found!");
        var Connection = ADBC.newConnection(DB);
        if (Connection == null) throw "Not Connected!";
        } else
            // no, display message to console.
            throw "Could not find the requested database.";
} catch (e) {
    console.println(e);
}

// alternatively, we could simple connect directly.
var Connection = ADBC.newConnection("q32000data");
```

Alerter Object

7.0			

Acrobat's multimedia plug-in displays error alerts under various conditions such as a missing media file. JavaScript code can customize these alerts, either for an entire document or for an individual media player.

In an alert situation, the internal function `app.media.alert` is called with parameters containing information about the alert. The `app.media.alert` methods handles the alert by looking for alerter objects and calling their `dispatch` methods, in this order:

```
args.alerter
doc.media.alerter
doc.media.stockAlerter
```

To handle alerts for a specific player, provide an alerter object in `args.alerter` when you call `app.media.createPlayer` (page 126) or `app.media.openPlayer` (page 136).

To handle alerts for an entire document, set `doc.media.alerter` to an alerter object.

All alerts can be suppressed for a player or document by setting `args.alerter` or `doc.media.alerter` to `null`.

`doc.media.stockAlerter` provides the default alerts that are used if a custom alerter is not specified. This property is initialized automatically by `app.media.alert`. Normally, `doc.media.stockAlerter` would not be referenced in developer code.

Alerter Methods

dispatch

7.0			

Called by `app.media.alert` to handle alert situations.

Parameters

alert	An Alert Object (page 15).

Returns

Boolean, `true` to stop further alert processing, `false` to continue processing.

Alert Object

Properties	type	Description
type	String	All alert types.
doc	Document Object (page 188)	All alert types.
fromUser	Boolean	All alert types.
error	Object	Available for the Exception type alert. The error object has a message property: error: { message: String }
errorText	String	Available for the PlayerError type alert.
fileName	String	Available for the FileNotFound type alert.
selection	MediaSelection Object (page 462)	Available for the SelectFailed type alert.

Example

Open a media player and suppress all alerts for this player.

```
app.media.openPlayer({ alerter: null });

// A more elaborate way to do the same thing
app.media.openPlayer(
{
   alerter:
   {
      dispatch() { return true; }
   }
});
```

Example

For all players in this document, log any alerts to a text field and allow the normal alert box to be displayed.

```
function logAlerts( doc )
{
   count = 0;
   doc.alerter =
   {
      dispatch( alert )
      {
         doc.getField("AlertLog").value += "Alert #"
            + ++count + ": " + alert.type + "\n";
      }
   }
}
logAlerts( this );
```

```
// Another way to keep the counter
function logAlerts( doc )
{
   doc.alerter =
   {
      count = 0,
      dispatch( alert )
      {
         doc.getField("AlertLog").value += "Alert #"
            + ++this.count + ": " + alert.type + "\n";
      }
   }
}
logAlerts( this );
```

Example

Handle the PlayerError alert here, with defaults for other alerts.

```
this.media.alerter =
{
   dispatch( alert )
   {
      switch( alert.type )
      {
         case "PlayerError":
         app.alert( "Player error: " + alert.errorText );
         return true;
      }
   }
}
```

AlternatePresentation Object

This object provides an interface to the document's particular alternate presentation. Use the Document Object (page 188) method `alternatePresentations` (page 189) to acquire an AlternatePresentation object.

See the *PDF Reference*, Section 9.4, for additional details on alternate presentations.

AlternatePresentation Properties

active

6.0			

This property is `true` if the presentation is currently active and `false` otherwise. When a presentation is active, it controls how the document that owns it is displayed.

Type: Boolean   *Access: R*

Example

See the `start` (page 17) method for an example.

type

6.0			

The type of the alternate presentation. Currently, the only supported type is "SlideShow".

Type: String   *Access: R*

AlternatePresentation Methods

start

6.0			

Switches the document view into the alternate presentation mode and sets the `active` (page 17) property to `true`. An exception is thrown if this or any other alternate presentation is already active.

Parameters

cOnStop	(optional) An expression to be evaluated by Acrobat when the presentation completes for any reason (as a result of a call to stop (page 18), an explicit user action, or the presentation logic itself).
cCommand	(optional) A command or script to pass to the alternate presentation. **Note:** This command is presentation-specific (not an Acrobat JavaScript expression).

Returns

Nothing

Example

Assume there is a named presentation called "MySlideShow" within the document.

```
// oMySlideShow is an AlternatePresentation object
oMySlideShow = this.alternatePresentations.MySlideShow;
if (!oMySlideShow.active) oMySlideShow.start();
```

Note that this.alternatePresentations (page 189) is used to access the specified presentation by property name.

stop

6.0			

Stops the presentation and switches the document into normal (PDF) presentation. An exception is thrown if this presentation is not active.

Parameters

None

Returns

Nothing

Example

In this example, oMySlideShow is an AlternatePresentations object. See start (page 17) for a related example.

```
// stop the show if already active
if (oMySlideShow.active) oMySlideShow.stop();
```

Annotation Object

This object represents an Acrobat annotation. Annotations can be created using the Acrobat annotation tool or by using the Document Object method `addAnnot` (page 209).

Before an annotation can be accessed, it must be bound to a JavaScript variable through a Document Object method such as `getAnnot` (page 244):

```
var a = this.getAnnot(0, "Important");
```

The script can then manipulate the annotation named "Important" on page 1 (0-based page numbering system) by means of the variable `a`. For example, the following code first stores the type of annotation in the variable `thetype`, then changes the author to "John Q. Public".

```
var thetype = a.type;              // read property
a.author = "John Q. Public";       // write property
```

Another way of accessing the Annotation object is through the Document Object `getAnnots` (page 245) method.

Note: In Adobe Reader 5.1 or later, you can get the value of any annotation property except `contents` (page 28). The ability to set these properties depends on Comments document rights, as indicated by the **Ⓒ** icon.

Note: The user interface in Acrobat refers to annotations as *comments*.

Annotation Types

Annotations are of different types, as reflected in the `type` (page 41) property. The each type is listed in the table below, along with all documented properties returned by the `getProps` (page 43) method.

Annotation Type	Properties
Text	`author` (page 27), `borderEffectIntensity` (page 27), `borderEffectStyle` (page 27), `contents` (page 28), `creationDate` (page 28), `delay` (page 29), `hidden` (page 30), `inReplyTo` (page 31), `intent` (page 31), `lock` (page 32), `modDate` (page 32), `name` (page 33), `noView` (page 34), `noteIcon` (page 33), `opacity` (page 34), `page` (page 34), `point` (page 34), `popupOpen` (page 35), `popupRect` (page 36), `print` (page 36), `readOnly` (page 37), `rect` (page 36), `refType` (page 37), `richContents` (page 37), `rotate` (page 38), `seqNum` (page 38), `state` (page 39), `stateModel` (page 39), `strokeColor` (page 39), `style` (page 40), `subject` (page 40), `toggleNoView` (page 41), `type` (page 41), `width` (page 42)

Annotation Type	Properties
FreeText	alignment (page 24), author (page 27), borderEffectIntensity (page 27), borderEffectStyle (page 27), callout (page 27), contents (page 28), creationDate (page 28), dash (page 28), delay (page 29), fillColor (page 30), hidden (page 30), inReplyTo (page 31), intent (page 31), lineEnding (page 32), lock (page 32), modDate (page 32), name (page 33), noView (page 34), opacity (page 34), page (page 34), print (page 36), readOnly (page 37), rect (page 36), refType (page 37), richContents (page 37), richDefaults (page 38), rotate (page 38), seqNum (page 38), strokeColor (page 39), style (page 40), subject (page 40), textFont (page 40), textSize (page 41), toggleNoView (page 41), type (page 41), width (page 42)
Line	arrowBegin (page 25), arrowEnd (page 26), author (page 27), borderEffectIntensity (page 27), borderEffectStyle (page 27), contents (page 28), creationDate (page 28), dash (page 28), delay (page 29), doCaption (page 29), fillColor (page 30), hidden (page 30), inReplyTo (page 31), intent (page 31), leaderExtend (page 31), leaderLength (page 32), lock (page 32), modDate (page 32), name (page 33), noView (page 34), opacity (page 34), page (page 34), points (page 35), popupOpen (page 35), popupRect (page 36), print (page 36), readOnly (page 37), rect (page 36), refType (page 37), richContents (page 37), rotate (page 38), seqNum (page 38), strokeColor (page 39), style (page 40), subject (page 40), toggleNoView (page 41), type (page 41), width (page 42)
Square	author (page 27), borderEffectIntensity (page 27), borderEffectStyle (page 27), contents (page 28), creationDate (page 28), dash (page 28), delay (page 29), fillColor (page 30), hidden (page 30), inReplyTo (page 31), intent (page 31), lock (page 32), modDate (page 32), name (page 33), noView (page 34), opacity (page 34), page (page 34), popupOpen (page 35), popupRect (page 36), print (page 36), readOnly (page 37), rect (page 36), refType (page 37), richContents (page 37), rotate (page 38), seqNum (page 38), strokeColor (page 39), style (page 40), subject (page 40), toggleNoView (page 41), type (page 41), width (page 42)

Annotation Type	Properties
Circle	author (page 27), borderEffectIntensity (page 27), borderEffectStyle (page 27), contents (page 28), creationDate (page 28), dash (page 28), delay (page 29), fillColor (page 30), hidden (page 30), inReplyTo (page 31), intent (page 31), lock (page 32), modDate (page 32), name (page 33), noView (page 34), opacity (page 34), page (page 34), popupOpen (page 35), popupRect (page 36), print (page 36), readOnly (page 37), rect (page 36), refType (page 37), richContents (page 37), rotate (page 38), seqNum (page 38), strokeColor (page 39), style (page 40), subject (page 40), toggleNoView (page 41), type (page 41), width (page 42)
Polygon	author (page 27), borderEffectIntensity (page 27), borderEffectStyle (page 27), contents (page 28), creationDate (page 28), dash (page 28), delay (page 29), fillColor (page 30), hidden (page 30), inReplyTo (page 31), intent (page 31), lock (page 32), modDate (page 32), name (page 33), noView (page 34), opacity (page 34), page (page 34), popupOpen (page 35), popupRect (page 36), print (page 36), readOnly (page 37), rect (page 36), refType (page 37), richContents (page 37), rotate (page 38), seqNum (page 38), strokeColor (page 39), style (page 40), subject (page 40), toggleNoView (page 41), type (page 41), vertices (page 42), width (page 42)
PolyLine	arrowBegin (page 25), arrowEnd (page 26), author (page 27), borderEffectIntensity (page 27), borderEffectStyle (page 27), contents (page 28), creationDate (page 28), dash (page 28), delay (page 29), fillColor (page 30), hidden (page 30), inReplyTo (page 31), intent (page 31), lock (page 32), modDate (page 32), name (page 33), noView (page 34), opacity (page 34), page (page 34), popupOpen (page 35), popupRect (page 36), print (page 36), readOnly (page 37), rect (page 36), refType (page 37), richContents (page 37), rotate (page 38), seqNum (page 38), strokeColor (page 39), style (page 40), subject (page 40), toggleNoView (page 41), type (page 41), vertices (page 42), width (page 42)

Annotation Type	Properties
Highlight	author (page 27), borderEffectIntensity (page 27), borderEffectStyle (page 27), contents (page 28), creationDate (page 28), delay (page 29), hidden (page 30), inReplyTo (page 31), intent (page 31), lock (page 32), modDate (page 32), name (page 33), noView (page 34), opacity (page 34), page (page 34), popupOpen (page 35), popupRect (page 36), print (page 36), quads (page 36), readOnly (page 37), rect (page 36), refType (page 37), richContents (page 37), rotate (page 38), seqNum (page 38), strokeColor (page 39), style (page 40), subject (page 40), toggleNoView (page 41), type (page 41), width (page 42)
Underline	author (page 27), borderEffectIntensity (page 27), borderEffectStyle (page 27), contents (page 28), creationDate (page 28), delay (page 29), hidden (page 30), inReplyTo (page 31), intent (page 31), lock (page 32), modDate (page 32), name (page 33), noView (page 34), opacity (page 34), page (page 34), popupOpen (page 35), popupRect (page 36), print (page 36), quads (page 36), readOnly (page 37), rect (page 36), refType (page 37), richContents (page 37), rotate (page 38), seqNum (page 38), strokeColor (page 39), style (page 40), subject (page 40), toggleNoView (page 41), type (page 41), width (page 42)
Squiggly	author (page 27), borderEffectIntensity (page 27), borderEffectStyle (page 27), contents (page 28), creationDate (page 28), delay (page 29), hidden (page 30), inReplyTo (page 31), intent (page 31), lock (page 32), modDate (page 32), name (page 33), noView (page 34), opacity (page 34), page (page 34), popupOpen (page 35), popupRect (page 36), print (page 36), quads (page 36), readOnly (page 37), rect (page 36), refType (page 37), richContents (page 37), rotate (page 38), seqNum (page 38), strokeColor (page 39), style (page 40), subject (page 40), toggleNoView (page 41), type (page 41), width (page 42)
StrikeOut	author (page 27), borderEffectIntensity (page 27), borderEffectStyle (page 27), contents (page 28), creationDate (page 28), delay (page 29), hidden (page 30), inReplyTo (page 31), intent (page 31), lock (page 32), modDate (page 32), name (page 33), noView (page 34), opacity (page 34), page (page 34), popupOpen (page 35), popupRect (page 36), print (page 36), quads (page 36), readOnly (page 37), rect (page 36), refType (page 37), richContents (page 37), rotate (page 38), seqNum (page 38), strokeColor (page 39), style (page 40), subject (page 40), toggleNoView (page 41), type (page 41), width (page 42)

Annotation Type	Properties
Stamp	AP (page 25), author (page 27), borderEffectIntensity (page 27), borderEffectStyle (page 27), contents (page 28), creationDate (page 28), delay (page 29), hidden (page 30), inReplyTo (page 31), intent (page 31), lock (page 32), modDate (page 32), name (page 33), noView (page 34), opacity (page 34), page (page 34), popupOpen (page 35), popupRect (page 36), print (page 36), readOnly (page 37), rect (page 36), refType (page 37), rotate (page 38), seqNum (page 38), strokeColor (page 39), style (page 40), subject (page 40), toggleNoView (page 41), type (page 41)
Caret	author (page 27), borderEffectIntensity (page 27), borderEffectStyle (page 27), caretSymbol (page 27), contents (page 28), creationDate (page 28), delay (page 29), hidden (page 30), inReplyTo (page 31), intent (page 31), lock (page 32), modDate (page 32), name (page 33), noView (page 34), opacity (page 34), page (page 34), popupOpen (page 35), popupRect (page 36), print (page 36), readOnly (page 37), rect (page 36), refType (page 37), richContents (page 37), rotate (page 38), seqNum (page 38), strokeColor (page 39), style (page 40), subject (page 40), toggleNoView (page 41), type (page 41), width (page 42)
Ink	author (page 27), borderEffectIntensity (page 27), borderEffectStyle (page 27), contents (page 28), creationDate (page 28), dash (page 28), delay (page 29), gestures (page 30), hidden (page 30), inReplyTo (page 31), intent (page 31), lock (page 32), modDate (page 32), name (page 33), noView (page 34), opacity (page 34), page (page 34), popupOpen (page 35), popupRect (page 36), print (page 36), readOnly (page 37), rect (page 36), refType (page 37), richContents (page 37), rotate (page 38), seqNum (page 38), strokeColor (page 39), style (page 40), subject (page 40), toggleNoView (page 41), type (page 41), width (page 42)
FileAttachment	attachIcon (page 26), author (page 27), borderEffectIntensity (page 27), borderEffectStyle (page 27), contents (page 28), creationDate (page 28), delay (page 29), hidden (page 30), inReplyTo (page 31), intent (page 31), lock (page 32), modDate (page 32), name (page 33), noView (page 34), opacity (page 34), page (page 34), point (page 34), print (page 36), readOnly (page 37), rect (page 36), refType (page 37), richContents (page 37), rotate (page 38), seqNum (page 38), strokeColor (page 39), style (page 40), subject (page 40), toggleNoView (page 41), type (page 41), width (page 42)

Annotation Type	Properties
Sound	author (page 27), borderEffectIntensity (page 27), borderEffectStyle (page 27), contents (page 28), creationDate (page 28), delay (page 29), hidden (page 30), inReplyTo (page 31), intent (page 31), lock (page 32), modDate (page 32), name (page 33), noView (page 34), opacity (page 34), page (page 34), point (page 34), print (page 36), readOnly (page 37), rect (page 36), refType (page 37), richContents (page 37), rotate (page 38), seqNum (page 38), soundIcon (page 39), strokeColor (page 39), style (page 40), subject (page 40), toggleNoView (page 41), type (page 41), width (page 42)

Annotation Properties

The *PDF Reference* documents all Annotation properties and specifies how they are stored.

Some property values are stored in the PDF document as names (see section 3.2.4 on name objects in the *PDF Reference*), and others are stored as strings (see section 3.2.3 on string objects in the *PDF Reference*). A property stored as a name can have only 127 characters.

Examples of properties that have a 127-character limit include AP, beginArrow, endArrow, attachIcon, noteIcon, and soundIcon.

alignment

Controls the alignment of the text for a FreeText annotation.

Alignment	Value
Left aligned	0
Centered	1
Right aligned	2

Type: Number   *Access: R/W*   *Annotations: FreeText*

AP

5.0	*D*		*C*

The named appearance of the stamp to be used in displaying a stamp annotation. The names of the standard stamp annotations are given below:

```
Approved
AsIs
Confidential
Departmental
Draft
Experimental
Expired
Final
ForComment
ForPublicRelease
NotApproved
NotForPublicRelease
Sold
TopSecret
```

Type: String   *Access: R/W*   *Annotations: Stamp*

Example

```
var annot = this.addAnnot({
    page: 0,
    type: "Stamp",
    author: "A. C. Robat",
    name: "myStamp",
    rect: [400, 400, 550, 500],
    contents: "Try it again, this time with order and method!",
    AP: "NotApproved"
});
```

Note: The name of a particular stamp can be found by opening the PDF file in the `Stamps` folder that contains the stamp in question. For a list of stamp names currently in use in the document, see the Document Object `icons` (page 196) property.

arrowBegin

Determines the line cap style that specifies the shape to be used at the beginning of a line annotation. Permissible values are listed below:

```
None (default)
OpenArrow
ClosedArrow
ROpenArrow     // Acrobat 6.0
RClosedArrow   // Acrobat 6.0
```

```
Butt           // Acrobat 6.0
Diamond
Circle
Square
Slash          // Acrobat 7.0
```

Type: String   *Access: R/W*   *Annotations: Line, PolyLine*

Example

See the setProps (page 45) method.

arrowEnd

Determines the line cap style that specifies the shape to be used at the end of a line annotation. Allowed values follow:

```
None (default)
OpenArrow
ClosedArrow
ROpenArrow     // Acrobat 6.0
RClosedArrow   // Acrobat 6.0
Butt           // Acrobat 6.0
Diamond
Circle
Square
Slash          // Acrobat 7.0
```

Type: String   *Access: R/W*   *Annotations: Line, PolyLine*

Example

See the setProps (page 45) method.

attachIcon

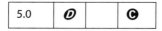

The name of an icon to be used in displaying the annotation. Recognized values are listed below:

```
Paperclip
PushPin (default)
Graph
Tag
```

Type: String   *Access: R/W*   *Annotations: FileAttachment*

author

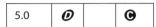

Gets or sets the author of the annotation.

Type: String *Access: R/W* *Annotations: all*

Example

See the `contents` (page 28) property.

borderEffectIntensity

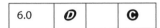

The intensity of the border effect, if any. This represents how cloudy a cloudy rectangle, polygon, or oval is.

Type: Number *Access: R/W* *Annotations: all*

borderEffectStyle

If non-empty, the name of a border effect style. Currently, the only supported border effects are the empty string (nothing) or "C" for cloudy.

Type: String *Access: R/W* *Annotations: all*

callout

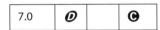

An array of four or six numbers specifying a callout line attached to the free text annotation. See Table 8.21 in the *PDF Reference* for additional details.

Type: Array *Access: R/W* *Annotations: FreeText*

caretSymbol

The symbol associated with a Caret annotation. Valid values are "" (nothing), "P" (paragraph symbol) or "S" (space symbol).

Type: String *Access: R/W* *Annotations: Caret*

---

contents

Accesses the contents of any annotation that has a pop-up window. For sound and file attachment annotations, specifies the text to be displayed as a description.

Type: String   *Access: R/W*   *Annotations: all*

Example

```
var annot = this.addAnnot({
    page: 0,
    type: "Text",
    point: [400,500],
    author: "A. C. Robat",
    contents: "Call Smith to get help on this paragraph.",
    noteIcon: "Help"
});
```

See also the Document Object `addAnnot` (page 209) method.

creationDate

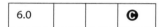

The date and time when the annotation was created.

Type: Date   *Access: R*   *Annotations: all*

dash

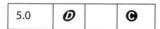

A dash array defining a pattern of dashes and gaps to be used in drawing a dashed border. For example, a value of [3, 2] specifies a border drawn with 3-point dashes alternating with 2-point gaps.

To set the dash array, the `style` property has to be set to D.

Type: Array   *Access: R/W*   *Annotations: FreeText, Line, PolyLine, Polygon, Circle, Square, Ink*

Example

Assuming `annot` is an Annotation Object (page 19), this example changes the border to dashed.

```
annot.setProps({ style: "D", dash: [3,2] });
```

See also the example following the `delay` (page 29) property.

---

delay

If `true`, property changes to the annotation are queued and then executed when `delay` is set back to `false`. (Similar to the Field Object `delay` (page 382) property.)

Type: Boolean   *Access: R/W*   *Annotations: all*

Example

Assuming `annot` is an Annotation Object (page 19), the code below changes the border to dashed.

```
annot.delay=true;
annot.style = "D";
annot.dash = [4,3];
annot.delay = false;
```

doc

The Document Object (page 188) of the document in which the annotation resides.

Type: Document Object   *Access: R*   *Annotations: all*

Example

```
var inch = 72;
var annot = this.addAnnot({
    page: 0,
    type: "Square",
    rect: [1*inch, 3*inch, 2*inch, 3.5*inch]
});
/* displays, for example,,
"file:///C|/Adobe/Annots/myDoc.pdf" */
console.println(annot.doc.URL);
```

doCaption

If `true`, draws the rich contents in the line appearance itself. In the UI, this property corresponds to **Show Text in Line** on the property dialog box.

Type: Boolean   *Access: R/W*   *Annotations: Line*

fillColor

5.0	*D*		**C**

Sets the background color for circle, square, line, polygon, polyline, and free text annotations. Values are defined by using `transparent`, `gray`, RGB or CMYK color. See "Color Arrays" on page 156 for information on defining color arrays and how values are used with this property.

Type: Color *Access: R/W* *Annotations: Circle, Square, Line, Polygon, PolyLine, FreeText*

Example

```
var annot = this.addAnnot(
{
    type: "Circle",
    page: 0,
    rect: [200,200,400,300],
    author: "A. C. Robat",
    name: "myCircle",
    popupOpen: true,
    popupRect: [200,100,400,200],
    contents: "Hi World!",
    strokeColor: color.red,
    fillColor: ["RGB",1,1,.855]
});
```

gestures

5.0	*D*		**C**

An array of arrays, each representing a stroked path. Each array is a series of alternating *x* and *y* coordinates in default user space, specifying points along the path. When drawn, the points are connected by straight lines or curves in an implementation-dependent way. See "Ink Annotations" in the *PDF Reference* for more details.

Type: Array *Access: R/W* *Annotations: Ink*

hidden

5.0	*D*		**C**

If `true`, the annotation is not shown and there is no user interaction, display, or printing of the annotation.

Type: Boolean *Access: R/W* *Annotations: all*

---

inReplyTo

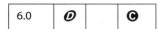

If non-empty, specifies the `name` (page 33) value of the annotation that this annotation is in reply to.

Type: String   *Access: R/W*   *Annotations: all*

intent

This property allows a markup annotation type to behave differently, depending on the intended use of the annotation. For example, the Callout Tool is a free text annotation with `intent` set to `FreeTextCallout`.

Though this property is defined for all annotations, currently, only free text, polygon, and line annotations have non-empty values for `intent`.

Type: String   *Access: R/W*   *Annotations: all*

The table below lists the tools available through the UI for creating annotations with special appearances.

UI	Annotation Type	intent
Callout Tool	`FreeText`	`FreeTextCallout`
Cloud Tool	`Polygon`	`PolygonCloud`
Arrow Tool	`Line`	`LineArrow`
Dimensioning Tool	`Line`	`LineDimension`

leaderExtend

Specifies the length of *leader line extensions* that extend from both endpoints of the line, perpendicular to the line. These lines extend from the line proper 180 degrees from the leader lines. The value should always be greater than or equal to zero.

The default is zero (no leader line extension).

Type: Number   *Access: R/W*   *Annotations: Line*

leaderLength

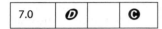

Specifies the length of *leader lines* that extend from both endpoints of the line, perpendicular to the line. The value may be negative to specify an alternate orientation of the leader lines.

The default is 0 (no leader line).

Type: Number　　　　*Access: R/W*　　*Annotations: Line*

lineEnding

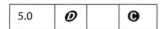

This property determines how the end of a callout line is stroked. It is relevant only for a free text annotation when the value of `intent` (page 31) is `FreeTextCallout`. Recognized values are listed below:

```
None (default)
OpenArrow
ClosedArrow
ROpenArrow         // Acrobat 6.0
RClosedArrow       // Acrobat 6.0
Butt               // Acrobat 6.0
Diamond
Circle
Square
Slash              // Acrobat 7.0
```

Type: String　　　　*Access: R/W*　　*Annotations: FreeText*

lock

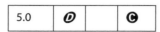

If `true`, the annotation is locked, which is equivalent to `readOnly` except that the annotation is accessible through the properties dialog box in the UI.

Type: Boolean　　　　*Access: R/W*　　*Annotations: all*

modDate

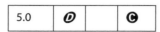

The last modification date for the annotation.

Type: Date　　　　*Access: R/W*　　*Annotations: all*

Example

```
// This example prints the modification date to the console
console.println(util.printd("mmmm dd, yyyy", annot.modDate));
```

name

The name of an annotation. This value can be used by the Document Object getAnnot (page 244) method to find and access the properties and methods of the annotation.

Type: String   *Access: R/W*   *Annotations: all*

Example

```
// This code locates the annotation named "myNote"
// and appends a comment.
var gannot = this.getAnnot(0, "myNote");
gannot.contents += "\r\rDon't forget to check with Smith";
```

noteIcon

The name of an icon to be used in displaying the annotation. Recognized values are given below:

```
Check
Circle
Comment
Cross
Help
Insert
Key
NewParagraph
Note(default)
Paragraph
RightArrow
RightPointer
Star
UpArrow
UpLeftArrow
```

Type: String   *Access: R/W*   *Annotations: Text*

Example

See the contents (page 28) property.

noView

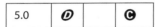

If `true`, the annotation is hidden, but if the annotation has an appearance, that appearance should be used for printing only.

Type: Boolean   *Access: R/W*   *Annotations: all*

Example

See the `toggleNoView` (page 41) property.

opacity

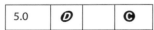

The constant opacity value to be used in painting the annotation. This value applies to all visible elements of the annotation in its closed state (including its background and border), but not to the pop-up window that appears when the annotation is opened. Permissible values are 0.0 - 1.0. A value of 0.5 makes the annotation semitransparent.

Type: Number   *Access: R/W*   *Annotations: all*

page

The page on which the annotation resides.

Type: Integer   *Access: R/W*   *Annotations: all*

Example

The following code moves the Annotation Object (page 19) `annot` from its current page to page 3 (0-based page numbering system).

```
annot.page = 2;
```

point

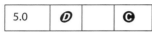

An array of two numbers, [*xul*, *yul*] that specifies the upper left-hand corner in default user space of the icon for a text, sound or file attachment annotation.

Type: Array   *Access: R/W*   *Annotations: Text, Sound, FileAttachment*

Example

```
var annot = this.addAnnot({
    page: 0,
    type: "Text",
    point: [400,500],
    contents: "Call Smith to get help on this paragraph.",
    popupRect: [400,400,550,500],
    popupOpen: true,
    noteIcon: "Help"
});
```

See also the `noteIcon` (page 33) property and the Document Object `addAnnot` (page 209) method.

points

An array of two points, [[x1, y1], [x2, y2]], specifying the starting and ending coordinates of the line in default user space.

Type: Array   *Access: R/W*   *Annotations: Line*

Example

```
var annot = this.addAnnot({
    type: "Line",
    page: 0,
    author: "A. C. Robat",
    contents: "Look at this again!",
    points: [[10,40],[200,200]],
});
```

See the `arrowBegin` (page 25) and `arrowEnd` (page 26) properties, the `setProps` (page 45) method, and the Document Object `addAnnot` (page 209) method.

popupOpen

If `true`, the pop-up text note appears open when the page is displayed.

Type: Boolean   *Access: R/W*   *Annotations: all except FreeText,*
                                         Sound, FileAttachment

Example

See the `print` (page 36) property.

popupRect

An array of four numbers [*xll*, *yll*, *xur*, *yur*] specifying the lower-left *x*, lower-left *y*, upper-right *x*, and upper-right *y* coordinates—in default user space—of the rectangle of the pop-up annotation associated with a parent annotation and defines the location of the pop-up annotation on the page.

Type: Array   *Access: R/W*   *Annotations: all except FreeText, Sound, FileAttachment*

Example

See the `print` (page 36) property.

print

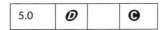

Indicates whether the annotation should be printed (`true`) or not (`false`).

Type: Boolean   *Access: R/W*   *Annotations: all*

quads

An array of 8 x *n* numbers specifying the coordinates of *n* quadrilaterals in default user space. Each quadrilateral encompasses a word or group of contiguous words in the text underlying the annotation. See Table 8.26 in the *PDF Reference* for more details. The `quads` for a word can be obtained through calls to the Document Object `getPageNthWordQuads` (page 255) method.

Type: Array   *Access: R/W*   *Annotations: Highlight, StrikeOut, Underline, Squiggly*

Example

See the Document Object `getPageNthWordQuads` (page 255) method.

rect

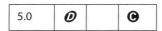

The `rect` array consists of four numbers [*xll*, *yll*, *xur*, *yur*] specifying the lower-left *x*, lower-left *y*, upper-right *x*, and upper-right *y* coordinates—in default user space—of the rectangle defining the location of the annotation on the page. See also the popupRect (page 36) property.

Type: Array   *Access: R/W*   *Annotations: all*

readOnly

If true, the annotation should display but not interact with the user.

Type: Boolean   *Access: R/W*   *Annotations: all*

refType

The reference type of the annotation. The property distinguishes whether inReplyTo (page 31) indicates a plain threaded discussion relationship or a group relationship. Recognized values are "R" and "Group". See Table 8.17 in the *PDF Reference* for additional details.

Type: String   *Access: R/W*   *Annotations: all*

richContents

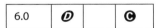

This property gets the text contents and formatting of an annotation. The rich text contents are represented as an array of Span Objects (page 601) containing the text contents and formatting of the annotation.

Type: Array of   *Access: R/W*   *Annotations: all except Sound,*
Span Objects   *FileAttachment*

Example

Create a text annotation and give it some rich text contents.

```
var annot = this.addAnnot({
    page: 0,
    type: "Text",
    point: [72,500],
    popupRect: [72, 500,6*72,500-2*72],
    popupOpen: true,
    noteIcon: "Help"
});

var spans = new Array();
spans[0] = new Object();
spans[0].text = "Attention:\r";
```

```
spans[0].textColor = color.blue;
spans[0].textSize = 18;

spans[1] = new Object();
spans[1].text = "Adobe Acrobat 6.0\r";
spans[1].textColor = color.red;
spans[1].textSize = 20;
spans[1].alignment = "center";

spans[2] = new Object();
spans[2].text = "will soon be here!";
spans[2].textColor = color.green;
spans[2].fontStyle = "italic";
spans[2].underline = true;
spans[2].alignment = "right";

// now give the rich field a rich value
annot.richContents = spans;
```

See also the Field Object `richValue` (page 392) method and the event
Object methods `richValue` (page 333), `richChange` (page 331), and
`richChangeEx` (page 332) for examples of using the Span Object.

richDefaults

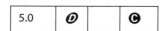

This property defines the default style attributes for a free text annotation.
See the description of the Field Object `defaultStyle` (page 380)
property for additional details.

Type: Span Object   *Access: R/W*   *Fields: FreeText*

rotate

The number of degrees (0, 90, 180, 270) the annotation is rotated
counterclockwise relative to the page. This property is only significant for
free text annotations.

Type: Integer   *Access: R/W*   *Annotations: FreeText*

seqNum

A read-only sequence number for the annotation on the page.

Type: Integer   *Access: R*   *Annotations: all*

soundIcon

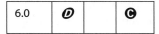

The name of an icon to be used in displaying the sound annotation. A value of "Speaker" is recognized.

Type: String   *Access: R/W*   *Annotations: Sound*

state

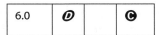

The state of the text annotation. The values of this property depend on the stateModel. For a state model of Marked, values are Marked and Unmarked. For a Review state model, the values are Accepted, Rejected, Cancelled, Completed and None.

Type: String   *Access: R/W*   *Annotations: Text*

stateModel

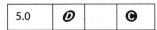

Beginning with Acrobat 6.0, annotations may have an author-specific state associated with them. The state is specified a separate text annotation that refers to the original annotation by means of its **IRT** entry (see the `inReplyTo` (page 31) property). There are two types of state models, "Marked" and "Review".

Type: String   *Access: R/W*   *Annotations: Text*

See also the `getStateInModel` (page 44) method.

strokeColor

Sets the appearance color of the annotation. Values are defined by using `transparent`, `gray`, `RGB`, or `CMYK` color. In the case of a free text annotation, `strokeColor` sets the border and text colors. See "Color Arrays" on page 156 for information on defining color arrays and how values are used with this property.

Type: Color   *Access: R/W*   *Annotations: all*

Example

```
// Make a text note red
var annot = this.addAnnot({type: "Text"});
annot.strokeColor = color.red;
```

style

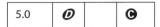

This property gets and sets the border style. Recognized values are **s** (solid) and **D** (dashed). The style property is defined for all annotation types but is only relevant for line, free text, circle, square, polyline, polygon and ink annotations.

Type: String   *Access: R/W*   *Annotations: all*

See the `dash` (page 28) property for an example.

subject

Text representing a short description of the subject being addressed by the annotation. The text appears in the title bar of the pop-up window, if there is one, or the properties dialog box.

Type: String   *Access: R/W*   *Annotations: all*

textFont

Determines the font that is used when laying out text in a free text annotation. Valid fonts are defined as properties of the `font` Object (page 396) (see the Field Object `textFont` (page 396) property).

An arbitrary font can be used when laying out a free text annotation by setting the value of `textFont` equal to a string that represents the PostScript name of the font.

Type: String   *Access: R/W*   *Annotations: FreeText*

Example

The following example shows the use of this property and the font object.

```
// Create FreeText annotation with Helvetica
var annot = this.addAnnot({
    page: 0,
    type: "FreeText",
    textFont: font.Helv,   // or, textFont: "Viva-Regular",
```

```
        textSize: 10,
        rect: [200, 300, 200+150, 300+3*12],
                                // height for three lines
        width: 1,
        alignment: 1
    });
```

textSize

The text size (in points) for a free text annotation. Valid text sizes include zero and the range from 4 to 144, inclusive. Zero indicates the largest point size that allows all the text to fit in the annotation's rectangle.

Type: Number   *Access: R/W*   *Annotations: FreeText*

Example

See the textFont (page 40) property.

toggleNoView

If true, the noView (page 34) flag is toggled when the mouse hovers over the annotation or the annotation is selected.

If an annotation has both the noView and toggleNoView flags set, the annotation is usually invisible. However, when the mouse is over it or it is selected, it becomes visible.

Type: Boolean   *Access: R/W*   *Annotations: all*

type

The type of annotation. The type of an annotation can only be set within the object-literal argument of the Document Object addAnnot (page 209) method. The valid values are:

```
Text
FreeText
Line
Square
Circle
Polygon
PolyLine
Highlight
Underline
```

```
Squiggly
StrikeOut
Stamp
Caret
Ink
FileAttachment
Sound
```

Type: String   *Access: R*   *Annotations: all*

vertices

An array of coordinate arrays representing the alternating horizontal and vertical coordinates, respectively, of each vertex, in default user space of a polygon or polyline annotation. See Table 8.25 in the *PDF Reference* for details.

Type: Array of arrays   *Access: R/W*   *Annotations: Polygon, PolyLine*

width

The border width in points. If this value is 0, no border is drawn. The default value is 1.

Type: Number   *Access: R/W*   *Annotations: Square, Circle, Line, Ink, FreeText*

Annotation Methods

destroy

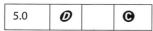

Destroys the annotation, removing it from the page. The object becomes invalid.

Parameters

None

Returns

Nothing

Example

```
// remove all "FreeText" annotations on page 0
var annots = this.getAnnots({ nPage:0 });
for (var i = 0; i < annots.length; i++)
    if (annots[i].type == "FreeText") annots[i].destroy();
```

getProps

5.0			

Get the collected properties of an annotation. Can be used to copy an annotation.

Parameters

None

Returns

An object literal of the properties of the annotation. The object literal is just like the one passed to the Document Object addAnnot (page 209) method.

Example 1

```
var annot = this.addAnnot({
    page: 0,
    type: "Text",
    rect: [40, 40, 140, 140]
});

    // Make a copy of the properties of annot
var copy_props = annot.getProps();

// Now create a new annot with the same properties on every
page
var numpages = this.numPages;
for (var i=0; i < numpages; i++) {
    var copy_annot = this.addAnnot(copy_props);
    // but move it to page i
    copy_annot.page=i;
}
```

Example 2

Display all properties and values of an annotation.

```
var a = this.getAnnots(0); // get all annots on page 0
if ( a != null ) {
    var p = a[0].getProps();// get the properties of first one
    for ( o in p ) console.println( o + " : " + p[o] );
}
```

getStateInModel

6.0			

Gets the current state of the annotation in the context of a state model. See also the `transitionToState` (page 45) method.

Parameters

`cStateModel`	The state model to determine the state of the annotation.

Returns

The result is an array of the identifiers for the current state of the annotation:

- If the state model was defined to be exclusive, there is only a single state (or no states if the state has not been set).
- If the state model is non-exclusive, there may be multiple states (or no entries if the state has not been set and there is no default).

Exceptions

None

Example

Report on the status of all annotations on all pages of this document.

```
annots = this.getAnnots()
for ( var i= 0; i< annots.length; i++) {
    states = annots[i].getStateInModel("Review");
    if ( states.length > 0 ) {
        for(j = 0; j < states.length; j++)
        {
            var d = util.printd(2, states[j].modDate);
            var s = states[j].state;
            var a = states[j].author;

            console.println(annots[i].type + ": " + a + " "
                + s + " " + d + "on page "
                + (annots[i].page+1) );
        }

    }
}
```

setProps

5.0	*Ⓓ*		Ⓒ

Sets many properties of an annotation simultaneously.

Parameters

object literal	A generic object that specifies the properties of the Annotation Object (page 19) to be created such as type (page 41), rect (page 36), and page (page 34). This object is the same as the parameter of the Document Object addAnnot (page 209) method.

Returns

The Annotation Object (page 19)

Example

```
var annot = this.addAnnot({type: "Line"})
annot.setProps({
   page: 0,
   points: [[10,40],[200,200]],
   strokeColor: color.red,
   author: "A. C. Robat",
   contents: "Check with Jones on this point.",
   popupOpen: true,
   popupRect: [200, 100, 400, 200], // place rect at tip of the
arrow
   arrowBegin: "Diamond",
   arrowEnd: "OpenArrow"
});
```

transitionToState

6.0	*Ⓓ*		Ⓒ

Sets the state of the annotation to cState by performing a state transition. The state transition is recorded in the audit trail of the annotation.

See also the getStateInModel (page 44) method.

Note: For the states to work correctly in a multiuser environment, all users must have the same state model definitions. Therefore, it is best to place state model definitions in a folder-level JavaScript file that can be distributed to all users or installed on all systems.

Parameters

cStateModel	The state model in which to perform the state transition. cStateModel must have been previously added by calling the Collab method addStateModel (page 153).
cState	A valid state in the state model to transition to.

Returns

Nothing

Exceptions

None

Example

```
try {
    // Create a document
    var myDoc = app.newDoc();
    // Create an annot
    var myAnnot = myDoc.addAnnot
    ({
        page: 0,
        type: "Text",
        point: [300,400],
        name: "myAnnot",
    });


    // Create the state model
    var myStates = new Object();
    myStates["initial"] = {cUIName: "Haven't reviewed it"};
    myStates["approved"] = {cUIName: "I approve"};
    myStates["rejected"] = {cUIName: "Forget it"};
    myStates["resubmit"] = {cUIName: "Make some changes"};
    Collab.addStateModel({
        cName: "ReviewStates",
        cUIName: "My Review",
        oStates: myStates,
        cDefault: "initial"
    });
} catch(e) { console.println(e); }

// Change the states
myAnnot.transitionToState("ReviewStates", "resubmit");
myAnnot.transitionToState("ReviewStates", "approved");
```

Annot3D Object

An Annot3D object represents a particular Acrobat 3D annotation; that is, an annotation created using the Acrobat 3D Tool. The Annot3D object can be acquired from the Document Object methods `getAnnot3D` (page 245) and `getAnnots3D` (page 246).

Annot3D Properties

activated

7.0			

A Boolean that indicates whether the annotation is displaying the 3D artwork (`true`) or just the posterboard picture (`false`).

See the `context3D` (page 47) property.

Type: Boolean   *Access: R/W*

context3D

7.0			

If `activated` (page 47) is `true`, this property returns the context of the 3D annotation (a SceneContext3d object containing the 3D scene. (See the Acrobat *3D JavaScript Reference* for more information.) If `activated` is `false`, this property returns `undefined`.

Type: SceneContext3d object   *Access: R*

innerRect

7.0			

An array of four numbers $[x_{ll}, y_{ll}, x_{ur}, y_{ur}]$ specifying the lower-left x, lower-left y, upper-right *x* and upper-right *y* coordinates, in the coordinate system of the annotation (lower-left is [0, 0], top right is [width, height]), of the 3D annotation's **3DB** box, where the 3D artwork is rendered.

Type: Array   *Access: R*

name

The name of the annotation.

Type: String   *Access: R*

page

The 0-based page number of the page containing the annotation.

Type: Integer   *Access: R*

rect

7.0

Returns an array of four numbers [x_{ll}, y_{ll}, x_{ur}, y_{ur}] specifying the lower-left x, lower-left y, upper-right *x* and upper-right *y* coordinates, in default user space, of the rectangle defining the location of the annotation on the page.

Type: Array   *Access: R/W*

app Object

A static JavaScript object that represents the Acrobat application. It defines a number of Acrobat-specific functions plus a variety of utility routines and convenience functions.

app Properties

activeDocs

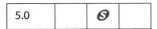

An array containing the Document Object (page 188) for each active document. If no documents are active, `activeDocs` returns nothing; that is, it has the same behavior as `d = new Array(0)` in core JavaScript.

In versions of Acrobat earlier than 7.0, executing the script `d = app.activeDocs` in the console returned `[object Global]` to the console. Beginning with Acrobat 7.0, no `toString()` value is output to the console.

The following notes relate to Security 🔒:

- In Acrobat 5.0, this property returns an array containing the Document Object (page 188) for each active document.

- In Acrobat 5.0.5, this property was changed to return an array of Document Objects (page 188) of only those open documents that have the Document Object `disclosed` (page 193) property set to `true`.

- Beginning with the Acrobat 5.0.5 Accessibility and Forms Patch and continuing with Acrobat 6.0 or later, the behavior is as follows: During a batch, console or menu event, `activeDocs` ignores the `disclosed` property and returns an array of Document Objects (page 188) of the active documents. During any other event, `activeDocs` returns an array of Document Objects of only those active documents that have `disclosed` (page 193) set to `true`.

- Beginning with Acrobat 7.0, execution of JavaScript through a menu event is no longer privileged. See "Privileged versus Non-privileged Context" on page 8 for details.

The array returned by `app.activeDocs` includes any documents opened by `app.openDoc` (page 97) with the `bHidden` parameter set to `true`, subject to the security restrictions described above.

Type: Array   *Access: R*

Example

This example searches among the open documents for the document with a title of "myDoc", then inserts a button in that document using the Document Object `addField` (page 211) method. Whether the documents must be `disclosed` depends on the version of Acrobat executing this code and on the placement of the code (for example, console versus mouse-up action).

```
var d = app.activeDocs;
for (var i=0; i < d.length; i++)
if (d[i].info.Title == "myDoc") {
    var f = d[i].addField("myButton", "button", 0 , \
        [20, 100, 100, 20]);
    f.setAction("MouseUp","app.beep(0)");
    f.fillColor=color.gray;
}
```

calculate

If `true` (the default value), calculations can be performed. If `false`, calculations are not permitted.

The use of this property is discouraged; the Document Object property `calculate` (page 191) is preferred.

Type: Boolean   *Access: R/W*

constants

7.0			

A wrapper object for holding various constant values. Currently, this property returns an object with a single property, `align`.

`app.constants.align` is an object that has the possible properties `left`, `center`, `right`, `top`, and `bottom`, indicating the type of alignment. These values can be used to specify alignment, such as when adding a watermark.

Type: Object   *Access: R*

Example

See the Document Object methods `addWatermarkFromFile` (page 218) and `addWatermarkFromText` (page 221) for examples.

focusRect

4.05	*P*		

Turns the focus rectangle on and off. The focus rectangle is the faint dotted line around buttons, check boxes, radio buttons, and signatures to indicate that the form field has the keyboard focus. A value of `true` turns on the focus rectangle.

Type: Boolean   *Access: R/W*

Example

```
app.focusRect = false; // don't want faint dotted lines around
fields
```

formsVersion

4.0			

The version number of the viewer forms software. Check this property to determine whether objects, properties, or methods in newer versions of the software are available if you want to maintain backward compatibility in your scripts.

Type: Number   *Access: R*

Example

```
if (typeof app.formsVersion != "undefined" &&
app.formsVersion >= 5.0)
{
    // Perform version specific operations here.
    // For example, toggle full screen mode
    app.fs.cursor = cursor.visible;
    app.fs.defaultTransition = "";
    app.fs.useTimer = false;
    app.fs.isFullScreen = !app.fs.isFullScreen;
}
else app.fullscreen = !app.fullscreen;
```

fromPDFConverters

6.0			

An array of file type conversion ID strings. A conversion ID string can be passed to the Document Object `saveAs` (page 282) method.

Type: Array   *Access: R*

Example

List all currently supported conversion ID strings.

```
for ( var i = 0; i < app.fromPDFConverters.length; i++)
    console.println(app.fromPDFConverters[i]);
```

fs

A FullScreen Object (page 425), which can be used to access the fullscreen properties.

Type: object　　　　*Access: R*

Example

```
// This code puts the viewer into fullscreen
// (presentation) mode.
app.fs.isFullScreen = true;
```

See also `fullScreenObject.isFullScreen` (page 426).

fullscreen

Note: The use of this property is discouraged; it has been superseded by the FullScreen Object property `isFullScreen` (page 426). The `fs` (page 52) method returns a FullScreen Object (page 425) that can be used to access the fullscreen properties.

Controls whether the viewer is in fullscreen mode or regular viewing mode.

Note: A PDF document being viewed from within a web browser cannot be put into fullscreen mode. Fullscreen mode can be initiated from within the browser, but applies only to a document open in the Acrobat viewer application, if any, not to the browser itself.

Type: Boolean　　　　*Access: R/W*

language

3.01			

The language of the running Acrobat viewer. It can be one of the following strings.

String	Language
CHS	Chinese Simplified
CHT	Chinese Traditional
DAN	Danish
DEU	German
ENU	English
ESP	Spanish
FRA	French
ITA	Italian
KOR	Korean
JPN	Japanese
NLD	Dutch
NOR	Norwegian
PTB	Brazilian Portuguese
SUO	Finnish
SVE	Swedish

Type: String   *Access: R*

media

6.0			

Defines an extensive number of properties and methods useful for setting up and controlling multimedia player.

See the `app.media` Object (page 115) for a listing of the properties and methods of this object, as well as numerous examples of use.

Type: Object   *Access: R/W*

---

monitors

6.0			

A Monitors Object (page 477), which is an array containing one or more Monitor Objects representing each of the display monitors connected to the user's system. Each access to `app.monitors` returns a new, up-to-date copy of this array.

A Monitors object also has several methods that can be used to select a display monitor. Alternatively, JavaScript code can look through the array explicitly. See the Monitors Object (page 477) for details.

Type: Monitors Object   Access: R

Example

Count the number of display monitors connected to the user's system.

```
var monitors = app.monitors;
console.println("There are " + monitors.length
   + " monitor(s) connected to this system.");
```

numPlugIns

Note: This method has been superseded by the `plugIns` (page 55) property.

Indicates the number of plug-ins that have been loaded by Acrobat.

Type: Number   Access: R

openInPlace

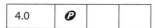

Determines whether cross-document links are opened in the same window or opened in a new window.

Type: Boolean   Access: R/W

Example

```
app.openInPlace = true;
```

platform

4.0			

The platform that the script is currently executing on. Valid values are

```
WIN
MAC
UNIX
```

Type: String   *Access: R*

plugIns

5.0			

An array of PlugIn Objects (page 498) representing the plug-ins that are currently installed in the viewer.

Type: Array   *Access: R*

Example

```
// Get array of PlugIn objects
var aPlugins = app.plugIns;
// Get number of plug-ins
var nPlugins = aPlugins.length;
// Enumerate names of all plug-ins
for ( var i = 0; i < nPlugins; i++)
    console.println("Plugin \#"+i+" is " + aPlugins[i].name);
```

printColorProfiles

6.0			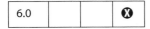

A list of available printer color spaces. Each of these values is suitable to use as the value of the `colorProfile` (page 501) property of a PrintParams Object (page 500).

Type: Array of Strings   *Access: R*

Example

Print out a listing of available printer color spaces:

```
var l = app.printColorProfiles.length
for ( var i = 0; i < l; i++)
    console.println("(" + (i+1) + ") " +
            app.printColorProfiles[i]);
```

printerNames

A list of available printers. Each of these values is suitable to use in the `printerName` (page 512) property of the PrintParams Object (page 500). If no printers are installed on the system, an empty array is returned.

Type: Array of Strings   Access: R

Example

Print out a listing of available printers:

```
var l = app.printerNames.length
for ( var i = 0; i < l; i++)
    console.println("(" + (i+1) + ") " + app.printerNames[i]);
```

runtimeHighlight

If `true`, the background color and hover color for form fields are shown.

Type: Boolean   Access: R/W

Example

If run-time highlighting is off (`false`), do nothing, otherwise change the preferences.

```
if (!app.runtimeHighlight)
{
    app.runtimeHighlight = true;
    app.runtimeHighlightColor = color.red;
}
```

runtimeHighlightColor

Sets the color for runtime highlighting of form fields.

The value of this property is a color array. (See "Color Arrays" on page 156 for details.)

Type: Color array   Access: R/W

Example

See the `runtimeHighlight` (page 56) property.

thermometer

6.0		

A Thermometer Object (page 628), which is a combined status window/progress bar that indicates to the user that a lengthy operation is in progress.

Type: object   *Access: R*

Example

See the Thermometer Object (page 628).

toolbar

3.01		

Allows a script to show or hide both the horizontal and vertical Acrobat toolbars. It does not hide the toolbar in external windows (that is, in an Acrobat window within a web browser).

Type: Boolean   *Access: R/W*

Example

```
// Opened the document, now remove the toolbar.
app.toolbar = false;
```

toolbarHorizontal

Note: This property has been deprecated in Acrobat 5.0 and later. If accessed, it acts like `toolbar` (page 57).

Allows a script to show or hide the Acrobat horizontal toolbar. It does not hide the toolbar in external windows (that is, in an Acrobat window within a web browser).

Type: Boolean   *Access: R/W*

toolbarVertical

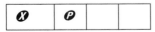

Note: This property has been deprecated in Acrobat 5.0 and later. If accessed, it acts like `toolbar` (page 57).

Allows a script to show or hide the Acrobat vertical toolbar. It does not hide the toolbar in external windows (that is, in an Acrobat window within a web browser).

Type: Boolean   *Access: R/W*

viewerType

3.01			

A string that indicates which viewer application is running. It can be one of these values.

Value	Description
Reader	Acrobat Reader version 5.0 or earlier / Adobe Reader version 5.1 or later
Exchange	Adobe Acrobat earlier than version 6.0 / Acrobat Standard version 6.0 or later
Exchange-Pro	Acrobat Professional version 6.0 or later

Type: String   *Access: R*

viewerVariation

5.0			

Indicates the packaging of the running viewer application. Values are:

```
Reader
Fill-In
Business Tools
Full
```

Type: String   *Access: R*

viewerVersion

4.0			

Indicates the version number of the current viewer application.

Type: Number   *Access: R*

app Methods

addMenuItem

5.0		🄢	

Adds a menu item to a menu.

Note: (Security 🄢): This method can only be executed during application initialization or console events. See the `event` Object (page 314) for a discussion of Acrobat JavaScript events.

See also the `addSubMenu` (page 61), `execMenuItem` (page 84), `hideMenuItem` (page 88), and `listMenuItems` (page 90) methods.

Parameters

cName	The language-independent name of the menu item. This name can be used by other methods (for example, `hideMenuItem` (page 88) to access the menu item.
cUser	(optional) The user string (language-dependent name) to display as the menu item name. If `cUser` is not specified, `cName` is used.
cParent	The name of the parent menu item. Its submenu will have the new menu item added to it. If `cParent` has no submenu, an exception is thrown. Menu item names can be obtained with the `listMenuItems` (page 90) method.
nPos	(optional) The position within the submenu to locate the new menu item. The default behavior is to append to the end of the submenu. Specifying `nPos` as `0` adds the menu to the top of the submenu. Beginning with Acrobat 6.0, the value of `nPos` can also be the language-independent name of a menu item. (Acrobat 6.0) If the value `nPos` is a string, this string is interpreted as a named item in the menu (a language-independent name of a menu item). The named item determines the position at which the new menu item is to be inserted. See `bPrepend` for additional details. **Note:** The `nPos` parameter is ignored in certain menus that are alphabetized. The alphabetized menus are • The first section of **View > Navigation Tabs**. • The first section of **View > Toolbars**. • The first section of the **Advanced** submenu. **Note:** When `nPos` is a number, `nPos` is not obeyed in the **Tools** menu. A menu item introduced into the **Tools** menu comes in at the top of the menu. `nPos` is obeyed when it is a string referencing another user-defined menu item.

cExec	An expression string to evaluate when the menu item is selected by the user. **Note:** Beginning with Acrobat 7.0, execution of JavaScript through a menu event is no longer privileged. See "Privileged versus Non-privileged Context" on page 8 for details.
cEnable	(optional) An expression string that is evaluated to determine whether to enable the menu item. The default is that the menu item is always enabled. This expression should set `event.rc` to `false` to disable the menu item.
cMarked	(optional) An expression string that determines whether the menu item has a check mark next to it. The expression should set `event.rc` to `false` to uncheck the menu item and `true` to check it. The default is that the menu item is not marked.
bPrepend	(optional, Acrobat 6.0) Determines the position of the new menu item relative to the position specified by `nPos`. The default value is `false`. If `bPrepend` is `true`, the rules for insertion are as follows: • If `nPos` is a string, the new item is placed before the named item. • If `nPos` is a number, the new item is placed before the numbered item. • If the named item cannot be found or `nPos` is not between zero and the number of items in the list, inclusive, the new item is inserted as the first item in the menu (rather than at the end of the menu). `bPrepend` is useful when the named item is the first item in a group.

Returns

Nothing

Example 1

```
// This example adds a menu item to the top of the
// File menu that puts up an alert dialog box displaying
// the active document title.
// This menu is only enabled if a document is opened.
app.addMenuItem({ cName: "Hello", cParent: "File",
    cExec: "app.alert(event.target.info.title, 3);",
    cEnable: "event.rc = (event.target != null);",
    nPos: 0
});
```

Example 2 (Acrobat 6.0)

Place two menu items in the **File** menu, one before the **Close** item and the other after the **Close** item.

```
// insert after the "Close" item (the default behavior)
app.addMenuItem( { cName: "myItem1", cUser: "My Item 1",\
    cParent: "File", cExec: "_myProc1()", nPos: "Close"});
// insert before the "Close" item, set bPrepend to true.
app.addMenuItem( { cName: "myItem2", cUser: "My Item 2",\
    cParent: "File", cExec: "_myProc2()", nPos: "Close",\
    bPrepend: true });
```

addSubMenu

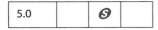

5.0		𝕊	

Adds a menu item with a submenu to the application.

See also the `addMenuItem` (page 59), `execMenuItem` (page 84), `hideMenuItem` (page 88), and `listMenuItems` (page 90) methods.

Note: (Security 𝕊): This method can only be executed during application initialization or console events. See the `event` Object (page 314) for a discussion of Acrobat JavaScript events.

Parameters

cName	The language-independent name of the menu item. This language-independent name is used to access the menu item (for example, for `hideMenuItem`, page 88).
cUser	(optional) The user string (language-dependent name) to display as the menu item name. If cUser is not specified, cName is used.
cParent	The name of the parent menu item to receive the new submenu. Menu item names can be discovered with `listMenuItems` (page 90).

<table>
<tr><td>nPos</td><td>(optional) The position within the parent's submenu to locate the new submenu. The default is to append to the end of the parent's submenu. Specifying nPos as 0 adds the submenu to the top of the parent's submenu.</td></tr>
</table>

> **Note:** The nPos parameter is ignored in certain menus that are alphabetized. The alphabetized menus are
>
> - The first section of **View > Navigational Tabs**.
> - The first section of **View > Toolbars**.
> - The first section of the **Advanced** submenu.
>
> **Note:** When nPos is a number, nPos is not obeyed in the **Tools** menu. A menu item introduced into the **Tools** menu comes in at the top of the menu. nPos is obeyed when nPos is a string referencing another user-defined menu item.

Returns

Nothing

Example

See the newDoc (page 94) method.

addToolButton

6.0			

Adds a toolbutton to the "Add-on" toolbar of Acrobat.

If there is an active document (for example, docA.pdf) open in Acrobat when this method is called to add a toolbutton, Acrobat will remove the toolbutton when docA.pdf is either no longer active or is closed. In the former case, the toolbutton will be automatically added to the toolbar if docA.pdf becomes the active document again.

The icon size is restricted to 20 by 20 pixels. If an icon of larger dimensions is used, an exception is thrown.

> **Note:** (Acrobat 7.0) A number of changes have been made with regard to the secure use of this method. Execution of addToolButton in the console and application initialization is considered privileged execution and is trusted.
>
> If this method is called from nonprivileged script, the warning "JavaScript Window" appears on the "Add-on" toolbar, which will not be dockable. (See "Privileged versus Non-privileged Context" on page 8.)

See also removeToolButton (page 102).

Parameters

cName	A unique language-independent identifier for the toolbutton. The language-independent name is used to access the toolbutton for other methods (for example, removeToolButton, page 102). **Note:** The value of cName must be unique. To avoid a name conflict, check listToolbarButtons (page 91), which lists all toolbar button names currently installed.
oIcon	An Icon Stream Object (page 435). Beginning with Acrobat 7.0, this parameter is optional if a cLabel is provided.
cExec	The expression string to evaluate when the toolbutton is selected.
cEnable	(optional) An expression string that determines whether to enable the toolbutton. The default is that the toolbutton is always enabled. This expression should set event.rc to false to disable the toolbutton.
cMarked	(optional) An expression string that determines whether the toolbutton is marked. The default is that the toolbutton is not marked. This expression should set event.rc to true to mark the toolbutton.
cTooltext	(optional) The text to display in the toolbutton help text when the mouse is over the toolbutton. The default is to not have a tool tip. **Note:** Avoid the use of extended characters in the cTooltext string as the string may be truncated.
nPos	(optional) The toolbutton number to place the added toolbutton before in the toolbar. If nPos is -1 (the default), the toolbutton is appended to the toolbar.
cLabel	(optional, Acrobat 7.0) A text label to be displayed on the button to the right of the icon. The default is to not have a label.

Returns

An integer.

Exceptions

None

Example

In this example, a toolbutton is created from a icon graphic on the user's hard drive. This script is executed from the console.

```
// Create a document
var myDoc = app.newDoc();

// import icon (20x20 pixels) from the file specified
myDoc.importIcon("myIcon", "/C/myIcon.jpg", 0);

// convert the icon to a stream.
oIcon = util.iconStreamFromIcon(myDoc.getIcon("myIcon"));

// close the doc now that we have grabbed the icon stream
myDoc.closeDoc(true);

// add a toolbutton
app.addToolButton({
     cName: "myToolButton",
     oIcon: oIcon,
     cExec: "app.alert('Someone pressed me!')",
     cTooltext: "Push Me!",
     cEnable: true,
     nPos: 0
});

app.removeToolButton("myToolButton")
```

See also the example following `util.iconStreamFromIcon` (page 639).

alert

3.01			

Displays an alert dialog box.

Parameters

cMsg	A string containing the message to be displayed.
nIcon	(optional) An icon type. Possible values are these:
	0: Error (default)
	1: Warning
	2: Question
	3: Status
	Note: On Macintosh, there is no distinction between warnings and questions.

nType	(optional) A button group type. Possible values are these: 0: OK (default) 1: OK, Cancel 2: Yes, No 3: Yes, No, Cancel
cTitle	(optional, Acrobat 6.0) The dialog box title. If not specified, the title "Adobe Acrobat" is used.
oDoc	(optional, Acrobat 6.0) The Document Object (page 188) that the alert should be associated with.
oCheckbox	(optional, Acrobat 6.0) If specified, a check box is created in the lower left region of the alert box. oCheckbox is a generic JavaScript object that has three properties. The first two property values are passed to the alert method; the third property returns a Boolean. ● cMsg (optional): A string to display with the check box. If not specified, the default string is "Do not show this message again". ● bInitialValue (optional): If true, the initial state of the check box is checked. The default is false. ● bAfterValue: When the alert method exits, contains the state of the check box when the dialog box is closed. If true, the check box was checked when the alert box is closed.

Returns

nButton, the type of the button that was pressed by the user:

1: OK

2: Cancel

3: No

4: Yes

Example 1

Display a simple alert box:

```
app.alert({
    cMsg: "Error! Try again!",
    cTitle: "Acme Testing Service"
});
```

Example 2

Close the document with the user's permission:

```
// A MouseUp action
var nButton = app.alert({
    cMsg: "Do you want to close this document?",
    cTitle: "A message from A. C. Robat",
    nIcon: 2, nType: 2
});
if ( nButton == 4 ) this.closeDoc();
```

Example 3 (Acrobat 6.0)

In this example, one document creates an alert box in another document. There are two documents, DocA and DocB, one open in a browser and the other in the viewer.

```
// The following is a declaration at the document level in DocA
var myAlertBoxes = new Object;
myAlertBoxes.oMyCheckbox = {
    cMsg: "Care to see this message again?",
    bAfterValue: false
}
```

The following is a mouse-up action in DocA. The variable theOtherDoc is the Document Object (page 188) of DocB. The alert box asks if the user wants to see this alert box again. If the user clicks the check box, the alert does not appear again.

```
if ( !myAlertBoxes.oMyCheckbox.bAfterValue )
{
    app.alert({
        cMsg: "This is a message from the DocA?",
        cTitle: "A message from A. C. Robat",
        oDoc:theOtherDoc,
        oCheckbox: myAlertBoxes.oMyCheckbox
    });
}
```

beep

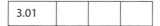

3.01			

Causes the system to play a sound.

Note: On Apple Macintosh and UNIX systems the beep type is ignored.

Parameters

nType	(optional) The sound type. Values are associated with sounds as follows:
	0: Error
	1: Warning
	2: Question
	3: Status
	4: Default (default value)

Returns

Nothing

beginPriv

Raises the execution privilege of the current stack frame such that methods marked secure can execute without security exceptions. For the method to succeed, there must be a frame on the stack representing the execution of a trusted function, and all frames (including the frame making the call) between the currently executing frame and that frame must represent the execution of trust propagator functions.

Use app.endPriv (page 70) to revoke privilege. The app.trustedFunction (page 107) method can create a trusted function, and app.trustPropagatorFunction (page 110) can create a trust propagator function. The term *stack frame* is discussed following the description of app.trustedFunction (page 107).

Parameters

None

Returns

undefined on success, exception on failure.

Example

For examples of usage, see trustedFunction (page 107) and trustPropagatorFunction (page 110).

browseForDoc

7.0		◎	

Presents a file system browser and returns an object containing information concerning the user's response.

Note: (Security ◎): This method can only be executed during batch or console events. See the `event` Object (page 314) for a discussion of Acrobat JavaScript events.

Parameters

bSave	(optional) A Boolean that, if `true`, specifies that the file system browser should be presented as it would be for a save operation. The default is `false`.
cFilenameInit	(optional) A string that specifies the default file name for the file system browser to be populated with.
cFSInit	(optional) A string that specifies the file system that the file system browser operates on initially. Two values are supported: "" (the empty string) representing the default file system and "CHTTP". The default is the default file system. This parameter is only relevant if the web server supports WebDAV.

Returns

On success, returns an object that has three properties.

Property	Description
cFS	A string containing the resulting file system name for the chosen file.
cPath	A string containing the resulting path for the chosen file.
cURL	A string containing the resulting URL for the chosen file

If the user cancels, the return value is `undefined`. On error, throws an exception.

Example 1

Browse for a document and report the results to the console.

```
var oRetn = app.browseForDoc({
    cFilenameInit: "myComDoc.pdf",
    cFSInit: "CHTTP",
});
```

```
if ( typeof oRetn != "undefined" )
   for ( var o in oRetn )
      console.println( "oRetn." + o + "=" + oRetn[o]);
else console.println("User cancelled!");
```

If the user selects a file on a WebDAV server, a possible output of this code is given below:

```
oRetn.cFS=CHTTP
oRetn.cPath=http://www.myCom.com/WebDAV/myComDoc.pdf
oRetn.cURL=http://www.myCom.com/WebDAV/myComDoc.pdf
```

Should the user select a file in the default file system, a typical output of this code is given below:

```
oRetn.cFS=DOS
oRetn.cPath=/C/temp/myComDoc.pdf
oRetn.cURL=file:///C|/temp/myComDoc.pdf
```

The script can go on to open the selected file using app.openDoc (page 97).

```
var myURL = (oRetn.cFS=="CHTTP") ? encodeURI(oRetn.cPath) :\
      oRetn.cPath;
var oDoc = app.openDoc({cPath: myURL, cFS: oRetn.cFS});
```

Note: app.openDoc (page 97) requires cPath to be an escaped string when retrieving a file from a WebDAV server. See app.openDoc (page 97) for a brief description and example.

Example 2

Browse and save a document.

```
var oRetn = app.browseForDoc({
   bSave: true,
   cFilenameInit: "myComDoc.pdf",
   cFSInit: "CHTTP",
});
if ( typeof oRetn != "undefined" ) this.saveAs({
   cFS: oRetn.cFS, cPath: oRetn.cPath, bPromptToOverwrite:
false});
```

clearInterval

5.0			

Cancels a previously registered interval initially set by the setInterval (page 104) method.

See also setTimeOut (page 105) and clearTimeOut (page 70).

Parameters

oInterval	The registered interval to cancel.

Returns

Nothing

Example

See setTimeOut (page 105).

clearTimeOut

5.0			

Cancels a previously registered time-out interval. Such an interval is initially set by setTimeOut (page 105).

See also setInterval (page 104) and clearInterval (page 69).

Parameters

oTime	The previously registered time-out interval to cancel.

Returns

Nothing

Example

See setTimeOut (page 105).

endPriv

7.0		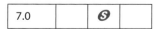	

Revokes any privilege bestowed upon the current stack frame by app.beginPriv (page 67). Does not revoke privilege bestowed by the current event.

Related methods are app.trustedFunction (page 107), app.trustPropagatorFunction (page 110) and app.beginPriv (page 67).

Parameters

None

Returns

undefined on success, exception on failure.

Example

For examples of usage, see `trustedFunction` (page 107) and `trustPropagatorFunction` (page 110).

execDialog

7.0			

Presents a modal dialog box to the user. Modal dialog boxes must be dismissed by the user before the host application can be directly used again.

The `monitor` parameter specifies a *dialog descriptor*, which is a generic object literal that consists of a set of handler functions for various events and a set of properties that describe the contents of the dialog box.

Dialog items are identified by an *ItemID*, which is a unique 4-character string. An *ItemID* is necessary only if the element must be referred to elsewhere in the dialog description (for example, to set or get a value for the element, to add a handler for the element, or to set a tab order including the element).

Note: To distinguish Acrobat dialog boxes from those created by JavaScript, dialogs that are added at the document level have a title of "JavaScript Dialog" and display the text "Warning: JavaScript Dialog" at the bottom.

Adobe Dialog Manager Programmer's Guide and Reference explains in detail the modal dialog and its properties (see "References" on page 2).

Parameters

`monitor`	An object literal. It consists of several handlers (see "Dialog Handlers" on page 72) and a `description` property that describes the dialog elements (see "description Property" on page 72).
`inheritDialog`	(optional) A Dialog Object (page 175) that should be reused when displaying this dialog box. It is useful when displaying a series of dialog boxes (such as a wizard) to prevent one from disappearing before the new one is displayed. The default is to not reuse a dialog.
`parentDoc`	(optional) A Document Object (page 188) to use as the parent for this dialog. The default parent is the Acrobat application.

Returns

A string, which is the *ItemID* of the element that caused the dialog box to be dismissed. The return value is "ok" or "cancel" if the dismissing element is the `ok` or `cancel` button.

Note: Debugging is disabled while a modal dialog box created by `app.execDialog` is active.

Dialog Handlers

The dialog handlers are called when specific dialog events occur. Each handler is optional and is passed a Dialog Object (page 175) that can be used to query or set values in the dialog. The supported handlers are listed in the table that follows.

Dialog Handler	Description
`initialize`	Called when the dialog is being initialized.
`validate`	Called when a field is modified to determine if the value is acceptable (by returning `true`) or unacceptable (by returning `false`).
`commit`	Called when the OK button of the dialog box is clicked.
`destroy`	Called when the dialog is being destroyed.

ItemID	Called when the dialog element *ItemID* is modified. For a text box, it is when the text box loses focus. For other controls, it is when the selection changes. If *ItemID* is not a JavaScript identifier, the name must be enclosed in double quotes when the method is defined, for example,
	     `"bt:1": function () { .... }`
	 If *ItemID* is a JavaScript identifier, the double quotes are optional. For example,
	     `"butn": function () { .... }`
	     `butn: function () { .... }`
	 are both correct.

description Property

The `description` property is an object literal that contains properties describing the dialog. Its `elements` property specifies the elements of the dialog, and each of the elements in turn can have an `elements` property describing subelements.

The dialog properties at the root level of the `description` property are listed in the table that follows.

Property	Type	Description
name	String	The title bar of the dialog box, which should be localized.
first_tab	String	An *ItemID* for the dialog item that should be first in the tab order. This dialog item will also be active when the dialog is created. This property is required for setting up a tabbing order. See the `next_tab` property defined below.
width	Numeric	The width of the dialog box in pixels. If no width is specified, the combined width of the contents is used.
height	Numeric	The height of the dialog box in pixels. If no height is specified, the combined height of the contents is used.
char_width	Numeric	The width of the dialog box in characters. If no width is specified, the combined width of the contents is used.
char_height	Numeric	The height of the dialog box in characters. If no height is specified, the combined height of the contents is used.
align_children	String	The alignment for all descendants. Must be one of the following values: • "align_left": Left aligned • "align_center": Center aligned • "align_right": Right aligned • "align_top": Top aligned • "align_fill": Align to fill the parent's width; may widen objects. • "align_distribute": Distribute the contents over the parent's width. • "align_row": Distribute the contents over the parent's width with a consistent baseline. • "align_offscreen": Align items one on top of another.
elements	Array	An array of *object literals* that describe the dialog elements contained within this dialog (see "elements Property" on page 73).

elements Property

A dialog `elements` property specifies an object literal with the following set of properties.

Property	Type	Description
name	String	The displayed name of the dialog element, which should be localized. **Note:** This property is ignored for the "edit_text" type.
item_id	String	An *ItemID* for this dialog, which is a unique 4-character string.

Property	Type	Description
type	String	The type of this dialog element. It must be one of the following strings: • "button" - A push button. • "check_box" - A check box. • "radio" - A radio button. • "list_box" - A list box. • "hier_list_box" - A hierarchical list box. • "static_text" - A static text box. • "edit_text" - An editable text box. • "popup" - A pop-up control. • "ok" - An OK button. • "ok_cancel" - An OK and Cancel Button. • "ok_cancel_other" - An OK, Cancel, and Other button. • "view" - A container for a set controls. • "cluster" - A frame for a set of controls. • "gap" - A place holder.
next_tab	String	An *ItemID* for the next dialog item in the tab order. **Note:** Tabbing does not stop at any dialog item that is not the target of the next_tab (or first_tab) property. Tabbing should form a circular linked list.
width	Numeric	Specifies the width of the element in pixels. If no width is specified, the combined width of the contents is used.
height	Numeric	Specifies the height of the element in pixels. If no height is specified, the combined height of the contents is used.
char_width	Numeric	Specifies the width of the element in characters. If no width is specified, the combined width of the contents is used.
char_height	Numeric	Specifies the height of the element in characters. If no height is specified, the combined height of the contents is used.
font	String	The font to use for this element. Must be one of the following strings: • "default" - Default Font • "dialog" - Dialog Font • "palette" - Palette (small) Font
bold	Boolean	Specify if the font is bold.
italic	Boolean	Specify if the font is italic.

Property	Type	Description
alignment	String	Sets the alignment for this element. Must be one of the following values: ● "align_left": Left aligned ● "align_center": Center aligned ● "align_right": Right aligned ● "align_top": Top aligned ● "align_fill": Align to fill the parent's width; may widen objects. ● "align_distribute": Distribute the contents over the parent's width. ● "align_row": Distribute the contents over the parent's width with a consistent baseline. ● "align_offscreen": Align items one on top of another.
align_child ren	String	Sets the alignment for all descendants. Possible values are the same as for alignment.
elements	Array	An array of object literals that describe the subelements of this dialog element. Its properties are the same as those described in this table.

Additional Attributes of Some Dialog Elements

Some of the element types have additional attributes, as listed below.

Element type	Property	Type	Description
static_text	multiline	Boolean	If true, this static text element is multiline.
edit_text	multiline	Boolean	If true, this static text element is multiline.
	readonly	Boolean	If true, this text element is read only. **Note:** This property is ignored when password is set to true.
	password	Boolean	If true, this text element is a password field.
	PopupEdit	Boolean	If true, it is a pop-up edit text element.
	SpinEdit	Boolean	If true, it is a spin edit text element.
radio	group_id	String	The group name to which this radio button belongs.
ok, ok_cancel, ok_cancel_other	ok_name	String	The name for the OK button.
	cancel_name	String	The name for the cancel button.
	other_name	String	The name for the other button.

Example 1

The following dialog descriptor can be a document-level or folder-level JavaScript.

```
var dialog1 = {

    initialize: function (dialog) {
        // create a static text containing the current date.
        var todayDate = dialog.store()["date"];
        todayDate = "Date: " + util.printd("mmmm dd, yyyy",
                new Date());
        dialog.load({ "date": todayDate });
    },
    commit:function (dialog) { // called when OK pressed
        var results = dialog.store();
        // now do something with the data collected,
        // for example,
        console.println("Your name is " + results["fnam"]
            + " " + results["lnam"] );
    },
    description:
    {
        name: "Personal Data",    // dialog title
        align_children: "align_left",
        width: 350,
        height: 200,
        elements:
        [
            {
                type: "cluster",
                name: "Your Name",
                align_children: "align_left",
                elements:
                [
                    {
                        type: "view",
                        align_children: "align_row",
                        elements:
                        [
                            {
                                type: "static_text",
                                name: "First Name: "
                            },
                            {
                                item_id: "fnam",
                                type: "edit_text",
                                alignment: "align_fill",
                                width: 300,
                                height: 20
                            }
                        ]
                    },
                    {
```

```
                         type: "view",
                         align_children: "align_row",
                         elements:
                         [
                             {
                                 type: "static_text",
                                 name: "Last Name: "
                             },
                             {
                                 item_id: "lnam",
                                 type: "edit_text",
                                 alignment: "align_fill",
                                 width: 300,
                                 height: 20
                             }
                         ]
                     },
                     {
                         type: "static_text",
                         name: "Date: ",
                         char_width: 25,
                         item_id: "date"
                     },
                 ]
             },
             {
                 alignment: "align_right",
                 type: "ok_cancel",
                 ok_name: "Ok",
                 cancel_name: "Cancel"
             }
         ]
     }
};
```

Now, the following line can be executed from actions such as the mouse-up action of a button or a menu action.

```
app.execDialog(dialog1);
```

Example 2

The following example uses a check box and a radio button field. This code might be a document-level JavaScript.

```
var dialog2 =
{
    initialize: function(dialog) {
        // set a default value for radio button field
        dialog.load({"rd01": true });
        this.hasPet = false;
        // disable radio button field
        dialog.enable({
            "rd01" : this.hasPet,
            "rd02" : this.hasPet,
```

```
                "rd03" : this.hasPet
            });
        },
        commit: function(dialog) {
            // when user presses "Ok", this handler will
            //execute first
            console.println("commit");
            var results = dialog.store();
            // do something with the data, for example,
            var hasPet = (this.hasPet) ? "have" : "don't have";
            console.println("You " + hasPet + " a pet.");
            if (this.hasPet)
                console.println("You have " +
    this.getNumPets(results)
                    + " pet(s).");
        },
        getNumPets: function (results) {
            for ( var i=1; i<=3; i++) {
                if ( results["rd0"+i] ) {
                    switch (i) {
                        case 1:
                            var nPets = "one";
                            break;
                        case 2:
                            var nPets = "two";
                            break;
                        case 3:
                            var nPets = "three or more";
                    }
                }
            };
            return nPets;
        },
        ok: function(dialog) {
            // the handler for the Ok button will be handed after
    commit
            console.println("Ok!");
        },
        ckbx: function (dialog) {
            // process the checkbox, if user has pet, turn on radios
            this.hasPet = !this.hasPet;
            dialog.enable({
                "rd01" : this.hasPet,
                "rd02" : this.hasPet,
                "rd03" : this.hasPet
            });
        },
        cancel: function(dialog) { // handle handle the cancel
    button
            console.println("Cancel!");
        },
        other: function(dialog){ // handle the other button
            app.alert("Thanks for pressing me!");
```

```
            dialog.end("other"); // end the dialog, return
"other"!
    },
    // The Dialog Description
    description:
    {
        name: "More Personal Information",
        elements:
        [
            {
                type: "view",
                align_children: "align_left",
                elements:
                [
                    {
                        type: "static_text",
                        name: "Personal Information",
                        bold: true,
                        font: "dialog",
                        char_width: 30,
                        height: 20
                    },
                    {
                        type: "check_box",
                        item_id: "ckbx",
                        name: "Pet Owner"
                    },
                    {
                        type: "view",
                        align_children: "align_row",
                        elements:
                        [
                            {
                                type: "static_text",
                                name: "Number of pets: "
                            },
                            {
                                type: "radio",
                                item_id: "rd01",
                                group_id: "rado",
                                name: "One"

                            },
                            {
                                type: "radio",
                                item_id: "rd02",
                                group_id: "rado",
                                name: "Two",
                            },
                            {
                                type: "radio",
                                item_id: "rd03",
```

```
                                group_id: "rado",
                                name: "Three or more",
                            }
                        ]
                    }
                ]
            },
            {
                type: "gap", //add a small vertical gap between
                height: 10 //..radio fields and buttons
            },
            {
                type: "ok_cancel_other",
                ok_name: "Ok",
                cancel_name: "Cancel",
                other_name: "Press Me"
            }
        ]
    }
};
```

The following line can be executed in situations such as the mouse-up action of a button or a menu action.

```
var retn = app.execDialog(dialog2);
```

The value of `retn` is "ok" if the ok button was pressed, "cancel" if the cancel button was pressed, and "other" if the button labeled "Press Me" was pressed.

Example 3

This example uses a list box.

```
var dialog3 = {
    // This dialog gets called when the dialog is created
    initialize: function(dialog) {
        this.loadDefaults(dialog);
    },
    // This dialog gets called when the OK button is hit.
    commit: function(dialog) {
        // See the Dialog object for a description of how
dialog.load
        // and dialog.store work.
        var elements = dialog.store()["subl"];
        // do something with the data.
    },
    // Callback for when the button "butn" is hit.
    butn: function(dialog) {
        var elements = dialog.store()["subl"]
        for(var i in elements) {
            if ( elements[i] > 0 ) {
                app.alert("You chose \"" + i
                + "\", which has a value of " + elements[i] );
            }
```

```
            }
        },
        loadDefaults: function (dialog) {
            dialog.load({
                sub1:
                {
                    "Acrobat Professional": +1,
                    "Acrobat Standard": -2,
                    "Adobe Reader": -3
                }
            })
        },
        // The Dialog Description
        description:
        {
            name: "Adobe Acrobat Products", // Title of dialog
            elements: // Child Element Array
            [
                {
                    type: "view",
                    align_children: "align_left",
                    elements: // Child Element Array
                    [
                        {
                            type: "cluster",
                            name: "Select",
                            elements: // Child Element Array
                            [
                                {
                                    type: "static_text",
                                    name: "Select Acrobat you use",
                                    font: "default"
                                },
                                {
                                    type: "list_box",
                                    item_id: "sub1",
                                    width: 200,
                                    height: 60
                                },
                                {
                                    type: "button",
                                    item_id: "butn",
                                    name: "Press Me"
                                }
                            ]
                        },
                        {
                            type: "ok_cancel"
                        }
                    ]
                }
            ]
        }
    }
```

Then execute

```
app.execDialog(dialog3);
```

In the example above, if the line `type: "list_box"` is replaced by `type: "popup"` and the `height` specification is removed, the example will run with a pop-up control rather than a list box.

Example 4

This example shows a hierarchical list box. After the dialog box is opened, a hierarchical list is presented. After a selection is made and the user clicks the Select buttons, the document jumps to the destination chosen by the user. The Document Object (page 188) is passed to the dialog by making it a property of the dialog.

```
var dialog4 = {
    initialize: function(dialog) {
        dialog.load({
            subl:
                {
                    "Chapter 1":
                    {
                        "Section 1":
                        {
                            "SubSection 1": -1,
                            "SubSection 2": -2,
                        },
                        "Section 2":
                        {
                            "SubSection 1": -3,
                            "SubSection 2": -4,
                        }
                    },
                    "Chapter 3": -5,
                    "Chapter 4": -6
                }
        })
    },
    subl: function(dialog) {
        console.println("Selection Box Hit");
    },
    getHierChoice: function (e)
    {
        if (typeof e == "object") {
            for ( var i in e ) {
                if ( typeof e[i] == "object" ) {
                    var retn = this.getHierChoice(e[i]);
                    if ( retn ) {
                        retn.label = i + ", " + retn.label;
                        return retn;
                    }
                }
```

```
                    // if e[i] > 0, we've found the selected item
                    } else  if ( e[i] > 0 ) return { label:i, value:
e[i] };
            }
        } else {
            if ( e[i] > 0 ) return e[i];
        }
    },
    butn: function (dialog)
    {
        var element = dialog.store()["subl"]
        var retn = this.getHierChoice(element);
        if ( retn ) {
        // write to the console the full name of the item
selected
            console.println("The selection you've chosen is \""
              + retn.label + "\", its value is " + retn.value );
            dialog.end("ok");
         // this.doc is the doc object of this document
            this.doc.gotoNamedDest("dest"+retn.value);
        }
        else app.alert("Please make a selection, or cancel");
    },
    cncl: function (dialog) { dialog.end("cancel") },
    // Dialog Description
    description:
    {
        name: "My Novel",
        elements:
        [
            {
                type: "view",
                align_children: "align_left",
                elements:
                [
                    {
                        type: "cluster",
                        name: "Book Headings",
                        elements:
                        [
                            {
                                type: "static_text",
                                name: "Make a selection",
                            },
                            {
                                type: "hier_list_box",
                                item_id: "subl",
                                char_width: 20,
                                height: 200
                            }
                        ]
                    },
```

```
                    {
                        type: "view",
                        align_children: "align_row",
                        elements:
                        [
                            {
                                type: "button",
                                item_id: "cncl",
                                name: "Cancel"
                            },
                            {
                                item_id: "butn",
                                type: "button",
                                name: "Select"
                            }
                        ]
                    }
                ]
            }
        ]
    }
};
```

This function attaches the document object to the dialog, then passes the dialog to the `app.execDialog` method. The `dialog4` object and this function can be at the document level.

```
function dotheDialog(dialog,doc)
{
    dialog.doc = doc;
    var retn = app.execDialog( dialog )
}
```

Finally, the following script can be executed from a mouse-up action, for example.

```
dotheDialog( dialog4, this );
```

Example 5

See "Example 2" on page 112, which shows how to execute privileged code from a non-privileged context.

execMenuItem

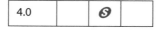

Executes the specified menu item.

Beginning with Acrobat 5.0, `app.execMenuItem("SaveAs")` can be called, subject to the restrictions described below. Executing the **Save As** menu item saves the current file to the user's hard drive after presenting a dialog box asking the user to select a folder and file name. The file is saved as a linearized file if **Save As optimizes for Fast Web View** is checked in the General preferences.

Note: (Security ☯, Acrobat 7.0) In previous versions of Acrobat,

```
app.execMenuItem("SaveAs");
```

could only be executed during batch, console or menu events. Acrobat 7.0 removes this restriction, so that `app.execMenuItem("SaveAs")` can be executed during a mouse-up event, for example.

Note: If the user preferences are set to **Save As optimizes for Fast Web View**, a form object will not survive a **Save As** operation. Field Objects (page 371) are no longer valid, and an exception may be thrown when trying to access a Field Object immediately after saving. See the examples that follow.

For security reasons, scripts are not allowed to execute the **Quit** menu item. Beginning with Acrobat 6.0, scripts are not allowed to execute the **Paste** menu item.

See also `addMenuItem` (page 59), `addSubMenu` (page 61), and `hideMenuItem` (page 88). Use `listMenuItems` (page 90) to have the console list the names of all menu items.

Parameters

cMenuItem	The menu item to execute.
	A list of menu item names can be obtained with `listMenuItems` (page 90).
oDoc	(optional, Acrobat 7.0) oDoc is the document object of a document that is not hidden (see the Document Object hidden method, page 195). If this parameter is present, `execMenuItem` executes the menu item in the document's context.

Returns

Nothing

Example 1

This example executes the **File > Open** menu item. It displays a dialog box asking for the file to be opened.

```
app.execMenuItem("Open");
```

Example 2 (Acrobat 5.0)

```
var f = this.getField("myField");
// Assume preferences set to save linearized
app.execMenuItem("SaveAs");
// exception thrown, field not updated
f.value = 3;
```

Example 3 (Acrobat 5.0)

```
var f = this.getField("myField");
// Assume preferences set to save linearized
app.execMenuItem("SaveAs");
// get the field again after the linear save
var f = getField("myField");
// field updated to a value of 3
f.value = 3;
```

getNthPlugInName

Note: This method has been superseded by the `plugIns` (page 55) property.

Obtains the name of the *n*th plug-in that has been loaded by the viewer.

Parameters

nIndex	The *n*th plug-in loaded by the viewer.

Returns

cName, the plug-in name that corresponds to nIndex.

getPath

Returns the path to folders created during installation. A distinction is made between application folders and user folders. The method throws a GeneralError exception (see "Error Object" on page 311) if the path does not exist.

Note: (Security ⊘, Acrobat 7.0) This method can only be executed during batch or console events (see "event Object" on page 314). See also "Privileged versus Non-privileged Context" on page 8.

Parameters

cCategory	(optional) The category of folder sought. Valid values are `app` (the default) and `user`.
cFolder	(optional) A platform-independent string that indicates the folder. Valid values are `root`, `eBooks`, `preferences`, `sequences`, `documents` `javascript`, `stamps`, `dictionaries`, `plugIns`, `spPlugIns` `help`, `temp`, `messages`, `resource`, `update` The default is `root`.

Returns

The path to the folder determined by the parameters. An exception is thrown if the folder does not exist.

Example 1

Find the path to the user's Sequences folder.

```
try {
    var userBatch = app.getPath("user","sequences");
} catch(e) {
    var userBatch = "User has not defined any custom batch
sequences";
}
console.println(userBatch);
```

Example 2

Create and save a document to My Documents on a Windows platform.

```
var myDoc = app.newDoc();
var myPath = app.getPath("user", "documents") + "/myDoc.pdf"
myDoc.saveAs(myPath);
myDoc.closeDoc();
```

goBack

3.01			

Goes to the previous view on the view stack, which is equivalent to pressing the go back button on the Acrobat toolbar.

Parameters

None

Returns

Nothing

Example

Create a go-back button. This code could be part of a batch sequence, for example, to place navigation buttons on the selected PDF documents.

```
var aRect = this.getPageBox();
var width = aRect[2] - aRect[0];
// rectangle is 12 points high and 18 points width,
// centered at bottom
rect = [width/2-8, 10, width/2+8, 22];
f = this.addField("goBack", "button", 0, rect);
f.textFont="Wingdings";
f.textSize=0;
f.buttonSetCaption("\u00E7");          // left pointing arrow
f.setAction("MouseUp", "app.goBack()");// add an action
```

goForward

3.01			

Goes to the next view on the view stack, which is equivalent to pressing the go forward button on the Acrobat toolbar.

Parameters

None

Returns

Nothing

Example

See the example following `app.goBack` (page 87).

hideMenuItem

Removes a specified menu item.

See also `addMenuItem` (page 59), `addSubMenu` (page 61), `execMenuItem` (page 84), and `listMenuItems` (page 90).

Note: (Security ⊘): This method can only be executed during application initialization or console events. See the `event` Object (page 314) for a discussion of Acrobat JavaScript events.

Parameters

cName	The menu item name to remove.
	Menu item names can be discovered with listMenuItems (page 90).

Returns

Nothing

hideToolbarButton

4.0			

Removes a specified toolbar button.

Note: (Security ): This method can only be executed during application initialization or console events. See the event Object (page 314) for a discussion of Acrobat JavaScript events.

Parameters

cName	The name of the toolbar button to remove.
	Toolbar item names can be discovered with listToolbarButtons (page 91).

Returns

Nothing

Example

A file named, myConfig.js, containing the following script is placed in one of the folder-level JavaScripts folders.

```
app.hideToolbarButton("Hand");
```

When the viewer is started, the "Hand" icon does not appear.

launchURL

7.0			

Launches a URL in a browser window.

Parameters

cURL	A string that specifies the URL to launch.
bNewFrame	(optional) If true, this method launches the URL in a new window of the browser application. The default is false.

Returns

The value `undefined` is returned on success. An exception is thrown on failure.

Example 1

```
app.launchURL("http://www.adobe.com/", true);
```

Example 2

Add a online help item to the menu system. This code should be placed in a folder-level JavaScript file, or executed from the JavaScript Debugger console.

```
app.addMenuItem({
    cName: "myHelp", cUser: "Online myHelp",
    cParent: "Help",
    cExec: "app.launchURL('www.myhelp.com/myhelp.html');",
    nPos: 0
});
```

Related methods are `openDoc` (page 97) and the Document Object `getURL` (page 259) method.

listMenuItems

5.0			

Beginning with Acrobat 6.0, returns an array of TreeItem Objects (page 90), which describes a menu hierarchy.

Prior to Acrobat 6.0, this method returned a list of menu item names to the console.

See also `addMenuItem` (page 59), `addSubMenu` (page 61), `execMenuItem` (page 84), and `hideMenuItem` (page 88).

Parameters

None

Returns

Array of TreeItem Objects (page 90)

TreeItem Object

A generic JavaScript object that represents a menu or toolbar item hierarchy. An array of these objects is returned by `app.listMenuItems` (page 90) and app.listToolbarButtons (page 91) (starting in Acrobat 6.0). It contains the following properties.

cName	The name of a menu item or toolbar button.
oChildren	(optional) An array of treeItem objects containing the submenus or flyout buttons.

Example 1

List all menu item names to the console.

```
var menuItems = app.listMenuItems()
for( var i in menuItems)
    console.println(menuItems[i] + "\n")
```

Example 2

List all menu items to console, fancy format.

```
function FancyMenuList(m, nLevel)
{
    var s = "";
    for (var i = 0; i < nLevel; i++) s += " ";
    console.println(s + "+-" + m.cName);
    if ( m.oChildren != null )
        for ( var i = 0; i < m.oChildren.length; i++ )
            FancyMenuList(m.oChildren[i], nLevel + 1);
}
var m = app.listMenuItems();
for ( var i=0; i < m.length; i++ ) FancyMenuList(m[i], 0);
```

listToolbarButtons

5.0			

Beginning with Acrobat 6.0, returns an array of treeItem objects that describes a toolbar hierarchy (with flyout toolbars).

Prior to Acrobat 6.0, this method displayed a list of toolbar button names in the console.

Parameters

None

Returns

Array of TreeItem Objects (page 90)

Example

List all toolbar names in the console.

```
var toolbarItems = app.listToolbarButtons()
for( var i in toolbarItems)
   console.println(toolbarItems[i] + "\n")
```

See also the `hideToolbarButton` (page 89) method.

mailGetAddrs

6.0		🚫	ⓧ

Note: This method is a Windows-only feature.

Displays an address book dialog box to let the user choose e-mail recipients. The dialog box is optionally prepopulated with semicolon-separated lists of addressees in the `cTo`, `cCc`, and `cBcc` strings. The `bCc` and `bBcc` Booleans control whether the user should be allowed to choose CC and BCC recipients.

See also `mailMsg` (page 93), the Document Object methods `mailDoc` (page 268) and `mailForm` (page 270), the FDF Object `mail` (page 366) method, and the Report Object `mail` (page 527) method.

Note: (Security 🚫, Acrobat 7.0) This method can only be executed during batch or console events. See also "Privileged versus Non-privileged Context" on page 8. See the `event` Object (page 314) for a discussion of Acrobat JavaScript events.

Parameters

cTo	(optional) A semicolon-separated list of "To" addressees to use.
cCc	(optional) A semicolon-separated list of CC addressees to use.
cBcc	(optional) A semicolon-separated list of BCC addressees to use.
cCaption	(optional) A string to appear on the caption bar of the address dialog box.
bCc	(optional) A Boolean to indicate whether the user can choose CC recipients.
bBcc	(optional) A Boolean to indicate whether the user can choose BCC recipients. This Boolean should only be used when `bCc` is `true`; otherwise, the method fails (and returns `undefined`).

Returns

On failure (the user canceled), returns undefined. On success, returns an array of three strings for To, CC, and BCC.

Example

```
var attempts = 2;
while (attempts > 0)
{
    var recipients = app.mailGetAddrs
    ({
        cCaption: "Select Recipients, Please",
        bBcc: false
    })
    if (typeof recipients == "undefined" ) {
        if (--attempts == 1)
            app.alert("You did not choose any recipients,"
                + " try again");
    } else break;
}
if (attempts == 0)
    app.alert("Cancelling the mail message");
else {
    JavaScript statements to send mail
}
```

mailMsg

4.0			

Sends out an e-mail message with or without user interaction.

See also the Document Object `mailDoc` (page 268) and `mailForm` (page 270) methods, the FDF Object `mail` (page 366) method, and the Report Object `mail` (page 527) method.

Note: On Windows: The client machine must have its default mail program configured to be MAPI enabled to use this method.

Parameters

bUI	Indicates whether user interaction is required. If `true`, the remaining parameters are used to seed the compose-new-message window that is displayed to the user. If `false`, the `cTo` parameter is required and others are optional.
cTo	A semicolon-separated list of addressees.
cCc	(optional) A semicolon-separated list of CC addressees.
cBcc	(optional) A semicolon-separated list of BCC addressees.
cSubject	(optional) Subject line text. The length limit is 64 KB.
cMsg	(optional) Mail message text. The length limit is 64 KB.

Returns

Nothing

Example

Open the compose new message window.

```
app.mailMsg(true);
```

Send out the mail to fun1@fun.com and fun2@fun.com.

```
app.mailMsg(false, "fun1@fun.com; fun2@fun.com", "", "",
"This is the subject", "This is the body of the mail.");
```

It is possible to compose a message containing form data.

```
var cMyMsg = "Below are the current budget figures:\n\n";
cMyMsg += "Date Compiled: " + \
          this.getField("date").value + "\n";
cMyMsg += "Current Estimate: " + \
          this.getField("budget").value + "\n";
app.mailMsg({
    bUI: true,
    cTo: "myBoss@greatCo.com",
    cSubject: "The latest budget figures",
    cMsg: cMyMsg
} );
```

newDoc

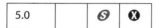

5.0		🅢	⊗

Creates a new document and returns its Document Object (page 188). The optional parameters specify the media box dimensions of the document in points.

Note: (Security 🅢): This method can only be executed during batch, console or menu events. See "Privileged versus Non-privileged Context" on page 8. See the event Object (page 314) for a discussion of Acrobat JavaScript events.

Parameters

nWidth	(optional) The width (in points) for the new document. The default value is 612.
nHeight	(optional) The height (in points) for the new document. The default value is 792.

Returns

The object of the newly created document.

Adobe® Acrobat® Official JavaScript Reference

Example

Add a **New** item to the Acrobat **File** menu. Within **New**, there are three menu items: **Letter**, **A4**, and **Custom**. This script should go in a folder-level JavaScripts .js file.

```
app.addSubMenu({ cName: "New", cParent: "File", nPos: 0 })
app.addMenuItem({ cName: "Letter", cParent: "New", \
    cExec: "app.newDoc();"});
app.addMenuItem({ cName: "A4", cParent: "New", \
    cExec: "app.newDoc(420,595)"});
app.addMenuItem({ cName: "Custom...", cParent: "New", \
    cExec: "var nWidth = \
        app.response({ cQuestion:'Enter Width in Points',\
            cTitle: 'Custom Page Size'});"
    +"if (nWidth == null) nWidth = 612;"
    +"var nHeight = \
        app.response({ cQuestion:'Enter Height in Points',\
            cTitle: 'Custom Page Size'});"
    +"if (nHeight == null) nHeight = 792;"
    +"app.newDoc({ nWidth: nWidth, nHeight: nHeight })"});
```

The script above works for versions of Acrobat prior to 7.0. For Acrobat 7.0, it works correctly if the user JavaScript preference **Enable menu items JavaScript execution privileges** is enabled.

If this item is not checked, the app.newDoc method must be executed through a trustedFunction (page 107) because execution of JavaScript through a menu event is no longer privileged beginning with Acrobat 7.0. See "Privileged versus Non-privileged Context" on page 8.

The same example can be worked as follows:

```
trustedNewDoc = app.trustedFunction( function (nWidth,
nHeight)
{
    app.beginPriv();
        switch( arguments.length ) {
            case 2:
                app.newDoc( nWidth, nHeight );
                break;
            case 1:
                app.newDoc( nWidth );
                break;
            default:
                app.newDoc();
        }
    app.endPriv();
})
app.addSubMenu({ cName: "New", cParent: "File", nPos: 0 })
app.addMenuItem({ cName: "Letter", cParent: "New", cExec:
    "trustedNewDoc();"});
app.addMenuItem({ cName: "A4", cParent: "New", cExec:
    "trustedNewDoc(420,595)"});
```

```
app.addMenuItem({ cName: "Custom...", cParent: "New", cExec:
    "var nWidth = \
        app.response({ cQuestion:'Enter Width in Points',\
            cTitle: 'Custom Page Size'});"
    +"if (nWidth == null) nWidth = 612;"
    +"var nHeight = \
        app.response({ cQuestion:'Enter Height in Points',\
            cTitle: 'Custom Page Size'});"
    +"if (nHeight == null) nHeight = 792;"
    +"trustedNewDoc(nWidth, nHeight) "});
```

The code is a little incomplete. In the case of the **Custom** menu item, additional lines can be inserted to prevent the user from entering the empty string, or a value too small or too large. See Appendix C in the *PDF Reference* for the current limitations.

Example

Create a blank document and acquire the Document Object (page 188), then insert a watermark.

```
var myNewDoc = app.newDoc();
myNewDoc.addWatermarkFromText("Confidential",0,font.Helv,24,
color.red);
```

This example uses the Document Object addWatermarkFromText (page 221) method.

newFDF

| 6.0 | | | |

Creates a new FDF Object that contains no data.

Note: (Security 🟊) : This method is available only during batch, console, application initialization and menu events. Not available in Adobe Reader. See "Privileged versus Non-privileged Context" on page 8.

Parameters

None

Returns

A new FDF Object

Example

Create a FDF with an embedded PDF file.

```
var fdf = app.newFDF();
fdf.addEmbeddedFile( "/c/myPDFs/myFile.pdf", 1);
fdf.save( "/c/myFDFs/myFile.fdf" );
```

This example continues following the description of `app.openFDF` (page 99).

openDoc

5.0			

Opens a specified PDF document and returns its Document Object (page 188). This object can be used by the script to call methods, or to get or set properties in the newly opened document.

Note: When a batch sequence is running, a modal dialog box is open, which prevents user interference while processing. Consequently, this method cannot be executed through a batch sequence.

Note: An exception is thrown and an invalid Document Object (page 188) is returned when an HTML document is opened using this method. To catch the exception, enclose `app.openDoc` in a `try/catch` construct. See **Example 2** below.

Parameters

cPath	A device-independent path to the document to be opened. If `oDoc` is specified, the path can be relative to it. The target document must be accessible in the default file system.
	Note: When `cFS` is set to "CHTTP", the `cPath` string should be escaped, perhaps using the core JavaScript global function `encodeURI`. See Example 5 below.
oDoc	(optional) A Document Object (page 188) to use as a base to resolve a relative `cPath`. Must be accessible in the default file system.
cFS	(optional, Acrobat 7.0) A string that specifies the source file system name. Two values are supported: "" (the empty string, which is the default), representing the default file system, and "CHTTP". This parameter is relevant only if the web server supports WebDAV.
bHidden	(optional, Acrobat 7.0) A Boolean that if `true`, opens the PDF file with its window hidden. The default is `false`.
bUseConv	(optional, Acrobat 7.0) A Boolean that is used when `cPath` references a non-PDF file. If **true**, the method tries to convert the non-PDF file to a PDF document. The default is `false`.
	Note: (Security 🛡, Acrobat 7.0) `bUseConv` can only be set to `true` during console and batch events. See also "Privileged versus Non-privileged Context" on page 8.

Returns

A Document Object (page 188) or `null`:

- In Acrobat 5.0, this method returns a Document Object (page 188).
- In Acrobat 5.0.5, the method returns the Document Object (page 188) unless the `disclosed` (page 193) property of the target document is not `true`, in which case it returns `null`.
- Beginning with the Acrobat 5.0.5 Accessibility and Forms Patch and continuing with Acrobat 6.0 and later, `openDoc` behaves as follows:
  - During a batch, console or menu event, `openDoc` ignores the `disclosed` property and returns the Document Object (page 188) of the file specified by `cPath`.
  - During any other event, `openDoc` returns the Document Object (page 188), if `disclosed` is `true`, and `null`, otherwise.

Example 1

This example opens another document, inserts a prompting message into a text field, sets the focus in the field, and then closes the current document.

```
var otherDoc = app.openDoc("/c/temp/myDoc.pdf");
otherDoc.getField("name").value="Enter your name here: "
otherDoc.getField("name").setFocus();
this.closeDoc();
```

Same example as above, but a relative path is used.

```
var otherDoc = app.openDoc("myDoc.pdf", this);
otherDoc.getField("name").value="Enter your name here: "
otherDoc.getField("name").setFocus();
this.closeDoc();
```

This example uses the Document Object `closeDoc` (page 225) method and the Field Object `setFocus` (page 412) method.

Example 2

Open an HTML document on your hard drive and convert it to PDF.

```
try {
    app.openDoc("/c/myWeb/myHomePage.html");
} catch (e) {};
```

Example 3 (Acrobat 7.0)

Open a hidden PDF document, extract information from it, and close it.

```
oDoc = app.openDoc({
    cPath:"/C/myDocs/myInfo.pdf",
    bHidden: true
});
var v = oDoc.getField("myTextField").value;
```

```
this.getField("yourTextField").value = v;
oDoc.closeDoc();
```

Example 4 (Acrobat 7.0)

Open a non-PDF file by converting it to a PDF document. The following script can be executed successfully from the console.

```
app.openDoc({
    cPath: "/c/temp/myPic.jpg",
    bUseConv: true
})
```

Example 5 (Acrobat 7.0)

Open a file from a WebDAV server. The `app.openDoc` method requires the path to the file to be escaped.

```
var myURL = encodeURI("http://www.myCom.com/My Folder/Com
Doc.pdf");
app.openDoc({cPath: myURL, cFS: "CHTTP" });
```

See also `app.browseForDoc` (page 68).

openFDF

Creates a new FDF Object (page 362) by opening the specified file. The FDF object has methods and properties that can be used on the data that this file contains.

Note: (Security 🅢): This method is available only during batch, console, application initialization and menu events. See also "Privileged versus Non-privileged Context" on page 8.

Parameters

cDIPath	The device-independent path to the file to be opened.

Returns

The FDF Object (page 362) for the FDF file that is opened.

Example

Create a FDF with an embedded PDF file.

```
var fdf = app.newFDF();
fdf.addEmbeddedFile( "/c/myPDFs/myFile.pdf", 1);
fdf.save( "/c/myFDFs/myFile.fdf" ); // save and close this FDF
```

```
// now open the fdf and embed another PDF doc.
var fdf = app.openFDF( "/c/myFDFs/myFile.fdf" );
fdf.addEmbeddedFile( "/c/myPDFs/myOtherFile.pdf", 1);
fdf.save( "/c/myFDFs/myFile.fdf" ); // save and close this FDF
```

See the FDF Object `signatureSign` (page 368) method for another example of usage.

popUpMenu

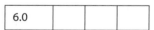

Note: `popUpMenuEx` (page 100) is preferred over this method.

Creates a pop-up menu at the current mouse position, containing the specified items.

Parameters

cItem	(optional) If the argument is a string, it is listed in the menu as a menu item. The menu item name "-" is reserved to draw a separator line in the menu.
Array	(optional) If the argument is an array, it appears as a submenu where the first element in the array is the parent menu item. This array can contain further submenus.

Returns

The name of the menu item that was selected, or `null` if no item was selected.

Example

```
var cChoice = app.popUpMenu("Introduction", "-", "Chapter 1",
    [ "Chapter 2", "Chapter 2 Start", "Chapter 2 Middle",
    ["Chapter 2 End", "The End"]]);
app.alert("You chose the \"" + cChoice + "\" menu item");
```

popUpMenuEx

Creates a pop-up menu at the current mouse position. Each of the parameters is a MenuItem Object (page 101) that describes a menu item to be included in the pop-up menu.

This method is preferred over the use of `popUpMenu` (page 100).

Adobe® Acrobat® Official JavaScript Reference

Parameters

One or more MenuItem Objects (page 101).

Returns

The `cReturn` value of the menu item that was selected, or its `cName` if `cReturn` was not specified for that item. The method returns `null` if no selection was made.

MenuItem Object

This generic JavaScript object represents a menu item. It has the following properties.

cName	The menu item name, which is the string to appear on the menu item. The value of "-" is reserved to draw a separator line in the menu.
bMarked	(optional) A Boolean specifying whether the item is to be marked with a check. The default is `false` (not marked).
bEnabled	(optional) A Boolean specifying whether the item is to appear enabled or grayed out. The default is `true` (enabled).
cReturn	(optional) A string to be returned when the menu item is selected. The default is the value of `cName`.
oSubMenu	(optional) A MenuItem Object (page 101) representing a submenu item or an array of submenu items, each represented by a MenuItem Object.

Example 1

The following example shows all the features of the `popUpMenuEx` method.

```
var cChoice = app.popUpMenuEx
(
    {cName: "Item 1", bMarked:true, bEnabled:false},
    {cName: "-"},
    {cName: "Item 2", oSubMenu:
        [ {cName: "Item 2, Submenu 1"},
            {
                cName: "Item 2, Submenu 2",
                oSubMenu: {cName:"Item 2, Submenu 2,
                    Subsubmenu 1", cReturn: "0"}
            }
        ]
    },
    {cName: "Item 3"},
    {cName: "Item 4", bMarked:true, cReturn: "1"}
)
app.alert("You chose the \"" + cChoice + "\" menu item");
```

Example 2

Because the `popupMenuEx` method takes a list of MenuItem Objects (page 101), its parameters cannot be passed to it as a JavaScript variable. As a workaround, you can create an array of menu items and use the Function object method `apply` from core JavaScript. This method allows arguments to be passed as an array.

```
// Declare pop-up menu properties as an array.
var aParams = [
    {cName: "Adobe Web Page", cReturn: "www.adobe.com"},
    {cName: "-"},
    {cName: "The Adobe Acrobat family",
     cReturn:
"http://www.adobe.com/products/acrobat/main.html"},
    {cName: "Adobe Reader",
     cReturn:
"http://www.adobe.com/products/acrobat/readstep2.html"}
];
// apply the function app.popUpMenuEx to the app object,
// with an array of parameters aParams
var cChoice = app.popUpMenuEx.apply( app, aParams );
if ( cChoice != null ) app.launchURL(cChoice);
```

removeToolButton

6.0			

Removes a previously added button from the toolbar.

Note: (Acrobat 7.0) To remove a toolbutton added by the `addToolButton` (page 62) method, `removeToolButton` must be executed within the same context as when `addToolButton` was executed.

If no document was open in Acrobat when the button was added, there must be no document open in Acrobat when the button is removed. See Example 2 below.

Similarly, if a certain document was the active document when a toolbutton was added, that same document must be active for the button to be removed using `removeToolButton`.

In the case of a document that is active when the toolbutton is added, the button is automatically removed when this document is closed. See also the notes following the description of `addToolButton` (page 62).

Parameters

cName	The language-independent identifier provided when `addToolButton` (page 62) was called.

Returns

Nothing

Exceptions

None

Example 1

See the example following `addToolButton` (page 62).

Example 2

This example shows the removal of a toolbutton with the same context as `addToolButton`. Initially, there is no document open in the Acrobat. Execute the following code from the console:

```
app.addToolButton({cName: "button1",
cExec:"app.alert('pressed');",
    cTooltext:"Button1"});
```

Open a PDF document in Acrobat and execute the next line from the console:

```
app.removeToolButton({cName:"button1"});
```

An exception is thrown and the removal of the button fails.

If you close the PDF document and execute the `removeToolButton` script again, the button is removed.

response

3.01			

Displays a dialog box containing a question and an entry field for the user to reply to the question.

Parameters

cQuestion	The question to be posed to the user.
cTitle	(optional) The title of the dialog box.
cDefault	(optional) A default value for the answer to the question. If not specified, no default value is presented.
bPassword	(optional) If `true`, indicates that the user's response should show as asterisks (*) or bullets (•) to mask the response, which might be sensitive information. The default is `false`.
cLabel	(optional, Acrobat 6.0) A short string to appear in front of and on the same line as the edit text field.

Returns

A string containing the user's response. If the user clicks the **Cancel** button, the response is the `null` object.

Example

This example asks for a response from the user and reports back the response.

```
var cResponse = app.response({
    cQuestion: "How are you today?",
        cTitle: "Your Health Status",
        cDefault: "Fine",
        cLabel: "Response:"
});
if (cResponse == null)
    app.alert("Thanks for trying anyway.");
else
    app.alert("You responded, \""+cResponse+"\",
        to the health " + "question.",3);
```

setInterval

5.0			

Specifies a JavaScript script and a time period. The script is executed every time the period elapses.

The return value of this method must be held in a JavaScript variable. Otherwise, the interval object is subject to garbage-collection, which would cause the clock to stop.

To terminate the periodic execution, pass the returned interval object to `clearInterval` (page 69).

Note: Beginning with Acrobat 7.05, an interval is automatically terminated when the document whose script called `setInterval` is closed (assuming it was not previously terminated).

Note: Opening and closing the document JavaScripts dialog box causes the JavaScript interpreter to re-read the document JavaScripts and consequently to re-initialize any document-level variables. Resetting document-level variables in this way after JavaScript expressions have been registered to be evaluated by `setInterval` (page 104) or `setTimeOut` (page 105) may cause JavaScript errors if those scripts use document-level variables.

See also `clearInterval` (page 69), `setTimeOut` (page 105), and `clearTimeOut` (page 70).

Adobe® Acrobat® Official JavaScript Reference

Parameters

cExpr	The JavaScript script to be executed.
nMilliseconds	The time period in milliseconds.

Returns

An interval object

Example

For example, to create a simple color animation on a field called "Color" that changes every second:

```
function DoIt() {
    var f = this.getField("Color");
    var nColor = (timeout.count++ % 10 / 10);
    // Various shades of red.
    var aColor = new Array("RGB", nColor, 0, 0);
    f.fillColor = aColor;
}
// save return value as a variable
timeout = app.setInterval("DoIt()", 1000);
// Add a property to our timeout object so that DoIt() can keep
// a count going.
timeout.count = 0;
```

See setTimeOut (page 105) for an additional example.

setTimeOut

5.0			

Specifies a JavaScript script and a time period. The script is executed one time only, after the period elapses.

The return value of this method must be held in a JavaScript variable. Otherwise, the timeout object is subject to garbage-collection, which would cause the clock to stop.

To cancel the timeout event , pass the returned timeout object to clearTimeOut (page 70).

Note: Beginning with Acrobat 7.05, an interval is automatically terminated when the document whose script called setInterval is closed (assuming it was not previously terminated).

Note: Opening and closing the document JavaScripts dialog box causes the JavaScript interpreter to re-read the document JavaScripts and consequently to re-initialize any document-level variables. Resetting document-level variables in this way after JavaScript expressions have been registered to be evaluated by `setInterval` (page 104) or `setTimeOut` (page 105) may cause JavaScript errors if those scripts use document-level variables.

See also `clearTimeOut` (page 70), `setInterval` (page 104), and `clearInterval` (page 69).

Parameters

cExpr	The JavaScript script to be executed.
nMilliseconds	The time period in milliseconds.

Returns

A `timeout` object

Example

This example creates a simple running marquee. Assume there is a text field named "marquee". The default value of this field is "Adobe Acrobat version 7.0 will soon be here!".

```
// Document-level JavaScript function
function runMarquee() {
    var f = this.getField("marquee");
    var cStr = f.value;
    // get field value
    var aStr = cStr.split("");       // convert to an array
    aStr.push(aStr.shift());         // move first char to last
    cStr = aStr.join("");            // back to string again
    f.value = cStr;                  // put new value in field
}

// Insert a mouse-up action into a "Go" button
run = app.setInterval("runMarquee()", 100);
// stop after a minute
stoprun=app.setTimeOut("app.clearInterval(run)",6000);

// Insert a mouse-up action into a "Stop" button
try {
    app.clearInterval(run);
    app.clearTimeOut(stoprun);
} catch (e){}
```

The "Stop" button code is protected with a `try/catch` construct. If the user presses the "Stop" button without having first pressed "Go", `run` and `stoprun` will be undefined and the "Stop" code will throw an exception. When the exception is thrown, the `catch` code is executed. In this example, the code does nothing if the user presses "Stop" first.

trustedFunction

7.0		🔊	

Marks a function as trusted. Trusted functions can explicitly increase the current *privilege level* for their stack frame. Typically, the stack frame (which corresponds to the body of the function) contains security-restricted methods that require a privileged context in which to run. By increasing the privilege level, these restricted methods can be executed in non-privileged contexts. See "Privileged versus Non-privileged Context" on page 8.

Within the body of the function definition, calls to the `app.beginPriv` (page 67) and `app.endPriv` (page 70) methods must enclose any code that normally executes in a privileged context, as the examples below show.

Note: (Security 🔊): This method is available only during batch, console, and application initialization.

Parameters

oFunc	A function object that specifies the function to mark as trusted.

Returns

On success, returns the same function object that was passed in. After successful execution, the function object will be trusted. On error, throws `NotAllowedError`.

Method Syntax

This method can be called in two ways.

```
myTrustedFunction = app.trustedFunction(
    function()
    {
        <function body>
    }
);
```

or

```
function myOtherTrustedFunction()
{
    <function body>
};
app.trustedFunction(myOtherTrustedFunction);
```

The following examples, along with the examples following the `app.trustPropagatorFunction` (page 110) method, contain many comments that clarify the notion of trusted function and highlight some of the nuances of the topic.

Example 1

`app.newDoc` (page 94) is a security-restricted method that needs a privileged context in which to run. For example, it cannot normally be executed from a mouse-up event. This example shows how this method can be executed from a mouse-up event by creating a trusted function.

Place the following script in a `.js` in the User (or App) JavaScript folder.

```
trustedNewDoc = app.trustedFunction( function (nWidth,
nHeight)
{
    // additional code may appear above
    app.beginPriv();        // explicitly raise privilege
    app.newDoc( nWidth, nHeight );
    app.endPriv();
    // additional code may appear below.
})
```

After Acrobat is restarted, the `trustedNewDoc` function can be executed from anywhere. The following script for a mouse-up action of a button creates a new document that is 200 points by 200 points.

```
trustedNewDoc( 200, 200 );
```

Because of security restrictions, `app.newDoc(200,200)` cannot normally be executed from a mouse-up event. The trusted function permits the creation of a new document.

Note: This example is simplified. The trusted function could be modified so that it also has the two optional arguments of the `app.newDoc` method.

The `trustedNewDoc` function can also be executed as a menu item.

```
app.addMenuItem( {
    cName: "myTrustedNewDoc",
    cUser: "New Doc", cParent: "Tools",
    cExec: "trustedNewDoc(200,200)", nPos: 0
} );
```

Again, `trustedNewDoc` could be enhanced by having the user input the dimensions for the new document, either through a series of `app.response` (page 103) dialogs, or a full dialog, created by `app.execDialog` (page 71).

Note: If `app.newDoc` is not enclosed in the `app.beginPriv/app.endPriv` pair, executing `trustedNewDoc` from a non-privileged context will fail and an exception will be thrown. You must explicitly raise the privilege level in the way shown.

Example 2

The `app.activeDocs` (page 49) property behaves differently depending on the setting:

- During a console or batch event, it returns an array of all active documents.
- In a non-privileged context, it returns an array of only those active documents that have their `disclosed` (page 193) property set to `true`.

To overcome this limitation in non-privileged context, you can define a trusted function that raises the privilege level and calls `activeDocs`. This function would be defined in a `.js` file in the User (or App) JavaScript folder:

```
trustedActiveDocs = app.trustedFunction (
    function()
    {
        app.beginPriv(); // explicitly raise privilege
        var d = app.activeDocs;
        app.endPriv();
        return d;
    }
)
```

The following code can be executed from a mouse-up action of a form button, for example:

```
var d = trustedActiveDocs();
console.println("There are d = " + d.length
    + " files open in the viewer.")
for ( var i=0; i< d.length; i++)
    console.println((i+1) + ". " + d[i].documentFileName )
```

The console reports the number and file name of all documents—disclosed or not—open in the viewer.

Example 3

A trusted function is capable of explicitly increasing the current privilege level only for its own stack frame. This example shows some related issues.

The following code attempts to make a trusted function more modular:

```
function mySaveAs(doc, path)
{
    doc.saveAs(doc, path);
}
myFunc = app.trustedFunction( function (doc, path)
{
    // privileged and/or non-privileged code here
    app.beginPriv();
    mySaveAs(doc, path);
    app.endPriv();
    // privileged and/or non-privileged code here
}
```

A problem occurs because when the privileged code `doc.saveAs(doc, path)` is executed, it is not within the stack frame (function body) of the calling trusted function `myFunc` but rather within the stack frame of `mySaveAs`, which is not a trusted function. Therefore, when `myFunc` is executed in a non-privileged context, it throws an exception.

A possible solution is to make `mySaveAs` into a trusted function so that `myFunc` succeeds. However, this exposes the privileged `doc.saveAs` function to non-privileged execution by anyone that knows this function is on your system.

You cannot simply enclose `doc.saveAs(doc,path)` in a `beginPriv/endPriv` pair. When `myFunc` is run from a non-privileged context, an exception will be thrown by the `app.beginPriv` within the body of the `mySaveAs` function. This is because `mySaveAs` is not trusted and therefore is not authorized to request an increased privilege level.

To summarize the observations above, there is a need for a kind of function that has the following characteristics:

- It can be called by a trusted function.
- It is not trusted itself and therefore cannot be directly called from a non-privileged context.

A *trust propagator* function satisfies these criteria (see trustPropagatorFunction, below).

trustPropagatorFunction

7.0		🅢	

Marks a function as a *trust propagator*. Such a function is not itself trusted but can inherit trust if called from a trusted function.

A trust propagator function propagates trust, not privilege. Therefore, as with the method `app.trustedFunction` (page 107), an `app.beginPriv` (page 67)/`app.endPriv` (page 70) pair must enclose any code within the function body that normally executes in a privileged context.

Trust propagator functions can play the role of utility functions. They can be called by a trusted function and by another trust propagator function, but they cannot successfully be called by a function that is not trusted in a non-privileged context.

Note: Functions defined in `.js` files in the App JavaScript folder are implicitly trust propagator functions. Functions defined in `.js` files in the User JavaScript folder are not.

Note: (Security ⊘): This method is available only during batch, console, and application initialization.

Method Syntax

This method can be called in two ways.

```
myPropagatorFunction = app.trustPropagatorFunction(
    function()
    {
        <function body>
    }
);
```

or

```
function myOtherPropagatorFunction()
{
    <function body>
};
app.trustPropagatorFunction(myOtherPropagatorFunction);
```

Parameters

oFunc	A function object that specifies the function to mark as a trust propagator.

Returns

On success, returns the same function object that was passed in. After successful execution, the function object will be a trust propagator. On error, throws `NotAllowedError`.

Example 1

For background, see "Example 3" on page 109.

This example defines a trust propagator function, `mySaveAs`, to save a file to a folder, and a trusted function, `myTrustedSpecialTaskFunc`, to perform various tasks involving privileged and non-privileged code. The `mySaveAs` function cannot be called directly in a non-privileged context.

```
mySaveAs = app.trustPropagatorFunction(function(doc,path)
{
    app.beginPriv();
        doc.saveAs(path);
    app.endPriv();
})
myTrustedSpecialTaskFunc =
app.trustedFunction(function(doc,path)
{
    // privileged and/or non-privileged code above
    app.beginPriv();
        mySaveAs(doc,path);
```

```
    app.endPriv();
    // privileged and/or non-privileged code below
});
```

Executing the code

```
myTrustedSpecialTaskFunc(this, "/c/temp/mySavedDoc.pdf");
```

from a mouse-up button, for example, saves the current document to the
specified path.

Example 2

This example develops a simple dialog using the `app.execDialog` (page 71)
method and executes privileged code.

The dialog box asks for your name and asks you to browse for a document
from your local hard drive (or a network drive). When you click the **OK**
button, the selected file is loaded into the viewer and your name is placed in
the author field of the document properties. (The insertion of the name only
occurs if the author field is empty.) The dialog also displays the value of
`identity.email`, which is privileged information.

Any privileged code is enclosed by a `beginPriv`/`endPriv` pair.

Note the use of the `ANTrustPropagateAll` function, which is useful for
creating dialogs that use privileged code. It takes a single object as its
argument, turns every function in the object into a trust propagator
function, then returns that object.

```
myDialog = app.trustedFunction(function()
{
    app.beginPriv();
    var dialog = ANTrustPropagateAll({
        initialize:function(dialog) {
            this.data = {}; // an object to hold dialog data
            app.beginPriv();
            dialog.load({ "emai": "Email: " + identity.email });
            app.endPriv();
        },
        commit:function (dialog) { // called when OK pressed
            var results = dialog.store();
            console.println("Your name is " + results["name"] );
            this.data.name = results["name"];
        },
        brws: function (dialog) {
            app.beginPriv();
            var oRetn = app.browseForDoc();
            if ( typeof oRetn != "undefined")
              this.data.oRetn = oRetn;
            app.endPriv();
        },
        doDialog:function() {
            app.beginPriv();
```

```
            var retn = app.execDialog(this);
            app.endPriv();
            return retn;
        },
        description: {
            name: "Open File & Populate Info Field",
            align_children: "align_left",
            elements:
            [
                {
                    type: "view",
                    align_children: "align_left",
                    elements:
                    [
                        {
                            type: "view",
                            align_children: "align_row",
                            elements:
                            [
                                {
                                    type: "static_text",
                                    name: "Name: "
                                },
                                {
                                    item_id: "name",
                                    type: "edit_text",
                                    alignment: "align_fill",
                                    width: 300,
                                    height: 20
                                },
                            ]
                        },
                        {
                            type: "static_text",
                            item_id: "emai",
                            name: "Email: ",
                            char_width: 25
                        },
                        {
                            type: "gap",
                            height: 10
                        },
                        {
                            type: "view",
                            align_children: "align_row",
                            elements:
                            [
                                {
                                    type: "button",
                                    name: "Browse",
                                    item_id: "brws"
                                },
                                {
                                    type: "ok_cancel",
```

```
                                    ok_name: "Ok",
                                    cancel_name: "Cancel"
                                }
                            ]
                        }
                    ]
                }
            ]
        }
    });
    app.endPriv();
    try { // protect against user pressing the "Esc" key
        // After everything is set up, run the dialog
        // using the doDialog function, defined in the
        // object dialog.
        var retn = dialog.doDialog();
        app.beginPriv();
        // if use clicked the ok button and there is oRetn
        //  data, we load the requested file using
        //  app.openDoc(), a restricted method.
        if ( (retn == "ok") && dialog.data.oRetn ) {
            var oDoc = app.openDoc({
              cPath: dialog.data.oRetn.cPath,
              cFS: dialog.data.oRetn.cFS
            });
            if ( !oDoc.info.Author )
              oDoc.info.Author = dialog.data.name;
        }
        app.endPriv();
    } catch(e) {}
})
```

This dialog can be activated from a button or, more appropriately, from a menu item or a toolbar button. For example, place the following code in a User JavaScript file to add a menu item to the **Tools** menu.

```
app.addMenuItem( { cName: "myDialog",
cUser: "My Cool Dialog", cParent: "Tools",
cExec: "myDialog()", nPos: 0 } );
```

app.media Object

This object defines properties and functions useful in multimedia JavaScript code.

Several `app.media` properties are enumeration objects that list the values allowed in various properties. Future versions of Acrobat may add more such values, and JavaScript code should be prepared to encounter values other than the ones listed here. Similarly, JavaScript code may be run on an older version of Acrobat than it was designed for, in which case it must fall back to using the values available in that version.

app.media Properties

align

6.0			

Enumerates the values that may be found in the `MediaSettings.floating.align` (page 467) property. The alignment is relative to the window specified by the `MediaSettings.floating.over` (page 467) property. (See the values for `app.media.over`, page 118.)

Valid values are listed in the table below.

Value	Position of floating window
`app.media.align.topLeft`	At the top left corner
`app.media.align.topCenter`	At the top center
`app.media.align.topRight`	At the top right corner
`app.media.align.centerLeft`	At the center left
`app.media.align.center`	At the center
`app.media.align.centerRight`	At the center right
`app.media.align.bottomLeft`	At the bottom left corner
`app.media.align.bottomCenter`	At the bottom center
`app.media.align.bottomRight`	At the bottom right corner

Type: Object (enumeration)   *Access: R*

canResize

6.0			

Enumerates the values that may be found in the
`MediaSettings.floating.canResize` (page 467) property, which
specifies whether a floating window may be resized by the user.

These values are listed in the table below.

Value	Description
app.media.canResize.no	May not be resized
app.media.canResize.keepRatio	May be resized only if the aspect ratio is preserved
app.media.canResize.yes	May be resized without preserving the aspect ratio

Type: Object (enumeration)   *Access: R*

closeReason

6.0			

Enumerates the values that may be found in the `event.reason` property for
a Close event. These values are:

```
app.media.closeReason.general
app.media.closeReason.error
app.media.closeReason.done
app.media.closeReason.stop
app.media.closeReason.play
app.media.closeReason.uiGeneral
app.media.closeReason.uiScreen
app.media.closeReason.uiEdit
app.media.closeReason.docClose
app.media.closeReason.docSave
app.media.closeReason.docChange
```

See the `afterClose` (page 340) and `onClose` (page 349) methods of the
EventListener Object.

Type: Object (enumeration)   *Access: R*

defaultVisible

6.0			

This property is defined as `true`, which is the default value for
`MediaSettings.visible` (page 473).

Type: Boolean   *Access: R*

ifOffScreen

6.0			

Enumerates the values allowed in a
`MediaSettings.floating.ifOffScreen` (page 467) property, which
specifies what action should be taken if the floating window is positioned
totally or partially offscreen.

These values and their descriptions are given in the table below.

Value	Description
`app.media.ifOffScreen.allow`	Take no action
`app.media.ifOffScreen.forceOnScreen`	Move and/or resize the window so that it is on-screen
`app.media.ifOffScreen.cancel`	Cancel playing the media clip

Type: Object (enumeration)   *Access: R*

layout

6.0			

Enumerates the values allowed in a `MediaSettings.layout` (page 468)
property.

The table below contains the values and their descriptions.

Value	Description
`app.media.layout.meet`	Scale to fit all content, preserve aspect, no clipping, background fill
`app.media.layout.slice`	Scale to fill the window, preserve aspect, and clip X or Y as needed
`app.media.layout.fill`	Scale X and Y separately to fill the window
`app.media.layout.scroll`	Natural size with scrolling
`app.media.layout.hidden`	Natural size with clipping
`app.media.layout.standard`	Use the player's default settings

Type: Object (enumeration)   *Access: R*

monitorType

6.0			

Enumerates the values allowed in a `MediaSettings.monitorType`
(page 469) property.

The table below contains the values and their descriptions:

Value	Description
`app.media.monitorType.document`	The monitor containing the largest section of the document window
`app.media.monitorType.nonDocument`	The monitor containing the smallest section of the document window
`app.media.monitorType.primary`	Primary monitor
`app.media.monitorType.bestColor`	Monitor with the greatest color depth
`app.media.monitorType.largest`	Monitor with the greatest area (in pixels squared)
`app.media.monitorType.tallest`	Monitor with the greatest height (in pixels)
`app.media.monitorType.widest`	Monitor with the greatest width (in pixels)

Type: Object (enumeration)   *Access: R*

openCode

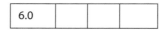

Enumerates the values that may be found in the code property of the return value from `MediaPlayer.open` (page 454). The values are:

```
app.media.openCode.success
app.media.openCode.failGeneral
app.media.openCode.failSecurityWindow
app.media.openCode.failPlayerMixed
app.media.openCode.failPlayerSecurityPrompt
app.media.openCode.failPlayerNotFound
app.media.openCode.failPlayerMimeType
app.media.openCode.failPlayerSecurity
app.media.openCode.failPlayerData
```

Type: Object (enumeration)   *Access: R*

over

6.0			

Enumerates the values allowed in a `MediaSettings.floating.over` (page 467) property, the value of which is used to align a floating window. See `app.media.align` (page 115).

Value	Description
`app.media.over.pageWindow`	Align the floating window relative to the document (page) window
`app.media.over.appWindow`	Align the floating window relative to the application window

---

Value	Description
app.media.over.desktop	Align the floating window relative to the full virtual desktop
app.media.over.monitor	Align the floating window relative to the (selected) monitor display screen

Type: Object (enumeration)   *Access: R*

pageEventNames

6.0			

Enumerates the values that may be found in the event.name property for a page-level action. Event names that represent direct user actions are not included here. This enumeration is used to distinguish page-level actions from user actions. The values are:

```
app.media.pageEventNames.Open
app.media.pageEventNames.Close
app.media.pageEventNames.InView
app.media.pageEventNames.OutView
```

Type: Object (enumeration)   *Access: R*

Example

app.media.pageEventNames can be used to distinguish between a page-level action and a direct user action. The script below is folder-level or document-level JavaScript that can be called from anywhere in a document.

```
function myMMfunction () {
    if ( app.media.pageEventNames[event.name] ) {
        console.println("Page Event: " + event.name);
        ...
    } else {
        console.println("User Generated Event: " + event.name);
        ...
    }
}
```

raiseCode

6.0			

Enumerates values that may be found in the error.raiseCode property when an exception is thrown. This property exists only when error.name is "RaiseError". Other values may be encountered in addition to these.

```
app.media.raiseCode.fileNotFound
app.media.raiseCode.fileOpenFailed
```

Type: Object (enumeration)   *Access: R*

---

raiseSystem

Enumerates values that may be found in the `error.raiseSystem` property when an exception is thrown. This property exists only when `error.name` is "RaiseError".

```
app.media.raiseSystem.fileError
```

```
Other values may be added to the above property.
```

Type: Object (enumeration)   *Access: R*

renditionType

Enumerates the values that may be found in `Rendition.type` (page 521). The values and their descriptions are given below.

Value	Description
`app.media.renditionType.unknown`	A type not known by this version of Acrobat
`app.media.renditionType.media`	A media rendition
`app.media.renditionType.selector`	A rendition selector

Type: Object (enumeration)   *Access: R*

status

Enumerates the values that may be found in the `event.media.code` property for a Status event (see `onStatus`, page 357/`afterStatus`, page 348). Most of these values have additional information that is found in the `event.text` property. The values are:

Value	Description
`app.media.status.clear`	Empty string—this status event clears any message
`app.media.status.message`	General message
`app.media.status.contacting`	Hostname being contacted
`app.media.status.buffering`	Progress message or nothing
`app.media.status.init`	Name of the engine being initialized
`app.media.status.seeking`	Empty string

Along with the `event.media.status` code, there is also the `event.media.text`, a string that reflects the current status, as described above.

Type: Object (enumeration)   *Access: R*

See `afterStatus` (page 348) and `onStatus` (page 357).

trace

6.0			

Set this property to `true` to print trace messages to the JavaScript console during player creation and event dispatching.

Note: `app.media.trace` is for test purposes only. Do not use this property in a PDF file that you publish. It will change in future versions of Acrobat.

Type: Boolean   *Access: R/W*

version

6.0			

The version number of the multimedia API, currently 7.0.

Type: Number   *Access: R*

windowType

6.0			

Enumerates the values allowed in a `MediaSettings.windowType` (page 473) property. These values are given in the table below.

Value	Description
`app.media.windowType.docked`	Docked to a PDF page
`app.media.windowType.floating`	Floating (pop-up) window
`app.media.windowType.fullScreen`	Full screen mode

Type: Object (enumeration)   *Access: R*

app.media Methods

addStockEvents

6.0			

Adds stock EventListeners to a MediaPlayer Object (page 448) and sets `player.stockEvents` as a reference to these listeners for later removal.

If the optional `annot` parameter is provided, a reference to the annotation is saved in `MediaPlayer.annot` (page 448). Later, when the player is opened with `MediaPlayer.open` (page 454), stock EventListeners will also be added to this annotation and `annot.player` (page 536) will be set as a reference to the player.

Parameters

player	A required MediaPlayer Object (page 448)
annot	(optional) A ScreenAnnot Object (page 533)

Returns

Nothing.

The stock EventListeners provide standard Acrobat behavior such as focus handling.

If `app.media.trace` (page 121) is `true`, debug trace listeners are also included with the stock EventListeners.

Use the `removeStockEvents` (page 138) method to remove EventListeners that were added with `addStockEvents`.

The `app.media.createPlayer` (page 126) and `app.media.openPlayer` (page 136) methods call `addStockEvents` internally, so in most cases it is not necessary to call this method yourself.

alertFileNotFound

6.0			

Displays the standard file not found alert, with an optional **Don't show again** check box.

Parameters

oDoc	oDoc is the document object the alert is associated with.
cFilename	cFilename is the name of the missing file.
bCanSkipAlert	(optional) If bCanSkipAlert is true and the user checks the check box, returns true, otherwise returns false. The default is false.

Returns

If bCanSkipAlert is true, returns true if the check box is checked, otherwise returns false.

Example

```
if ( !doNotNotify )
{
    var bRetn = app.media.alertFileNotFound(
        this, cFileClip, true );
    var doNotNotify = bRetn;
}
```

alertSelectFailed

6.0			

Displays the standard alert for a rendition.select (page 523) failure.

Parameters

oDoc	The Document Object (page 188) the alert is associated with
oRejects	(optional) If provided, an array of MediaReject Objects (page 461) as returned by PlayerInfoList.select (page 496).
bCanSkipAlert	(optional) If true and the user checks the check box, the method returns true; otherwise, the method returns false. The default is false.
bFromUser	(optional) A Boolean that affects the wording of the alert message. It should be true if a direct user action triggered this code, or false if some other action, such as selecting a bookmark, triggered it. The default is false.

Returns

If bCanSkipAlert is true, returns true if the check box is checked, otherwise returns false.

Note: When rendition.select fails to find a usable player, and the select parameter bWantRejects is set to true, the returned MediaSelection Object (page 462) will contain an array of

---

MediaReject Objects (page 461), which can be passed to this method as the `oRejects` parameter. The `alertSelectFailed` method will, in turn, ask the user to go to the web to download an appropriate player.

Example

Displays **Cannot play media clip**, with check box.

```
var bRetn = app.media.alertSelectFailed({
    oDoc: this,
    bCanSkipAlert: true
});
```

argsDWIM

This method is a "do what I mean" function that is used by `app.media.createPlayer` (page 126), `app.media.openPlayer` (page 136), and `app.media.startPlayer` (page 138). It fills in default values for properties that are not provided in the PlayerArgs Object (page 127), picking them out of the `event` Object (page 314), so that these functions may be used as rendition action event handlers with no arguments or in custom JavaScript with explicit arguments.

Parameters

args	A PlayerArgs Object (see PlayerArgs Object, page 127, and `app.media.createPlayer`, page 126).

Returns

PlayerArgs Object (page 127)

Example

See "Example 1" on page 128 for an example of usage.

canPlayOrAlert

Determines whether any media playback is allowed and returns `true` if it is. If playback is not allowed, it alerts the user and returns `false`.

Parameters

args	A PlayerArgs Object (see PlayerArgs Object, page 127, and `app.media.createPlayer`, page 126).

Returns

`true` if media playback is allowed, otherwise `false`.

Note: The `createPlayer` (page 126) method calls this function before attempting to create a player. If you write your own code to substitute for `createPlayer`, you can call `canPlayOrAlert` to alert the user in situations where playback is not allowed, such as in multimedia authoring mode.

The only property in the `args` object that is used is `doc`, so you can use:

```
// There is a document object in myDoc
if ( app.media.canPlayOrAlert({ doc: myDoc })
/* OK to create player here */ ;
```

The above code displays "Cannot play media while in authoring mode", or other alerts, as appropriate.

computeFloatWinRect

6.0			

Calculates and returns the rectangle in screen coordinates needed as specified by its parameters.

Parameters

`doc`	The Document Object (page 188) for the document.
`floating`	The floating parameters from the object returned by `MediaSettings.floating` (page 467).
`monitorType`	A number indicating which monitor to use. See the `app.media.monitorType` (page 117) property.
`uiSize`	(optional) The user interface size given as an array of four numbers [w, x, y, z] representing the size, as returned by `MediaPlayer.uiSize` (page 452).

Returns

The rectangle in screen coordinates.

Example

```
var floating =
{
    over: app.media.over.monitor,
    align: app.media.align.center,
    canResize: app.media.canResize.no,
    hasClose: false,
    hasTitle: true,
```

```
            width: 400,
            height: 400
      }
      var rect = app.media.computeFloatWinRect
            (this, floating, app.media.monitorType.primary);
```

constrainRectToScreen

6.0			

Returns a rectangle of screen coordinates, moved and resized if needed to place it entirely on some display monitor. If `anchorPt` is provided and `rect` must be shrunk to fit, it shrinks proportionally toward `anchorPt` (which is an array of two numbers representing a point as [x, y]).

Parameters

rect	An array of four numbers representing the screen coordinates of the d rectangle.
anchorPt	(optional) An array of two points [x, y] that is to be an anchor point.

Returns

A rectangle in screen coordinates.

createPlayer

6.0			

Creates a MediaPlayer Object (page 448) without opening the player.

Note: To open the player, call `MediaPlayer.open` (page 454). You can combine these two steps into one by calling `app.media.openPlayer` (page 136) instead of `createPlayer`.

If `createPlayer` is called inside a rendition action (for example, in custom JavaScript entered from the Actions tab in the Multimedia Properties panel), default values are taken from the action's `event` Object (page 314). The `args` parameter is not required in this case unless you want to override the rendition action's values. `createPlayer` calls `argsDWIM` (page 124) to process the `event` Object (page 314) and `args` (see "PlayerArgs Object" on page 127) parameter.

Unless `noStockEvents` of the PlayerArgs Object (page 127) is set to `true`, the MediaPlayer Object (page 448) is equipped with stock EventListeners that provide the standard behavior required to interact properly with

Acrobat. Additional EventListeners can be provided in the PlayerArgs object or may be added afterward with `MediaPlayer.events.add` (page 449).

If `args.annot.player` (page 536) is an open `MediaPlayer`, `createPlayer` closes that player, which triggers events.

Parameters

args	A PlayerArgs object, whose required and optional properties are described below. If `createPlayer` is executed within a Rendition action with an associated rendition, this parameter is optional and its properties are populated by the defaults and by options selected in the UI. Otherwise, this parameter is required.

PlayerArgs Object

Property	Type	Description
doc	Object	The Document Object (page 188) of the document. Required if both `annot` and `rendition` are omitted, for example, for URL playback.
annot	Object	A ScreenAnnot Object (page 533). Required for docked playback unless it is found in the `event` Object (page 314) or `MediaSettings.page` (page 470) is provided. The new player is associated with the annotation. If a player was already associated with the annotation, it is stopped and closed.
rendition	Object	(optional) A Rendition Object (page 520) (either a MediaRendition or a RenditionList). Required unless `rendition` is found in the `event` Object (page 314) or URL is present.
URL	String	Either URL or `rendition` is required, with URL taking precedence.
mimeType	String	(optional) Ignored unless URL is present. If URL is present, either `mimeType` or `settings.players` (page 470), as returned by `app.media.getPlayers` (page 131), is required.
settings	Object	(optional) A MediaSettings Object (page 464). Overrides the `rendition` settings.
events	Object	(optional) An EventListener Object (page 338). Optional if stock events are used, added after stock events.
noStockEvents	Boolean	(optional) If `true`, do not use stock events. The default is `false`.
fromUser	Boolean	(optional) It should be `true` if a direct user action will trigger this code, or `false`, otherwise. The default depends on the `event` Object (page 314).

Property	Type	Description
showAltText	Boolean	(optional) If true, show alternate text (see Rendition.altText, page 520) if the media cannot be played. The default is true.
showEmptyAltText	Boolean	(optional) If true and alternate text (see Rendition.altText, page 520) is empty, show the alternate text as an empty box; if false, respond with an alert. The default value is true if fromUser is false, and false if fromUser is true.

Returns

MediaPlayer Object (page 448)

Example 1

The following code is the definition of openPlayer (page 136), which uses createPlayer in its definition.

```
app.media.openPlayer = function( args )
{
    var player = null;
    try
    {
        args = app.media.argsDWIM( args );

        player = app.media.createPlayer( args );
        if( player )
        {
            var result = player.open();
            if( result.code != app.media.openCode.success )
            {
                player = null;
                app.media.alert
                    ( "Open", args, { code: result.code } );
            }
            else if( player.visible )
                player.setFocus();  // triggers Focus event
        }
    }
    catch( e )
    {
        player = null;
        app.media.alert( 'Exception', args, { error: e } );
    }

    return player;
}
```

Adobe® Acrobat® Official JavaScript Reference

Example 2

See the examples at the end of the description of `openPlayer` (page 136) for examples of PlayerArgs usage.

getAltTextData

6.0			

Returns a MediaData object (see `MediaSettings.data`, page 465) that represents alternate text data for the given text. This object can be used to create a player to display the alternate text.

Parameters

`cAltText`	A string that is to be used as alternate text data.

Returns

MediaData object (see `MediaSettings.data`, page 465).

Example

See the embedded example following the `getAltTextSettings` method.

getAltTextSettings

6.0			

Takes a PlayerArgs Object (page 127) containing at least `settings`, `showAltText`, and `showEmptyAltText` properties, along with a selection object as returned by `rendition.select` (page 523), and finds the first available alternate text rendition if there is one. It then creates and returns a new MediaSettings Object (page 464) suitable for playback of the alternate text. Otherwise it returns `null`.

Parameters

`args`	A PlayerArgs Object (page 127)
`selection`	A MediaSelection Object (page 462)

Returns

MediaSettings Object (page 464) or `null`

Example

This example plays back the alternate text of the rendition. The code plays back the alternate text in a screen annotation, but can be modified for playback in a floating window.

```
var rendition = this.media.getRendition("myClip");
var settings = rendition.getPlaySettings();
var args = {
    settings: settings,
    showAltText: true,
    showEmptyAltText: true
};
var selection = rendition.select();
settings = app.media.getAltTextSettings( args, selection );

// You can also play custom alternate text by uncommenting
// the next line
// settings.data = app.media.getAltTextData("A. C. Robat");

// Uncomment the code below to obtain a floating window
// to playback the alternate text
/*
settings.windowType = app.media.windowType.floating
settings.floating = {
    canResize: app.media.canResize.keepRatio,
    hasClose: true,
    width: 400,
    height: 100
} */

// now define an args parameter for use with openPlayer,
// which will play the alternate text.
args = {
    rendition: rendition,
    annot: this.media.getAnnot({nPage: 0,\
        cAnnotTitle:"myScreen"}),
    settings: settings
};
app.media.openPlayer(args);
```

getAnnotStockEvents

Returns an event Object (page 314) containing the stock EventListeners required in a screen annotation for normal playback in Acrobat. The stock EventListeners provide standard Acrobat behavior such as focus handling.

If app.media.trace (page 121) is true, debug trace listeners are also included with the stock EventListeners.

Parameters

settings	A number corresponding to the window type (see app.media.windowType, page 121).

Returns

event Object (page 314)

getAnnotTraceEvents

6.0			

Returns an Events Object (page 358) containing EventListeners that provide a debugging trace as events are dispatched.

Parameters

None

Returns

Events Object (page 358)

getPlayers

6.0			

Returns a PlayerInfoList Object (page 496), which is an array of PlayerInfo Objects (page 489) representing the available media players.

The PlayerInfoList may be filtered using its select (page 496) method, and it may be used in the settings.players (page 470) property when creating a media player with createPlayer (page 126).

See PlayerInfoList Object (page 496) and PlayerInfo Object (page 489) for more details.

Parameters

cMimeType	(optional) An optional MIME type such as "audio/wav". If cMimeType is omitted, the list includes all available players. If cMimeType is specified, the list includes only players that can handle that MIME type.

Returns

PlayerInfoList Object (page 496)

Example 1

List MP3 players to the debug console.

```
var mp = app.media.getPlayers("audio/mp3")
for ( var i = 0; i < mp.length; i++) {
    console.println("\nmp[" + i + "] Properties");
    for ( var p in mp[i] ) console.println(p + ": " + mp[i][p]);
}
```

Example 2

Choose any player that can play Flash media by matching the MIME type. The code assumes the code below is executed as a Rendition action with associated rendition (so no arguments for createPlayer are required).

```
var player = app.media.createPlayer();
player.settings.players
    = app.media.getPlayers( "application/x-shockwave-flash" );
player.open();
```

getPlayerStockEvents

6.0			

Returns an Events Object (page 358) containing the stock EventListeners required in a media player for normal playback in Acrobat. The stock EventListeners provide standard Acrobat behavior such as focus handling.

Use MediaPlayer.events.add (page 449) to add these stock events to a media player.

The app.media.createPlayer (page 126) and app.media.openPlayer (page 136) methods automatically call getPlayerStockEvents internally, so it is not necessary to call this method yourself unless you are writing code that sets up all EventListeners explicitly.

If app.media.trace (page 121) is true, debug trace listeners are also included with the stock EventListeners.

Parameters

settings	A MediaSettings Object (page 464).

Returns

Events Object (page 358)

getPlayerTraceEvents

6.0			

Returns an Events Object (page 358) containing EventListeners that provide a debugging trace as events are dispatched.

Parameters

None

Returns

An Events Object (page 358)

getRenditionSettings

6.0			

Calls `Rendition.select` (page 523) to get a MediaSelection Object (page 462), then `MediaSelection.rendition.getPlaySettings` (page 522) to get a MediaSettings Object (page 464) for playback. If either of these fails, it calls the `getAltTextSettings` (page 129) method to get a MediaSettings Object for alternate text playback. Finally, it returns the resulting MediaSettings Object, or `null` if `getAltTextSettings` returned `null` (that is, alternate text was not specified or not allowed).

Parameters

args	A PlayerArgs Object (page 127).

Returns

MediaSettings Object (page 464) or `null`

Example

See "Example 3" on page 137.

getURLData

6.0			

Returns a MediaData object (see `MediaSettings.data`, page 465) that represents data to be retrieved for a URL and optional MIME type. This MediaData object can be used to create a player that accesses data from that URL.

Parameters

cURL	The URL from which media data is to be retrieved.
cMimeType	(optional) The MIME type of the data.

Returns

MediaData object

Example

The following example retrieves a media clip from the internet and plays it in a floating window.

```
var myURLClip = "http://www.mywebsite.com/myClip.mpg";
var args = {
    URL: myURLClip,
    mimeType: "video/x-mpg",
    doc: this,
    settings: {
        players: app.media.getPlayers("video/x-mpg"),
        windowType: app.media.windowType.floating,
        data: app.media.getURLData(myURLClip,"video/x-mpg"),
        floating: { height: 400, width: 600 }
    }
}
app.media.openPlayer(args);
```

getURLSettings

6.0			

Takes a PlayerArgs Object (page 127) that contains a settings property and returns a MediaSettings Object (page 464) suitable for playback of a URL. The settings property must contain a URL property and may contain a mimeType property. It may also contain additional settings that are copied into the resulting settings object.

Parameters

args	A PlayerArgs Object (page 127).

Returns

MediaSettings Object (page 464)

Example 1

Same example as above. getURLSettings calls getURLData and inserts the return MediaData object into the data property into the setting, which it then returns.

Adobe® Acrobat® Official JavaScript Reference

```
var myURLClip = "http://www.mywebsite.com/myClip.mpg";
args = {
   URL: myURLClip,
   mimeType: "video/x-mpg",
   doc: this,
   settings:
   {
       players: app.media.getPlayers("video/x-mpg"),
       windowType: app.media.windowType.floating,
       floating: { height: 400, width: 600 }
   }
};
settings = app.media.getURLSettings(args)
args.settings = settings;
app.media.openPlayer(args);
```

Example 2

The example below is a custom keystroke action of a combo box. The combo box is a simple playlist of streamed audio and video websites. The export value of each element in the list has the form "URL,mimeType", for example

```
http://www.mySite.com/streaming/radio.asx,video/x-ms-asx
```

The script below splits the export value into a 2-element array, where the first element is the URL and the second is the mimeType. Any video is shown in the screen annotation "myScreen". Otherwise, only audio is heard.

```
if (!event.willCommit)
{
    var aURLMime = event.changeEx.split(",")
    console.println("aURLMime[0] = " + aURLMime[0]);
    console.println("aURLMime[1] = " + aURLMime[1]);
    var args = {
       annot:this.media.getAnnot({ nPage:0,cAnnotTitle:\
           "myScreen" }),
       URL: aURLMime[0],
       mimeType: aURLMime[1],
       doc: this,
       settings: {
          players: app.media.getPlayers(aURLMime[1]),
          windowType: app.media.windowType.docked
       }
    };
    settings = app.media.getURLSettings(args);
    args.settings = settings;
    var player = app.media.openPlayer(args);
}
```

getWindowBorderSize

6.0			

Returns an array of four numbers representing the size in pixels of the left, top, right, and bottom borders that would be used for a floating window with the properties specified in the parameters.

The `hasTitle` and `hasClose` parameters are Booleans, and `canResize` may be any of the values in `app.media.canResize` (page 116).

These parameters have the same names as properties of a `MediaSettings.floating` (page 467) object, so you can simply pass in a floating object as a single parameter:

```
var size = doc.media.getWindowBorderSize( settings.floating
);
```

Parameters

hasTitle	(optional) The default is `true`.
hasClose	(optional) The default is `true`.
canResize	(optional) The default is `app.media.canResize.no` (page 116).

Returns

An array of 4 numbers.

openPlayer

6.0			

Calls `app.media.createPlayer` (page 126) to create a MediaPlayer Object (page 448) and then calls `MediaPlayer.open` to open the player.

This method triggers several events, which may include `Ready` (see `onReady`, page 355, and `afterReady`, page 344), `Play` (see `onPlay`, page 355, and `afterPlay`, page 344), and `Focus` (see `onFocus`, page 353, and `afterFocus`, page 343). See the EventListener Object (page 338) for a general description of these events.

The method alerts the user and returns `null` on failure. It does not throw exceptions.

Parameters

args	(optional) A PlayerArgs Object (page 127).

Returns

A MediaPlayer Object (page 448), or `null` on failure

Example 1

This minimal example is a custom JavaScript from the Actions tab in the Multimedia Properties panel of a screen annotation. To override the parameters specified by the UI of the screen annotation, the `args` parameter is passed.

```
app.media.openPlayer();
```

Override `settings.repeat`: if repeat is set to 1, change it to 2. Otherwise, set it to 1.

```
var nRepeat =
    ( event.action.rendition.getPlaySettings().repeat == 1 ) \
        ? 2 : 1;
var args = { settings: { repeat: nRepeat } };
app.media.openPlayer(args);
```

See the `event` Object (page 314) for an explanation of `event.action.rendition`. The above example also uses `Rendition.getPlaySettings` (page 522) to access the settings associated with the rendition to be played (the one associated with the screen annotation).

Example 2

The following script is executed from a mouse-up action of a form button. It plays a docked media clip in a screen annotation.

```
app.media.openPlayer({
    rendition: this.media.getRendition( "myClip" ),
    annot: this.media.getAnnot( {nPage:0,\
        cAnnotTitle:"myScreen"} ),
    settings: { windowType: app.media.windowType.docked }
});
```

Example 3

This example is a custom JavaScript from the Actions tab in the Multimedia Properties of a screen annotation. The user clicks the annotation and a randomly chosen movie clip is played.

```
// these are placed at the top level of the
// document JavaScripts
var myRenditions = new Array();
myRenditions[0] = "myClip1";
myRenditions[1] = "myClip2";
myRenditions[2] = "myClip3";
```

```
// this code is a Custom JavaScript of a ScreenAnnot.
// All renditions are docked and are played in the ScreenAnnot.
var l = myRenditions.length;
randomIndex = Math.floor( Math.random() * l ) % l;

var rendition =
this.media.getRendition(myRenditions[randomIndex]);
var settings = app.media.getRenditionSettings({ rendition:
rendition });

var args = { rendition: rendition, settings: settings }
app.media.openPlayer(args);
```

removeStockEvents

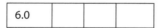

Removes any stock EventListeners from a MediaPlayer Object (page 448) and from any associated ScreenAnnot Object (page 533) and deletes the `player.stockEvents`, `player.annot`, `annot.stockEvents`, and `annot.player` properties. This undoes the effect of a previous `addStockEvents` (page 122) call.

Parameters

player	A MediaPlayer Object (page 448)

Returns

Nothing

startPlayer

6.0			

Checks whether an annotation is provided in the PlayerArgs Object (page 127) and the annotation already has a player open. If so, it calls `player.play` (page 456) on that player to start or resume playback. If not, it calls `app.media.openPlayer` (page 136) to create and open a new MediaPlayer Object (page 448). See `openPlayer` (page 136) for more details.

Note: `app.media.startPlayer` is the default mouse-up action when you use the Acrobat user interface to create a multimedia annotation and rendition and you do not specify any custom JavaScript.

Parameters

args	(optional) A PlayerArgs Object (page 127)

Returns

A MediaPlayer Object (page 448) or `null` on failure

Example

Start a screen annotation from a form button.

```
var args = {
    rendition: this.media.getRendition( "myClip" ),
    annot: this.media.getAnnot({ nPage: 0, cAnnotTitle:
"myScreen" }),
};
app.media.startPlayer(args);
```

Bookmark Object

A Bookmark Object represents a node in the bookmark tree that appears in the bookmarks navigational panel. Bookmarks are typically used as a table of contents allowing the user to navigate quickly to topics of interest.

Bookmark Properties

children

An array of Bookmark Objects (page 140) that are the children of this bookmark in the bookmark tree. If there are no children of this bookmark, this property has a value of `null`.

See also the `parent` (page 142) and `bookmarkRoot` (page 190) properties.

Type: Array | null   *Access: R*

Example

Dump all bookmarks in the document.

```
function DumpBookmark(bkm, nLevel)
{
    var s = "";
    for (var i = 0; i < nLevel; i++) s += " ";
    console.println(s + "+-" + bkm.name);
    if (bkm.children != null)
        for (var i = 0; i < bkm.children.length; i++)
            DumpBookmark(bkm.children[i], nLevel + 1);
}
console.clear(); console.show();
console.println("Dumping all bookmarks in the document.");
DumpBookmark(this.bookmarkRoot, 0);
```

color

Specifies the color for a bookmark. Values are defined by using gray, RGB or CMYK color. See "Color Arrays" on page 156 for information on defining color arrays and how values are used with this property. See also the `style` (page 142) property.

Type: Array   *Access: R/W (Adobe Reader: R only)*

Example

The following fun script colors the top-level bookmark red, green, and blue.

```
var bkm = this.bookmarkRoot.children[0];
bkm.color = color.black;
var C = new Array(1, 0, 0);
var run = app.setInterval(
    'bkm.color = ["RGB",C[0],C[1],C[2]]; C.push(C.shift());',\
        1000);
var stoprun = app.setTimeOut(
    "app.clearInterval(run); bkm.color=color.black",12000);
```

doc

The Document Object (page 188) that the bookmark resides in.

Type: object   *Access: R*

name

The text string for the bookmark that the user sees in the navigational panel.

Type: String   *Access: R/W (Adobe Reader: R only)*

Example

The following code puts the top-level bookmark in bold.

```
var bkm = this.bookmarkRoot.children[0];
console.println( "Top-level bookmark name: " + bkm.name );
```

The example that follows the children (page 140) property also uses the name property.

open

Determines whether the bookmark shows its children in the navigation panel (open) or whether the children subtree is collapsed (closed).

Type: Boolean   *Access: R/W (Adobe Reader: R only)*

parent

The parent bookmark of the bookmark or `null` if the bookmark is the root bookmark. See also the `children` (page 140) and `bookmarkRoot` (page 190) properties.

Type: object | `null`   *Access: R*

style

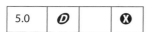

Specifies the style for the bookmark's font: 0 is normal, 1 is italic, 2 is bold, and 3 is bold-italic. See also the `color` (page 140) property.

Type: Integer   *Access: R/W (Adobe Reader: R only)*

Example

The following code puts the top-level bookmark in bold.

```
var bkm = this.bookmarkRoot.children[0];
bkm.style = 2;
```

Bookmark Methods

createChild

Creates a new child bookmark at the specified location.

See also the `children` (page 140) property and the `insertChild` (page 144) and `remove` (page 144) methods.

Parameters

cName	The name of the bookmark that the user sees in the navigation panel.
cExpr	(optional) An expression to be evaluated whenever the user clicks the bookmark. It is equivalent to creating a bookmark with a JavaScript action, as described in the *PDF Reference*, section 8.6.4. The default is no expression.
nIndex	(optional) The 0-based index into the children array of the bookmark at which to create the new child. The default is 0.

Returns

Nothing

Example

Create a bookmark at the top of the bookmark panel that takes you to the next page in the document.

```
this.bookmarkRoot.createChild("Next Page",
"this.pageNum++");
```

execute

5.0			

Executes the action associated with this bookmark. This can have a variety of behaviors. See Section 8.5.3, "Action Types," in the *PDF Reference*, for a list of common action types. See also the `createChild` (page 142) method.

Parameters

None

Returns

Nothing

Example

This example implements a simple search of the bookmarks. If successful, the action associated with the bookmark is executed.

```
// Document-level or folder-level JavaScript.
function searchBookmarks(bkm, nLevel, bkmName)
{
    if ( bkm.name == bkmName ) return bkm;
    if (bkm.children != null) {
        for (var i = 0; i < bkm.children.length; i++)
        {
            var bkMark = searchBookmarks(
                bkm.children[i], nLevel + 1, bkmName);
            if ( bkMark != null ) break;
        }
        return bkMark;
    }
    return null;
}
// Redefine this function for a more sophisticated compare.
function bmkCompare( name1, name2 )
{
    return ( name1 == name2 );
}
```

The following code initiates the search. This code could be executed as field-level JavaScript or be executed as a menu action.

```
var bkmName = app.response({
    cQuestion: "Enter the name of the bookmark to find",
    cTitle: "Bookmark Search and Execute"
});
if ( bkmName != null ) {
    var bkm = searchBookmarks(this.bookmarkRoot, 0, bkmName );
    if ( bkm != null ) bkm.execute();
    else app.alert("Bookmark not found");
}
```

insertChild

Inserts the specified bookmark as a child of this bookmark. If the bookmark already exists in the bookmark tree, it is unlinked before inserting it back into the tree. In addition, the insertion is checked for circularities and disallowed if one exists. This prevents users from inserting a bookmark as a child or grandchild of itself. See also the `children` (page 140) property and the `createChild` (page 142) and `remove` (page 144) methods.

Parameters

oBookmark	A bookmark object to add as the child of this bookmark.
nIndex	(optional) The 0-based index into the children array of the bookmark at which to insert the new child. The default is 0.

Returns

Nothing

Example

Take the first child bookmark and move it to the end of the bookmarks.

```
var bm = bookmarkRoot.children[0];
bookmarkRoot.insertChild(bm, bookmarkRoot.children.length);
```

remove

Removes the bookmark and all its children from the bookmark tree. See also the `children` (page 140) property and the `createChild` (page 142) and `insertChild` (page 144) methods.

Parameters

None

Returns

Nothing

Example

Remove all bookmarks from the document.

```
bookmarkRoot.remove();
```

setAction

6.0			

Sets a JavaScript action for a bookmark.

See also the Document Object `addRequirement` (page 215) and `setPageAction` (page 288) methods and the Field Object `setAction` (page 411) method.

Note: This method overwrites any action already defined for this bookmark.

Parameters

`cScript`	Defines the JavaScript expression that is to be executed whenever the user clicks the bookmark.

Returns

Nothing

Example

Attach an action to the topmost bookmark.

```
var bm = bookmarkRoot.children[0]
bm.setAction("app.beep(0);");
```

catalog Object

A static object that accesses the functionality provided by the Acrobat Catalog plug-in. This plug-in must be installed to interface with the `catalog` object.

Note: The Catalog plug-in (and the `catalog` object) is available only in Acrobat Professional.

See also the Index Object (page 437), which is used to invoke various indexing operations provided by the Catalog plug-in, and the CatalogJob Object (page 148).

catalog Properties

isIdle

Returns `true` when Catalog is not busy with an indexing job.

Type: Boolean   *Access: R*

jobs

Gets information about the Catalog jobs. Catalog maintains a list of its pending, in-progress, and completed jobs for each Acrobat session. Returns an array of CatalogJob Objects (page 148).

Type: Array   *Access: R*

catalog Methods

getIndex

Uses a specified path of a Catalog index to get an Index Object (page 437). The returned object can be used to perform various indexing operations such as building or deleting an index.

Parameters

cDIPath	The device-independent path of a Catalog index.

Returns

The Index Object (page 437).

remove

Removes the specified CatalogJob Object (page 148) from Catalog's job list. Catalog maintains a list of pending, in-progress, and completed jobs for each Acrobat session.

Parameters

oJob	The CatalogJob Object (page 148) to remove, as returned by the jobs property and various methods of the Index Object (page 437).

Returns

Nothing

Example

Delete all jobs that are pending and need complete rebuild.

```
if (typeof catalog != undefined)  {
    for (var i=0; i<catalog.jobs.length; i++){
        var job = catalog.jobs[i];
        console.println("Index: ", job.path);

        if (job.status == "Pending" && job.type == "Rebuild")
            catalog.remove(job);
    }
}
```

CatalogJob Object

This generic JavaScript object provides information about a job submitted to Catalog. It is returned by the `build` (page 438) method of the Index Object (page 437) and the `catalog.jobs` (page 146) property, and passed to `catalog.remove` (page 147).

It has the following properties:

Property	Type	Access	Description
path	String	R	Device-independent path of the index associated with the job
type	String	R	Type of indexing operation associated with the job. Possible values are: Build Rebuild Delete
status	String	R	The status of the indexing operation. Possible values are: Pending Processing Completed CompletedWithErrors

Certificate Object

The Certificate object provides read-only access to the properties of an X.509 public key certificate.

Related objects and methods are:

- security Object: `importFromFile` (page 555) and `getSecurityPolicies` (page 554)
- DirConnection Object: `search` (page 180)
- Field Object: `signatureInfo` (page 416)
- FDF Object: `signatureValidate` (page 369)
- RDN Object (page 518)
- Usage Object (page 152)

Note: There are no security restrictions on this object.

Certificate Properties

binary

5.0			

The raw bytes of the certificate, as a hex encoded string.

Type: String   *Access: R*

issuerDN

5.0			

The distinguished name of the issuer of the certificate, returned as an RDN Object (page 518).

Type: RDN object   *Access: R*

keyUsage

6.0			

An array of strings indicating the value of the certificate key usage extension. Possible values are

```
kDigitalSignaturekDataEnciphermentkCRLSign
kNonRepudiationkKeyAgreementkEncipherOnly
kKeyEnciphermentkKeyCertSignkDecipherOnly
```

Type: Array of Strings   *Access: R*

MD5Hash

5.0			

The MD5 digest of the certificate, represented as a hex-encoded string. This provides a unique fingerprint for this certificate.

Type: String   *Access: R*

SHA1Hash

5.0			

The SHA1 digest of the certificate, represented as a hex-encoded string. This provides a unique fingerprint for this certificate.

Type: String   *Access: R*

serialNumber

5.0			

A unique identifier for this certificate, used in conjunction with `issuerDN` (page 149).

Type: String   *Access: R*

subjectCN

5.0			

The common name of the signer.

Type: String   *Access: R*

subjectDN

5.0			

The distinguished name of the signer, returned as an RDN Object (page 518).

Type: RDN object   *Access: R*

ubRights

7.0			

The application rights that can be enabled by this certificate, returned as a generic Rights Object (page 151).

Type: Rights Object   *Access: R*

Rights Object

A `Rights` object has the following properties.

Property	Type	Access	Description
mode	String	R	Possible values are: • `Evaluation`: Rights enabled by this certificate for this document are valid as long as this certificate is valid. • `Production`: Rights enabled by this certificate for this document are valid for eternity. Currently, this value is not used by Adobe's PDF viewer.
rights	Array of Strings	R	Array of strings indicating the application rights that can be enabled by this certificate. Possible values are: • `FormFillInAndSave`: The right to fill in forms, excluding signature fields, and to save the modified file. • `FormImportExport`: The right to import and export form data. • `FormAddDelete`: The right to add or delete a form field. • `SubmitStandalone`: The right to submit a document outside a browser. • `SpawnTemplate`: The right to spawn page templates. • `Signing`: The right to sign existing form fields in a document. • `AnnotModify`: The right to create, delete, and modify comments. • `AnnotImportExport`: The right to import and export annotations. • `BarcodePlaintext`: The right to encode the appearance of a form field as a plain text barcode. • `AnnotOnline`: Allow online commenting. Enables uploading of any annotations in the document to a server and downloading of annotations from a server. Does not enable the addition of these annotations into the document. • `FormOnline`: Enable forms-specific online mechanisms such as SOAP or Active Data Object. • `EFModify`: The right to create, delete, modify, and import named embedded files. Does not apply to file attachment annotations.

usage

6.0			

The purposes for which this certificate may be used within the Acrobat environment returned as a Usage Object (page 152).

Type: Usage Object   *Access: R*

Usage Object

This generic JavaScript object represents a certificate usage value in the certificate.usage (page 151) property. It has the following properties.

Property	Type	Access	Description
endUserSigning	Boolean	R	true if the certificate is usable for end-user signing.
endUserEncryption	Boolean	R	true if the certificate is usable for end-user encryption.

Example

The following example shows how the usage (page 151) property can be used. The result of this script execution is that the currently open document is encrypted for everyone in the addressbook. Addressbook entries that contain sign-only certificates, CA certificates, no certificates at all, or are otherwise unsuitable for encryption, are not included in the final recipient list.

```
var eng = security.getHandler( "Adobe.AAB" );
var dc = eng.directories[0].connect();
var recipients = dc.search();

var filteredRecipients = new Array();
for( i = 0; i < recipients.length; ++i ) {
  if( recipients[i].defaultEncryptCert &&
    recipients[i].defaultEncryptCert.usage.endUserEncryption ) {
    filteredRecipients[filteredRecipients.length]
      = recipients[i];
    continue;
  }
  if(recipients[i].certificates) {
    for( j = 0; j < recipients[i].certificates.length; ++j )
      if( recipients[i].certificates[j].usage.endUserEncryption )
      {
        filteredRecipients[filteredRecipients.length]
          = recipients[i];
        continue;
      }
  }
}
this.encryptForRecipients({
    [userEntities: filteredRecipients] });
```

Collab Object

This static object represents the collaboration functionality.

Collab Methods

addStateModel

6.0				

Adds a new state model to Acrobat. A state model describes the valid states that an annotation using the model can have (see "Annotation Object" on page 19 for details about getting and setting the state of an annotation). State models can be used to describe the workflow that a document review goes through and can be used for review management.

See also `removeStateModel` (page 155), `getStateInModel` (page 44), and `transitionToState` (page 45).

Parameters

cName	A unique, language-independent identifier for the State Model.
cUIName	The display name of the state model used in the user interface and should be localized.
oStates	The states in the state model, described by a States Object (page 154).
cDefault	(optional) One of the states in the model to be used as a default state if no other state is set. The default is for there to be no default state.
bHidden	(optional) Specifies whether the state model should be hidden in the state model user interface. The default is `false` (the State Model is shown).
bHistory	(optional) Specifies whether an audit history is maintained for the state model. Keeping an audit history requires more space in the file. The default is `true`.

Returns

Nothing

States Object

This generic object represents a set of states in a state model and is passed as the `oStates` parameter. The elements in the object literal are the unique state identifiers and the values are objects having the following properties:

cUIName	The UI (display name) for the state.
oIcon	(optional) An Icon Stream Object (page 435) that is displayed in the UI for the state.

Example

Add a new state model with a unique name of "ReviewStates":

```
Collab.addStateModel({
    cName: "ReviewStates",
    cUIName: "My Review",
    oStates:
    {
        "initial": {cUIName: "Haven't reviewed it"},
        "approved": {cUIName: "I approve"},
        "rejected": {cUIName: "Forget it"},
        "resubmit": {cUIName: "Make some changes"}
    },
    cDefault: "initial"
});
```

A state model can be removed with `Collab.removeStateModel` (page 155).

documentToStream

7.0.5			⑤

Saves a copy of a Document Object (page 188) and returns the contents as a stream object.

The document `dirty` (page 192) property is preserved after this method is called and the original document is not modified.

Parameters

oDocument	The Document Object (page 188).

Returns

A ReadStream Object.

removeStateModel

6.0				

Removes a state model that was previously added by calling addStateModel. Removing a state model does not remove the state information associated with individual annotations. If the model is removed and added again, all of the state information for the annotations is still available.

See also addStateModel (page 153), getStateInModel (page 44), and transitionToState (page 45).

Parameters

cName	A unique, language-independent identifier for the state model that was used in addStateModel (page 153).

Returns

Nothing

Example

Continuing the example in addStateModel (page 153), remove the state model "ReviewStates":

```
// Remove the state model
Collab.removeStateModel("ReviewStates");
```

color Object

The `color` object is a convenience static object that defines the basic colors. Use this object to set a property or call a method that requires a color array.

Color Arrays

A color is represented in JavaScript as an array containing 1, 2, 4, or 5 elements corresponding to a Transparent, Gray, RGB, or CMYK color space, respectively. The first element in the array is a string denoting the color space type. The subsequent elements are numbers that range between zero and one inclusive. For example, the color red can be represented as `["RGB", 1, 0, 0]`.

Invalid strings or insufficient elements in a color array cause the color to be interpreted as the color black.

Color Space	String	Number of Additional Elements	Description
Transparent	"T"	0	A *transparent* color space indicates a complete absence of color and allows those portions of the document underlying the current field to show through.
Gray	"G"	1	Colors are represented by a single value—the intensity of achromatic light. In this color space, 0 is black, 1 is white, and intermediate values represent shades of gray. For example, .5 represents medium gray.
RGB	"RGB"	3	Colors are represented by three values: the intensity of the *red, green*, and *blue* components in the output. RGB is commonly used for video displays, which are generally based on red, green, and blue phosphors.
CMYK	"CMYK"	4	Colors are represented by four values, the amounts of the cyan, magenta, yellow, and black components in the output. This color space is commonly used for color printers, where they are the colors of the inks used in four-color printing. Only cyan, magenta, and yellow are necessary, but black is generally used in printing because black ink produces a better black than a mixture of cyan, magenta, and yellow inks and because black ink is less expensive than the other inks.

color Properties

The `color` object defines the following colors.

Color Object	Keyword	Equivalent JavaScript	Version
Transparent	color.transparent	["T"]	
Black	color.black	["G", 0]	
White	color.white	["G", 1]	
Red	color.red	["RGB", 1,0,0]	
Green	color.green	["RGB", 0,1,0]	
Blue	color.blue	["RGB", 0, 0, 1]	
Cyan	color.cyan	["CMYK", 1,0,0,0]	
Magenta	color.magenta	["CMYK", 0,1 0,0]	
Yellow	color.yellow	["CMYK", 0,0,1,0]	
Dark Gray	color.dkGray	["G", 0.25]	4.0
Gray	color.gray	["G", 0.5]	4.0
Light Gray	color.ltGray	["G", 0.75]	4.0

Example

This example sets the text color of the field to red if the value of the field is negative, or to black if the field value is nonnegative.

```
var f = event.target; /* field that the event occurs at */
f.target.textColor = event.value < 0 ? color.red :
color.black;
```

color Methods

convert

Converts the colorspace and color values specified by the `color` (page 156) to the specified colorspace:

- Conversion to the gray colorspace is lossy (in the same fashion that displaying a color TV signal on a black-and-white TV is lossy).
- The conversion of RGB to CMYK does not take into account any black generation or undercolor removal parameters.

Parameters

colorArray	Array of color values. See "Color Arrays" on page 156.
cColorspace	The colorspace to which to convert.

Returns

A color array.

Example

The return value of the code line below is the array ["CMYK", 0, 1, 1, 0].

```
color.convert(["RGB",1,0,0], "CMYK");
```

equal

5.0			

Compares two Color Arrays (page 156) to see if they are the same. The routine performs conversions, if necessary, to determine if the two colors are indeed equal (for example, ["RGB",1,1,0] is equal to ["CMYK",0,0,1,0]).

Parameters

colorArray1	The first color array for comparison.
colorArray2	The second color array for comparison.

Returns

true if the arrays represent the same color, false otherwise.

Example

```
var f = this.getField("foo");
if (color.equal(f.textColor, f.fillColor))
    app.alert("Foreground and background color are the
same!");
```

Column Object

This generic JavaScript object contains the data from every row in a column. A column object is returned by the getColumn (page 620) and getColumnArray (page 620) methods of the Statement Object (page 619). See also the ColumnInfo Object (page 160).

It has the following properties.

Property	Type	Access	Description
columnNum	number	R	The number identifying the column.
name	string	R	The name of the column.
type	number	R	One of the SQL Types for the data in the column.
typeName	string	R	The name of the type of data the column contains.
value	various	R/W	The value of the data in the column, in the format in which the data was originally retrieved.

ColumnInfo Object

This generic JavaScript object contains basic information about a column of data. It is returned by the `getColumnList` (page 161) method of the Connection Object. See also the Column Object (page 159).

It has the following properties.

Property	Type	Access	Description
name	string	R	A string that represents the identifying name of a column. This string can be used in a call to the `getColumn` (page 620) method of the Statement Object identify the associated column.
description	string	R	A string that contains database-dependent information about the column.
type	number	R	A numeric value identifying one of the ADBC SQL Types (page 10) that applies to the data contained in the column associated with the ColumnInfo Object (page 160).
typeName	string	R	A string identifying the type of the data contained in the associated column. It is not one of the SQL Types (see page 10, and see `type` above), but a database-dependent string representing the data type. This property may give useful information about user-defined data types.

Connection Object

This object encapsulates a session with a database. Connection objects are returned by `ADBC.newConnection` (page 12). See also the ADBC Object (page 10), Statement Object (page 619), Column Object (page 159), ColumnInfo Object (page 160), Row Object (page 532), and TableInfo Object (page 624).

Connection Methods

close

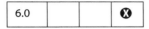

Closes an active connection and invalidates all the objects created from the connection.

Parameters

None

Returns

Nothing

getColumnList

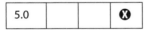

Gets information about the various columns in the table

Parameters

cName	The name of the table to get column information about.

Returns

An array of ColumnInfo Objects (page 160). This method never fails but may return a zero-length array.

Example

Given the Connection object `con`, get a list of all column names.

```
var con = ADBC.newConnection("q32000data");
var columnInfo = con.getColumnList("sales");
console.println("Column Information");
```

```
for (var i = 0; i < columnInfo.length; i++) {
    console.println(columnInfo[i].name);
    console.println("Description: "+
columnInfo[i].description);
}
```

getTableList

Gets information about the various tables in a database.

Parameters

None

Returns

It returns an array of TableInfo Objects (page 624). This method never fails but may return a zero-length array.

Example

Assuming a Connection Object (page 161) con has been obtained (see getColumnList, page 161, and newConnection, page 12), this example gets the list of tables.

```
var tableInfo = con.getTableList();
console.println("A list of all tables in the database.");
for (var i = 0; i < tableInfo.length; i++) {
    console.println("Table name: "+ tableInfo[i].name);
    console.println("Description: "+
tableInfo[i].description);
}
```

newStatement

Creates a Statement Object (page 619) through which database operations may be performed.

Parameters

None

Returns

A Statement Object (page 619) on success or null on failure.

Adobe® Acrobat® Official JavaScript Reference

Example

```
// get a connection object
var con = ADBC.newConnection("q32000data");
// now get a statement object
var statement = con.newStatement();
var msg = (statement == null) ?
    "Failed to obtain newStatement!" : "newStatement Object
obtained!";
console.println(msg);
```

console Object

The `console` object is a static object that enables access to the JavaScript console for executing JavaScript and displaying debug messages.

This object does not function in Adobe Reader versions earlier than 7.0. Beginning with version 7.0, Adobe Reader has a console window. Its primary function is to report errors and messages. This capability is controlled by the JavaScript preference **Show console on errors and messages**. Though the console is not interactive, the methods of the `console` object function as they do in Acrobat Professional and Standard.

The debugging capability of the JavaScript Debugging window can be made available for Adobe Reader for the Windows and Macintosh platforms. To debug within Adobe Reader, the JavaScript file `debugger.js` must be installed and the Windows registry must be edited appropriately. See the *Acrobat JavaScript Scripting Guide* for the technical details.

See also the `dbg` Object (page 170).

console Methods

clear

3.01			

Clears the console windows buffer of any output.

Parameters

None

Returns

Nothing

hide

4.0			

Closes the console window.

Parameters

None

Returns

Nothing

println

3.01			

Prints a string value to the console window with an accompanying carriage return.

Parameters

cMessage	A string message to print.

Returns

Nothing

Example 1

This example prints the value of a field to the console window. The script could be executed during a mouse-up event.

```
var f = this.getField("myText");
console.clear(); console.show();
console.println("Field value = " + f.value);
```

Example 2

The console can be used as a debugging tool. For example, you can write values of variables to the console. The following script is at the document level:

```
var debugIsOn = true;
function myFunction ( n, m )
{
    if (debugIsOn)
    {
        console.println("Entering function: myFunction");
        console.println(" Parameter 1: n = " + n);
        console.println(" Parameter 2: m = " + m);
    }
    ....
    ....
    if (debugIsOn) console.println(" Return value: rtn = " +
rtn);
    return rtn;
}
```

Beginning with Acrobat 6.0, debugging can also be accomplished with the JavaScript Debugger. See the dbg Object (page 170).

show

3.01			

Shows the console window.

Parameters

None

Returns

Nothing

Example

Clear and show the console window:

```
console.clear();
console.show();
```

Data Object

5.0			

The Data object is the representation of an embedded file or data stream that is stored in the document. See the section 3.10.3, "Embedded File Streams," in the *PDF Reference* for details.

Using Data objects is a good way to associate and embed source files, metadata, and other associated data with a document. Data objects can be inserted from the external file system, queried, and extracted.

See the following Document Object properties and methods:

createDataObject (**page 226**), dataObjects (**page 191**), exportDataObject (**page 238**), getDataObject (**page 247**), importDataObject (**page 262**), removeDataObject (**page 275**), openDataObject (**page 272**), getDataObjectContents (**page 247**), and setDataObjectContents (**page 286**).

Note: The Data object methods were implemented in Acrobat 5.0. However, the ability to use them in Adobe Reader with additional usage rights only became available in Adobe Reader 6.0.

Data Properties

creationDate

The creation date of the file that was embedded.

Type: Date   *Access: R*

description

7.0.5			

The description associated with this data object.

Type: String   *Access: R/W*

MIMEType

The MIME type associated with this data object.

Type: String   *Access: R*

modDate

The modification date of the file that was embedded.

Type: Date *Access: R*

name

The name associated with this data object.

Type: String *Access: R*

Example

```
console.println("Dumping all data objects in the document.");
var d = this.dataObjects;
for (var i = 0; i < d.length; i++)
    console.println("DataObject[" + i + "]=" + d[i].name);
```

path

The device-independent path to the file that was embedded.

Type: String *Access: R*

size

The size, in bytes, of the uncompressed data object.

Type: Number *Access: R*

DataSourceInfo Object

This generic JavaScript object contains basic information about a database. The `ADBC.getDataSourceList` (page 12) method returns an array of these objects. The object has the following properties.

Property	Type	Access	Description
name	String	R	A string that represents the identifying name of a database. This string can be passed to `newConnection` (page 12) to establish a connection to the database that the DataSourceInfo object is associated with.
description	String	R	A string that contains database-dependent information about the database.

dbg Object

The dbg object is a static object that can be used to control the JavaScript Debugger from a command-line console. Its methods provide the same functionality as the buttons in the JavaScript Debugger dialog toolbar. In addition, breakpoints can be created, deleted, and inspected using the dbg object.

The dbg object and the JavaScript Debugger are only available in Acrobat Professional.

Note: If the viewer locks up during a debugging session, pressing Esc may resolve the problem.

Debugging is not possible with a modal dialog open; for example, when debugging a batch sequence.

Debugging a script with a running event initiated by either app.setInterval (page 104) or app.setTimeOut (page 105) may cause recurring alert boxes to appear. Use Esc after the modal dialog is dismissed to resolve the problem.

(Acrobat 7.0) While the Debugger is open and a debugging session is under way, the Acrobat application is unavailable.

dbg Properties

bps

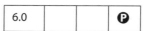

An array of *breakpoint generic objects* corresponding to breakpoints set in the debugger. This object contains the following properties and methods.

Property	Type	Access	Description
fileName	string	R	A string that identifies the script in the debugger.
condition	string	R	A JavaScript expression evaluated by the debugger to decide to whether to stop at a breakpoint. Used to create conditional breakpoints. The default value for this property is the string "true".
lineNum	number	R	The line number in the script for which the breakpoint is set.

Method	Parameters	Returns	Description
toString	none	String	A string describing the breakpoint.

Type: Array   *Access: R*

Example

List all currently active breakpoints.

```
var db = dbg.bps
for ( var i = 0; i < db.length; i++ )
{
    for ( var o in db[i] ) console.println(o + ": " + db[i][o]);
    console.println("-----------------------------------");
}
```

See sb (page 172) for another example of usage.

dbg Methods

c

The c (continue) method resumes execution of a program stopped in the debugger. The JavaScript program may either stop again, depending on where the breakpoints are set, or reach execution end.

Parameters

None

Returns

Nothing

cb

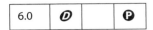

The cb (clear breakpoint) method clears a breakpoint in the debugger.

Parameters

fileName	The name of the script from where the breakpoint is going to be deleted.
lineNum	The line number for the breakpoint that is going to be cleared in the script.

Returns

Nothing

q

| 6.0 | | |  |

The q (quit) method quits debugging and executing the current JavaScript. It additionally dismisses the debugger dialog box.

Parameters

None

Returns

Nothing

sb

| 6.0 | *D* | | 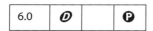 |

The sb (set breakpoint) method sets a new breakpoint in the debugger.

Parameters

fileName	The name of the script where the breakpoint is to be set.
lineNum	The line number in the script to create the breakpoint.
condition	(optional) a JavaScript expression to be evaluated when the debugger reaches the breakpoint. If the expression evaluates to true, the debugger stops at the breakpoint. If the expression evaluates to false, the debugger continues executing the script and does not stop at the breakpoint. The default value is true.

Returns

Nothing

Example 1

Some script is run and an exception is thrown due to some error. A breakpoint is programmatically set using the information given in the error message.

```
SyntaxError: missing ; before statement 213:Document-Level:
myDLJS
// now set a breakpoint using the console
dbg.sb({
    fileName: "Document-Level: myDLJS",
    lineNum: 213,
    condition: "true"
});
```

Example 2

This example simulates the functionality of the **Store breakpoints in PDF file** check box in the JavaScript user preferences.

```
// save breakpoints in PDF file
this.addScript("myBreakpoints", "var myBPS = " +\
    dbg.bps.toSource());

// now reset the breakpoints
for ( var i = 0; i < myBPS.length; i++ ) dbg.sb( myBPS[i] );
```

Example 3

Set a conditional break. Consider the following code, which is a mouse-up action.

```
for (var i=0; i<100; i++)
    myFunction(i);  // defined at document level

// In the console, set a conditional break. Here, we break when
// the index of the loop is greater than 30.
dbg.sb({
    fileName:"AcroForm:Button1:Annot1:MouseUp:Action1",
    lineNum:2,
    condition:"i > 30"
})
```

si

The `si` (step in) method advances the program pointer to the next instruction in the JavaScript program, entering each function call for which there is a script defined. (Native JavaScript calls cannot be stepped into.)

Parameters

None

Returns

Nothing

sn

The `sn` (step instruction) method advances the program pointer to the next bytecode in the JavaScript program. (Each JavaScript instruction is made up of several bytecodes as defined by the JavaScript interpreter.)

Parameters

None

Returns

Nothing

so

The so (step out) method executes the program until it exits the current function. Execution stops at the instruction immediately following the call to the current function. If the scope currently under debug is the top-level scope, the program either continues executing until it ends or stops again when it reaches a breakpoint.

Parameters

None

Returns

Nothing

sv

The sv (step over) method advances the program pointer to the next instruction in the JavaScript program. If a function call is encountered, the debugger does not step into the instructions defined inside that function.

Parameters

None

Returns

Nothing

Dialog Object

An instance of this object is passed as a parameter to dialog handlers (see "Dialog Handlers" on page 72). These handlers include the `initialize`, `validate`, `commit`, `destroy` and *ItemID* methods of the dialog descriptor object literal that is passed to `app.execDialog` (page 71). The Dialog object allows the current state of the Dialog to be queried and set.

Dialog Methods

enable

7.0			

Enables or disables various dialog elements using the object literal passed in.

Typically, `enable` is called in the `initialize` method (see "Dialog Handlers" on page 72) of the object literal passed to `app.execDialog` (page 71) to preset whether various dialog elements are enabled or not.

Parameters

object literal	For each dialog item to modify, there should be an entry in the object literal with the Dialog *ItemID* as the label and a Boolean as the value indicating if it is enabled or not.

Returns

Nothing

Example

See the examples following `app.execDialog` (page 71).

end

7.0			

Terminates a currently executing dialog (as if the cancel button had been pressed). This method takes an optional parameter of the *ItemID*, a string, of the dialog element that will be reported as dismissing the dialog. This *ItemID* will be the return value of the `app.execDialog` (page 71) call that created the dialog.

Parameters

`String`	(optional) The *ItemID* of the dialog element that will be reported as dismissing the dialog.

Returns

Nothing

Example

See the examples following `app.execDialog` (page 71).

load

7.0			

Sets the values of dialog elements using the object literal passed in. Dialog items are identified by an *ItemID* which is a unique 4-character string.

Typically, `load` is called in the `initialize` method (see "Dialog Handlers" on page 72) of the object literal passed to `app.execDialog` (page 71) to preset the value of various dialog elements.

Parameters

`object literal`	For each dialog item to be modified, there should be an entry in the object literal with the *ItemID* as the label and the dialog element setting as the contents. If the dialog element takes multiple values (for example, a `list_box` or a `popup`), the value should be an object literal consisting of the displayed entry as the label and a numeric value as the contents. Similarly, if the dialog element is hierarchical in nature (for example, a `hier_list_box`),the value should be a set of nested object literals. If the numeric value is greater than 0, the item is selected, otherwise it is not selected.

Returns

Nothing

Example

See the examples following `app.execDialog` (page 71).

store

7.0			

Gets the values of dialog elements as an object literal returned. Dialog items are identified by an *ItemID*, which is a unique 4-character string. For each dialog element, there will be an entry in the object literal with the *ItemID* as the label and the dialog element setting as the contents. If the dialog element takes multiple values (for example, a `list_box` or a `popup`), the value should be an object literal consisting of the displayed entry as the label and a numeric value as the contents. If the numeric value is greater than 0, the item was selected, otherwise it was not selected.

Typically, `store` is called in the `commit` method (see "Dialog Handlers" on page 72) of the object literal passed to `app.execDialog` (page 71) to extract the value of various dialog elements.

Parameters

None

Returns

object literal

DirConnection Object

6.0

This object represents an open connection to a directory: a repository of user information, including public-key certificates. Directory connections are opened using the Directory Object `connect` (page 187) method. A directory with a particular name can have more than one connection open at a time. All DirConnection objects must support all properties and methods listed here, unless otherwise specified.

Note: (Security ❺) : This object can only be obtained from a Directory Object (page 184) and is thus governed by the security restrictions of the Directory object. The DirConnection object is therefore available only for batch, console, application initialization and menu execution, including in Adobe Reader. See also "Privileged versus Non-privileged Context" on page 8.

DirConnection Properties

canList

6.0

Indicates whether the directory connection is capable of listing all of its entries. Some directories may contain too many entries for this operation to be practical.

Type: Boolean   *Access: R*

Example

The AAB directory allows listing of the local trusted identity list:

```
var sh = security.getHandler( "Adobe.AAB" );
var dc = sh.directories[0].connect();
console.println( "CanList = " + dc.canList );
```

canDoCustomSearch

6.0

Specifies whether the directory connection supports searching using directory-specific search parameter attributes. For example, directory-specific attributes for an LDAP directory include o (organization), c (country), cn (common name), givenname, sn (surname), uid, st, postalcode, mail, and telephonenumber.

Type: Boolean   *Access: R*

canDoCustomUISearch

Specifies whether the directory connection supports searching using its own custom user interface to collect the search parameters.

Type: Boolean   *Access: R*

canDoStandardSearch

Specifies whether the directory connection supports search using standard search parameter attributes. The standard attributes are

```
firstName
lastName
fullName
email
certificates
```

Some directory database implementations may not support these attributes, but directory handlers are free to translate these attributes to names understood by the directory.

Type: Boolean   *Access: R*

groups

An array of language-dependent names for groups that are available through this connection.

Type: Array   *Access: R*

name

Type: 6.0

The language-independent name of the directory that this object is connected to. An example of this would be `Adobe.PPKMS.ADSI.dir0`. All DirConnection objects must support this property.

Type: String   *Access: R*

uiName

The language-dependent string of the directory this object is connected to. This string is suitable for user interfaces. All DirConnection objects must support this property.

Type: String   *Access: R*

DirConnection Methods

search

Searches the directory and returns an array of UserEntity Objects (page 181) that match the search parameters. A UserEntity Object is a generic object that contains properties for all attributes that were requested by the `setOutputFields` (page 182) method. If the setOutputFields method is not called prior to a search, it would return a UserEntity Object containing no entries.

Parameters

oParams	(optional) A generic object containing an array of key-value pairs consisting of search attribute names and their corresponding strings. If oParams is not provided and canList (page 178) is true for this directory, all entries in the directory will be returned. If oParams is not provided and canList (page 178) is false, an exception occurs.
cGroupName	(optional) The name of a group (not to be confused with Group Objects, page 231). If specified, the search will be restricted to this group.
bCustom	(optional) If false (the default), oParams contains standard search attributes. If true, oParams contains directory-specific search parameters. If the canDoCustomSearch (page 178) property is not true, an exception occurs.
bUI	(optional) If true, the handler displays the user interface to allow collection of search parameters. The results of the search are returned by this method. canDoCustomUISearch (page 179) must also be true if bUI is true, or an exception will occur. If bUI is specified, bCustom must also be specified, though its value is ignored.

Returns

An array of UserEntity Objects (page 181).

Example 1

Directory search

```
var sh = security.getHandler( "Adobe.PPKMS" );
var dc= sh.directories[0].connect();
dc.setOutputFields( {oFields:["certificates","email"]} )
var retVal = dc.search({oParams:{lastName:"Smith"}});
if( retVal.length )
console.println( retVal[0].email );
```

Example 2

List all entries in local Acrobat Address Book. The script searches the directory and returns an array of users, along with their certificate information.

```
var sh = security.getHandler( "Adobe.AAB" );
var dc = sh.directories[0].connect();
if( dc.canList ) {
    var x = dc.search();
    for( j=0; j<x.length; ++j ) {
        console.println("Entry[" + j + "] = " + x[j].fullName +
            ":");
        for(i in x[j]) console.println("  " + i + " = " +
            x[j][i]);
    }
}
```

UserEntity Object

A generic JavaScript object that describes a user in a directory and the user's associated certificates. It contains standard properties that have a specific meaning for all directory handlers. Directory handlers translate these entries to the ones that are specific to them when required. An array of these objects is returned by the `search` (page 180) method of the DirConnection Object.

It has the following properties.

Property	Type	Access	Description
firstName	String	R/W	The first name for the user.
lastName	String	R/W	The last name of the user.
fullName	String	R/W	The full name of the user.

Property	Type	Access	Description
certificates	Array of Certificate Objects	R/W	An array of certificates that belong to this user. To find a certificate that is to be used for a particular use, the caller should inspect the certificate's keyUsage (page 149) property.
defaultEncryptCert	Array of Certificate Objects	R/W	The preferred certificate to use when encrypting documents for this user entity. Routines that process user entity objects will look first to this property when choosing an encryption certificate. If this property is not set, the first valid match in the certificates property will be used.

setOutputFields

Defines the list of attributes that should be returned when executing the search (page 180) method.

Note: This method is not supported by the Adobe.AAB directory handler. Custom options are not supported by the Adobe.PPKMS.ADSI directory handler.

Parameters

oFields	An array of strings containing the names of attributes that should be returned from the directory when calling the search method. The names in this array must either be names of standard attributes that can be used for all directory handlers or custom attributes that are defined for a particular directory. The standard attributes are the property names defined for the UserEntity Object (page 181). Directory handlers can, when needed, translate standard attribute names to names that it understands.
bCustom	(optional) A Boolean indicating that the names in oFields are standard output attribute names. If true, the names represent directory-specific attributes that are defined for a particular directory handler. The default is false.

Adobe® Acrobat® Official JavaScript Reference

Returns

An array of strings, containing the names of attributes from `oFields` that are not supported by this directory. An empty array is returned if the `oFields` array is empty.

Example

In this example, `dc.setOutputFields` returns the array of strings `["x", "y"]`.

```
var sh = security.getHandler("Adobe.PPKMS");
var dc = sh.directories[0].connect();
var w = dc.setOutputFields( [ "certificates", "email", "x",\
        "y"] );
console.println( w );
```

See also the examples that follow the `DirConnection.search` (page 180) method.

Directory Object

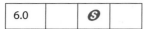

Directories are a repository of user information, including public-key certificates. Directory objects provide directory access and are obtained using the `directories` (page 559) property or the `newDirectory` (page 566) method of the SecurityHandler Object.

Acrobat 6.0 provides several directories. The Adobe.AAB Security Handler has a single directory named Adobe.AAB.AAB. This directory provides access to the local Acrobat Address Book, also called the *trusted identity store*. On Windows, the Adobe.PPKMS Security Handler provides access through the Microsoft Active Directory Script Interface (ADSI) to as many directories as have been created by the user. These directories are created sequentially with names `Adobe.PPKMS. ADSI.dir0`, `Adobe.PPKMS.ADSI.dir1`, and so on.

Note: (Security ◯) This object can only be obtained from a SecurityHandler Object (page 557) and is thus governed by the security restrictions of the SecurityHandler Object. The Directory object is therefore available only for batch, console, application initialization, and menu execution, including in Adobe Reader. See also "Privileged versus Non-privileged Context" on page 8.

Directory Properties

info

The value of this property is a DirectoryInformation Object (page 185), a generic object used to set and get the properties for this Directory Object (page 184).

Type: Object   *Access: R/W*

Example

```
// Create and activate a new directory
var oDirInfo = { dirStdEntryID: "dir0",
    dirStdEntryName: "Employee LDAP Directory",
    dirStdEntryPrefDirHandlerID: "Adobe.PPKMS.ADSI",
    dirStdEntryDirType: "LDAP",
    server: "ldap0.acme.com",
    port: 389 };
var sh = security.getHandler( "Adobe.PPKMS" );
var newDir = sh.newDirectory();
```

```
newDir.info = oDirInfo;
```

DirectoryInformation Object

A directory information object is a generic object representing the properties for a directory and has the following standard properties.

Standard Directory Information Object properties				
Property	Type	Access	Required	Description
dirStdEntryID	String	R/W	Yes	A unique, language-independent name for the directory. Must be alphanumeric and can include underscores, periods and hyphens. For new directory objects, it is suggested that the ID not be provided, in which case a new unique name will be automatically generated.
dirStdEntryName	String	R/W	Yes	A user-friendly name for the directory.
dirStdEntryPrefDirHandlerID	String	R/W	No	The name of the directory handler to be used by this directory. Security handlers can support multiple directory handlers for multiple directory types (for example, local directories and LDAP directories).
dirStdEntryDirType	String	R/W	No	The type of directory. Examples of this are LDAP, ADSI, and WINNT.
dirStdEntryVersion	String	R	No	The version of the data. The default value is 0 if this is not set by the directory. The value for Acrobat 6.0 directories for the Adobe.AAB and Adobe.PPKMS.ADSI directory handlers is 0x00010000.

Directory information objects can include additional properties that are specific to a particular directory handler. The Adobe.PPKMS.ADSI directory handler includes the following additional properties:

Adobe.PPKMS.ADSI additional directory information object properties			
Property	**Type**	**Access**	**Description**
server	String	R/W	The server that hosts the data. For example, addresses.employees.xyz.com.
port	Number	R/W	The port number for the server. The standard LDAP port number is 389.
searchBase	String	R/W	Narrows the search to a particular section of the directory. An example of this is o=XYZ Systems,c=US.
maxNumEntries	Number	R/W	The maximum number of entries to be retrieved in a single search.
timeout	Number	R/W	The maximum time allowed for a search.

Example 1

Create and activate a new directory.

```
var oDirInfo = { dirStdEntryID: "dir0",
    dirStdEntryName: "Employee LDAP Directory",
    dirStdEntryPrefDirHandlerID: "Adobe.PPKMS.ADSI",
    dirStdEntryDirType: "LDAP",
    server: "ldap0.acme.com",
    port: 389
};
var sh = security.getHandler( "Adobe.PPKMS" );
var newDir = sh.newDirectory();
newDir.info = oDirInfo;
```

Example 2

Get information for existing directory.

```
var sh = security.getHandler("Adobe.PPKMS");
var dir0 = sh.directories[0];
// Get directory info object just once for efficiency
var dir0Info = dir0.info;
console.println( "Directory " + dir0Info.dirStdEntryName );
console.println( "address " + dir0Info.server + ":" +
    dir0Info.port );
```

Directory Methods

connect

6.0		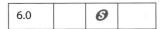	

Returns a DirConnection Object (page 178) that is a connection to the directory with the specified name. There can be more than one active connection for a directory.

See also the DirConnection Object (page 178) and the SecurityHandler Object's `directories` (page 559) property.

Parameters

oParams	(optional) A generic object that can contain parameters that are necessary to create the connection. Properties of this object are dependent on the particular directory handler and can include `userid` and `password`.
bUI	(optional) A Boolean value whose default is `false`. It specifies whether the directory handler can bring its UI, if required for establishing the connection.

Returns

A DirConnection Object (page 178), or `null` if there is no directory with the specified name.

Example

Enumerate available directories and connect.

```
var sh = security.getHandler( "Adobe.PPKMS" );
var dirList = sh.directories;
for ( var i=0; i< dirList.length; i++)
    for ( var o in dirList[i].info )
        console.println( o + " = " + dirList[i].info[o]);
var dirConnection = dirList[0].connect();
```

Document Object

This object provides the interface between a PDF document open in the viewer and the JavaScript interpreter. It provides methods and properties for accessing the PDF document.

You can access Document Objects from JavaScript in a variety of ways:

- The `this` Object (page 631) usually points to the Document Object of the underlying document.

- Some properties and methods, such as `extractPages` (page 242), `app.activeDocs` (page 49), and `app.openDoc` (page 97), return Document Objects.

- Document Objects can often be accessed through `event` Objects (page 314), which are created for each event by which a JavaScript is executed:

  - For `mouse`, `focus`, `blur`, `calculate`, `validate`, and `format` events, `event.target` (page 334) returns the Field Object (page 371) that initiated the event. You can then access the Document Object through the `doc` (page 384) method of the Field Object.

  - For all other events, `event.target` (page 334) points to the Document Object.

Example 1: Access through this object

Use `this` to get the number of pages in this document:

```
var nPages = this.numPages;
// get the crop box for "this" document:
var aCrop = this.getPageBox();
```

Example 2: Access through return values

Return values from one document to open, modify, save and close another.

```
// path relative to "this" doc:
var myDoc = app.openDoc("myNovel.pdf", this);
myDoc.info.Title = "My Great Novel";
myDoc.saveAs(myDoc.path);
myDoc.closeDoc(true);
```

Example 3: Access through the event object.

For mouse, calculate, validate, format, focus, and blur events:

```
var myDoc = event.target.doc;
```

For all other events (for example, batch or console events):

```
var myDoc = event.target;
```

Document Properties

alternatePresentations

6.0			

References the document's AlternatePresentation Object (page 17). If the functionality needed to display alternate presentations is not available, this property is `undefined`.

The AlternatePresentation Object provides access to the document's alternate presentations. The PDF language extension specifies that each document can potentially have many named alternate presentations. Each alternate presentation with a known `type` will have a corresponding `alternatePresentations` property in the document. This property should have the same name as its alternate presentation and should reference its alternate presentation's AlternatePresentation Object. If there are no recognized alternate presentations in the document, this object is empty (does not have any properties).

Section 9.4 in the *PDF Reference* provides details on alternate presentations.

Note: For compatibility with the current implementation, the alternate presentation name must be an ASCII string. The only alternate presentation type currently implemented is "SlideShow".

See the AlternatePresentation Object (page 17) for properties and methods that can be used to control an alternate presentation.

Type: Object | undefined Access: R

Example 1

Test whether the AlternatePresentation Object (page 17) is present:

```
if ( typeof this.alternatePresentations != "undefined" )
{
    // assume AlternatePresentations are present
    // list the names of all alternate presentations in the doc
    for ( var ap in this.alternatePresentations )
console.println(ap);
}
```

Example 2

This example assumes there is a named presentation "MySlideShow" in the document.

```
// oMySlideShow is an AlternatePresentation object
oMySlideShow = this.alternatePresentations["MySlideShow"];
oMySlideShow.start();
```

author

> **Note:** This property has been superseded by the `info` (page 197) property.
>
> The author of the document.
>
> *Type: String*   *Access: R/W (Adobe Reader: R only)*

baseURL

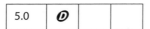

> The base URL for the document is used to resolve relative web links within the document. See also URL (page 208).
>
> *Type: String*   *Access: R/W*

Example

> This example sets the base URL, creates a link to go to a page relative to the base URL.
>
> ```
> console.println("Base URL was " + this.baseURL);
> this.baseURL = "http://www.adobe.com/products/";
> console.println("Base URL is " + this.baseURL);
> // add a link to the first page
> var link = this.addLink(0, [200,200, 400, 300])
> // set action that goes to the Acrobat page on
> // the Adobe website.
> link.setAction("this.getURL('acrobat',false)")
> ```

bookmarkRoot

> The root bookmark for the bookmark tree. This bookmark is not displayed to the user but is a programmatic construct used to access the tree and the child bookmarks.
>
> *Type: object*   *Access: R*

Example

> See the Bookmark Object (page 140) for an example.

calculate

If `true` (the default value), calculations can be performed for this document. If `false`, calculations cannot be performed for this document. This property supersedes the `app.calculate` (page 50) property, whose use is now discouraged.

Type: Boolean   *Access: R/W*

creationDate

Note: This property has been superseded by the `info` (page 197) property.

The document's creation date.

Type: Date   *Access: R*

creator

Note: This property has been superseded by the `info` (page 197) property.

The creator of the document (for example, "Adobe FrameMaker" or "Adobe PageMaker").

Type: String   *Access: R*

dataObjects

An array containing all the named Data Objects (page 167) in the document.

Related properties and methods are `openDataObject` (page 272), `getDataObject` (page 247), `createDataObject` (page 226), `importDataObject` (page 262), `removeDataObject` (page 275), `getDataObjectContents` (page 247), and `setDataObjectContents` (page 286).

Type: Array   *Access: R*

Example

List all embedded files in the document.

```
var d = this.dataObjects;
for (var i = 0; i < d.length; i++)
    console.println("Data Object[" + i + "]=" + d[i].name);
```

delay

4.0			

This property can delay the redrawing of any appearance changes to every field in the document. It is generally used to buffer a series of changes to fields before requesting that the fields regenerate their appearance. If `true`, all changes are queued until `delay` is reset to `false`, at which time all the fields on the page are redrawn.

See also the Field Object `delay` (page 382) property.

Type: Boolean   *Access: R/W*

dirty

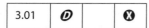

Specifies whether the document needs to be saved as the result of a changes to the document. It is useful to reset the `dirty` flag when performing changes that do not warrant saving, such as updating a status field.

Note: If the document is temporary or newly created, setting `dirty` to `false` has no effect. That is, the user is still asked to save changes before closing the document. See `requiresFullSave` (page 205).

Type: Boolean   *Access: R/W*

Example 1

This example resets a form and sets `dirty` to `false`. After the reset, the user can close the document without having to dismiss a Save dialog box.

```
var f = this.getField("MsgField");
f.value = "You have made too many mistakes, I'm resetting the form. "
    + "Start over, this time follow the directions!";
this.resetForm();
this.dirty = false;
```

Example 2

In this example, a text field is filled to instruct the user to complete the form. The script is constructed so that populating the field does not change the save state of the document.

```
var f = this.getField("MsgField");
var b = this.dirty;
f.value = "Please fill in the fields below.";
this.dirty = b;
```

disclosed

Specifies whether the document should be accessible to JavaScripts in other documents.

The app.openDoc (page 97) and app.activeDocs (page 49) methods check the disclosed property of the document before returning its Document Object (page 188).

Note: (Security ✆): The disclosed property can only be set during batch, console, Page/Open and Doc/Open events. See the event Object (page 314) for a discussion of Acrobat JavaScript events. See also "Privileged versus Non-privileged Context" on page 8.

Type: Boolean   *Access: R/W*

Example 1

A document can be disclosed to others by placing the code at the document level (or as a page open action) at the top level:

```
this.disclosed = true;
```

Example 2

The following code can be used in an Execute JavaScript Batch Sequence to disclose all selected documents.

this.addScript("Disclosed", "this.disclosed = true;");

docID

An array of two strings in hex-encoded binary format. The first string is a permanent identifier based on the contents of the file at the time it was originally created; it does not change when the file is incrementally updated. The second string is a changing identifier based on the file's contents at the time it was last updated. These identifiers are defined by the optional `ID` entry in a PDF file's trailer dictionary. (See Section 10.3 in the *PDF Reference*.)

Type: Array   *Access: R*

See "Example 6 (Acrobat 7.0)" on page 300 for an example of usage.

documentFileName

6.0			

The base file name, with extension, of the document referenced by the Document Object (page 188). The device-independent path is not returned. See also the `path` (page 203) and `URL` (page 208) properties. The file size of the document can be obtained from the `filesize` (page 195) property.

Type: String   *Access: R*

Example

Executing the script

```
console.println('"The file name of this document is '
    + this.documentFileName +'."');
```

on this document, the *Acrobat JavaScript Scripting Reference*, yields

```
"The file name of this document is AcroJS.pdf."
```

dynamicXFAForm

7.0			

Returns `true` if the document is a dynamic XFA form and `false` otherwise.

A dynamic XFA form is one in which some of the fields can grow or shrink in size to accommodate the values they contain.

Type: Boolean   *Access: R*

Example

See the XFA Object (page 649) for an example of usage.

external

4.0			

Specifies whether the current document is being viewed in the Acrobat application or in an external window (such as a web browser).

Type: Boolean   *Access: R*

Example

```
if ( this.external )
{
    // viewing from a browser
}
else
{
    // viewing in the Acrobat application.
}
```

filesize

3.01			

The file size of the document in bytes.

Type: Integer   *Access: R*

Example (Acrobat 5.0)

Get a readout of the difference in file sizes before and after saving a document:

```
// add the following code to the "Document Will Save" section
var filesizeBeforeSave = this.filesize
console.println("File size before saving is " +
        filesizeBeforeSave);

// add the following code to the "Document Did Save" section
var filesizeAfterSave = this.filesize
console.println("File size after saving is " +
        filesizeAfterSave);
var difference = filesizeAfterSave - filesizeBeforeSave;
console.println("The difference is " + difference );
if ( difference < 0 )
    console.println("Reduced filesize!");
else
    console.println("Increased filesize!");
```

hidden

7.0			

This property is `true` if the document's window is hidden. A window may be hidden, for example, because it is being operated on in batch mode or if it was explicitly opened hidden. The `openDataObject` (page 272) and `app.openDoc` (page 97) methods can be used to open a document with a hidden window.

Type: Boolean   *Access: R*

Example

Open a document and verify its hidden status.

```
oDoc = app.openDoc({
    cPath:"/C/myDocs/myHidden.pdf",
    bHidden: true
});
console.println("It is " + oDoc.hidden +
        " that this document hidden.");
oDoc.closeDoc();
```

hostContainer

7.0.5			

An instance of the HostContainer Object (page 431) if the PDF document is embedded in another container such as a web browser, otherwise undefined.

Note: This property is not implemented on the Macintosh platform.

Type: Object   *Access: R/W*

icons

5.0			

An array of named Icon Objects (page 434) that are present in the document-level named icons tree. If there are no named icons in the document, the property has a value of `null`.

See also `addIcon` (page 212), `getIcon` (page 249), `importIcon` (page 263), `removeIcon` (page 276), the Field Object properties `buttonGetIcon` (page 401), `buttonImportIcon` (page 401), `buttonSetIcon` (page 403), and the Icon Object (page 434).

Type: Array | null   *Access: R*

Example 1

```
if (this.icons == null)
    console.println("No named icons in this doc");
else
    console.println("There are " + this.icons.length
        + " named icons in this doc");
```

Example 2

```
// list all named icons
for (var i = 0; i < this.icons.length; i++) {
    console.println("icon[" + i + "]=" + this.icons[i].name);
}
```

---

info

5.0	*Ⓓ*		

Specifies an object with properties from the document information dictionary in the PDF file. (See Table 10.2 in the *PDF Reference.*) Standard entries are:

```
Title
Author
Subject
Keywords
Creator
Producer
CreationDate
ModDate
Trapped
```

For Acrobat, properties of this object are writeable and setting a property dirties the document. Additional document information fields can be added by setting non-standard properties.

In Adobe Reader, writing to any property in this object throws an exception.

Note: Standard entries are case insensitive, that is, `info.Keywords` is the same as `info.keywords`.

Type: object   *Access: R/W (Adobe Reader: R only)*

Example 1

```
// get title of document
var docTitle = this.info.Title;
```

Example 2

The following script

```
this.info.Title = "JavaScript, The Definitive Guide";
this.info.ISBN = "1-56592-234-4";
this.info.PublishDate = new Date();
for (var i in this.info)
    console.println(i + ": "+ this.info[i]);
```

could produce the following output:

```
CreationDate: Mon Jun 12 14:54:09 GMT-0500 (Central Daylight Time) 2000
Producer: Acrobat Distiller 4.05 for Windows
Title: JavaScript, The Definitive Guide
Creator: FrameMaker 5.5.6p145
ModDate: Wed Jun 21 17:07:22 GMT-0500 (Central Daylight Time) 2000
SavedBy: Adobe Acrobat 4.0 Jun 19 2000
PublishDate: Tue Aug 8 10:49:44 GMT-0500 (Central Daylight Time) 2000
ISBN: 1-56592-234-4
```

innerAppWindowRect

6.0			

This property returns an array of screen coordinates (a rectangle) for the Acrobat inner application window. This rectangle does not include items such as the title bar and resizing border, which are part of the outer rectangle of the application window.

Type: Array of Numbers   *Access: R*

Example

```
var coords = this.innerAppWindowRect;
console.println(coords.toSource())
// possible output: [115, 154, 1307, 990]
```

See also innerDocWindowRect (page 198), outerAppWindowRect (page 203), and outerDocWindowRect (page 203).

innerDocWindowRect

6.0			

This property returns an array of screen coordinates (a rectangle) for the Acrobat inner document window. This rectangle does not include items such as the title bar and resizing border, which are part of the outer rectangle of the document window.

The document and application rectangles may differ on different platforms. For example, on Windows, the document window is always inside the application window; on Macintosh, they are the same.

Type: Array of Numbers   *Access: R*

See also innerAppWindowRect (page 198), outerAppWindowRect (page 203), outerDocWindowRect (page 203), and pageWindowRect (page 204).

isModal

7.0.5			

A Boolean value indicating whether the document is currently in a modal state (for example, displaying a modal dialog using app.execDialog, page 71).

Type: Object   *Access: R*

keywords

Note: This property has been superseded by the `info` (page 197) property.

The keywords that describe the document (for example, "forms", "taxes", "government").

Type: object   *Access: R/W (Adobe Reader: R only)*

layout

Changes the page layout of the current document. Valid values are:

```
SinglePage
OneColumn
TwoColumnLeft
TwoColumnRight
```

In Acrobat 6.0, there are two additional properties:

```
TwoPageLeft
TwoPageRight
```

Type: String   *Access: R/W*

Example

Put the document into a continuous facing layout where the first page of the document appears in the left column:

```
this.layout = "TwoColumnLeft";
```

media

An object that contains multimedia properties and methods for the document. The properties and methods are described under the Doc.media Object (page 302).

Type: Doc.media Object   *Access: R/W*

metadata

Allows you to access the XMP metadata embedded in a PDF document. Returns a string containing the metadata as XML. For information on embedded XMP metadata, see section 10.2.2 in the *PDF Reference*.

Type: String   Access: R/W

Exceptions

RaiseError is thrown if setting metadata to a string not in XMP format.

Example 1

Try to create metadata not in XMP format.

```
this.metadata = "this is my metadata";
RaiseError: The given metadata was not in the XMP format
Global.metadata:1:Console undefined:Exec
 ===> The given metadata was not in the XMP format
```

Example 2

Create a PDF report file with metadata from a document.

```
var r = new Report();
r.writeText(this.metadata);
r.open("myMetadataReportFile");
```

modDate

Note: This property has been superseded by the info (page 197) property.

The date the document was last modified.

Type: Date   Access: R

mouseX

Gets the x coordinate of the mouse coordinates in default user space in relation to the current page.

Type: Number   Access: R

Example

Get the coordinates of the mouse as the user moves it around the viewer.

```
function getMouseCoor() {
    console.println( "("+this.mouseX+","+ this.mouseY+")" );
}
var ckMouse = app.setInterval("getMouseCoor()", 100);
var timeout = app.setTimeOut(
    "app.clearInterval(ckMouse);\
    app.clearTimeOut(timeout)",2000);
```

mouseY

7.0			

Gets the *y* coordinate of the mouse coordinates in default user space in relation to the current page.

Type: Number　　　　*Access: R*

noautocomplete

7.0			

This property can be used to turn off the auto-complete feature of Acrobat Forms, for this document only:

- If `true`, no suggestions are made as the user enters data into a field.
- If `false`, auto-complete respects the user preference **Forms > Auto-Complete**.

Setting this property does not change the user's auto-complete preferences.

Initially, this property has a value of `undefined`.

Type: Boolean　　　　*Access: R/W*

Example

The following script could be executed from an open page action or as a top-level document JavaScript. It turns off the auto-complete feature:

```
this.noautocomplete = true;
```

nocache

7.0			

This property is used to turn off forms data caching for this document only:

- If `true`, Acrobat is prevented from retaining forms data in an internet browser
- If `false`, Acrobat respects the Forms user preference **Keep forms data temporarily available on disk**

Note: The value of the `nocache` property does not affect the check box item **Keep forms data temporarily available on disk**.

Before this property is set for the first time, it has a value of `undefined`.

Type: Boolean　　　　*Access: R/W*

Example

The following script turns off caching of form data, so that sensitive data are not left on the local hard drive. It can be executed from an open page action or as a top-level document JavaScript.

```
this.nocache = true;
```

numFields

4.0			

The total number of fields in the document. See also `getNthFieldName` (page 252).

Type: Integer   *Access: R*

Example 1

```
console.println("There are " + this.numFields + " in this
document");
```

Example 2

This script uses the `numFields` property and `getNthFieldName` (page 252) method to loop through all fields in the document. All button fields are changed so that they have a beveled appearance (other modifications to the buttons of the document can also be made).

```
for ( var i = 0; i < this.numFields; i++) {
   var fname = this.getNthFieldName(i);
   if ( fname.type = "button" ) f.borderStyle = border.b;
}
```

numPages

3.01			

The number of pages in the document.

Type: Integer   *Access: R*

Example 1

```
console.println("There are " + this.numPages + \
   " in this document");
```

Example 2

Delete the last page from the document. The (0-based) page number of the last page in the document is `this.numPages - 1`.

```
this.deletePages({ nStart: this.numPages - 1 });
```

numTemplates

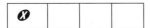

Note: This property has been superseded by `templates` (page 207).

The number of templates in the document.

Type: Integer   *Access: R*

path

| 3.01 | | | |

The device-independent path of the document, for example,
`/c/Program Files/Adobe/Acrobat 5.0/Help/AcroHelp.pdf`.

Type: String   *Access: R*

The file name of the document can be acquired by the `documentFileName` (page 194) property. See also the `URL` (page 208) property.

outerAppWindowRect

| 6.0 | | | |

This property returns an array of screen coordinates (a rectangle) for the Acrobat outer application window. This rectangle includes items such as the title bar and resizing border, which are not part of the inner rectangle of the application window.

Type: Array of Numbers   *Access: R*

See also `innerAppWindowRect` (page 198), `outerDocWindowRect` (page 203), `outerDocWindowRect` (page 203), and `pageWindowRect` (page 204).

outerDocWindowRect

| 6.0 | | | |

This property returns an array of screen coordinates (a rectangle) for the Acrobat outer document window. This rectangle includes items such as the title bar and resizing border, which are not part of the inner rectangle of the document window.

The application and document rectangles may differ on different platforms. For example, on Windows, the document window is always inside the application window. On the Macintosh, the windows are the same.

Type: Array of Numbers   *Access: R*

See also `innerAppWindowRect` (page 198), `outerDocWindowRect` (page 203), `outerAppWindowRect` (page 203), and `pageWindowRect` (page 204).

pageNum

3.01			

Gets or sets the current page of the document. When setting `pageNum` to a specific page, remember that the values are 0-based.

Type: Integer   *Access: R/W*

Example

This example goes to the first page of the document.

```
this.pageNum = 0;
```

This example advances the document to the next page.

```
this.pageNum++;
```

pageWindowRect

6.0			

An array of screen coordinates (a rectangle) for the Acrobat page view window. The page view window is the area inside the inner document window in which the PDF content is displayed.

Type: Array of Numbers   *Access: R*

See also `innerAppWindowRect` (page 198), `outerDocWindowRect` (page 203), `outerAppWindowRect` (page 203), and `outerDocWindowRect` (page 203).

permStatusReady

6.0			

A Boolean specifying whether the permissions for this document have been resolved.

When downloading over a network connection, `false` can indicate that the document is not available, in the case where permissions must be determined based on an author signature that covers the entire document.

Type: Boolean   *Access: R*

---

producer

Note: This property has been superseded by the `info` (page 197) property.

The producer of the document (for example, "Acrobat Distiller" or "PDFWriter").

Type: String   *Access: R*

requiresFullSave

7.0			

This property is `true` if the document requires a full save because it is temporary or newly created. Otherwise, it is `false`.

Type: Boolean   *Access: R*

Example

```
var oDoc = app.newDoc();
console.println("It is " + oDoc.requiresFullSave
    + " that this document requires a full save.");
```

securityHandler

5.0			

The name of the security handler used to encrypt the document. Returns `null` if there is no security handler (for example, the document is not encrypted).

Type: String   *Access: R*

Example

```
console.println(this.securityHandler != null ?
    "This document is encrypted with " + this.securityHandler
    + " security." : "This document is unencrypted.");
```

This script could print the following if the document was encrypted with the standard security handler.

```
This document is encrypted with Standard security.
```

selectedAnnots

5.0			

An array of Annotation Objects (page 19) corresponding to all currently selected markup annotations.

See also getAnnot (page 244) and getAnnots (page 245).

Type: Array   *Access: R*

Example

Show all the comments of selected annotations in console.

```
var aAnnots = this.selectedAnnots;
for (var i=0; i < aAnnots.length; i++)
    console.println(aAnnots[i].contents);
```

sounds

5.0			

An array containing all of the named Sound Objects Sound Object (page 599) in the document.

See also getSound (page 258), importSound (page 265), deleteSound (page 229), and the Sound Object (page 599).

Type: Array   *Access: R*

Example

```
var s = this.sounds;
for (i = 0; i < s.length; i++)
    console.println("Sound[" + i + "]=" + s[i].name);
```

spellDictionaryOrder

5.0			

An array specifying the dictionary search order for this document. For example, the form designer of a medical form may want to specify a medical dictionary to be searched first before searching the user's preferred order.

The Spelling plug-in first searches for words in this array, then searches the dictionaries the user has selected on the Spelling Preference panel. The user's preferred order is available from spell.dictionaryOrder (page 606). An array of the currently installed dictionaries can be obtained using spell.dictionaryNames (page 605).

Note: When setting this property, an exception is thrown if any of the elements in the array is not a valid dictionary name.

Type: Array   *Access: R/W*

spellLanguageOrder

An array specifying the language array search order for this document. The Spelling plug-in first searches for words in this array, then it searches the languages the user has selected on the Spelling Preferences panel. The user's preferred order is available from `spell.languageOrder` (page 607). An array of currently installed languages can be obtained using the `spell.languages` (page 606) property.

Type: Array   *Access: R/W*

subject

Note: This property has been superseded by the `info` (page 197) property.

The document's subject. This property is read-only in Adobe Reader.

Type: String   *Access: R/W*

templates

An array of all of the Template Objects (page 625) in the document. See also `createTemplate` (page 227), `getTemplate` (page 259), and `removeTemplate` (page 278).

Type: Array   *Access: R*

Example

List all templates in the document.

```
var t = this.templates
for ( var i=0; i < t.length; i++)
{
    var state = (t[i].hidden) ? "visible" : "hidden"
    console.println("Template: \"" + t[i].name
        + "\", current state: " + state);
}
```

title

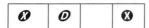

> **Note:** This property has been superseded by the `info` (page 197) property.
>
> The title of the document.
>
> *Type: String*   *Access: R/W (Adobe Reader: R only)*

URL

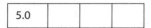

> The document's URL. If the document is local, it returns a URL with a `file:///` scheme for Windows and UNIX and `file://localhost/` for Macintosh. This may be different from the `baseURL` (page 190).
>
> *Type: String*   *Access: R*
>
> See also the `path` (page 203) and `documentFileName` (page 194) properties.

viewState

> An opaque string representing the current view state of the document. The state includes, at minimum, information about the current page number, scroll position, zoom level, and field focus.
>
> To set this value, you must use what was previously returned from a read of the value. It can be used to restore the view state of a document.
>
> *Type: String*   *Access: R/W*

Example

> This example gets the view state and sends it to the host application, which can store it and pass it back to the viewer later to restore the view to the original state.
>
> ```
> var myViewState = this.viewState;
> this.hostContainer.postMessage("viewState", myViewState);
> ```

zoom

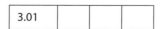

> The current page zoom level. Allowed values are between 8.33% and 6400%, specified as a percentage number. For example, a zoom value of 100 specifies 100%.

Type: Number   *Access: R/W*

Example

This example zooms to twice the current zoom level.

```
this.zoom *= 2;
```

This sets the zoom to 200%.

```
this.zoom = 200;
```

zoomType

The current zoom type of the document. The table below lists the valid zoom types.

The convenience `zoomtype` object defines all the valid zoom types and is used to access all zoom types.

Zoom Type	Keyword	Version
NoVary	zoomtype.none	
FitPage	zoomtype.fitP	
FitWidth	zoomtype.fitW	
FitHeight	zoomtype.fitH	
FitVisibleWidth	zoomtype.fitV	
Preferred	zoomtype.pref	
ReflowWidth	zoomtype.refW	6.0

Type: String   *Access: R/W*

Example

This example sets the zoom type of the document to fit the width.

```
this.zoomType = zoomtype.fitW;
```

Document Methods

addAnnot

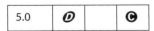

Creates an Annotation Object (page 19) having the specified properties. Properties not specified are given their default values for the specified `type` (page 41) of annotation.

Parameters

object literal	A generic object that specifies the properties of the Annotation Object (page 19), such as `type` (page 41), `rect` (page 36), and `page` (page 34), to be created.

Returns

The new Annotation Object (page 19).

Example 1

This minimal example creates a square annotation.

```
var sqannot = this.addAnnot({type: "Square", page: 0});
```

`sqannot` will be created as a square annotation on the first page (using 0-based page numbering).

Example 2

```
var annot = this.addAnnot
({
    page: 0,
    type: "Text",
    author: "A. C. Robat",
    point: [300,400],
    strokeColor: color.yellow,
    contents: "Need a little help with this paragraph.",
    noteIcon: "Help"
});
```

Example 3

```
var annot = this.addAnnot({
    page: 0,
    type: "Square",
    rect: [0, 0, 100, 100],
    name: "OnMarketShare",
    author: "A. C. Robat",
    contents: "This section needs revision."
});
```

Example 4

Below is a fancy ink annotation in the shape of a three-leaf rose.

```
var inch = 72, x0 = 2*inch, y0 = 4*inch;
var scaledInch = .5*inch;
var nNodes = 60;
var theta = 2*Math.PI/nNodes;
var points = new Array();
for (var i = 0; i <= nNodes; i++) {
    Theta = i*theta;
```

```
        points[i] = [x0 +\
            2*Math.cos(3*Theta)*Math.cos(Theta)*scaledInch,
        y0 + 2*Math.cos(3*Theta)*Math.sin(Theta)*scaledInch];
    }
    var annot = this.addAnnot({
        type: "Ink",
        page: 0,
        name: "myRose",
        author: "A. C. Robat",
        contents: "Three leaf rose",
        gestures: [points],
        strokeColor: color.red,
        width: 1
    });
```

addField

Creates a new form field and returns it as a Field Object (page 371).

Note: (**F**, Acrobat 6.0): Beginning with Acrobat 6.0, this method can be used from within Adobe Reader for documents with forms usage rights enabled. Prior to 6.0, it was not available from Adobe Reader.

Parameters

cName	The name of the new field to create. This name can use the dot separator syntax to denote a hierarchy (for example, name.last creates a parent node, name, and a child node, last).
cFieldType	The type of form field to create. Valid types are: text button combobox listbox checkbox radiobutton signature
nPageNum	The 0-based index of the page to which to add the field.
oCoords	An array of four numbers in rotated user space that specifies the size and placement of the form field. These four numbers are the coordinates of the bounding rectangle, in the following order: upper-left *x*, upper-left *y*, lower-right *x* and lower-right *y*. See also the Field Object rect (page 390) property. **Note:** If you use the **Info** panel to obtain the coordinates of the bounding rectangle, you must transform them from info space to rotated user space. To do this, subtract the info space *y* coordinate from the on-screen page height.

Returns

The newly created Field Object (page 371).

Example

The following code might be used in a batch sequence to create a navigational icon on every page of a document, for each document in a selected set of documents.

```
var inch = 72;
for (var p = 0; p < this.numPages; p++) {
    // position rectangle (.5 inch, .5 inch)
    var aRect = this.getPageBox( {nPage: p} );
    aRect[0] += .5*inch;   // from upper left hand corner of page.
    aRect[2] = aRect[0]+.5*inch; // Make it .5 inch wide
    aRect[1] -= .5*inch;
    aRect[3] = aRect[1] - 24;     // and 24 points high

    // now construct button field with a right arrow
    // from ZapfDingbats
    var f = this.addField("NextPage", "button", p, aRect )
    f.setAction("MouseUp", "this.pageNum++");
    f.delay = true;
    f.borderStyle = border.s;
    f.highlight = "push";
    f.textSize = 0;     // auto sized
    f.textColor = color.blue;
    f.fillColor = color.ltGray;
    f.textFont = font.ZapfD
    f.buttonSetCaption("\341")   // a right arrow
    f.delay = false;
}
```

See the Field Object setAction (page 411) method for another example.

addIcon

Adds a new named Icon Object (page 434) to the document-level icon tree, storing it under the specified name.

See also icons (page 196), getIcon (page 249), importIcon (page 263), removeIcon (page 276), and the Field Object methods buttonGetIcon (page 401), buttonImportIcon (page 401), and buttonSetIcon (page 403).

Parameters

cName	The name of the new object.
icon	The Icon Object (page 434) to add.

Returns

Nothing

Example

This example takes an icon already attached to a form button field in the document and assigns a name to it. This name can be used to retrieve the icon object with getIcon (page 249) for use in another button, for example.

```
var f = this.getField("myButton");
this.addIcon("myButtonIcon", f.buttonGetIcon());
```

addLink

Adds a new link to the specified page with the specified coordinates, if the user has permission to add links to the document. See also getLinks (page 251), removeLinks (page 277), and the Link Object (page 440).

Parameters

nPage	The page on which to add the new link.
oCoords	An array of four numbers in rotated user space specifying the size and placement of the link. The numbers are the coordinates of the bounding rectangle in the following order: upper-left *x*, upper-left *y*, lower-right *x* and lower-right *y*.

Returns

The newly created Link Object (page 440).

Example 1

Create simple navigational links in the lower left and right corners of each page of the current document. The link in lower left corner goes to the previous page; the one in the lower right corner goes to the next page.

```
var linkWidth = 36, linkHeight = 18;
for ( var i=0; i < this.numPages; i++)
{
    var cropBox = this.getPageBox("Crop", i);
    var linkRect1 = [0,linkHeight,linkWidth,0];
    var offsetLink = cropBox[2] - cropBox[0] - linkWidth;
    var linkRect2 = [offsetLink,linkHeight,linkWidth
        + offsetLink,0]
    var lhLink = this.addLink(i, linkRect1);
    var rhLink = this.addLink(i, linkRect2);
    var nextPage = (i + 1) % this.numPages;
    var prevPage = (i - 1) % this.numPages;
```

```
            var prevPage = (prevPage>=0) ? prevPage : -prevPage;
            lhLink.setAction( "this.pageNum = " + prevPage);
            lhLink.borderColor = color.red;
            lhLink.borderWidth = 1;
            rhLink.setAction( "this.pageNum = " + nextPage);
            rhLink.borderColor = color.red;
            rhLink.borderWidth = 1;
    }
```

See the Link Object (page 440) for information on setting the properties and the action of a link.

Example 2

Search through the document for the word "Acrobat" and create a link around that word.

```
for (var p = 0; p < this.numPages; p++)
{
    var numWords = this.getPageNumWords(p);
    for (var i=0; i<numWords; i++)
    {
        var ckWord = this.getPageNthWord(p, i, true);
        if ( ckWord == "Acrobat")
        {
            var q = this.getPageNthWordQuads(p, i);
            // convert quads in default user space to rotated
            // user space used by Links.
            m = (new Matrix2D).fromRotated(this,p);
            mInv = m.invert()
            r = mInv.transform(q)
            r=r.toString()
            r = r.split(",");
            l = addLink(p, [r[4], r[5], r[2], r[3]]);
            l.borderColor = color.red
            l.borderWidth = 1

l.setAction("this.getURL('http://www.adobe.com/');");
        }
    }
}
```

addRecipientListCryptFilter

Adds a crypt filter to the document. The crypt filter is used for encrypting Data Objects (page 167).

See also the cCryptFilter parameter of the importDataObject (page 262), createDataObject (page 226), and setDataObjectContents (page 286) methods.

Note: (Security ⑤): Can only be executed during batch, application initialization, menu or console events. See also "Privileged versus Non-privileged Context" on page 8.

Parameters

`cCryptFilter`	The language-independent name of the crypt filter. This same name should be used as the value of the `cCryptFilter` parameter of the Document Object methods `importDataObject` (page 262), `createDataObject` (page 226), and `setDataObjectContents` (page 286).
`oGroup`	An array of Group Objects (page 231) that lists the recipients for whom the data is to be encrypted.

Returns

Nothing

Example

This script encrypts the current document and embeds it into a PDF document.

```
var Note = "Select the list of people that you want to send
this"
    + " document to. Each person must have both an email
address"
    + " and a certificate that you can use when creating the"
    + "envelope.";
var oOptions = { bAllowPermGroups: false, cNote: Note,
    bRequireEmail: true };
var oGroups = security.chooseRecipientsDialog( oOptions );
var env = app.openDoc( "/c/temp/ePaperMailEnvelope.pdf" );
env.addRecipientListCryptFilter( "MyFilter", oGroups );
env.importDataObject( "secureMail0", this.path, "MyFilter" );
var envPath = "/c/temp/outMail.pdf";
env.saveAs( envPath );
```

Note: This script was executed in the console but is best executed a folder JavaScript as part of larger script for sending PDF documents securely.

addRequirement

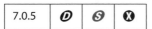

Allows a PDF document to be authored so that a certain requirement is needed for the document to properly function in Acrobat.

When Acrobat opens a document containing a requirement, it will try to satisfy the requirement before allowing the user to freely interact with the

---

document. If the requirement is not fulfilled, the application may limit the functionality of the document.

Note: (Security ⊘): This method can only be called from console or batch events.

Parameters

cType	The type of document requirement. The types are described by the Requirements Enumerator Object (page 216).
oReq	(Optional) A Requirement object.

Returns

Nothing

Requirements Enumerator Object

This object lists all the possible types of requirements that a document may contain to properly function in Acrobat.

Property	Description
requirements. EnableJavaScripts	Some documents may contain data validation scripts that may never run if the **Enable JavaScript Execution** user preference is disabled. This property allows a PDF document to enforce the execution of its JavaScripts in Acrobat. The user will be prompted to either enable JavaScript execution for the particular document or to open the document in read-only mode.

Requirement Object

This generic object contains properties that describe the nature of the requirement.

Property	Description
aRH	(Optional) An array of ReqHandler Objects (page 216).

ReqHandler Object

This generic object contains information about a requirement handler that can be used when Acrobat finds an unrecognized requirement. The viewer should delegate requirement checking for the unrecognized requirement to the first handler in the array that supports the type. If no requirement handler can be found to deal with the unrecognized requirement, a generic message should be provided by the viewer.

Property	Description
cType	A string specifying the type of the requirement handler (see the ReqHandlers Enumerator Object (page 217) for a lists of possible names).
cScriptName	(Optional) A string specifying the name of a document-level JavaScript present in the document. It may be present if the value of cType is reqHandlers.JS. The named script will not be executed in case the requirement is satisfied.

ReqHandlers Enumerator Object

This object enumerates the types of requirement handlers a document may contain.

Property	Description
reqHandlers.JS	This handler manages document-level JavaScripts that deal with unrecognized requirements in the PDF document.
reqHandlers.NoOp	This handler allows older viewers to ignore unrecognized requirements.

Example

Add a requirement to enable JavaScript in a document.

```
addRequirement(this.requirements.EnableJavaScripts,
    {[{cType: reqHandlers.JS, cScriptName: "requirement"}]});
```

addScript

Sets a document-level script for a document. See also setAction (page 285), setPageAction (page 288), the Bookmark Object setAction (page 145) method, and the Field Object setAction (page 411) method.

Note: This method overwrites any script already defined for cName.

Parameters

cName	The name of the script. If a script with this name already exists, the new script replaces the old one.
cScript	A JavaScript expression to be executed when the document is opened.

Returns

Nothing

Example

Create a beeping sound every time the document is opened.

```
this.addScript("My Code", "app.beep(0);");
```

See "Example 2" on page 193 following the disclosed (page 193) property for another example.

addThumbnails

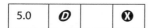

Creates thumbnails for the specified pages in the document. See also the removeThumbnails (page 279) method.

Parameters

nStart	(optional) A 0-based index that defines the start of an inclusive range of pages. If nStart and nEnd are not specified, the range of pages is for all pages in the document. If only nStart is specified, the range of pages is the single page specified by nStart. If only nEnd is specified, the range of a pages is 0 to nEnd.
nEnd	(optional) A 0-based index that defines the end of an inclusive range of pages. See nStart for details.

Returns

Nothing

addWatermarkFromFile

Adds a page as a watermark to the specified pages in the document and places the watermark in an optional content group (OCG). See also the OCG Object (page 485).

Note: (Security ⑤): Can only be executed during batch or console events. See also "Privileged versus Non-privileged Context" on page 8.

Parameters

cDIPath	The device-independent path of the source file to use for the watermark. If the file at this location is not a PDF file, Acrobat attempts to convert the file to a PDF file.
nSourcePage	(optional) The 0-based index of the page in the source file to be used as the watermark. The default is 0.
nStart	(optional) The 0-based index of the first page in the range of pages to which the watermark should be added. If nStart and nEnd are not specified, the range of pages is for all pages in the document. If only nStart is specified, the range of pages is the single page specified by nStart. If only nEnd is specified, the range of a pages is 0 to nEnd.
nEnd	(optional) The last page in the range of pages to which the watermark should be added. See nStart for details.
bOnTop	(optional) A Boolean specifying the z-ordering of the watermark. If true (the default), the watermark is added above all other page content. If false, the watermark is added below all other page content. This parameter is ignored if bFixedPrint is true.
bOnScreen	(optional) A Boolean to indicate whether the watermark should be displayed when viewing the document on screen. The default is true.
bOnPrint	(optional) A Boolean to indicate whether the watermark should be displayed when printing the document. The default is true.
nHorizAlign	(optional) A number indicating how the watermark should be aligned horizontally. See app.constants.align (page 50) for possible values. The default is app.constants.align.center (page 50).
nVertAlign	(optional) A number indicating how the watermark should be aligned vertically. See app.constants.align (page 50) for possible values. The default is app.constants.align.center (page 50).
nHorizValue	(optional) A number used to shift the horizontal position of the watermark on the page. If bPercentage is true, this number represents a percentage of the horizontal page size. If bPercentage is false, this number represents the number of points to be offset. The default is 0.

nVertValue	(optional) A number used to shift the vertical position of the watermark on the page. If bPercentage is true, this number represents a percentage of the vertical page size. If bPercentage is false, this number represents the number of points to be offset. The default is 0.
bPercentage	(optional) A Boolean that indicates whether nHorizValue and nVertValue represent a percentage of the page size or an explicit number of points. The default is false.
nScale	(optional) The scale to be used for the watermark, where 1.0 is 100%. A value of -1 specifies that the watermark should fit to the page while maintaining its proportions. The default is 1.0.
bFixedPrint	(optional) A Boolean that indicates that this watermark should be added as a FixedPrint Watermark annotation. This allows watermarks to be printed at a fixed size/position regardless of the size of the page being printed to. If true, bOnTop is ignored. The default is false.
nRotation	(optional) The number of degrees to rotate the watermark counterclockwise. The default is 0.
nOpacity	(optional) The opacity to be used for the watermark, where 0 is transparent and 1.0 is opaque. The default is 1.0.

Returns

Nothing

Example 1

Adds the first page of watermark.pdf as a watermark to the center all pages of the current document.

```
this.addWatermarkFromFile("/C/temp/watermark.pdf");
```

Example 2

Adds the second page of watermark.pdf as a watermark to the first 10 pages of the current document. The watermark is rotated counterclockwise 45 degrees and positioned 1 inch down and 2 inches over from the upper-left corner of the page.

```
this.addWatermarkFromFile({
    cDIPath: "/C/temp/watermark.pdf",
    nSourcePage: 4, nEnd: 9,
    nHorizAlign: app.constants.align.left,
    nVertAlign: app.constants.align.top,
    nHorizValue: 144, nVertValue: -72,
    nRotation: 45
});
```

addWatermarkFromText

7.0	*𝕯*		*𝕏*

Adds the given text as a watermark to the specified pages in the document and places the watermark in an optional content group (OCG).

See the OCG Object (page 485).

Parameters

cText	The text to use as the watermark. Multiline text is allowed. A newline can be specified with the characters "\r".
nTextAlign	(optional) The text alignment to use for cText within the watermark. See app.constants.align (page 50) for possible values. This parameter has no effect if cText is only one line.
cFont	(optional) The font to be used for this watermark. Valid fonts are defined as properties of the font Object (page 396), as listed in the textFont (page 396) property of the Field Object (page 371). An arbitrary font can be used by passing a string that represents the PostScript name of the font. The default is font.Helv.
nFontSize	(optional) The point size of the font to use for the watermark. The default is 24.
aColor	(optional) The color to use for the watermark. See "Color Arrays" on page 156. The default is color.black.
nStart	(optional) The 0-based index of the first page in the range of pages to which the watermark should be added. If nStart and nEnd are not specified, the range of pages is for all pages in the document. If only nStart is specified, the range of pages is the single page specified by nStart.
nEnd	(optional) The last page in the range of pages to which the watermark should be added. If nStart and nEnd are not specified, the range of pages is for all pages in the document. If only nEnd is specified, the range of a pages is 0 to nEnd.
bOnTop	(optional) A Boolean specifying the z-ordering of the watermark. A value of true will result in the watermark being added above all other page content. A value of false will result in the watermark being added below all other page content. This parameter is ignored if bFixedPrint is true. The default is true.
bOnScreen	(optional) A Boolean to indicate whether the watermark should be displayed when viewing the document on screen.

`bOnPrint`	(optional) A Boolean to indicate whether the watermark should be displayed when printing the document.
`nHorizAlign`	(optional) A number indicating how the watermark should be aligned horizontally. See `app.constants.align` (page 50) for possible values. The default is `app.constants.align.center` (page 50).
`nVertAlign`	(optional) A number indicating how the watermark should be aligned vertically. See `app.constants.align` (page 50) for possible values. The default is `app.constants.align.center` (page 50).
`nHorizValue`	(optional) Number used to shift the horizontal position of the watermark on the page. If `bPercentage` is `true`, this number represents a percentage of the horizontal page size. If `bPercentage` is `false`, this number represents the number of points to be offset. The default is 0.
`nVertValue`	(optional) Number used to shift the vertical position of the watermark on the page. If `bPercentage` is `true`, this number represents a percentage of the vertical page size. If `bPercentage` is `false`, this number represents the number of points to be offset. The default is 0.
`bPercentage`	(optional) A Boolean used to indicate whether `nHorizValue` and `nVertValue` represent a percentage of the page size or an explicit number of points. The default is `false`.
`nScale`	(optional) The scale to be used for the watermark, where 1.0 is 100%. A value of -1 specifies that the watermark should fit to the page while maintaining its proportions. The default is 1.0.
`bFixedPrint`	(optional) A Boolean that indicates that the watermark should be added as FixedPrint Watermark annotation. This prints the watermark at a fixed size and position regardless of the size of the page being printed to. If `true`, `bOnTop` is ignored. The default is `false`.
`nRotation`	(optional) The number of degrees to rotate the watermark counterclockwise. The default is 0.
`nOpacity`	(optional) The opacity to be used for the watermark, where 0 is transparent and 1.0 is opaque. The default is 1.0.

Returns

Nothing

Example 1

Adds "Confidential" as a watermark to the center of all pages of the current document.

```
this.addWatermarkFromText("Confidential", 0, font.Helv, 24,
color.red);
```

Example 2

Adds a multiline watermark to each page of the current document 1 inch
down and 1 inch over from the upper-right corner.

```
this.addWatermarkFromText({
    cText: "Confidential Document\rA. C. Robat",
    nTextAlign: app.constants.align.right,
    nHorizAlign: app.constants.align.right,
    nVertAlign: app.constants.align.top,
    nHorizValue: -72, nVertValue: -72
});
```

addWeblinks

Scans the specified pages looking for instances of text with an `http:`
scheme and converts them into links with URL actions.

See also the `removeWeblinks` (page 279) method

Parameters

nStart	(optional) A 0-based index that defines the start of an inclusive range of pages. If nStart and nEnd are not specified, the range of pages is for all pages in the document. If only nStart is specified, the range of pages is the single page specified by nStart.
nEnd	(optional) A 0-based index that defines the end of an inclusive range of pages. If nStart and nEnd are not specified, the range of pages is for all pages in the document. If only nEnd is specified, the range of a pages is 0 to nEnd.

Returns

The number of web links added to the document.

Example

Search the entire document and convert all content that appears to be a web
address into a web link. Report back the number of links created.

```
var numWeblinks = this.addWeblinks();
console.println("There were " + numWeblinks +
    " instances of text that looked like a web address,"
    +" and converted as such.");
```

bringToFront

5.0			

Brings an open document to the front.

Parameters

None

Returns

Nothing

Example

This example searches among the open documents for one with a title of "Annual Report" and brings it to the front.

```
var d = app.activeDocs;
for (var i = 0; i < d.length; i++)
    if (d[i].info.Title == "Annual Report")
d[i].bringToFront();
```

calculateNow

3.01			

Forces computation of all calculation fields in the current document.

When a form contains many calculations, there can be a significant delay after the user inputs data into a field, even if it is not a calculation field. One strategy is to turn off calculations at some point and turn them back on later (see example).

Parameters

None

Returns

Nothing

Example

```
// turn off calculations
this.calculate = false;
. . . . .
// turn on calculations
this.calculate = true;
// Unless the user committed data after this.calculate is set
// to true, automatic calculation does not occur.
```

```
// Calculation can be forced to occur by using...
this.calculateNow();
```

closeDoc

| 5.0 | | | ❽ |

Closes the document.

For Adobe Reader 5.1 or later, the method is always allowed:

- If the document was changed and no Document Save Rights ❽ are available, the document is closed without any warnings and changes are lost.
- If Document Save Rights are available, the user has the option of saving the changed file.

It is important to use this method carefully, because it is an abrupt change in the document state that can affect any JavaScript executing after the close. Triggering this method from a Page event or Document event could cause the application to behave strangely.

In versions of Acrobat earlier than 7.0, a document that closes itself by executing `this.closeDoc` terminates any script that follows it. In Acrobat 7.0, the script is allowed to continue and to terminate naturally. However, if the Document Object (page 188) of the closed document is referenced, an exception will be thrown.

Parameters

bNoSave	(optional) A Boolean indicating whether to close the document without saving:
	• If `false` (the default), the user is prompted to save the document if it has been modified.
	• If `true`, the document is closed without prompting the user and without saving, even if the document has been modified. Be careful in using this feature because it can cause data loss without user approval.

Returns

Nothing

Example 1

From the console, close all open documents.

```
var d = app.activeDocs;
for( var i in d ) d[i].closeDoc();
```

The following code can be executed as a mouse-up action from an open document. It closes all *disclosed* open documents. The code is designed to close the active document last so that the execution of the code will not be abruptly terminated.

```
var d = app.activeDocs;
for( var i in d )
    if( d[i] != this ) d[i].closeDoc();
if ( this.disclosed ) this.closeDoc();
```

Example 2

Create a series of three test files and save them to a directory. This code must be executed in the console, because saveAs (page 282) has a security restriction.

```
var myDoc = app.newDoc();
for (var i=0; i < 3; i++) {
    myDoc.info.Title = "Test File " + i;
    myDoc.saveAs("/c/temp/test"+i+".pdf");
}
myDoc.closeDoc(true);
```

See saveAs (page 282) for an another example of closeDoc.

createDataObject

Creates a Data Object (page 167).

Data objects can be constructed *ad hoc*. This is useful if the data is being created in JavaScript from sources other than an external file (for example, ADBC database calls).

Related objects, properties, and methods are dataObjects (page 191), getDataObject (page 247), openDataObject (page 272), importDataObject (page 262), removeDataObject (page 275), getDataObjectContents (page 247), and setDataObjectContents (page 286), and the Data Object (page 167).

Parameters

cName	The name to associate with the data object.
cValue	A string containing the data to be embedded.
cMIMEType	(optional) The MIME type of the data. The default is "text/plain".

cCryptFilter	(optional, Acrobat 6.0) The language-independent name of a crypt filter to use when encrypting this data object. This crypt filter must have previously been added to the document's list of crypt filters, using the Document Object `addRecipientListCryptFilter` (page 214) method, otherwise an exception will be thrown. The predefined **Identity** crypt filter can be used so that this data object is not encrypted in a file that is otherwise encrypted by the Document Object `encryptForRecipients` (page 230) method.

Returns

Nothing

Example

```
this.createDataObject("MyData.txt", "This is some data.");
```

See also the example that follows `addRecipientListCryptFilter` (page 214).

createTemplate

Note: In Adobe Reader 5.1 and later, this method was allowed with Advanced Form Features rights (**F**). Beginning with version 7.0 of Adobe Reader, this method is not allowed and will throw a `NotAllowedError` exception.

Creates a visible template from the specified page. See also the `templates` (page 207) property, the `getTemplate` (page 259) and `removeTemplate` (page 278) methods, and the Template Object (page 625).

Note: (Security **S**): This method can only be executed during batch, console, or menu events. (See "Privileged versus Non-privileged Context" on page 8.) The `event` Object (page 314) contains a discussion of Acrobat JavaScript events.

Parameters

cName	The name to be associated with this page.
nPage	(optional) The 0-based index of the page to operate on. The default is 0, the first page in the document.

Returns

The newly created Template Object (page 625).

Example

Convert all pages beginning with page 2 to hidden templates. As the templates are hidden, `this.numPages` is updated to reflect that change in the number of (visible) pages. Notice that in the loop below, only page 2 is made a template and then hidden. The next page will become the new page 2.

```
numNewTemplates = this.numPages - 2;
for ( var i = 0; i < numNewTemplates; i++)
{
    var t = this.createTemplate({cName:"myTemplate"+i, nPage:2
});
    t.hidden = true;
}
```

deletePages

Deletes pages from the document. If neither page of the range is specified, the first page (page 0) is deleted. See also `insertPages` (page 267), `extractPages` (page 242), and `replacePages` (page 280).

Note: You cannot delete all pages in a document: there must be at least one page remaining.

Note: (**F**, Acrobat 6.0): Beginning with version 6.0, this method deletes *spawned* pages from within Adobe Reader for documents with forms usage rights enabled.

Parameters

nStart	(optional) The 0-based index of the first page in the range of pages to be deleted. The default is 0, the first page in the document.
nEnd	(optional) The last page in the range of pages to be deleted. If nEnd is not specified, only the page specified by nStart is deleted.

Returns

Nothing

Example

Delete pages 1 through 3 (base 0), inclusive.

```
this.deletePages({nStart: 1, nEnd: 3});
```

deleteSound

5.0	*⊘*		**⊗**

Deletes the Sound Object (page 599) with the specified name from the document.

See also `sounds` (page 206), `getSound` (page 258), `importSound` (page 265), and the Sound Object (page 599).

Parameters

cName	The name of the sound object to delete.

Returns

Nothing

Example

```
this.deleteSound("Moo");
```

embedDocAsDataObject

7.0			**Ⓓ**

Embeds the specified document as a Data Object in the document.

Note: For Adobe Reader 7.0 and later, this method is allowed if the document has file attachment rights **Ⓓ**, but the document to be embedded must have document Save rights **Ⓢ** in case it has changed.

Parameters

cName	The name to associate with the data object.
oDoc	The document to embed as a data object.
cCryptFilter	(optional) The language-independent name of a crypt filter to use when encrypting this data object. This crypt filter must have previously been added to the document's list of crypt filters, using the `addRecipientListCryptFilter` (page 214) method, otherwise an exception will be thrown. The predefined **Identity** crypt filter can be used so that this data object is not encrypted in a file that is otherwise encrypted by the `encryptForRecipients` (page 230) method.
bUI	(optional) If `true`, an alert may be shown if `oDoc` requires saving and the permissions do not allow it to be saved. Default value is `false`.

Returns

Nothing

Example

An envelope file that includes a "myFilter" crypt filter has been previously authored and has been included in the current document.

```
var authorEmail = "johndoe@acme.com";
var envelopeDoc = this.openDataObject( "envelope" );
envelopeDoc.embedDocAsDataObject( "attachment", this,\
    "myFilter" );
envelopeDoc.title.Author = authorEmail;
envelopeDoc.mailDoc({
    cTo: "support@mycompany.com",
    cSubject: "Application from " + authorEmail
});
```

encryptForRecipients

Encrypts the document for the specified lists of recipients, using the public-key certificates of each recipient. Encryption does not take place until the document is saved. Recipients can be placed into groups and each group can have its own unique permission settings. This method throws an exception if it is unsuccessful.

Note: (Security ☑): This method is available from batch, console, app initialization, and menu events. See also "Privileged versus Non-privileged Context" on page 8.

See also the `createDataObject` (page 226) method, the `security`.chooseRecipientsDialog (page 549) method, and the Data Object (page 167).

Parameters

oGroups	An array of generic Group Objects (page 231) that list the recipients for which the document is to be encrypted.
bMetaData	(optional) If `true` (the default), document metadata should be encrypted. Setting this value to `false` will produce a document that can only be viewed in Acrobat 6.0 or later.
bUI	(optional) If **true**, the handler displays the user interface, in which the user can select the recipients for whom to encrypt the document. The default value is `false`.

Adobe® Acrobat® Official JavaScript Reference

Returns

`true`, if successful, otherwise an exception is thrown.

Group Object

A generic JavaScript object that allows a set of permissions to be attached to a list of recipients for which a document or data is to be encrypted. This object is passed to `encryptForRecipients` (page 230) and returned by `security.chooseRecipientsDialog` (page 549). It contains the following properties.

Property	Description
`permissions`	A Group Object (page 231) with the permissions for the group.
`userEntities`	An array of UserEntity Objects (page 181), the users to whom the permissions apply.

Permissions Object

A generic JavaScript object that contains a set of permissions, used in a Group Object (page 231). It contains the following properties. The default value for all Boolean properties is `false`.

Property	Type	Access	Description
`allowAll`	Boolean	R/W	Specifies whether full, unrestricted access is permitted. If `true`, overrides all other properties.
`allowAccessibility`	Boolean	R/W	Specifies whether content access for the visually impaired is permitted. If `true`, allows content to be extracted for use by applications that, for example, read text aloud.
`allowContentExtraction`	Boolean	R/W	Specifies whether content copying and extraction is permitted.

`allowChanges`	String	R/W	What changes are allowed to be made to the document. Values are:
			
			`none`
			`documentAssembly`
			`fillAndSign`
			`editNotesFillAndSign`
			`all`

`allowPrinting`	String	R/W	What the allowed printing security level is for the document. Values are:
			
			`none`
			`lowQuality`
			`highQuality`

Example

Encrypt all strings and streams in the document. This will produce a file that can be opened with Acrobat 5.0 and later:

```
var sh = security.getHandler( "Adobe.PPKMS" );
var dir = sh.directories[0];
var dc = dir.connect();

dc.setOutputFields({oFields:["certificates"]});
var importantUsers = dc.search({oParams:{lastName:"Smith"}});
var otherUsers = dc.search({oParams: {lastName:"jones" }});

this.encryptForRecipients({
   oGroups :
   [
      {oUserEntities:
            importantUsers,oPermissions:{allowAll:true }},
      {oUserEntities:
      otherUsers,
      oPermissions:{allowPrinting:"highQuality"}
      }
   ],
   bMetaData : true
});
```

encryptUsingPolicy

7.0		$\mathcal{S}$	$\mathbf{X}$

Encrypts the document using a specified policy object and handler. This method may require user interaction and may result in a new security policy being created.

Note: (Security $\mathcal{S}$) This method can be executed only during batch, console or application initialization events. See also "Privileged versus Non-privileged Context" on page 8.

Parameters

`oPolicy`	The policy object to use when encrypting the document. It may be a SecurityPolicy Object (page 569) returned from `chooseSecurityPolicy` (page 551) or `getSecurityPolicies` (page 554).
	This parameter may also be a generic object with the `policyId` property defined. If a predefined policy ID is passed, the associated policy is retrieved and used. If the policy ID passed is unknown, an error is returned.
	There is a predefined policy ID that has a special behavior. If `policyId` is set to "adobe_secure_for_recipients", a new policy will be created by the Adobe Policy Server.
	Note: If this special policy ID is used and `oGroups` is `null`, an error will be returned.
`oGroups`	(optional) An array of Group Objects (page 231) that the handler should use when applying the policy. The exact behavior depends on the policy used and the handler involved. The Group object may have embedded permission information. Whether that information is used depends on the policy and associated security handler.
	Default value is `null`.
`oHandler`	(optional) The SecurityHandler Object (page 557) to be used for encryption. This will result in failure if this handler does not match the handler name specified in the `oPolicy` object. If not specified, the default object associated with this handler will be used.
	If you are using the APS security handler, you can create a new SecurityHandler ahead of time, authenticate to a server not configured in Acrobat through the `login` call, and then pass that SecurityHandler in `oHandler`. This would allow you to use policies that are not defined on the server Acrobat is configured to use.
	If you are using the PPKLite security handler, you could create a new SecurityHandler ahead of time, open a digital ID file not configured in Acrobat through the `login` call, and then pass that SecurityHandler in `oHandler`. This would allow you to use certificates contained in the digital ID file but not in Acrobat.
`bUI`	(optional) If `true`, the user interface may be displayed (for example, for authentication). If `false`, the user interface will not be displayed. If user interaction is required but not allowed, an error is returned.
	Default value is `false`.

Returns

The value returned is a SecurityPolicyResults object, which has the following properties.

Property	Type	Description

errorCode	Integer	The error code returned from the handler implementing the policy. There are three possible errors:
		
		0 = Success.
		    errorText is not defined.
		    unknownRecipients may be defined.
		    policyApplied is defined.
		
		1 = Failure.
		    errorText is defined. unknownRecipients may be defined. policyApplied is not defined.
		
		2 = Abort, the user aborted the process.
		    errorText is not defined. unknownRecipients is not defined. policyApplied is not defined.

errorText	String	The localized error description, if defined. See errorCode for when this is defined.
policyApplied	Object	The SecurityPolicy Object (page 569) applied, if defined. If the policy passed in was "adobe_secure_for_recipients", a new policy was created by the call and the corresponding policy object will be returned here. See errorCode for when this is defined.
unknownRecipients	RecipientsObject	Recipients passed in that could not be used when applying the policy, if defined. See errorCode for when this is defined.

Example 1

In this example, a newly created document is encrypted using a chosen policy.

```
var doc = app.newDoc();
var policy = security.chooseSecurityPolicy();
var results = doc.encryptUsingPolicy( { oPolicyId: policy } );
console.println("The policy applied was: "
    + results.policyApplied.name);
```

Example 2

In this example a newly created document is encrypted using a template policy.

```
var doc = app.newDoc();
var groups = [ { userEntities: [{email:"jdoe@mycorp.com"},
    {email:"bsmith@mycorp.com"} ] }
];
```

```
var policy = { policyId: "adobe_secure_for_recipients" };
var results = doc.encryptUsingPolicy({
   oPolicy: policy,
   oGroups: groups,
   bUI: true
});
console.println("The policy applied was: "
   + results.policyApplied.name);
```

exportAsFDF

Exports form fields as a FDF file to the local hard drive.

Note: (Security **S**): If the cPath parameter is specified, this method can only be executed during batch, console, or menu events. See also "Privileged versus Non-privileged Context" on page 8. The event Object contains a discussion of Acrobat JavaScript events.

Parameters

bAllFields	(optional) If true, all fields are exported, including those that have no value. If false (the default), excludes those fields that currently have no value.
bNoPassword	(optional) If true (the default), do not include text fields that have the password flag set in the exported FDF.
aFields	(optional) The array of field names to submit or a string containing a single field name: • If specified, only these fields are exported, except those excluded by bNoPassword. • If aFields is an empty array, no fields are exported. The FDF might still contain data, depending on the bAnnotations parameter. • If this parameter is omitted or is null, all fields in the form are exported, except those excluded by bNoPassword. Specify non-terminal field names to export an entire subtree of fields (see the example below).
bFlags	(optional) If true, field flags are included in the exported FDF. The default is false.

cPath	(optional) A string specifying the device-independent pathname for the file. The pathname may be relative to the location of the current document. If the parameter is omitted, a dialog box is shown to let the user select the file.
	Note: (Security ☯): The parameter cPath must have a safe path (see "Safe Path" on page 8) and have a .fdf extension. This method will throw a NotAllowedError (see "Error Object" on page 311) exception if these security conditions are not met, and the method will fail.
bAnnotations	(optional, Acrobat 6.0) If true, annotations are included in the exported FDF. The default is false.

Returns

Nothing

Example 1

Export the entire form (including empty fields) with flags.

```
this.exportAsFDF(true, true, null, true);
```

Example 2

Export the *name* subtree with no flags.

```
this.exportAsFDF(false, true, "name");
```

This example shows a shortcut to exporting a whole subtree. By passing "name" as part of the aFields parameter, fields such as "name.title", "name.first", "name.middle", and "name.last" are exported.

exportAsText

| 6.0 | | ☯ | ❺ |

Exports form fields as a tab-delimited text file to a local hard disk. The text file that is created follows the conventions specified by Microsoft Excel. In particular, exportAsText correctly handles quotes and multiline text fields.

This method writes two lines to the text file, the first line a tab-delimited list of the names of the fields specified by aFields, the second line is a tab-delimited list of the values of the fields.

Note: (Security ☯): If the cPath parameter is specified, this method can only be executed during batch, console or menu events. See also "Privileged versus Non-privileged Context" on page 8. The event Object (page 314) includes a discussion of Acrobat JavaScript events.

Parameters

bNoPassword	(optional) If `true` (the default), do not include text fields that have the password flag set in the exported text file.
aFields	(optional) The array of field names to submit or a string containing a single field name: ● If specified, only these fields are exported, except those excluded by bNoPassword. ● If aFields is an empty array, no fields are exported. ● If this parameter is omitted or is `null`, all fields in the form are exported, except those excluded by bNoPassword.
cPath	(optional) A string specifying the device-independent pathname for the file. The pathname may be relative to the location of the current document. If the parameter is omitted, a dialog box is shown to let the user select the file. **Note:** (Security **S**): The parameter cPath is must have a safe path (see "Safe Path" on page 8) and have a `.txt` extension. This method will throw a `NotAllowedError` (see "Error Object" on page 311) exception if these security conditions are not met, and the method will fail.

Returns

Nothing

Example

To export all fields to a tab-delimited file, execute the following script in the console:

```
this.exportAsText();
```

To create a tab-delimited file with more than just one data line, see "Example" on page 248.

exportAsXFDF

Exports form fields an XFDF file to the local hard drive.

XFDF is an XML representation of Acrobat form data. See the document *XML Form Data Format Specification* (see "References" on page 2).

There is an import version of this same method, `importAnXFDF` (page 261).

Note: (Security **S**): If the cPath parameter is specified, this method can only be executed during batch, console or menu events. See "Privileged versus Non-privileged Context" on page 8 for details. The `event` Object (page 314) contains a discussion of Acrobat JavaScript events.

Parameters

bAllFields	(optional) If `true`, all fields are exported, including those that have no value. If `false` (the default), excludes those fields that currently have no value.
bNoPassword	(optional) If `true` (the default), do not include text fields that have the password flag set in the exported XFDF.
aFields	(optional) The array of field names to submit or a string containing a single field name: • If specified, only these fields are exported, except those excluded by `bNoPassword`. • If `aFields` is an empty array, no fields are exported. The XFDF might still contain data, depending on the `bAnnotations` parameter. • If this parameter is omitted or is `null`, all fields in the form are exported, except those excluded by `bNoPassword`. Specify non-terminal field names to export an entire subtree of fields.
cPath	(optional) A string specifying the device-independent pathname for the file. The pathname may be relative to the location of the current document. If the parameter is omitted, a dialog box is shown to let the user select the file. **Note:** (Security ): The parameter `cPath` must have a safe path (see "Safe Path" on page 8) and have a `.xfdf` extension. This method will throw a `NotAllowedError` (see "Error Object" on page 311) exception if these security conditions are not met, and the method will fail.
bAnnotations	(optional, Acrobat 6.0) If `true`, annotations are included in the exported XFDF. The default is `false`.

Returns

Nothing

exportDataObject

5.0			

Extracts the specified data object to an external file.

Related objects, properties, and methods are `dataObjects` (page 191), `openDataObject` (page 272), `createDataObject` (page 226), `removeDataObject` (page 275), `importDataObject` (page 262),

---

getDataObjectContents (page 247), and setDataObjectContents (page 286), and the Data Object (page 167).

Note: (Security ☯): Beginning with Acrobat 6.0, if the parameter cDIPath is non-null, a NotAllowedError (see "Error Object" on page 311) exception is thrown and the method fails.

If cDIPath is not passed to this method, a file selection dialog box opens to allow the user to select a save path for the embedded data object.

Parameters

cName	The name of the data object to extract.
cDIPath	(optional) A device-independent path to which to extract the data object. This path may be absolute or relative to the current document. If not specified, the user is prompted to specify a save location. **Note:** (Acrobat 6.0) The use of this parameter is no longer supported and should not be used. See the security notes above.
bAllowAuth	(optional, Acrobat 6.0) If true, a dialog box is used to obtain user authorization. Authorization may be required if the data object was encrypted using the encryptForRecipients (page 230) method. Authorization dialogs are allowed if bAllowAuth is true. The default value is false.
nLaunch	(optional, Acrobat 6.0) nLaunch controls whether the file is launched, or opened, after it is saved. Launching may involve opening an external application if the file is not a PDF file. The values of nLaunch are • If the value is 0, the file will not be launched after it is saved. • If the value is 1, the file will be saved and then launched. Launching will prompt the user with a security alert warning if the file is not a PDF file. The user will be prompted for a save path. • If the value is 2, the file will be saved and then launched. Launching will prompt the user with a security alert warning if the file is not a PDF file. A temporary path is used, and the user will not be prompted for a save path. The temporary file that is created will be deleted by Acrobat upon application shutdown. The default value is 0.

Returns

Nothing

Example 1

Prompt the user for a file and location to extract to.

```
this.exportDataObject("MyData");
```

Example 2 (Acrobat 6.0)

Extract PDF document and launch it in the viewer.

```
this.exportDataObject({ cName: "MyPDF.pdf", nLaunch: 2 });
```

Example 3

When a file attachment is imported using the `importDataObject` (page 262) method, the value of its `Data.name` (page 168) property is assigned by that method's `cName` parameter. However, when a file is attached using the UI, its `name` (page 168) is automatically assigned. The attachments are assigned the sequential names "Untitled Object", "Untitled Object 2", "Untitled Object 3", and so on.

To export a file attached through the UI, the `name` of the attachment must be found. For the code that follows, the last file attached by the UI, if any, is exported.

```
var d = this.dataObjects;
if ( d == null ) console.println("No file attachments");
else {
    for ( var i = d.length - 1; i>=0; i--)
        if ( d[i].name.indexOf("Untitled Object") != -1 )
            break;
    if ( i != -1 ) this.exportDataObject(d[i].name);
    else console.println("No attachment was embedded by UI");
}
```

exportXFAData

Exports the XFA data (if any) from the document and saves it as an XDP file.

Form Rights (**F**): When exporting XFA data from Adobe Reader, the document must have export form rights.

Note: (Security **S**): If the `cPath` parameter is specified, this method can only be executed during batch, console or menu events. See "Privileged versus Non-privileged Context" on page 8 for details. The event Object contains a discussion of Acrobat JavaScript events.

Parameters

cPath	(optional) A device-independent pathname for the file. The pathname may be relative to the document. If this parameter is omitted, a dialog box is shown to let the user select the file. (Security ❂): The path must meet the following conditions: ● It must be a safe path (see "Safe Path" on page 8). ● If bXDP is true, the file name must have an .xdp extension. ● If bXDP is false,the file name must have an .xml extension. This method throws a NotAllowedError (see "Error Object" on page 311) exception if these conditions are not met.
bXDP	(optional) If true (the default), the data is exported in XDP format. Otherwise, it is exported in plain XML data format.
aPackets	(optional) An array of strings specifying the packets to include in the XDP export. This parameter is applicable only if bXDP is true. Possible strings are: ``` template datasets stylesheet xfdf sourceSet pdf config * ``` If pdf is specified, the PDF is embedded. Otherwise, only a link to the PDF is included in the XDP. If xfdf is specified, annotations are included in the XDP (since that packet uses XFDF format). If * is specified, all packets are included in the XDP. However, the default for the pdf packet is to include it as a *reference*. To embed the PDF file in the XDP, explicitly specify pdf as one of the packets. **Note:** (Save rights required ❂): When exporting in the XDP format from Adobe Reader, the document must have document save rights only in the case where pdf is listed explicitly. The default for this parameter is: ["datasets", "xfdf"].

Returns

Nothing

Example

In the following example, all packets are included. However, the PDF document is referenced, not embedded:

```
this.exportXFAData({
    cPath: "/c/temp/myData.xdp",
    bXDP: true,
    aPackets: ["*"]
})
```

In this example, all packets are included, with the PDF document embedded in the XDP.

```
this.exportXFAData({
    cPath: "/c/temp/myData.xdp",
    bXDP: true,
    aPackets: ["*","pdf"]
})
```

extractPages

Creates a new document consisting of pages extracted from the current document. If a page range is not specified, the method extracts all pages in the document.

See also deletePages (page 228), insertPages (page 267), and replacePages (page 280).

Note: (Security ☯) If the cPath parameter is specified, this method can only be executed during batch, console or menu events, or through an external call (for example, OLE). See "Privileged versus Non-privileged Context" on page 8 for details. The event Object (page 314) contains a discussion of Acrobat JavaScript events.

Parameters

nStart	(optional) A 0-based index that defines the start of the range of pages to extract from the source document. If only nStart is specified, the range of pages is the single page specified by nStart.
nEnd	(optional) A 0-based index that defines the end of the range of pages to extract from the source document. If only nEnd is specified, the range of pages is 0 to nEnd.

cPath		(optional) The device-independent pathname to save the new document. The path name may be relative to the location of the current document.
	Note:	(Security 🔒): The parameter cPath must have a safe path (see "Safe Path" on page 8) and have a .pdf extension. This method will throw a NotAllowedError (see "Error Object" on page 311) exception if these security conditions are not met, and the method will fail.

Returns

If cPath is not specified, returns the Document Object (page 188) for the new document; otherwise, returns the null object.

Example

The following batch sequence takes each of the selected files, extracts each page, and save the page in a folder with a unique name. It could be used, for example, when the client's one-page bills are produced by an application and placed in a single PDF file. The client wants to separate the pages for distribution or separate printing jobs.

```
/* Extract Pages to Folder */
// regular expression used to acquire the base name of file
var re = /\.pdf$/i;
// filename is the base name of the file Acrobat is working on
var filename = this.documentFileName.replace(re,"");
try {for (var i = 0; i < this.numPages; i++)
        this.extractPages({
            nStart: i,
            cPath: "/F/temp/"+filename+"_" + i +".pdf"
        });
} catch (e) { console.println("Aborted: " + e) }
```

flattenPages

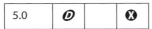

Converts all annotations in a page range to page contents. If a page range is not specified, all annotations in the document are converted.

Note: Great care must be used when using this method. All annotations—including form fields, comments, and links—on the specified range of pages are flattened. They may have appearances, but they will no longer be annotations.

Parameters

nStart	(optional) A 0-based index that defines the start of an inclusive range of pages in the current document. If only nStart is specified, the page range is the single page specified by nStart.
nEnd	(optional) A 0-based index that defines the end of an inclusive range of pages in the current document.
nNonPrint	(optional, Acrobat 6.0) This parameter determines how to handle non-printing annotations. Values are 0 (default): Non-printing annotations are flattened. 1: Non-printing annotations are left as is. 2: Non-printing annotations are removed from the document.

Returns

Nothing

Example

Flatten all pages in the document.

```
this.flattenPages();
```

getAnnot

5.0			

Returns an Annotation Object (page 19) contained on a specific document page.

Parameters

nPage	The page that contains the Annotation Object (page 19).
cName	The name of the Annotation Object (page 19).

Returns

The Annotation Object (page 19), or null if there is no such annotation.

Example

```
var ann = this.getAnnot(0, "OnMarketShare");
if (ann == null)
    console.println("Not Found!")
else
    console.println("Found it! type: " + ann.type);
```

getAnnot3D

7.0			

Gets an Annot3D Object (page 47) with a given name from a given page.

Parameters

nPage	The 0-based page number that contains the Annot3D Object (page 47).
cName	The name of the Annot3D Object (page 47).

Returns

The Annot3D Object (page 47), or undefined if there is no such annotation.

getAnnots

5.0			

Gets an array of Annotation Objects (page 19) satisfying specified criteria. See also getAnnot (page 244) and syncAnnotScan (page 300).

Parameters

nPage	(optional) A 0-based page number. If specified, gets only annotations on the given page. If not specified, gets annotations that meet the search criteria from all pages.
nSortBy	(optional) A sort method applied to the array. Values are: ANSB_None: (default) Do not sort; equivalent to not specifiying this parameter. ANSB_Page: Use the page number as the primary sort criteria. ANSB_Author: Use the author as the primary sort criteria. ANSB_ModDate: Use the modification date as the primary sort criteria. ANSB_Type: Use the annotation type as the primary sort criteria.
bReverse	(optional) If true, causes the array to be reverse sorted with respect to nSortBy.

nFilterBy	(optional) Gets only annotations satisfying certain criteria. Values are:
	ANFB_ShouldNone: (default) Get all annotations. Equivalent of not specifying this parameter.
	ANFB_ShouldPrint: Only include annotations that can be printed.
	ANFB_ShouldView: Only include annotations that can be viewed.
	ANFB_ShouldEdit: Only include annotations that can be edited.
	ANFB_ShouldAppearInPanel: Only annotations that appear in the annotations pane.
	ANFB_ShouldSummarize: Only include annotations that can be included in a summary.
	ANFB_ShouldExport: Only include annotations that can be included in an export.

Returns

An array of Annotation Objects (page 19), or null if none are found.

Example

```
this.syncAnnotScan();
var annots = this.getAnnots({
    nPage:0,
    nSortBy: ANSB_Author,
    bReverse: true
});
console.show();
console.println("Number of Annotations: " + annots.length);
var msg = "%s in a %s annot said: \"%s\"";
for (var i = 0; i < annots.length; i++)
    console.println(util.printf(msg, annots[i].author,
annots[i].type,
        annots[i].contents));
```

getAnnots3D

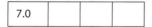

7.0			

Returns an array of Annot3D Objects (page 47) for a page.

Parameters

nPage	The 0-based page number that contains the Annot3D Objects (page 47).

Returns

An array of Annot3D Objects (page 47), or `undefined` if none is found.

getDataObject

5.0			

Obtains a specific Data Object (page 167). See also `dataObjects` (page 191), `createDataObject` (page 226), `exportDataObject` (page 238), `importDataObject` (page 262), and `removeDataObject` (page 275).

Parameters

cName	The name of the `data` object to obtain.

Returns

The Data Object (page 167) corresponding to the specified name.

Example

```
var MyData = this.getDataObject("MyData");
console.show(); console.clear();
for (var i in MyData) console.println("MyData." + i + "="
    + MyData[i]);
```

getDataObjectContents

7.0			

Allows access to the contents of the file attachment associated with a DataObject.

Parameters

cName	The name associated with the Data Object (page 167) to get.
bAllowAuth	(optional) The default value is `false`. If `true`, a dialog box is used to obtain user authorization. Authorization may be required if the data object was encrypted using `encryptForRecipients` (page 230). Authorization dialogs are allowed if `bAllowAuth` is `true`.

Returns

ReadStream Object (page 519)

Related objects, properties, and methods are `dataObjects` (page 191), `getDataObject` (page 247), `openDataObject` (page 272), `createDataObject` (page 226), `importDataObject` (page 262),

---

setDataObjectContents (page 286), removeDataObject (page 275), and the Data Object (page 167).

Example

This code is part of a circulating memo. A PDF file is circulated among members on an email list. Each recipient enters a budget figure, then forwards the document on to the next person on the list. Before the document is sent, the budget number is appended to an embedded tab-delimited document, budget.xls, an attachment to this document. The last recipient can open the attachment, budget.xls, in a spreadsheet application to view the various budget numbers.

```
// get the name and department of the current recipient
var firstName = this.getField("Name.First").value;
var lastName =  this.getField("Name.Last").value;
var deptName =  this.getField("Dept.Name").value;
// get the budget number
var deptBudget =  this.getField("Dept.Budget").value;
if ( app.viewerVersion >= 7 ) {
    // get the file stream object of the embedded file
    var oFile = this.getDataObjectContents("budget.xls");
    // convert to a string
    var myBudget = util.stringFromStream(oFile, "utf-8");
    // append current data to the end, using tabs to
    //separate info
    var myBudget = myBudget + "\r\n" + firstName
        + "\t" + lastName + "\t" + deptName + "\t" + deptBudget;
    // convert back to a file stream
    var oFile = util.streamFromString(myBudget, "uft-8");
    // now "overwrite" budget.xls
    this.setDataObjectContents("budget.xls", oFile);
} else {
    app.alert("Acrobat 7.0 or later is required."
        + " Your budget data will not be included. "
        + "Will e-mail on to the next correspondent, sorry. "
        + "Send in your budget request using traditional\
            methods.");
}
```

The rest of the code, not shown, is to save the document and sent to the next person on the mailing list.

This example uses getDataObjectContents, setDataObjectContents (page 286), util.stringFromStream (page 647), and util.streamFromString (page 646).

getField

3.01			

Maps a Field Object (page 371) in the PDF document to a JavaScript variable.

Beginning with Acrobat 6.0, this method can return the Field Object of an individual widget. For more information, see "Field Object" on page 371.

Parameters

cName	The name of the field of interest.

Returns

A Field Object (page 371) representing a form field in the PDF document.

Example 1

Make a text field multiline and triple its height

```
var f = this.getField("myText");
var aRect = f.rect;// get bounding rectangle
f.multiline = true;// make it multiline
var height = aRect[1]-aRect[3];// calculate height
aRect[3] -= 2* height;// triple the height of the text field
f.rect = aRect;    // and make it so
```

Example 2 (Acrobat 6.0)

Attach a JavaScript action to an individual widget, in this case, a radio button:

```
var f = this.getField("myRadio.0");
f.setAction("MouseUp",
    "app.alert('Thanks for selecting the first choice.');");
```

Example 3

The following code lists all properties of a field. This technique can be used to programmatically duplicate a field.

```
f = this.getField("myField");
for ( var i in f ) {
    try {
        if ( typeof f[i] != "function" ) // remove a field
methods
            console.println( i + ":" + f[i] )
    } catch(e) {} // an exception occurs when we get a property
that
}            // does not apply to this field type.
```

getIcon

5.0			

Obtains a specific icon object. See also the icons (page 196) property, the addIcon (page 212), importIcon (page 263), and removeIcon (page 276) methods, and the Field Object methods `buttonGetIcon` (page 401), `buttonImportIcon` (page 401), and `buttonSetIcon` (page 403).

Parameters

cName	The name of the `icon` object to obtain.

Returns

An Icon Object (page 434) associated with the specified name in the document or `null` if no icon of that name exists.

Example

The following is a custom keystroke script from a combo box. The face names of the items in the combo box are the names of some of the icons that populate the document. As the user chooses different items from the combo box, the corresponding icon appears as the button face of the field "myPictures".

```
if (!event.willCommit) {
    var b = this.getField("myPictures");
    var i = this.getIcon(event.change);
    b.buttonSetIcon(i);
}
```

See the Field Object `buttonSetIcon` (page 403) method or a more elaborate variation on this example.

getLegalWarnings

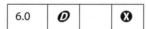

Returns the legal warnings for this document in the form of an object with entries for each warning that has been found in the document. Legal warnings can be embedded in a file at the time that a file is signed by an author signature. Legal warnings can be embedded using the `cLegalAttest` of the Field Object `signatureSign` (page 421) method.

The process that analyzes a file to determine this list of warnings is not available in Adobe Reader. The value of each entry is the number of occurrences of this warning in the document. (See section 8.7.4 in the *PDF Reference*.)

Parameters

bExecute	If `true`, the file is examined and all detected warnings are returned. If `false` (the default value), the warnings that have been embedded in the file are returned.

Returns

A object containing property names and values of legal warnings.

Example

Process a document and get legal PDF warnings.

```
var w = this.getLegalWarnings( true );
console.println( "Actual Legal PDF Warnings:" );
for(i in w) console.println( i + " = " + w[i] );

var w1 = this.getLegalWarnings( false );
console.println( "Declared Legal PDF Warnings:" );
for(i in w1) console.println( i + " = " + w1[i] );

// For an author signature, note also if annotations are
// allowed by MDP settings

var f = this.getField( "AuthorSig" );
var s = f.signatureInfo();
if( s.mdp == "defaultAndComments" )
   console.println( "Annotations are allowed" );

// What does author have to say about all this?

console.println( "Legal PDF Attestation:" );
console.println( w1.Attestation );
```

getLinks

6.0			

Gets an array of Link Objects (page 440) that are enclosed within specified coordinates on a page. See also `addLink` (page 213) and `removeLinks` (page 277).

Parameters

nPage	The page that contains the Link Objects (page 440). The first page is 0.
oCoords	An array of four numbers in rotated user space, the coordinates of a rectangle listed in the following order: upper-left *x*, upper-left *y*, lower-right *x* and lower-right *y*.

Returns

An array of Link Objects (page 440).

Example

Count the number of links in a document and report to the console.

```
var numLinks=0;
for ( var p = 0; p < this.numPages; p++)
{
    var b = this.getPageBox("Crop", p);
     var l = this.getLinks(p, b);
    console.println("Number of Links on page " + p +" is "
        + l.length);
     numLinks += l.length;
}
console.println("Number of Links in Document is " + numLinks);
```

getNthFieldName

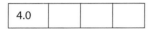

Gets the name of the *n*th field in the document. See also `numFields` (page 202).

Parameters

nIndex	The index of the field whose name should be obtained.

Returns

The name of the field in the document.

Example

Enumerate through all of the fields in the document.

```
for (var i = 0; i < this.numFields; i++)
    console.println("Field[" + i + "] = "
        + this.getNthFieldName(i));
```

getNthTemplate

Note: This method is superseded by the `templates` (page 207) property, the `getTemplate` (page 259) method, and the Template Object (page 625).

Gets the name of the *n*th template within the document.

Parameters

nIndex	The index of the template to obtain.

Returns

The name of the specified template.

Adobe® Acrobat® Official JavaScript Reference

getOCGs

6.0			

Gets an array of OCG Objects (page 485) found on a specified page.

Related methods are getOCGOrder (page 253) and setOCGOrder (page 288), and the OCG Object (page 485).

Parameters

nPage	(optional) The 0-based page number. If not specified, all the OCGs found in the document are returned.

Returns

An array of OCG Objects OCG Object (page 485) or null if no OCGs are present.

Example

Turn on all the OCGs on the given document and page.

```
function TurnOnOCGsForPage(doc, nPage)
{
    var ocgArray = doc.getOCGs(nPage);
    for (var i=0; i < ocgArray.length; i++)
        ocgArray[i].state = true;
}
```

getOCGOrder

7.0			

Returns this document's OCGOrder array. This array represents how layers are displayed in the UI.

Related methods are getOCGs (page 253) and setOCGOrder (page 288) and the OCG Object (page 485).

Parameters

None

Returns

An array containing OCG objects, strings, and similar subarrays, or null if no OCGs are present.

See setOCGOrder (page 288) for a description of the order array.

getPageBox

5.0			

Gets a rectangle in rotated user space that encompasses the named box for the page. See also setPageBoxes (page 289).

Parameters

cBox	(optional) The type of box. Values are: Art Bleed BBox Crop (*default*) Trim For definitions of these boxes see section 10.10.1, "Page Boundaries," in the *PDF Reference*.
nPage	(optional) The 0-based index of the page. The default is 0, the first page in the document.

Returns

A rectangle in rotated user space that encompasses the named box for the page.

Example

Get the dimensions of the Media box.

```
var aRect = this.getPageBox("Media");
var width = aRect[2] - aRect[0];
var height = aRect[1] - aRect[3];
console.println("Page 1 has a width of " + width
       + " and a height of " + height);
```

getPageLabel

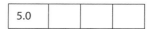

5.0			

Gets page label information for the specified page.

Parameters

nPage	(optional) The 0-based index of the page. The default is 0, the first page in the document.

Returns

Page label information for the specified page.

Example

See setPageLabels (page 290) for an example.

getPageNthWord

5.0		⊘	

Gets the *n*th word on the page.

See also getPageNumWords (page 256) and selectPageNthWord (page 285).

Note: (Security ⊘): This method throws an exception if the document security is set to prevent content extraction.

Parameters

nPage	(optional) The 0-based index of the page. The default is 0, the first page in the document.
nWord	(optional) The 0-based index of the word. The default is 0, the first word on the page.
bStrip	(optional) Specifies whether punctuation and whitespace should be removed from the word before returning. The default is true.

Returns

The *n*th word on the page.

Example

See "Example 2" on page 612 of spell.checkWord for an example.

getPageNthWordQuads

5.0		⊘	

Gets the quads list for the *n*th word on the page. The quads (page 36) property of the Annotation Object (page 19) can be used for constructing text markup, underline, strikeOut, highlight and squiggly annotations. See also getPageNthWord (page 255), getPageNumWords (page 256), and selectPageNthWord (page 285).

Note: (Security ⊘): This method throws an exception if the document security is set to prevent content extraction.

Parameters

nPage	(optional) The 0-based index of the page. The default is 0, the first page in the document.
nWord	(optional) The 0-based index of the word. The default is 0, the first word on the page.

Returns

The quads list for the *n*th word on the page.

Example

The following example underlines the fifth word on the second page of a document.

```
var annot = this.addAnnot({
    page: 1,
    type: "Underline",
    quads:  this.getPageNthWordQuads(1, 4),
    author: "A. C. Acrobat",
    contents: "Fifth word on second page"
});
```

See spell.checkWord (page 611) for an additional example.

getPageNumWords

5.0			

Gets the number of words on the page.

See also getPageNthWord (page 255), getPageNthWordQuads (page 255), and selectPageNthWord (page 285).

Parameters

nPage	(optional) The 0-based index of the page. The default is 0, the first page in the document.

Returns

The number of words on the page.

Example

```
// count the number of words in a document
var cnt=0;
for (var p = 0; p < this.numPages; p++)
   cnt += getPageNumWords(p);
console.println("There are " + cnt + " words in this doc.");
```

See "Example 2" on page 612 of `spell.checkWord` for an additional example.

getPageRotation

5.0			

Gets the rotation of the specified page. See also `setPageRotations` (page 291).

Parameters

nPage	(optional) The 0-based index of the page. The default is 0, the first page in the document.

Returns

The rotation value of 0, 90, 180, or 270.

getPageTransition

5.0			

Gets the transition of the specified page. See also `setPageTransitions` (page 292).

Parameters

nPage	(optional) The 0-based index of the page. The default is 0, the first page in the document.

Returns

An array of three values: [nDuration, cTransition, nTransDuration].

- nDuration is the maximum amount of time the page is displayed before the viewer automatically turns to the next page. A duration of -1 indicates that there is no automatic page turning.

- cTransition is the name of the transition to apply to the page. See the property app.fs.transitions (page 427) for a list of valid transitions.

- cTransDuration is the duration (in seconds) of the transition effect.

getPrintParams

6.0			

Gets a PrintParams Object (page 500) that reflects the default print settings. See the print method, which now takes the PrintParams Object (page 500) as its parameter.

Parameters

None

Returns

A PrintParams Object (page 500)

Example

Get the PrintParams Object (page 500) of the default printer.

```
var pp = this.getPrintParams();
                                    // set some properties
pp.colorOverride = pp.colorOverrides.mono;
this.print(pp);                     // print
```

getSound

5.0			

Gets the sound object corresponding to the specified name. See also sounds (page 206), importSound (page 265), deleteSound (page 229), and the Sound Object (page 599).

Parameters

cName	The name of the object to obtain.

Returns

The Sound Object (page 599) corresponding to the specified name.

Example

```
var s = this.getSound("Moo");
console.println("Playing the " + s.name + " sound.");
s.play();
```

getTemplate

| 5.0 | | | |

Gets the named template from the document. See also `templates` (page 207), `createTemplate` (page 227), `removeTemplate` (page 278), and the Template Object (page 625).

Parameters

cName	The name of the template to retrieve.

Returns

The Template Object (page 625) or `null` if the named template does not exist in the document.

Example

```
var t = this.getTemplate("myTemplate");
if ( t != null ) console.println( "myTemplate exists and is "
    + eval( '( t.hidden) ? "hidden" : "visible"' ) + "." );
else console.println( "myTemplate is not present!");
```

getURL

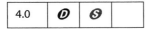

| 4.0 | 𝐷 | 𝘚 | |

Gets the specified URL over the internet using a GET. If the current document is being viewed inside the browser or Acrobat Web Capture is not available, the method uses the Acrobat Weblink plug-in to retrieve the requested URL. If running inside Acrobat, the method gets the URL of the current document either from the `baseURL` (page 190), from the URL of the first page (page 0) if the document was obtained by Web Capture, or from the file system.

Note: This method roughly corresponds to the "open a web page" action.

A related method is `app.launchURL` (page 89).

Parameters

cURL	A fully qualified URL or a relative URL. There can be a query string at the end of the URL.

bAppend	(optional) If `true` (the default), the resulting page or pages should be appended to the current document. This flag is considered to be `false` if the document is running inside the web browser, the Acrobat Web Capture plug-in is not available, or if the URL is of type `"file:///"`.
	Note: (Security ☯): Beginning with Acrobat 6.0, if `bAppend` is `true`, the `getURL` method can only be executed during a console, menu or batch event. See "Privileged versus Non-privileged Context" on page 8 for details.

Returns

Nothing

Example

```
this.getURL("http://www.adobe.com/", false);
```

gotoNamedDest

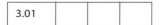

Goes to a named destination within the PDF document. For details on named destinations and how to create them, see Section 8.2, "Document-Level Navigation," in the *PDF Reference*.

Parameters

cName	The name of the destination within a document.

Returns

Nothing

Example

The following example opens a document, then goes to a named destination within that document.

```
// open new document
var myNovelDoc = app.openDoc("/c/fiction/myNovel.pdf");
// go to destination in this new doc
myNovelDoc.gotoNamedDest("chapter5");
// close old document
this.closeDoc();
```

importAnFDF

4.0	*Ɒ*		**Ꮐ**

Imports the specified FDF file. See also `importAnXFDF` (page 261) and `importTextData` (page 265).

Parameters

`cPath`	(optional) The device-independent pathname to the FDF file. It should look like the value of the **F** entry in an FDF file exported with the `submitForm` (page 295) method or with the **Advanced > Forms > Export Data From Form** menu item. The pathname may be relative to the location of the current document. If this parameter is omitted, a dialog box is shown to let the user select the file.

Returns

Nothing

Example

The following code, which is an action of a Page Open event, checks whether a certain function, `ProcResponse`, is already defined, if not, it installs a document-level JavaScript, which resides in an FDF file.

```
if(typeof ProcResponse == "undefined")
this.importAnFDF("myDLJS.fdf");
```

Here, the pathname is a relative one. This technique may be useful for automatically installing document-level JavaScripts for PDF files distilled from a PostScript file.

importAnXFDF

5.0	*Ɒ*	**Ꮐ**

Imports the specified XFDF file containing XML form data.

XFDF is an XML representation of Acrobat form data. See the document *XML Form Data Format (XFDF) Specification* (see "References" on page 2).

See also `exportAsXFDF` (page 237), `importAnFDF` (page 261) and `importTextData` (page 265).

Parameters

cPath	(optional) The device-independent pathname to the XFDF file. The pathname may be relative to the location of the current document. If the parameter is omitted, a dialog box is shown to let the user select the file.

Returns

Nothing

importDataObject

Imports an external file into the document and associates the specified name with the data object. Data objects can later be extracted or manipulated.

Related objects, properties, and methods are dataObjects (page 191), getDataObject (page 247), openDataObject (page 272), createDataObject (page 226), exportDataObject (page 238), removeDataObject (page 275), getDataObjectContents (page 247), and setDataObjectContents (page 286), and the Data Object.

Note: (Security **S**): If the cDIPath parameter is specified, this method can only be executed during batch, console or menu events, or through an external call (for example, OLE). See "Privileged versus Non-privileged Context" on page 8 for details. See the event Object (page 314) for a discussion of Acrobat JavaScript events.

When a file attachment is imported using importDataObject, the value of its Data.name (page 168) is assigned by the parameter cName. However, when a file is attached using the UI, its name (page 168) is automatically assigned. The attachments are assigned the sequential names "Untitled Object", "Untitled Object 2", "Untitled Object 3", and so on.

Parameters

cName	The name to associate with the data object.
cDIPath	(optional) A device-independent path to a data file on the user's hard drive. This path may be absolute or relative to the current document. If not specified, the user is prompted to locate a data file.

cCryptFilter	(optional, Acrobat 6.0) The language-independent name of a crypt filter to use when encrypting this data object. This crypt filter must have previously been added to the document's list of crypt filters, using the Document Object addRecipientListCryptFilter (page 214) method, otherwise an exception will be thrown. To leave this data object unencrypted in a file that is encrypted by the Document Object encryptForRecipients (page 230) method, the predefined **Identity** crypt filter can be used.

Returns

true on success. An exception is thrown on failure.

Example

```
function DumpDataObjectInfo(dataobj)
{
    for (var i in dataobj)
        console.println(dataobj.name + "[" + i + "]="
            + dataobj[i]);
}
// Prompt the user for a data file to embed.
this.importDataObject("MyData");
DumpDataObjectInfo(this.getDataObject("MyData"));
// Embed Foo.xml (found in parent director for this doc).
this.importDataObject("MyData2", "../Foo.xml");
DumpDataObjectInfo(this.getDataObject("MyData2"));
```

importIcon

5.0	𝐃	𝐒	𝐗

Imports an icon into the document and associates it with the specified name.

See also icons (page 196), addIcon (page 212), getIcon (page 249), removeIcon (page 276), field methods buttonGetIcon (page 401), buttonImportIcon (page 401), buttonSetIcon (page 403), and the Icon Object (page 434).

Beginning with version 6.0, Acrobat will first attempt to open cDIPath as a PDF. On failure, Acrobat will try to convert cDIPath to PDF from one of the known graphics formats (BMP, GIF, JPEG, PCX, PNG, TIFF) and then import the converted file as a button icon.

Note: (Security 𝐒): If cDIPath is specified, this method can only be executed during batch, console or menu events. See "Privileged versus Non-privileged Context" on page 8 for details. The event Object (page 314) contains a discussion of Acrobat JavaScript events.

Parameters

cName	The name to associate with the icon.
cDIPath	(optional) A device-independent path to a PDF file on the user's hard drive. This path may be absolute or relative to the current document. cDIPath may only be specified in a batch environment or from the console. If not specified, the nPage parameter is ignored and the user is prompted to locate a PDF file and browse to a particular page.
nPage	(optional) The 0-based index of the page in the PDF file to import as an icon. The default is 0.

Returns

An integer code indicating whether it was successful or not:

0: No error

1: The user canceled the dialog

-1: The selected file could not be opened

-2: The selected page was invalid

Example

This function is useful to populate a document with a series of named icons for later retrieval. For example, an author may want a picture of a list box state to appear next to the list box when the user selects the state in a list box. Without this function, it could be done by using a number of fields that could be hidden and shown. However, this is difficult to author. Instead, the appropriate script might be something like this:

```
var f = this.getField("StateListBox");
var b = this.getField("StateButton");
b.buttonSetIcon(this.getIcon(f.value));
```

This uses a single field to perform the same effect.

A simple user interface can be constructed to add named icons to a document. Assume the existence of two fields: a field called IconName that will contain the icon name and a field called IconAdd that will add the icon to the document. The mouse-up script for IconAdd would be:

```
var t = this.getField("IconName");
this.importIcon(t.value);
```

The same kind of script can be applied in a batch setting to populate a document with every selected icon file in a folder.

importSound

Imports a sound into the document and associates the specified name with the sound.

Note: (Security ): If `cDIPath` is specified, this method can only be executed during batch, console, or menu events. See "Privileged versus Non-privileged Context" on page 8 for details. The `event` Object (page 314) contains a discussion of Acrobat JavaScript events.

Parameters

cName	The name to associate with the sound object.
cDIPath	(optional) A device-independent path to a sound file on the user's hard drive. This path may be absolute or relative to the current document. If not specified, the user is prompted to locate a sound file.

Returns

Nothing

Example

```
this.importSound("Moo");
this.getSound("Moo").play();
this.importSound("Moof", "./moof.wav");
this.getSound("Moof").play();
```

See also `sounds` (page 206), `getSound` (page 258), `deleteSound` (page 229), and the Sound Object (page 599).

importTextData

Imports a row of data from a text file. Each row must be *tab delimited*. The entries in the first row of the text file are the column names of the tab delimited data. These names are also field names for text fields present in the PDF file. The data row numbers are 0-based; that is, the first row of data is row zero (this does not include the column name row). When a row of data is imported, each column datum becomes the field value of the field that corresponds to the column to which the data belongs.

See also the export version of this method, `exportAsText` (page 236).

Parameters

`cPath`	(optional) A relative device-independent path to the text file. If not specified, the user is prompted to locate the text data file.
`nRow`	(optional) The 0-based index of the row of the data to import, not counting the header row. If not specified, the user is prompted to select the row to import.

Returns

An integer return code.

Return Code	Description	Return Code	Description
-3	Warning: Missing Data	1	Error: Cannot Open File
-2	Warning: User Canceled Row Select	2	Error: Cannot Load Data
-1	Warning: User Canceled File Select	3	Error: Invalid Row
0	No Error		

Example 1

In this example, there are text fields named "First", "Middle", and "Last", and a data file whose first row consists of the three strings, "First", "Middle", and "Last", separated by tabs, along with four additional rows of tab-separated name data.

```
First     Middle     Last
A.        C.         Robat
T.        A.         Croba
A.        T.         Acrob
B.        A.         Tacro
// Import the first row of data from "myData.txt".
this.importTextData("/c/data/myData.txt", 0)
```

Example (continued)

The following code is a mouse-up action for a button. Clicking on the button cycles through the text file and populates the three fields "First", "Middle", and "Last" with the name data.

```
if (typeof cnt == "undefined") cnt = 0;
    this.importTextData("/c/data/textdata.txt", cnt++ % 4)
```

The same functionality can be obtained using the ADBC Object (page 10) and associated properties and methods. The data file can be a spreadsheet or a database.

importXFAData

Imports the specified XFA file. See also `importAnXFDF` (page 261) and `importTextData` (page 265).

Note: (Security 🟊): This method is only allowed in batch, console, and menu events. See "Privileged versus Non-privileged Context" on page 8 for details.

Parameters

cPath	(optional) The device-independent pathname of the XFA file. The pathname may be relative to the location of the current document. If this parameter is omitted, a dialog box is shown to let the user select the file.

Returns

Nothing

insertPages

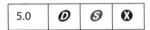

Inserts pages from the source document into the current document. If a page range is not specified, the method gets all pages in the source document.

See also `deletePages` (page 228) and `replacePages` (page 280).

Note: (Security 🟊) This method can only be executed during batch, console, or menu events. See "Privileged versus Non-privileged Context" on page 8 for details. The `event` Object (page 314) contains a discussion of Acrobat JavaScript events.

Parameters

nPage	(optional) The 0-based index of the page after which to insert the source document pages. Use -1 to insert pages before the first page of the document.
cPath	The device-independent pathname to the PDF file that will provide the inserted pages. The pathname may be relative to the location of the current document.

nStart	(optional) A 0-based index that defines the start of an inclusive range of pages in the source document to insert. If only `nStart` is specified, the range of pages is the single page specified by `nStart`.
nEnd	(optional) A 0-based index that defines the end of an inclusive range of pages in the source document to insert. If only `nEnd` is specified, the range of pages is 0 to `nEnd`.

Returns

Nothing

Example

Insert a cover page to the current document.

```
this.insertPages ({
    nPage: -1,
    cPath: "/c/temp/myCoverPage.pdf",
    nStart: 0
});
```

mailDoc

Saves the current PDF document and mails it as an attachment to all recipients, with or without user interaction.

See also `mailForm` (page 270), `app.mailGetAddrs` (page 92), `app.mailMsg` (page 93), the FDF Object `mail` (page 366) method and the Report Object `mail` (page 527) method.

Note: (Security ✪, Acrobat 7.0) When this method is executed in a non-privileged context, the `bUI` parameter is not honored and defaults to `true`. See "Privileged versus Non-privileged Context" on page 8 for details.

(Save Rights✪) For Adobe Reader 5.1 and later, this method is allowed, but document Save rights are required in case the document is changed.

On Windows, the client computer must have its default mail program configured to be MAPI enabled to use this method.

Parameters

bUI	(optional) If `true` (the default), the rest of the parameters are used in a compose-new-message window that is displayed to the user. If `false`, the `cTo` parameter is required and all others are optional. **Note:** (Security ❺, Acrobat 7.0) When this method is executed in a non-privileged context, the `bUI` parameter is not honored and defaults to `true`. See "Privileged versus Non-privileged Context" on page 8.
cTo	(optional) The semicolon-delimited list of recipients for the message.
cCc	(optional) The semicolon-delimited list of CC recipients for the message.
cBcc	(optional) The semicolon-delimited list of BCC recipients for the message.
cSubject	(optional) The subject of the message. The length limit is 64 KB.
cMsg	(optional) The content of the message. The length limit is 64 KB.

Returns

Nothing

Example

This opens the compose-new-message window.

```
this.mailDoc(true);
```

This sends email with the attached PDF file to `fun1@fun.com` and `fun2@fun.com`. Beginning with Acrobat 7.0, the code below would have to be executed in a privileged context if the `bUI` parameter (set to `false`) is to be honored.

```
this.mailDoc({
    bUI: false,
    cTo: "apstory@ap.com",
    cCC: "dpsmith@ap.com",
    cSubject: "The Latest News",
    cMsg: "A.P., attached is my latest news story in PDF."
});
```

mailForm

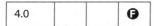

| 4.0 | | | **F** |

Exports the form data and mails the resulting FDF file as an attachment to all recipients, with or without user interaction. The method does not support signed signature fields.

See also `mailDoc` (page 268), `app.mailGetAddrs` (page 92), `app.mailMsg` (page 93), FDF Object `mail` (page 366) method, and the Report Object (page 525) mail method.

Note: On Windows, the client machine must have its default mail program configured to be MAPI enabled to use this method.

Parameters

bUI	If `true`, the rest of the parameters are used in a compose-new-message window that is displayed to the user. If `false`, the `cTo` parameter is required and all others are optional.
cTo	(required if `bUI` is `true`) A semicolon-delimited list of recipients for the message.
cCc	(optional) A semicolon-delimited list of CC recipients for the message.
cBcc	(optional) A semicolon-delimited list of BCC recipients for the message.
cSubject	(optional) The subject of the message. The length limit is 64 KB.
cMsg	(optional) The content of the message. The length limit is 64 KB.

Returns

Nothing

Example

Open the compose new message window.

```
this.mailForm(true);
```

This sends out the mail with the attached FDF file to `fun1@fun.com` and `fun2@fun.com`.

```
this.mailForm(false, "fun1@fun.com; fun2@fun.com", "", "",
    "This is the subject", "This is the body of the mail.");
```

movePage

5.0	*Ⓓ*		*Ⓧ*

Moves a page within the document.

Parameters

nPage	(optional) The 0-based index of the page to move. The default is 0.
nAfter	(optional) The 0-based index of the page after which to move the specified page. Use -1 to move the page before the first page of the document. The default is the last page in the document.

Returns

Nothing

Example

Reverse the pages in the document.

```
for (i = this.numPages - 1; i >= 0; i--) this.movePage(i);
```

newPage

6.0	*Ⓓ*	*Ⓢ*	*Ⓧ*

Adds a new page to the active document.

Note: (Security Ⓢ): This method can only be executed during batch, console or menu events. See "Privileged versus Non-privileged Context" on page 8 for details.

Parameters

nPage	(optional) The page after which to add the new page in a 1-based page numbering system. The default is the last page of the document. Use 0 to add a page before the first page. An invalid page range is truncated to the valid range of pages.
nWidth	(optional) The width of the page in points. The default value is 612.
nHeight	(optional) The height of the page in points. The default value is 792.

Returns

Nothing

Example

Add a new page to match the page size of the doc.

```
var Rect = this.getPageBox("Crop");
this.newPage(0, Rect[2], Rect[1]);
```

openDataObject

7.0			

Returns the Document Object (page 188) of a PDF document that is an embedded data object (an attachment) within the document that this method is being called for.

The method can throw an exception instead of returning a Document Object (page 188) if any of the following conditions are true:

- The document that this method is being called for does not contain the requested embedded data object.
- The data object is not a PDF document.
- Permissions forbid opening attachments by means of JavaScript.

The document should be closed (using closeDoc, page 225) after it is no longer needed.

Parameters

cName	The name of the data object.

The name of a data object is a property of the Data Object (page 167). A name is given to the object when it is embedded, automatically by the Acrobat UI, or programmatically by the JavaScript methods createDataObject (page 226) or importDataObject (page 262).

Returns

Document Object (page 188) or an exception is thrown.

Related objects, properties, and methods are dataObjects (page 191), setDataObjectContents (page 286), getDataObjectContents (page 247), createDataObject (page 226), and importDataObject (page 262), and the Data Object (page 167).

Example

Open a PDF attachment and extract form data from it.

```
var oDoc = this.openDataObject("myAttachment");
try {
    var myField = this.getField("myTextField");
```

```
// get the value of "yourTextField" in PDF attachment
var yourField = oDoc.getField("yourTextField");
// view this value in "myTextField"
myField.value = yourField.value;
oDoc.closeDoc();
} catch(e) { app.alert("Operation failed");}
```

See also "Example 5 (Acrobat 7.0)" on page 299 following the submitForm method.

print

Prints all or a specific number of pages of the document.

Beginning with Acrobat 6.0, the method can print the document using the settings contained in a PrintParams Object (page 500), rather than through the other parameters. The permanent print settings are not altered.

Note: (Security , Acrobat 6.0) When printing to a file, the path must be a safe path (see "Safe Path" on page 8). The print method will not overwrite an existing file.

(Security , Acrobat 7.0) Non-interactive printing can only be executed during batch, console, and menu events. Printing is made non-interactive by setting bUI is to false or by setting the interactive (page 506) property to silent, for example:

```
var pp = this.getPrintParams();
pp.interactive = pp.constants.interactionLevel.silent;
```

Outside of batch, console, and menu events, the values of bUI and of interactive (page 506) are ignored and a print dialog will always be presented.

See also "Privileged versus Non-privileged Context" on page 8.

Note: On a Windows platform, the file name must include an extension of .ps or .prn (case insensitive). Additionally, the print method will not create a file directly in the root directory, the windows directory, or the windows system directory.

An InvalidArgsError (see Error Object, page 311) exception will be thrown and print will fail if any of the above security restrictions are not met.

Parameters

bUI	(optional) If `true` (the default), will cause a UI to be presented to the user to obtain printing information and confirm the action.
nStart	(optional) A 0-based index that defines the start of an inclusive range of pages. If `nStart` and `nEnd` are not specified, all pages in the document are printed. If only `nStart` is specified, the range of pages is the single page specified by `nStart`. If `nStart` and `nEnd` parameters are used, `bUI` must be `false`.
nEnd	(optional) A 0-based index that defines the end of an inclusive page range. If `nStart` and `nEnd` are not specified, all pages in the document are printed. If only `nEnd` is specified, the range of a pages is 0 to `nEnd`. If `nStart` and `nEnd` parameters are used, `bUI` must be `false`.
bSilent	(optional) If `true`, suppresses the cancel dialog box while the document is printing. The default is `false`.
bShrinkToFit	(optional, Acrobat 5.0) If `true`, the page is shrunk (if necessary) to fit within the imageable area of the printed page. If `false`, it is not. The default is `false`.
bPrintAsImage	(optional, Acrobat 5.0) If `true`, print pages as an image. The default is `false`.
bReverse	(optional, Acrobat 5.0) If `true`, print from `nEnd` to `nStart`. The default is `false`.
bAnnotations	(optional, Acrobat 5.0) If `true` (the default), annotations are printed.
printParams	(optional, Acrobat 6.0) The PrintParams Object (page 500) containing the settings to use for printing. If this parameter is passed, any other parameters are ignored.

Returns

Nothing

Example 1

This example prints current page the document is on.

```
this.print(false, this.pageNum, this.pageNum);
// print a file silently
this.print({bUI: false, bSilent: true, bShrinkToFit: true});
```

Example 2 (Acrobat 6.0)

```
var pp = this.getPrintParams();
pp.interactive = pp.constants.interactionLevel.automatic;
pp.printerName = "hp officejet d series";
this.print(pp);
```

Note: If printerName (page 512) is an empty string and fileName (page 502) is nonempty, the current document is saved to disk as a PostScript file.

Example 3 (Acrobat 6.0)

Save the current document as a PostScript file.

```
var pp = this.getPrintParams();
pp.fileName = "/c/temp/myDoc.ps";
pp.printerName = "";
this.print(pp);
```

removeDataObject

Deletes the data object corresponding to the specified name from the document.

Related objects, properties, and methods are dataObjects (page 191), getDataObject (page 247), openDataObject (page 272), createDataObject (page 226), removeDataObject (page 275), importDataObject (page 262), getDataObjectContents (page 247), and setDataObjectContents (page 286), and the Data Object (page 167).

Parameters

cName	The name of the data object to remove.

The name of a data object is a property of the Data Object (page 167). A name is given to the object when it is embedded, either automatically by the Acrobat UI or programmatically by the JavaScript methods createDataObject (page 226) or importDataObject (page 262).

Returns

Nothing

Example

```
this.removeDataObject("MyData");
```

removeField

Removes the specified field from the document. If the field appears on more than one page, all representations are removed.

Note: (**⑤**, Acrobat 6.0): Beginning with Acrobat 6.0, `removeField` can now be used from within Adobe Reader for documents with forms usage rights.

Parameters

cName	The field name to remove.

Returns

Nothing

Example

```
this.removeField("myBadField");
```

removeIcon

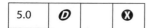

Removes the specified named icon from the document.

See also `icons` (page 196), `addIcon` (page 212), `getIcon` (page 249), and `importIcon` (page 263), the `field` methods `buttonGetIcon` (page 401), `buttonImportIcon` (page 401), and `buttonSetIcon` (page 403), and the Icon Object (page 434).

Parameters

cName	The name of the icon to remove.

The name of the icon is a property of the Icon Object (page 434). A name is given to the object either by `importIcon` (page 263), when the icon file is imported into the document, or by `addIcon` (page 212), which names an icon that is not in the document-level named icons tree.

Returns

Nothing

Example

Remove all named icons from the document.

```
for ( var i = 0; i < this.icons.length; i++)
    this.removeIcon(this.icons[i].name);
```

removeLinks

6.0	*Ⓓ*		*Ⓧ*

Removes all the links on the specified page within the specified coordinates, if the user has permission to remove links from the document.

See also `addLink` (page 213), `getLinks` (page 251), and the Link Object (page 440).

Parameters

`nPage`	The 0-based index of the page from which to remove links.
`oCoords`	An array of four numbers in rotated user space, the coordinates of a rectangle listed in the following order: upper-left *x*, upper-left *y*, lower-right *x*, and lower-right *y*.

Returns

Nothing

Example

Remove all links from the document.

```
// remove all links from the document
for ( var p = 0; p < this.numPages; p++)
{
    var b = this.getPageBox("Crop", p);
    this.removeLinks(p, b);
}
```

Use `getLinks` (page 251) to help count the number of links removed.

removeRequirement

7.0.5	*Ⓓ*	*Ⓢ*	*Ⓧ*

Removes an existing requirement present in a PDF document. Removing a requirement frees Acrobat from having to fulfill it to open the document. The document may not function properly if a requirement is removed.

Note: (Security 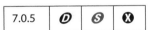): This method can only be called from console or batch events.

Parameters

`cType`	The type of requirement to be removed. The types are described by the Requirements Enumerator Object (page 216).

Returns

Nothing

removeScript

7.0			

Removes a document-level JavaScript, if permissions for script removal is granted.

Parameters

cName	A string that specifies the name of the script to be removed.

Returns

The value `undefined` on success. The method throws an exception if the script is not found.

Example

Add a document-level script, then remove it.

```
this.addScript("myScript",
    "app.alert('A.C. Robat welcomes you!')");
```

Now remove this script:

```
this.removeScript("myScript");
```

removeTemplate

5.0			

Removes the named template from the document.

See also `templates` (page 207), `createTemplate` (page 227), `getTemplate` (page 259), and the Template Object (page 625).

Note: (Security ⑤): This method can only be executed during batch or console events. See "Privileged versus Non-privileged Context" on page 8 for details. See `event` Object (page 314) for a discussion of Acrobat JavaScript events.

Parameters

cName	The name of the template to remove.

The template name is a property of the Template Object (page 625). A name is given to a template when it is created, either by the Acrobat UI or by the JavaScript method `getTemplate` (page 259).

Returns

Nothing

removeThumbnails

Deletes thumbnails for the specified pages in the document. See also `addThumbnails` (page 218).

Parameters

nStart	(optional) A 0-based index that defines the start of an inclusive range of pages. If nStart and nEnd are not specified, operates on all pages in the document. If only nStart is specified, the range of pages is the single page specified by nStart.
nEnd	(optional) A 0-based index that defines the end of an inclusive range of pages. If nStart and nEnd are not specified, operates on all pages in the document. If only nEnd is specified, the range of pages is 0 to nEnd.

Returns

Nothing

removeWeblinks

Scans the specified pages looking for links with actions to go to a particular URL on the web and deletes them. See also `addWeblinks` (page 223).

Note: This method only removes weblinks authored in the application using the UI. Web links that are executed through JavaScript (for example, using getURL, page 259) are not removed.

Parameters

nStart	(optional) A 0-based index that defines the start of an inclusive range of pages. If nStart and nEnd are not specified, operates on all pages in the document. If only nStart is specified, the range of pages is the single page specified by nStart.

nEnd	(optional) A 0-based index that defines the end of an inclusive range of pages. If nStart and nEnd are not specified, operates on all pages in the document. If only nEnd is specified, the range of a pages is 0 to nEnd.

Returns

The number of web links removed from the document.

Example

Remove all web links from the document and report results to the console window.

```
var numWeblinks = this.removeWeblinks();
console.println("There were " + numWeblinks +
    " web links removed from the document.");
```

replacePages

Replaces pages in the current document with pages from the source document.

See also deletePages (page 228), extractPages (page 242), and insertPages (page 267).

Note: (Security ): This method can only be executed during batch, console, or menu events. See "Privileged versus Non-privileged Context" on page 8 for details. See the event Object (page 314) for a discussion of Acrobat JavaScript events.

Parameters

nPage	(optional) The 0-based index of the page at which to start replacement. The default is 0.
cPath	The device-independent pathname to the PDF file that will provide the replacement pages. The pathname may be relative to the location of the current document.
nStart	(optional) A 0-based index that defines the start of an inclusive range of pages in the source document to be used for replacement.
	If nStart and nEnd are not specified, gets all pages in the source document. If only nStart is specified, the range of pages is the single page specified by nStart.

nEnd	(optional) A 0-based index that defines the end of an inclusive range of pages in the source document to be used for replacement.
	If nStart and nEnd are not specified, gets all pages in the source document. If only nEnd is specified, the range of pages is 0 to nEnd.

Returns

Nothing

resetForm

Resets the field values within a document. Resetting a field causes it to take on its default value (which, in the case of text fields, is usually blank).

Note: If the form contains signature fields, signature rights **⑥** are required to use the method in Adobe Reader.

Parameters

aFields	(optional) An array specifying the fields to reset. If not present or null, all fields in the form are reset. You can include non-terminal fields in the array.

Returns

Nothing

Example 1

Select fields to be reset and reset them.

```
var fields = new Array();
fields[0] = "P1.OrderForm.Description";
fields[1] = "P1.OrderForm.Qty";
this.resetForm(fields);
```

or, the same fields can be reset using only one line of code:

```
this.resetForm(["P1.OrderForm.Description","P1.OrderForm.Qty
"]);
```

Example 2

This example shows how to reset a whole subtree. For example, if you pass "name" as part of the fields array, all name fields, such as name.first and name.last, are reset.

```
this.resetForm(["name"]);
```

saveAs

5.0		🚫	🅂

Saves the file to the device-independent path specified by the required parameter, `cPath`. The file is not saved in linearized format. Beginning with Acrobat 6.0, the document can be converted to another file type (other than PDF) and saved as specified by the value of the `cConvID` parameter.

Note: (Security 🚫): This method can only be executed during batch, console, or menu events. See "Privileged versus Non-privileged Context" on page 8 for details. The `event` Object (page 314) contains a discussion of Acrobat JavaScript events.

Note: (Adobe Reader 🅂): This method is available in Adobe Reader for documents that have Save usage rights.

Parameters

`cPath`	The device-independent path in which to save the file. **Note:** (Security 🚫): The parameter `cPath` must have a safe path (see "Safe Path" on page 8) and an extension appropriate to the value of `cConvID`. See the table "Values of cConvID and Valid Extensions" on page 283. This method will throw a `NotAllowedError` (see "Error Object" on page 311) exception if these security conditions are not met, and the method will fail.
`cConvID`	(optional, Acrobat 6.0) A conversion ID string that specifies the conversion file type. Currently supported values for `cConvID` are listed by the app.`fromPDFConverters` (page 51). If `cConvID` is not specified, PDF is assumed.
`cFS`	(optional, Acrobat 7.0) A string that specifies the source file system name. Two values are supported: "" (the empty string) representing the default file system and "CHTTP". The default is the default file system. This parameter is only relevant if the web server supports WebDAV.
`bCopy`	(optional, Acrobat 7.0) A Boolean which, if `true`, saves the PDF file as a copy. The default is `false`.
`bPromptToOverwrite`	(optional, Acrobat 7.0) A Boolean which, if `true`, prompts the user if the destination file already exists. The default is `false`.

Returns

The value `undefined` is returned on success. An exception is thrown if an error occurs. For example, this method will throw a `NotAllowedError` (see Error Object, page 311) if the user disallows an overwrite.

Note: Prior to Acrobat 7.0, this method had no return value.

Values of cConvID and Valid Extensions

cConvID	Valid Extensions
com.adobe.acrobat.eps	eps
com.adobe.acrobat.html-3-20	html, htm
com.adobe.acrobat.html-4-01-css-1-00	html, htm
com.adobe.acrobat.jpeg	jpeg ,jpg, jpe
com.adobe.acrobat.jp2k	jpf,jpx,jp2,j2k,j2c,jpc
com.adobe.acrobat.doc	doc
com.adobe.acrobat.png	png
com.adobe.acrobat.ps	ps
com.adobe.acrobat.rtf	rft
com.adobe.acrobat.accesstext	txt
com.adobe.acrobat.plain-text	txt
com.adobe.acrobat.tiff	tiff, tif
com.adobe.acrobat.xml-1-00	xml

Note: When the conversion ID corresponds to `jpeg`, `jp2k`, `png`, or `tiff`, this method saves each page individually under a file name obtained by appending `"_Page_#"` to the basename of the file name provided. For example, if the value of the `cPath` is `"/C/temp/mySaveAsDocs/myJPGs.jpg"`, the names of the files generated will be `myJPGs_Page_1.jpg`, `myJPGs_Page_2.jpg`, and so on.

Example 1

The following code, which could appear as a batch sequence, is an outline of a script. It assumes a PDF file is open containing form fields. The fields must be populated from a database and the document saved.

```
// code lines to read from a database and populate the form
// with data. Now save file to a folder; use customerID from
// database record as name
var row = statement.getRow();
.......
```

```
this.saveAs("/c/customer/invoices/" + row.customerID +
".pdf");
```

Example 2

You can use `newDoc` (page 94) and `addField` (page 211) to dynamically layout a form, then populate it from a database and save.

```
var myDoc = app.newDoc()
// layout some dynamic form fields
// connect to database, populate with data, perhaps
// from a database
..........
// save the doc and/or print it; print it silently this time
// to default printer
myDoc.saveAs("/c/customer/invoices/" + row.customerID
    + ".pdf");
myDoc.closeDoc(true); // close the doc, no notification
```

Example 3 (Acrobat 6.0)

Save the current document in rich text format:

```
this.saveAs("/c/myDocs/myDoc.rtf", "com.adobe.acrobat.rtf");
```

See `fromPDFConverters` (page 51) for a listing of supported conversion ID strings.

Example 3 (Acrobat 7.0)

Save the document to a WebDAV folder.

```
this.saveAs({
    cPath: "http://www.myCom.com/WebDAV/myDoc.pdf",
    bPromptToOverwrite: true,
    cFS: "CHTTP"
});
```

scroll

3.01			

Scrolls the specified point on the current page into the middle of the current view. These coordinates must be defined in rotated user space. See section 4.2.1, "Coordinate Spaces," in the *PDF Reference* for details.

Parameters

nX	The *x* coordinate for the point to scroll.
nY	The *y* coordinate for the point to scroll.

Returns

Nothing

selectPageNthWord

5.0			

Changes the current page number and selects the specified word on the page.

See also getPageNthWord (page 255), getPageNthWordQuads (page 255), and getPageNumWords (page 256).

Parameters

nPage	(optional) The 0-based index of the page to operate on. The default is 0, the first page in the document.
nWord	(optional) The 0-based index of the word to obtain. The default is 0, the first word on the page.
bScroll	(optional) Specifies whether to scroll the selected word into the view if it is not already viewable. The default is true.

Returns

Nothing

Example

Get and select a particular word.

```
// get the 20th word on page 2 (page 1, 0-based)
var cWord = this.getPageNthWord(1, 20);
// Select that word (highlight) for the user to see,
// change page if necessary.
this.selectPageNthWord(1, 20);
```

setAction

6.0	𝕯		𝕏

Sets the JavaScript action of the document for a given trigger.

See also addRequirement (page 215), setPageAction (page 288), the Bookmark Object setAction (page 145) method, and the Field Object setAction (page 411) method.

Note: This method will overwrite any action already defined for the selected trigger.

Parameters

`cTrigger`	The name of the trigger point to which to attach the action. Values are:
	`WillClose` `WillSave` `DidSave` `WillPrint` `DidPrint`
`cScript`	The JavaScript expression to be executed when the trigger is activated.

Returns

Nothing

Example

This example inserts `WillSave` and `DidSave` actions. The code gets the filesize before saving and after saving, and compares the two.

```
// WillSave Script
var myWillSave = 'var filesizeBeforeSave = this.filesize;\r'
    + 'console.println("File size before saving is " + '
    + ' filesizeBeforeSave );';

// DidSave Script
var myDidSave = 'var filesizeAfterSave = this.filesize;\r'
    + 'console.println("File size after saving is "'
    + 'filesizeAfterSave);\r'
    + 'var difference =
            filesizeAfterSave - filesizeBeforeSave;\r'
    + 'console.println("The difference is " + difference );\r'
    + 'if ( difference < 0 )\r\t'
    + 'console.println("Reduced filesize!");\r'
    + 'else\r\t'
    + 'console.println("Increased filesize!");'

// Set Document Actions...
this.setAction("WillSave", myWillSave);
this.setAction("DidSave", myDidSave);
```

setDataObjectContents

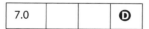

7.0			**ⓓ**

Replaces the file attachment specified by the parameter `cName` with the contents of the `oStream` parameter.

Adobe® Acrobat® Official JavaScript Reference

Parameters

cName	The name associated with the Data Object (page 167) that is to be replaced with oStream.
oStream	A ReadStream Object (page 519) representing the contents of the file attachment.
cCryptFilter	(optional) The language-independent name of a crypt filter to use when encrypting this data object. This crypt filter must have previously been added to the document's list of crypt filters, using the addRecipientListCryptFilter (page 214) method, otherwise, an exception will be thrown. The predefined **Identity** crypt filter can be used so that this data object is not encrypted in a file that is otherwise encrypted by the encryptForRecipients (page 230) method.

Returns

Nothing

Example 1

See the "Example" on page 248.

Example 2

This document has a file attachment named acrobat.xml. The attachment is opened, the XML data is updated, then the new XML document is saved back to the attachment. It is possible to submit this XML file attachment. See "Example 5 (Acrobat 7.0)" on page 299, following the submitForm method. This example uses the XML data defined in the Example following XMLData.applyXPath (page 650).

```
// get the file stream object of the attachment
var acrobat = this.getDataObjectContents("acrobat.xml");

// convert to a string
var cAcrobat = util.stringFromStream(acrobat, "utf-8");

// parse this and get XFAObject
var myXML = XMLData.parse(cAcrobat,false);

// change the value of grandad's income
myXML.family.grandad.personal.income.value = "300000";

// save XML document as string, cAcrobat
var cAcrobat = myXML.saveXML('pretty');

// convert to a file stream
var acrobat = util.streamFromString(cAcrobat, "utf-8");

// now "update" the attachment acrobat.xml with
```

```
// this file stream
this.setDataObjectContents("acrobat.xml", acrobat);
```

Related objects, properties, and methods are `dataObjects` (page 191), `getDataObject` (page 247), `openDataObject` (page 272), `createDataObject` (page 226), `importDataObject` (page 262), `getDataObjectContents` (page 247), and `removeDataObject` (page 275), and the Data Object (page 167).

setOCGOrder

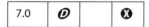

| 7.0 | *D* | | *X* |

Sets this document's OCGOrder array. This array represents how layers are displayed in the UI.

The simplest order array is a flat array of OCG objects. In this case, the listed OCGs are displayed in the UI as a flat list in the same order. If a subarray is present in the order array and the first element of the array is a string, the string will be listed with the rest of the array nested underneath it. If the first element if the array is not a string, the entire array will appear nested underneath the OCG preceding the subarray.

Related methods are `getOCGs` (page 253) and `getOCGOrder` (page 253), and the OCG Object (page 485).

Parameters

| oOrderArray | The array to be used as this document's OCG Order array. |

Returns

Nothing

Example

Reverse the order of OCGs as listed in the UI.

```
var ocgOrder = this.getOCGOrder();
var newOrder = new Array();
for (var j=0; j < ocgOrder.length; j++)
    newOrder[j] = ocgOrder[ocgOrder.length-j-1];
this.setOCGOrder(newOrder);
```

setPageAction

| 6.0 | *D* | | *X* |

Sets the action of a page in a document for a given trigger.

Adobe® Acrobat® Official JavaScript Reference

See also `setAction` (page 145), `addRequirement` (page 215), the Bookmark Object `setAction` (page 285) method, and the Field Object `setAction` (page 411) method.

Note: This method will overwrite any action already defined for the chosen page and trigger.

Parameters

nPage	The 0-based index of the page in the document to which an action is added.
cTrigger	The trigger for the action. Values are: Open Close
cScript	The JavaScript expression to be executed when the trigger is activated.

Returns

Nothing

Example

This example causes the application to beep when the first page is opened.

```
this.setPageAction(0, "Open", "app.beep(0);");
```

setPageBoxes

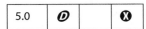

Sets a rectangle that encompasses the named box for the specified pages.

See also `getPageBox` (page 254).

Parameters

cBox	(optional) The box type value, one of: Art Bleed Crop Media Trim Note that the BBox box type is read-only and only supported in `getPageBox` (page 254). For definitions of these boxes, see Section 10.10.1, "Page Boundaries," in the *PDF Reference*.

nStart	(optional) A 0-based index that defines the start of an inclusive range of pages in the document to be operated on. If nStart and nEnd are not specified, operates on all pages in the document. If only nStart is specified, the range of pages is the single page specified by nStart.
nEnd	(optional) A 0-based index that defines the end of an inclusive range of pages in the document to be operated on. If nStart and nEnd are not specified, operates on all pages in the document.
rBox	(optional) An array of four numbers in rotated user space to which to set the specified box. If not provided, the specified box is removed.

Returns

Nothing

setPageLabels

Establishes the numbering scheme for the specified page and all pages following it until the next page with an attached label is encountered.

See also getPageLabel (page 254).

Parameters

nPage	(optional) The 0-based index for the page to be labeled.

aLabel	(optional) An array of three required items [cStyle, cPrefix, nStart]:
	
	• cStyle is the style of page numbering. It can be:
	    D: decimal numbering
	    R or r: roman numbering, upper or lower case
	    A or a: alphabetic numbering, upper or lower case
	    See the *PDF Reference*, Section 8.3.1, for the exact definitions of these styles.
	• cPrefix is a string to prefix the numeric portion of the page label.
	• nStart is the ordinal with which to start numbering the pages.
	
	If not supplied, any page numbering is removed for the specified page and any others up to the next specified label.
	
	The value of aLabel cannot be null.

Returns

Nothing

Example 1

10 pages in the document, label the first 3 with small roman numerals, the next 5 with numbers (starting at 1) and the last 2 with an "Appendix-" prefix and alphabetics.

```
this.setPageLabels(0, [ "r", "", 1]);
this.setPageLabels(3, [ "D", "", 1]);
this.setPageLabels(8, [ "A", "Appendix-", 1]);
var s = this.getPageLabel(0);
for (var i = 1; i < this.numPages; i++)
    s += ", " + this.getPageLabel(i);
console.println(s);
```

The example will produce the following output on the console:

```
i, ii, iii, 1, 2, 3, 4, 5, Appendix-A, Appendix-B
```

Example 2

Remove all page labels from a document.

```
for (var i = 0; i < this.numPages; i++) {
    if (i + 1 != this.getPageLabel(i)) {
        // Page label does not match ordinal page number.
        this.setPageLabels(i);
    }
}
```

setPageRotations

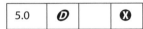

Rotates the specified pages in the current document.

See also getPageRotation (page 257).

Parameters

nStart	(optional) A 0-based index that defines the start of an inclusive range of pages in the document to be operated on. If nStart and nEnd are not specified, operates on all pages in the document. If only nStart is specified, the range of pages is the single page specified by nStart.
nEnd	(optional) A 0-based index that defines the end of an inclusive range of pages in the document to be operated on. If nStart and nEnd are not specified, operates on all pages in the document. If only nEnd is specified, the range of pages is 0 to nEnd.

nRotate	(optional) The amount of rotation that should be applied to the target pages. Can be 0, 90, 180, or 270. The default is 0.

Returns

Nothing

Example

Rotate pages 0 through 10 of the current document.

```
this.setPageRotations(0, 10, 90);
```

setPageTabOrder

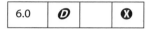

Sets the tab order of the form fields on a page. The tab order can be set by row, by column, or by structure.

If a PDF 1.4 documents is viewed in Acrobat 6.0, tabbing between fields is in the same order as it is in Acrobat 5.0. Similarly, if a PDF 1.5 document is opened in Acrobat 5.0, the tabbing order for fields is the same as it is in Acrobat 6.0.

Parameters

nPage	The 0-based index of the page number on which the tabbing order is to be set.
cOrder	The order to be used. Values are: rows columns structure

Returns

Nothing

Example

Set the page tab order for all pages to rows.

```
for (var i = 0; i < this.numPages; i++)
    this.setPageTabOrder(i, "rows");
```

setPageTransitions

Sets the page transition for a specific range of pages.

Adobe® Acrobat® Official JavaScript Reference

See also `getPageTransition` (page 257).

Parameters

nStart	(optional) A 0-based index that defines the start of an inclusive range of pages in the document to be operated on. If nStart and nEnd are not specified, operates on all pages in the document. If only nStart is specified, the range of pages is the single page specified by nStart.
nEnd	(optional) A 0-based index that defines the end of an inclusive range of pages in the document to be operated on. If nStart and nEnd are not specified, operates on all pages in the document. If only nEnd is specified, the range of pages is 0 to nEnd.
aTrans	(optional) The page transition array consists of three values: [nDuration, cTransition, nTransDuration]. • nDuration is the maximum amount of time the page is displayed before the viewer automatically turns to the next page. Set to -1 to turn off automatic page turning. • cTransition is the name of the transition to apply to the page. See `fullScreen.transitions` (page 427) for a list of valid transitions. • nTransDuration is the duration (in seconds) of the transition effect. If aTrans is not present, any page transitions for the pages are removed.

Returns

Nothing

Example

Put the document into fullscreen mode and apply some transitions:

```
this.setPageTransitions({ aTrans: [-1, "Random", 1] } );
app.fs.isFullScreen=true;
```

spawnPageFromTemplate

Note: This method has been superseded by `templates` (page 207), `createTemplate` (page 227), and the Template Object `spawn` (page 625) method.

Spawns a page in the document using the given template, as returned by `getNthTemplate` (page 252). The template feature does not work in Adobe Reader.

Parameters

cTemplate	The template name.
nPage	(optional) The 0-based page number before which or into which the template is spawned, depending on the value of bOverlay. If nPage is omitted, a new page is created at the end of the document.
bRename	(optional) Specifies whether fields should be renamed. The default is true.
bOverlay	(optional, Acrobat 4.0) If false, the template is inserted before the page specified by nPage. If true (the default) it is overlaid on top of that page.
oXObject	(optional, Acrobat 6.0) The value of this parameter is the return value of an earlier call to spawnPageFromTemplate.

Returns

Prior to Acrobat 6.0, this method returned nothing. Now, this method returns an object representing the page contents of the page spawned. This return object can then be used as the value of the optional parameter **oXObject** for subsequent calls to spawnPageFromTemplate.

Note: Repeatedly spawning the *same* page can cause a large increase in file size. To avoid this problem, spawnPageFromTemplate now returns an object that represents the page contents of the spawned page. This return value can be used as the value of the oXObject parameter in subsequent calls to the spawnPageFromTemplate method to spawn the same page.

Example 1

```
var n = this.numTemplates;
var cTempl;
for (i = 0; i < n; i++) {
    cTempl = this.getNthTemplate(i);
    this.spawnPageFromTemplate(cTempl);
}
```

Example 2 (Acrobat 6.0)

The following example spawns the same template 31 times using the oXObject parameter and return value. Using this technique avoids overly inflating the file size.

```
var t = this.getNthTemplate(0)
var XO = this.spawnPageFromTemplate(t, this.numPages,
    false, false);
```

```
for (var i=0; i < 30; i++)
    this.spawnPageFromTemplate(t,this.numPages, false,
        false, XO);
```

submitForm

3.01			

Submits the form to a specified URL. To call this method, you must be running inside a web browser or have the Acrobat Web Capture plug-in installed. (If the URL uses the "mailto" scheme, it will be honored even if not running inside a web browser, as long as the SendMail plug-in is present.) Beginning with Adobe Reader 6.0, you need not be inside a web browser to call this method.

Note: (Acrobat 6.0) Depending on the parameters passed, there are restrictions on the use of this method. See the notes embedded in the description of the parameters.

The `https` protocol is supported for secure connections.

Parameters

cURL	The URL to submit to. This string must end in #FDF if the result from the submission is FDF or XFDF (that is, the value of cSubmitAs is "FDF" or "XFDF") and the document is being viewed inside a browser window.
bFDF	✖ (optional) **Note:** This option has been deprecated; use cSubmitAs instead. If `true` (the default) form data is submitted as FDF. If `false`, it is submitted as URL-encoded HTML.
bEmpty	(optional) If `true`, submit all fields, including those that have no value. If `false` (the default), exclude fields that currently have no value. **Note:** If data is submitted as XDP, XML, or XFD (see the cSubmitAs parameter, below), this parameter is ignored. All fields are submitted, even fields that are empty. See aFields.

`aFields`	(optional) An array of field names to submit or a string containing a single field name: ● If supplied, only the fields indicated are submitted, except those excluded by `bEmpty`. ● If omitted or `null`, all fields are submitted, except those excluded by `bEmpty`. ● If an empty array, no fields are submitted. A submitted FDF might still contain data if `bAnnotations` is `true`. You can specify non-terminal field names to export an entire subtree of fields. **Note:** If data is submitted as XDP, XML, or XFD (see the `cSubmitAs` parameter), this parameter is ignored. All fields are submitted, even fields that are empty. See `bEmpty`.
`bGet`	(optional, Acrobat 4.0) If `true`, submit using the HTTP GET method. If `false` (the default), use a POST. GET is only allowed if using Acrobat Web Capture to submit (the browser interface only supports POST) and only if the data is sent as HTML (that is, `cSubmitAs` is `HTML`).
`bAnnotations`	(optional, Acrobat 5.0) If `true`, annotations are included in the submitted FDF or XML. The default is `false`. Only applicable if `cSubmitAs` is `FDF` or `XFDF`.
`bXML`	✪ (optional, Acrobat 5.0) **Note:** This option has been deprecated; use `cSubmitAs` instead. If `true`, submit as XML. The default is `false`.
`bIncrChanges`	(optional, Acrobat 5.0) If `true`, include the incremental changes to the PDF in the submitted FDF. The default is `false`. Only applicable if `cSubmitAs` is `FDF`. Not available in Adobe Reader.
`bPDF`	✪ (optional, Acrobat 5.0) **Note:** This option has been deprecated; use `cSubmitAs` instead. If `true`, submit the complete PDF document. The default is `false`. If `true`, all other parameters except `cURL` are ignored. Not available in Adobe Reader.
`bCanonical`	(optional, Acrobat 5.0) If `true`, convert any dates being submitted to standard format (that is, `D:YYYYMMDDHHmmSSOHH'mm'`; see section 3.8.3 in the *PDF Reference*). The default is `false`.
`bExclNonUserAnnots`	(optional, Acrobat 5.0) If `true`, exclude any annotations that are not owned by the current user. The default is `false`.
`bExclFKey`	(optional, Acrobat 5.0) If `true`, exclude the **F** entry. The default is `false`.

`cPassword`	(optional, Acrobat 5.0) The password to use to generate the encryption key, if the FDF needs to be encrypted before being submitted. Pass the value `true` (no quotes) to use the password that the user has previously entered (within this Acrobat session) for submitting or receiving an encrypted FDF. If no password has been entered, prompts the user to enter a password. Regardless of whether the password is passed in or requested from the user, this new password is remembered within this Acrobat session for future outgoing or incoming encrypted FDFs. Only applicable if `cSubmitAs` is `FDF`.
`bEmbedForm`	(optional, Acrobat 6.0) If `true`, the call embeds the entire form from which the data is being submitted in the FDF. Only applicable if `cSubmitAs` is `FDF`.
`oJavaScript`	(optional, Acrobat 6.0) Can be used to include `Before`, `After`, and `Doc` JavaScripts in a submitted FDF. If present, the value is converted directly to an analogous `CosObj` and used as the **JavaScript** attribute in the FDF. For example: ```\noJavaScript:\n{\n Before: 'app.alert("before!")',\n After: 'app.alert("after")',\n Doc: ["MyDocScript1", "myFunc1()",\n "MyDocScript2", "myFunc2()"]\n}\n``` Only applicable if `cSubmitAs` is `FDF`.
`cSubmitAs`	(optional, Acrobat 6.0) This parameter indicates the format for submission. Values are ● `FDF` (*default*): Submit as FDF ● `XFDF`: Submit as XFDF ● `HTML`: Submit as HTML ● `XDP`: Submit as XDP ● `XML`: submit as XML. In Acrobat 7.0, form data is submitted in XML format unless the parameter `oXML` (new to Acrobat 7.0) contains a valid XMLData Object (page 650), in which case that is what gets submitted instead. ● `XFD`: Submit as Adobe Form Client Data File ● `PDF`: Submit the complete PDF document; all other parameters except `cURL` are ignored. Save rights required (Ⓢ): This choice is not available in Adobe Reader, unless the document has save rights. This parameter supersedes the individual format parameters. However, they are considered in the following priority order, from high to low: `cSubmitAs`, `bPDF`, `bXML`, `bFDF`.

bInclNMKey	(optional, Acrobat 6.0) If `true`, include the **NM** entry of any annotations. The default is `false`.
aPackets	(optional, Acrobat 6.0) An array of strings, specifying which packets to include in an XDP submission. This parameter is only applicable if `cSubmitAs` is XDP. Possible strings are:
	• `config`
	• `datasets`
	• `sourceSet`
	• `stylesheet`
	• `template`
	• `pdf`: The PDF should be embedded; if pdf is not included here, only a link to the PDF is included in the XDP.
	• `xfdf`: Include annotations in the XDP (since that packet uses XFDF format)
	• *: All packets should be included in the XDP. However, the default for `pdf` is to include it as a *reference*. To embed the PDF file in the XDP, *explicitly* specify `pdf` as one of the packets.
	Note: (Save rights required **S**): When submitting a document as XDP from Adobe Reader with `pdf` explicitly listed, the document must have document save rights.
	The default is: `["datasets", "xfdf"]`.
cCharset	(optional, Acrobat 6.0) The encoding for the values submitted. String values are:
	`utf-8`
	`utf-16`
	`Shift-JIS`
	`BigFive`
	`GBK`
	`UHC`
	If not passed, the current Acrobat behavior applies. For XML-based formats, `utf-8` is used. For other formats, Acrobat tries to find the best host encoding for the values being submitted.
	XFDF submission ignores this value and always uses `utf-8`.
oXML	(optional, Acrobat 7.0) This parameter is only applicable if `cSubmitAs` equals XML. It should be an XMLData Object (page 650), which will get submitted.
cPermID	(optional, Acrobat 7.0) Specifies a permanent ID to assign to the PDF that is submitted if either the value of `cSubmitAs` is PDF or `bEmbedForm` is `true`. This permanent ID is the first entry in the `docID` (page 193) array (`docID[0]`).
	Does not affect the current document.

cInstID	(optional, Acrobat 7.0) Specifies an instance ID to assign to the PDF that is submitted if either the value of cSubmitAs is PDF or bEmbedForm is true. This instance ID is the second entry in the docID (page 193) array (docID[1]).
	Does not affect the current document.
cUsageRights	(optional, Acrobat 7.0) Specifies the additional usage rights to be applied to the PDF that is submitted if either the value of cSubmitAs is PDF or bEmbedForm is true. The only valid value is submitFormUsageRights.RMA.
	Does not affect the current document.

Returns

Nothing

Example 1

Submit the form to the server.

```
this.submitForm("http://myserver/cgi-bin/myscript.cgi#FDF");
```

Example 2

```
var aSubmitFields = new Array( "name", "id", "score" );
this.submitForm({
   cURL: "http://myserver/cgi-bin/myscript.cgi#FDF",
   aFields: aSubmitFields,
   cSubmitAs: "FDF" // the default, not needed here
});
```

Example 3

This example shows a shortcut to submitting a whole subtree. Passing "name" as part of the field parameter, submits "name.title", "name.first", "name.middle" and "name.last".

```
this.submitForm("http://myserver/cgi-bin/myscript.cgi#FDF",
   true, false, "name");
```

Example 4

```
this.submitForm({
   cURL: "http://myserver/cgi-bin/myscript.cgi#FDF",
   cSubmitAs: "XFDF"
});
```

Example 5 (Acrobat 7.0)

A PDF file contains several XFA forms as attachments, the following script gathers the XML data from each attachment and concatenates them. The combined data is then submitted.

```
var oParent = event.target;
```

```
var oDataObjects = oParent.dataObjects;
if (oDataObjects == null)
   app.alert("This form has no attachments!");
else {
   var nChildren = oDataObjects.length;
   var oFirstChild =
oParent.openDataObject(oDataObjects[0].name);
   var oSubmitData =
oFirstChild.xfa.data.nodes.item(0).clone(true);
   for (var iChild = 1; iChild < nChildren; iChild++) {
       var oNextChild = oParent.openDataObject(
           oDataObjects[iChild].name);

oSubmitData.nodes.append(oNextChild.xfa.data.nodes.item(0));
       oNextChild.closeDoc();
   }
   oParent.submitForm({
   cURL: "http://www.myCom.com/cgi-bin/myCGI.pl#FDF",
   cSubmitAs: "XML",
   oXML: oSubmitData
   });
   oFirstChild.closeDoc();
}
```

This example uses `dataObjects` (page 191), `openDataObject` (page 272) and properties and methods of the XFA Object (page 649).

Example 6 (Acrobat 7.0)

This script uses `cPermID`, `cInstID` and `cUsageRights`.

```
this.submitForm({
   cUrl: myURL,
   cSubmitAs: "PDF",
   cPermID: someDoc.docID[0],
   cInstID: someDoc.docID[1],
   cUsageRights: submitFormUsageRights.RMA
});
```

syncAnnotScan

Guarantees that all annotations will be scanned by the time this method returns.

To show or process annotations for the entire document, all annotations must have been detected. Normally, a background task runs that examines every page and looks for annotations during idle time, as this scan is a time-consuming task. Much of the annotation behavior works gracefully even when the full list of annotations is not yet acquired by background scanning.

In general, you should call this method if you want the entire list of annotations.

See also `getAnnots` (page 245).

Parameters

None

Returns

Nothing

Example

The second line of code is not executed until `syncAnnotScan` returns, which does not occur until the annotation scan of the document is completed.

```
this.syncAnnotScan();
annots = this.getAnnots({nSortBy:ANSB_Author});
// now, do something with the annotations.
```

Doc.media Object

The `media` property of each document specifies an object that contains multimedia properties and methods that apply to the document.

Doc.media Properties

canPlay

6.0			

Indicates whether multimedia playback is allowed for a document. Playback depends on the user's Trust Manager preferences and other factors. For example, playback is not allowed in authoring mode.

`doc.media.canPlay` returns an object that contains both a yes/no indication and a reason why playback is not allowed, if that is the case.

Type: Object   *Access: R*

If playback is allowed, `canPlay.yes` exists to indicate this. (It is an empty object, but it may contain other information in the future.) You can make a simple test like this:

```
if ( doc.media.canPlay.yes )
{
    // We can play back multimedia for this document
}
```

If playback is not allowed, the `canPlay.no` object exists instead. As with `canPlay.yes`, you can simply test for the existence of `canPlay.no` or you can look inside it for information about why playback is not allowed. At least one of these properties or other properties that may be added in the future will exist within `canPlay.no`:

Properties of canPlay.no	
Property	**Description**
authoring	Cannot play when in authoring mode
closing	Cannot play because the document is closing
saving	Cannot play because the document is saving
security	Cannot play because of security settings
other	Cannot play for some other reason

In addition, `canPlay.canShowUI` indicates whether any alert boxes or other user interface are allowed in response to this particular playback rejection.

Adobe® Acrobat® Official JavaScript Reference

Example

```
var canPlay = doc.media.canPlay;
if( canPlay.no )
{
    // We can't play, why not?
    if( canPlay.no.security )
    {
        // The user's security settings prohibit playback,
        // are we allowed to put up alerts right now?
        if( canPlay.canShowUI )
            app.alert( "Security prohibits playback" );
        else
            console.println( "Security prohibits playback" );
    }
    else
    {
        // Can't play for some other reason, handle it here
    }
}
```

Doc.media Methods

deleteRendition

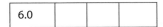

Deletes the named Rendition from the document. The Rendition is no longer accessible with JavaScript. It does nothing if the Rendition is not present.

Parameters

cName	A string that is the name of the Rendition.

Returns

Nothing

Example

```
this.media.deleteRendition("myMedia");
if ( this.media.getRendition("myMedia") == null)
    console.println( "Rendition successfully deleted" );
```

getAnnot

Looks for and returns a ScreenAnnot Object (page 533) in the document by page number and either name or title, or returns `null` if there is no matching screen annotation. If both name and title are specified, both must match.

Parameters

args	An object containing the properties to be passed to this method. The properties are described below.

This table describes the properties of `args`.

nPage	The page number (base 0) on which the annotation resides
cAnnotName	(optional) The name of the screen annotation. **Note:** cAnnotName is never used in PDF files generated by Acrobat.
cAnnotTitle	(optional) The title of the screen annotation.

Note: The parameters for this method must be passed as an object literal and not as an ordered listing of parameters.

Returns

ScreenAnnot Object (page 533)

Example

The Acrobat user interface allows you to specify the title for a screen annotation but not its name, so a typical use of `getAnnot` would be:

```
var annot= myDoc.media.getAnnot
    ({ nPage: 0,cAnnotTitle: "My Annot Title" });
```

See the example following `getRendition` (page 306) for an additional example.

getAnnots

6.0			

The `doc.media.getAnnots` method returns an array of all the ScreenAnnot Object (page 533)s on the specified page of the document, or all the ScreenAnnot Objects on all pages of the document if `nPage` is omitted. The array is empty if there are no such ScreenAnnots.

Parameters

nPage	The page number (base 0) on which the ScreenAnnots reside.

Returns

Array of ScreenAnnot Objects (page 533)

Example

Get a listing of the ScreenAnnots on page 0, then play a media clip in a screen annotation randomly chosen from the list.

```
var annots = this.media.getAnnots({ nPage: 0 });
var rendition = this.media.getRendition("myClip");
var settings = { windowType: app.media.windowType.docked }
var l = annots.length
var i = Math.floor( Math.random() * l ) % l
var args = { rendition:rendition, annot:annots[i],
settings:settings };
app.media.openPlayer( args );
```

getOpenPlayers

7.0			

Returns an array of MediaPlayer Objects (page 448), one for each currently open media player. The players in the array are listed in the order in which they were opened. Using this array, some or all of the open players can be manipulated. For example, you can stop or close all players that the document has opened, without having to keep a list of them yourself.

Each time `getOpenPlayers` is called, it returns a new copy of the array, listing the players open at that time. New players that are subsequently opened do not show up in an array already returned. If a player in the array is closed, the player object remains in the array and `player.isOpen` (page 450) becomes false. The `doc.media.getOpenPlayers` method can be called again to get a new, up-to-date player array.

Do not write code that iterates directly over `doc.media.getOpenPlayers`:

```
for( var i in doc.media.getOpenPlayers() ) // Wrong!
```

Instead, get a copy of the player array and iterate over that:

```
var players = doc.media.getOpenPlayers();
for( var i in players ) {
....
}
```

This insures that the loop works correctly even if players are opened or closed during the loop.

Parameters

None

Returns

Array of MediaPlayer Objects (page 448).

Example

The following two functions take a Document Object (page 188) as a parameter and operate on the running players associated with that Document Object.

```
// Stop all running players.
function stopAllPlayers( doc ) {
    var players = doc.media.getOpenPlayers();
    for( var i in players ) players[i].stop();
}
// Close all running players. Closing a player does not remove
it from // the array.
function closeAllPlayers( doc ) {
    var players = doc.media.getOpenPlayers();
    for( var i in players )
        players[i].close( app.media.closeReason.general );
}
```

getRendition

Looks up a Rendition in the document by name and returns it, or returns null if there is no Rendition with that name.

Parameters

cName	cName, a string, is the name of the Rendition.

Returns

Rendition Object (page 520)

Example

The following script is executed from a mouse-up action of a form button. It plays a docked media clip in a screen annotation.

```
app.media.openPlayer({
    rendition: this.media.getRendition( "myClip" ),
    annot: this.media.getAnnot(
        {nPage:0,cAnnotTitle:"myScreen"} ),
    settings: { windowType: app.media.windowType.docked }
});
```

newPlayer

This method creates and returns a MediaPlayer Object (page 448). The args parameter must contain a settings property and optionally can contain an

---

`events` property. It can also contain additional user-defined properties. The properties of `args` are copied into the new MediaPlayer Object. This is a shallow copy, which means that if any of the copied properties are objects themselves, those objects are shared between `args` and the new player.

The `newPlayer` method creates a bare-bones player that does not have any of the standard EventListeners required for standard Acrobat media player behavior. Use `app.media.addStockEvents` (page 122) to add the necessary EventListeners.

In most cases, it is better to use `app.media.createPlayer` (page 126) instead of `doc.media.newPlayer` to create a media player . The `createPlayer` method sets up the standard EventListeners and other player properties automatically.

Parameters

`args`	A PlayerArgs Object (page 127).

Returns

MediaPlayer Object (page 448).

Example

See `Events.dispatch` (page 359) for an example.

Embedded PDF Object

This object describes an API exposed to the object model of a container application that allows sending and receiving messages from an embedded PDF document. For example, when a PDF document is embedded in an HTML document using the <OBJECT> tag, the PDF object can be scripted in the browser scripting context.

The HostContainer Object (page 431) provides the corresponding interface in the PDF scripting model. Both the container and PDF document must explicitly allow this communication to occur for security reasons.

Embedded PDF Properties

messageHandler

7.0.5			

This property allows a script running in the web browser scripting context to register a notification object that will be called if a script in the PDF document calls the Document Object `hostContainer.postMessage (page 433)` method.

The value of this property is an object that may expose the following methods.

Method	Description
onMessage	If present, this method will be called in response to the Document Object `hostContainer.postMessage` (page 433) method. The message is delivered asynchronously. The method is passed a single array parameter containing the array passed to the `postMessage` (page 433) method.
onError	If present, this method will be called in response to an error. It is passed an Error Object (page 311) and an array of strings corresponding to the message that caused the error. If an error occurs and this property is undefined, the error will not be delivered (unlike messages, errors are not queued). The `name` property of the Error Object will be set to one of the following strings: • "MessageGeneralError": A general error occurred. • "MessageNotAllowedError": The operation failed for security reaons. • "MessageDocNotDisclosedError": The document has not been configured for disclosure to the host container. The `hostContainer.messageHandler.onDisclose` property of the Document Object (page 188) must be initialized correctly. • "MessageDocRefusedDisclosureError": The document has refused to disclose itself to the host container based on the URL because the `hostContainer.messageHandler.onDisclose` method returned `false`.

When the methods are invoked, the `this` Object (page 631) will be the `messageHandler` instance that the method is being called on. Properties on the `messageHandler` property that begin with `on` are reserved for future use as notification methods.

If the PDF document has had the `postMessage` method called on it prior to this method being registered, all of the queued messages will subsequently be passed to the `messageHandler` object once it is set.

Messages are guaranteed to be delivered in the order in which they are posted and errors are guaranteed to be delivered in the order in which they occurred. However, there is no correspondence between the delivery order of messages and errors.

Exceptions thrown from within the handler methods will be discarded. Messages and errors will not be delivered while inside an `onMessage` / `onError` handler.

Note: This property is not implemented on the Macintosh platform.

Type: Object　　　　　　*Access: R/W*

Embedded PDF Methods

postMessage

7.0.5			

Sends a message asynchronously to the PDF document message handler if the PDF document has disclosed itself by returning `true` from the `onDisclosed` method of the HostContainer Object `messageHandler` (page 431) property.

The message is passed to the `onMessage` method of the `messageHandler` (page 431).

If the PDF document does not disclose itself to the host container, an error will be passed to the `onError` method of the `messageHandler` (page 431) property at some later point after `postMessage` has returned. If the PDF document has not registered to receive events by setting the Document Object `hostContainer.messageHandler` property, the events will be queued until the PDF document sets the property.

The messages will be submitted to a queue of messages until they are delivered. If the queue size exceeds a maximum, an error will be thrown until some of the messages in the queue have been delivered.

Parameters

aMessage	An array of one or more strings that will be passed to onMessage.

Returns

Nothing

Note: This method is not implemented on the Macintosh platform.

Error Object

Error objects are dynamically created whenever an exception is thrown from methods or properties implemented in Acrobat JavaScript. Several subclasses of the Error object can be thrown by core JavaScript (`EvalError`, `RangeError`, `SyntaxError`, `TypeError`, `ReferenceError`, `URLError`). They all have the Error object as prototype. Acrobat JavaScript can throw some of these exceptions, or implement subclasses of the Error object at its convenience. If your scripts are using the mechanism of `try`/`catch` error handling, the object thrown should be one of the types listed in the following table.

Error Object	Brief Description
`RangeError`	Argument value is out of valid range
`TypeError`	Wrong type of argument value
`ReferenceError`	Reading a variable that does not exist
`MissingArgError`	Missing required argument
`NumberOfArgsError`	Invalid number of arguments to a method
`InvalidSetError`	A property set is not valid or possible
`InvalidGetError`	A property get is not valid or possible
`OutOfMemoryError`	Out of memory condition occurred
`NotSupportedError`	Functionality not supported in this configuration (for example, Adobe Reader)
`NotSupportedHFTError`	HFT is not available (a plug-in may be missing)
`NotAllowedError`	Method or property is not allowed for security reasons
`GeneralError`	Unspecified error cause
`RaiseError`	Acrobat internal error
`DeadObjectError`	Object is dead
`HelpError`	User requested for help with a method

Error object types implemented by Acrobat JavaScript inherit properties and methods from the core Error object. Some Acrobat JavaScript objects may implement their own specific types of exception. A description of the Error subclass (with added methods and properties, if any) should be provided in the documentation for the particular object.

Example

Print all properties of the Error object to the console.

```
try {
    app.alert(); // one argument is required for alert
} catch(e) {
    for (var i in e)
    console.println( i + ": " + e[i])
}
```

Error Properties

fileName

The name of the script that caused the exception to be thrown.

Type: String   *Access: R*

lineNumber

The offending line number from where an exception was thrown in the JavaScript code.

Type: Integer   *Access: R*

extMessage

A message providing additional details about the exception.

Type: String   *Access: R*

message

The error message providing details about the exception.

Type: String   *Access: R*

name

The name of the Error Object (page 311) subclass, indicating the type of the Error Object instance.

Type: String   *Access: R/W*

Error Methods

toString

6.0			

Gets the error message that provides details about the exception.

Parameters

None

Returns

The error message string. (See the message property, page 312.)

event Object

All JavaScripts are executed as the result of a particular event. For each of these events, Acrobat JavaScript creates an `event` object. During the occurrence of each event, you can access this object to get and possibly manipulate information about the current state of the event.

Each event has a `type` (page 335) and a `name` (page 330) property that uniquely identify the event. This section describes all the events, listed as type/name pairs, and indicates which additional properties, if any, they define.

The `rc` (page 331) property of an event is its return code. The description for each event describes whether it listens to (is affected by) the return code.

It is important for JavaScript writers to know when these events occur and in what order they are processed. Some methods or properties can only be accessed during certain events.

Event Type/Name Combinations

App/Init

This event (the *application initialization event*) occurs when the viewer is started. Script files, called *folder-level JavaScripts*, are read in from the application and user JavaScript folders. They load in the following order: `config.js`, `glob.js`, all other files, then any user files.

This event does not listen to the `rc` (page 331) return code.

Batch/Exec

5.0			

This event occurs during the processing of each document of a batch sequence. JavaScripts authored as part of a batch sequence can access the `event` object upon execution.

The `target` (page 334) for this event is the Document Object (page 188).

This event listens to the `rc` (page 331) return code. If rc is set to `false`, the batch sequence is stopped.

Bookmark/Mouse Up

5.0			

This event occurs whenever a user clicks a bookmark that executes a JavaScript.

The `target` (page 334) for this event is the bookmark object that was clicked.

This event does not listen to the `rc` (page 331) return code.

Console/Exec

5.0			

This event occurs whenever a user evaluates a JavaScript in the console.

This event does not listen to the `rc` (page 331) return code.

Doc/DidPrint

5.0			

This event is triggered after a document has printed.

The `target` (page 334) for this event is the Document Object (page 188).

This event does not listen to the `rc` (page 331) return code.

Doc/DidSave

5.0			

This event is triggered after a document has been saved.

The `target` (page 334) for this event is the Document Object (page 188)

This event does not listen to the `rc` (page 331) return code.

Doc/Open

4.0			

This event is triggered whenever a document is opened. When a document is opened, the document-level script functions are scanned and any exposed scripts are executed.

The `target` (page 334) for this event is the Document Object (page 188). This event also defines the `targetName` (page 335) property.

This event does not listen to the `rc` (page 331) return code.

Doc/WillClose

This event is triggered before a document is closed.

The `target` (page 334) for this event is the Document Object (page 188).

This event does not listen to the `rc` (page 331) return code.

Doc/WillPrint

This event is triggered before a document is printed.

The `target` (page 334) for this event is the Document Object (page 188).

This event does not listen to the `rc` (page 331) return code.

Doc/WillSave

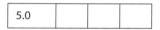

This event is triggered before a document is saved.

The `target` (page 334) for this event is the Document Object (page 188).

This event does not listen to the `rc` (page 331) return code.

External/Exec

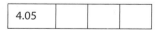

This event is the result of an external access, for example, through OLE, AppleScript, or loading an FDF.

This event does not listen to the `rc` (page 331) return code.

Field/Blur

This event occurs after all other events just as a field loses focus. This event is generated regardless of whether a mouse click is used to deactivate the field (for example, a tab key could be used instead).

Additional properties defined:

- `target` (page 334): The field whose validation script is being executed.
- `modifier` (page 330), `shift` (page 334), `targetName` (page 335), and `value` (page 336).

This event does not listen to the `rc` (page 331) return code.

Field/Calculate

3.01			

This event is defined when a change in a form requires that all fields that have a calculation script attached to them be executed. All fields that depend on the value of the changed field will now be recalculated. These fields may in turn generate additional `Field/Validate` (page 320), `Field/Blur` (page 316), and `Field/Focus` (page 317) events.

Calculated fields may have dependencies on other calculated fields whose values must be determined beforehand. The *calculation order array* contains an ordered list of all the fields in a document that have a calculation script attached. When a full calculation is needed, each of the fields in the array is calculated in turn starting with the zeroth index of the array and continuing in sequence to the end of the array.

To change the calculation order of fields, use the **Advanced>Forms>Set Field Calculation Order...** menu item in Acrobat.

The `target` (page 334) for this event is the field whose calculation script is being executed. This event also defines the `source` (page 334) and `targetName` (page 335) properties.

This event listens to the `rc` (page 331) return code. If the return code is set to `false`, the field's value is not changed. If true, the field takes on the value found in the `value` (page 336) property.

Field/Focus

4.05			

This event occurs after the mouse-down event but before the mouse-up event after the field gains the focus. It occurs regardless of whether a mouse click is used to activate the field (or, for example, the tab key) and is the best place to perform processing that must be done before the user can interact with the field.

The `target` (page 334) for this event is the field whose validation script is being executed. This event also defines the `modifier` (page 330), `shift` (page 334), and `targetName` (page 335) properties.

This event does not listen to the `rc` (page 331) return code.

Field/Format

3.01			

This event is triggered once all dependent calculations have been performed. It allows the attached JavaScript to change the way that the data value appears to a user (also known as its presentation or appearance). For example, if a data value is a number and the context in which it should be displayed is currency, the formatting script can add a dollar sign ($) to the front of the value and limit it to two decimal places past the decimal point.

The `target` (page 334) for this event is the field whose format script is being executed. This event also defines the `commitKey` (page 328), `targetName` (page 335), and `willCommit` (page 337) properties.

This event does not listen to the `rc` (page 331) return code. However, the resulting `value` (page 336) is used as the field's formatted appearance.

Field/Keystroke

3.01			

This event occurs whenever a user types a keystroke into a text box or combo box (including cut and paste operations) or selects an item in a combo box list or list box field. A keystroke script may limit the type of keys allowed. For example, a numeric field might only allow numeric characters.

The Acrobat user interface allows the author to specify a `Selection Change` script for list boxes. The script is triggered every time an item is selected. This is implemented as the keystroke event where the keystroke value is equivalent to the user selection. This behavior is also implemented for the combo box—the "keystroke" could be thought to be a paste into the text field of the value selected from the drop-down list.

There is a final call to the keystroke script before the validate event is triggered. This call sets the `willCommit` (page 337) to `true` for the event. With keystroke processing, it is sometimes useful to make a final check on the field value (pre-commit) before it is committed. This allows the script writer to gracefully handle particularly complex formats that can only be partially checked on a keystroke-by-keystroke basis.

The `keystroke` event of text fields is called in situations other than when the user is entering text with the keyboard or committing the field value. It is also called to validate the default value of a field when set through the UI or by JavaScript and to validate entries provided by autofill. In these situations not all properties of the event are defined. Specifically `event.target` (page 334) will be `undefined` when validating default values and event."richChange" on page 331 and `event.richValue` (page 333) will be `undefined` when validating autofill entries.

The `target` (page 334) for this event is the field whose keystroke script is being executed. This event also defines the `commitKey` (page 328), `change` (page 327), `changeEx` (page 327), `keyDown` (page 330), `modifier` (page 330), `selEnd` (page 333), `selStart` (page 334), `shift` (page 334), `targetName` (page 335), `value` (page 336), and `willCommit` (page 337) properties.

This event listens to the `rc` (page 331) return code. If set to `false`, the keystroke is ignored. The resulting `change` (page 327) is used as the keystroke if the script wants to replace the keystroke code. The resultant `selEnd` (page 333) and `selStart` (page 334) properties can change the current text selection in the field.

Field/Mouse Down

3.01			

This event is triggered when a user starts to click a form field and the mouse button is still down. A mouse-down event does not occur unless a mouse enter event has already occurred. It is advised that you perform very little processing during this event (for example, play a short sound).

The `target` (page 334) for this event is the field whose validation script is being executed. This event also defines the `modifier` (page 330), `shift` (page 334), and `targetName` (page 335) properties.

This event does not listen to the `rc` (page 331) return code.

Field/Mouse Enter

3.01			

This event is triggered when a user moves the pointer inside the rectangle of a field. This is the typical place to open a text field to display help text, for example.

The `target` (page 334) for this event is the field whose validation script is being executed. This event also defines the `modifier` (page 330), `shift` (page 334), and `targetName` (page 335) properties.

This event does not listen to the `rc` (page 331) return code.

Field/Mouse Exit

3.01			

This event occurs when a user moves the mouse pointer outside of the rectangle of a field. A `mouse exit` event will not occur unless a `mouse enter` event has already occurred.

The `target` (page 334) for this event is the field whose validation script is being executed. This event also defines the `modifier` (page 330), `shift` (page 334), and `targetName` (page 335) properties.

This event does not listen to the `rc` (page 331) return code.

Field/Mouse Up

3.01			

This event is triggered when the user clicks a form field and releases the mouse button. This is the typical place to attach routines such as the submit action of a form. A mouse-up event will not occur unless a mouse-down event has already occurred.

The `target` (page 334) for this event is the field whose validation script is being executed. This event also defines the `modifier` (page 330), `shift` (page 334), and `targetName` (page 335) properties.

This event does not listen to the `rc` (page 331) return code.

Field/Validate

3.01			

Regardless of the field type, user interaction with a field may produce a new value for that field. After the user has either clicked outside a field, tabbed to another field, or pressed the enter key, the user is said to have *committed* the new data value.

This event is the first event generated for a field after the value has been committed so that a JavaScript can verify that the value entered was correct. If the validate event is successful, the next event triggered is the `calculate` event.

The `target` (page 334) for this event is the field whose validation script is being executed. This event also defines the `change` (page 327), `changeEx` (page 327), `keyDown` (page 330), `modifier` (page 330), `shift` (page 334), `targetName` (page 335), and `value` (page 336) properties.

This event listens to the `rc` (page 331) return code. If the return code is set to `false`, the field value is considered to be invalid and the value of the field is unchanged.

Link/Mouse Up

5.0			

This event is triggered when a link containing a JavaScript action is activated by the user.

The `target` (page 334) for this event is the Document Object (page 188).

This event does not listen to the `rc` (page 331) return code.

Menu/Exec

5.0			

This event occurs whenever JavaScript that has been attached to a menu item is executed. The user can add a menu item and associate JavaScript actions with it. For example,

```
app.addMenuItem({ cName: "Hello", cParent: "File",
    cExec: "app.alert('Hello',3);", nPos: 0});
```

The script `app.alert('Hello',3)` will execute during a menu event. There are two ways for this to occur:

- The user can select the menu item in the user interface.
- Programmatically, when `app.execMenuItem("Hello")` is executed (perhaps, during a mouse-up event of a button field).

The `target` (page 334) for this event is the currently active document, if one is open. This event also defines the `targetName` (page 335) property.

This event listens to the `rc` (page 331) return code in the case of the enable and marked proc for menu items. (See the `cEnabled` and `cMarked` parameters of `app.addMenuItem`, page 59.) A return code of `false` will disable or unmark a menu item. A return code of `true` will enable or mark a menu item.

Page/Open

4.05			

This event occurs whenever a new page is viewed by the user and after page drawing for the page has occurred.

The `target` (page 334) for this event is the Document Object (page 188).

This event does not listen to the `rc` (page 331) return code.

Page/Close

4.05			

This event occurs whenever the page being viewed is no longer the current page; that is, the user switched to a new page or closed the document.

The `target` (page 334) for this event is the Document Object (page 188).

This event does not listen to the `rc` (page 331) return code.

Screen/Blur

6.0			

This event occurs after all other events, just as the screen annotation loses focus. This event is generated regardless of whether a mouse click is used to deactivate the screen annotation (for example, the tab key might be used).

The `target` (page 334) for this event is the ScreenAnnot Object (page 533) that initiated this event. `targetName` (page 335) is the title of the screen annotation. This event also defines the modifier and shift properties.

This event does not listen to the `rc` (page 331) return code.

Screen/Close

6.0			

This event occurs whenever the page being viewed is no longer the current page; that is, the user switched to a new page or closed the document.

The `target` (page 334) for this event is the ScreenAnnot Object (page 533) that initiated this event. `targetName` (page 335) is the title of the screen annotation. This event also defines the `modifier` (page 330), `shift` (page 334), and `target` (page 334) properties.

This event does not listen to the `rc` (page 331) return code.

Screen/Focus

6.0			

This event occurs after the mouse-down event but before the mouse-up after the field gains the focus. This routine is called regardless of whether a mouse click is used to activate the screen annotation (for example, the tab key might be used). It is the best place to perform processing that must be done before the user can interact with the field.

The `target` (page 334) for this event is the ScreenAnnot Object (page 533) that initiated this event. `targetName` (page 335) is the title of the screen annotation. This event also defines the `modifier` (page 330) and `shift` (page 334) properties.

This event does not listen to the `rc` (page 331) return code.

Screen/InView

6.0			

This event occurs whenever a new page first comes into view by the user. When the page layout is set to **Continuous** or **Continuous - Facing**, this event occurs before the Screen/Open event.

The `target` (page 334) for this event is the ScreenAnnot Object (page 533) that initiated this event. `targetName` (page 335) is the title of the screen annotation. This event also defines the `modifier` (page 330) and `shift` (page 334) properties.

This event does not listen to the `rc` (page 331) return code.

Screen/Mouse Down

6.0			

This event is triggered when a user starts to click a screen annotation and the mouse button is still down. It is advised that you perform very little processing (that is, play a short sound) during this event. A mouse-down event will not occur unless a `mouse enter` event has already occurred.

The `target` (page 334) for this event is the ScreenAnnot Object (page 533) that initiated this event. `targetName` (page 335) is the title of the screen annotation. This event also defines the `modifier` (page 330) and `shift` (page 334) properties.

This event does not listen to the `rc` (page 331) return code.

Screen/Mouse Enter

6.0			

This event is triggered when a user moves the mouse pointer inside the rectangle of an screen annotation.

The `target` (page 334) for this event is the ScreenAnnot Object (page 533) that initiated this event. `targetName` (page 335) is the title of the screen annotation. This event also defines the `modifier` (page 330) and `shift` (page 334) properties.

This event does not listen to the `rc` (page 331) return code.

Screen/Mouse Exit

6.0			

This event is the opposite of the Mouse Enter event and occurs when a user moves the mouse pointer outside of the rectangle of a screen annotation. A Mouse Exit event will not occur unless a Mouse Enter event has already occurred.

The `target` (page 334) for this event is the ScreenAnnot Object (page 533) that initiated this event. `targetName` (page 335) is the title of the screen annotation. This event also defines the `modifier` (page 330) and `shift` (page 334) properties.

This event does not listen to the `rc` (page 331) return code.

Screen/Mouse Up

6.0			

This event is triggered when the user clicks a screen annotation and releases the mouse button. This is the typical place to attach routines such as the starting a Multimedia clip. A mouse-up event will not occur unless a mouse-down event has already occurred.

The `target` (page 334) for this event is the ScreenAnnot Object (page 533) that initiated this event. `targetName` (page 335) is the title of the screen annotation. This event also defines the `modifier` (page 330) and `shift` (page 334) properties.

This event does not listen to the `rc` (page 331) return code.

Screen/Open

6.0			

This event occurs whenever a new page is viewed by the user and after page drawing for the page has occurred.

The `target` (page 334) for this event is the ScreenAnnot Object (page 533) that initiated this event. `targetName` (page 335) is the title of the screen annotation. This event also defines the `modifier` (page 330) and `shift` (page 334) properties.

This event does not listen to the `rc` (page 331) return code.

Screen/OutView

6.0			

This event occurs whenever a page first goes out of view from the user. When the page layout is set to **Continuous** or **Continuous - Facing**, this event occurs after the Screen/Close event.

The `target` (page 334) for this event is the ScreenAnnot Object (page 533) that initiated this event. `targetName` (page 335) is the title of the screen annotation. This event also defines the `modifier` (page 330) and `shift` (page 334) properties.

This event does not listen to the `rc` (page 331) return code.

Document Event Processing

When a document is opened, the `Doc/Open` (page 315) event occurs. Functions are scanned and any exposed (top-level) scripts are executed. Next, if the **NeedAppearances** entry in the PDF file is set to `true` in the **AcroForm** dictionary, the formatting scripts of all form fields in the document are executed. (See 8.6.1 in the *PDF Reference*.) Finally, the `Page/Close` (page 322) event occurs.

Note: For users who create PDF files containing form fields with the **NeedAppearances** entry set to `true`, be sure to do a **Save As** before posting such files on the web. Performing a **Save As** on a file generates the form appearances, which are saved with the file. This increases the performance of Adobe Reader when it loads the file within a web browser.

Form Event Processing

The order in which the form events occur is shown in the state diagram below. Certain dependencies are worth noting. For example, the mouse-up event cannot occur if the Focus event did not occur.

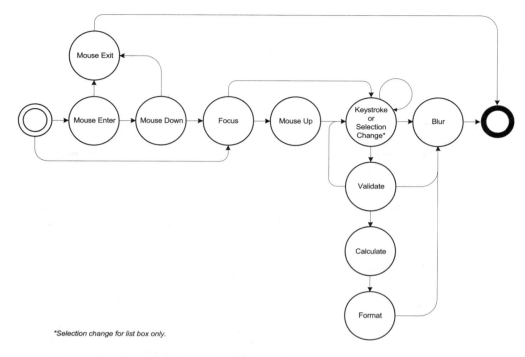

Selection change for list box only.

Multimedia Event Processing

Whenever an event is triggered and dispatched to an EventListener, a (multimedia) `event` Object (page 314) is passed as a parameter to the EventListener. This object is similar to the `event` object used elsewhere in Acrobat and it has the properties listed below.

Multimedia event Objects (page 314) triggered by rendition actions (for example, in custom JavaScript entered from the Actions tab in the Multimedia Properties panel) also include these properties:

`action.annot`	The ScreenAnnot Object (page 533) for this event
`action.rendition`	The Rendition Object (page 520) for this event

Multimedia event objects that have been dispatched by the standard multimedia event dispatcher also include these properties. These are not present if you provide your own `events.dispatch` (page 359) method.

`media.doc`	The document, same as `target.doc`
`media.events`	The events object, same as `target.events`
`media.id`	A copy of `event.name` with spaces removed

Individual events may have additional properties. See the description of each EventListener Object (page 338) method for details.

An event method called by the standard event dispatcher may set either of these properties to stop further event dispatching:

```
stopDispatch
stopAllDispatch
```

To stop the current event from being dispatched to any remaining EventListeners, an event method can set `event.stopDispatch` to `true`. If this is done in an `on` event method, no more `on` methods will be called for the event, but `after` methods will still be called. If you set `event.stopAllDispatch`, no more event methods of either type will be called. See the EventListener Object (page 338) for a description of the `on` and `after` EventListeners.

event Properties

change

3.01			

A string specifying the change in value that the user has just typed. A JavaScript may replace part or all of this string with different characters. The change may take the form of an individual keystroke or a string of characters (for example, if a paste into the field is performed).

Type: String   *Access: R/W*

Example

Change all keystrokes to upper case.

```
// Custom Keystroke for text field
event.change = event.change.toUpperCase();
```

changeEx

5.0			

Contains the export value of the change and is available only during a `Field/Keystroke` (page 318) event for list boxes and combo boxes.

For the list box , the keystroke script, if any, is entered under the **Selection Change** tab in the properties dialog box.

For the combo box, `changeEx` is only available if the pop-up list is used— that is, a selection (with the mouse or the keyboard) is being made from the list. If the combo is editable and the user types in an entry, the

`Field/Keystroke` (page 318) event behaves as for a text field (that is, there are no `changeEx` or `keyDown` (page 330) event properties).

Beginning with Acrobat 6.0, `event.changeEx` is defined for text fields. When `event.fieldFull` (page 329) is `true`, `changeEx` is set to the entire text string the user attempted to enter and `event.change` (page 327) is the text string cropped to what fits within the field. Use `event.richChangeEx` (page 332) (and `event.richChange`, page 331) to handle rich text fields.

Type: various   *Access: R*

Example 1

This example implements a simple HTML online help file system.

Here is a combo box, which is described programmatically.

```
var c = this.addField({
    cName: "myHelp",
    cFieldType: "combobox",
    nPageNum: 0,
    oCoords: [72,12+3*72, 3*72, 0+3*72]
})
```

Now set the items in the combo box.

```
c.setItems([
    ["Online Help", "http://www.myhelp.com/myhelp.html"],
    ["How to Print",
        "http://www.myhelp.com/myhelp.html#print"],
    ["How to eMail",
        "http://www.myhelp.com/myhelp.html#email"]
]);
```

Set the action.

```
c.setAction("Keystroke", "getHelp()");
```

This function is defined at the document level.

```
function getHelp() {
    if ( !event.willCommit && (event.changeEx != "") )
        app.launchURL(event.changeEx);
}
```

Example 2

For an example of the use of `changeEx` with text fields, see the example following `fieldFull` (page 329).

commitKey

4.0			

Determines how a form field will lose focus. Values are:

- 0 : Value was not committed (for example, escape key was pressed).
- 1: Value was committed because of a click outside the field using the mouse.
- 2: Value was committed because of hitting the Enter key.
- 3: Value was committed by tabbing to a new field.

Type: Number   *Access: R*

Example

To automatically display an alert dialog after a field has been committed, add the following to the field's format script:

```
if (event.commitKey != 0)
    app.alert("Thank you for your new field value.");
```

fieldFull

6.0			

Only available in keystroke events for text fields. Set to `true` when the user attempts to enter text that does not fit in the field due to either a space limitation (the Field Object property doNotScroll, page 382, is set to `true`) or the maximum character limit (the Field Object property charLimit, page 378, is set to a positive value). When `fieldFull` is true, event.changeEx (page 327) is set to the entire text string the user attempted to enter and event.change (page 327) is the text string cropped to what fits within the field.

Type: Boolean   *Access: R*   *Events:* Keystroke

Example 1

This is a custom keystroke script for a text field that has a character limit. When the field gets filled, or if the user commits the data entered, the focus moves to another field.

```
if ( event.fieldFull || event.willCommit )
    this.getField("NextTabField").setFocus();
```

Example 2

Test whether user has overfilled the text field. Custom Keystroke script for a text field. Initially, the field is set so that text does not scroll.

```
if ( event.fieldFull )
{
    app.alert("You've filled the given space with text,"
    + " and as a result, you've lost some text. \
        I'll set the field to"
```

```
                + " scroll horizontally, and paste in the rest of your"
                + " missing text.");
            // reset field to lose focus
            this.resetForm([event.target.name]);
            event.target.doNotScroll = false;    // make changes
            event.change = event.changeEx;
        }
```

Field properties generally cannot be changed during a keystroke event, so it is necessary for the field to lose focus as a way to commit the data. The user then has to reset the focus and continue entering data.

keyDown

5.0			

Available only during a keystroke event for list box and combo box. For a list box or the pop-up part of a combo box, the value is true if the arrow keys were used to make a selection, false otherwise.

For the combo box, keyDown (page 330) is only available if the pop-up part of it is used, that is, a selection (with the mouse or the keyboard) is being made from the pop-up. If the combo is editable and the user types in an entry, the Field/Keystroke (page 318) event behaves as for a text field (that is, there are no changeEx, page 327, or keyDown event properties).

Type: Boolean   *Access: R*

modifier

3.01			

Specifies whether the modifier key is down during a particular event. The modifier key on the Microsoft Windows platform is **Control** and on the Macintosh platform is **Option** or **Command**. This property is not supported on UNIX.

Type: Boolean   *Access: R*

name

4.05			

The name of the current event as a text string. The type (page 335) and name together uniquely identify the event. Valid names are:

```
Keystroke   Mouse Exit
Validate    WillPrint
Focus       DidPrint
Blur        WillSave
Format      DidSave
```

```
Calculate Init
Mouse Up   Exec
Mouse Down Open
Mouse EnterClose
```

Type: String　　　　　*Access: R*　　　*Events: all*

rc

3.01			

Used for validation. Indicates whether a particular event in the event chain should succeed. Set to `false` to prevent a change from occurring or a value from committing. The default is `true`.

Type: Boolean　　　　*Access: R/W*　　　*Events:* `Keystroke, Validate, Menu`

richChange

6.0			

Specifies the change in value that the user has just typed. The `richChange` property is only defined for rich text fields and mirrors the behavior of the `event.change` (page 327) property. The value of `richChange` is an array of Span Objects (page 601) that specify both the text entered into the field and the formatting. Keystrokes are represented as single member arrays, while rich text pasted into a field is represented as an array of arbitrary length.

When `event.fieldFull` (page 329) is `true`, `richChangeEx` (page 332) is set to the entire rich formatted text string the user attempted to enter and `event.richChange` is the rich formatted text string cropped to what fits within the field. Use `event.changeEx` (page 327) (and `event.change`, page 327) to handle (plain) text fields.

Type: Array of Span Objects　*Access: R/W*　　*Events:* `Keystroke`

Related objects and properties are `event.richValue` (page 333), the Span Object (page 601), the Field Object `defaultStyle` (page 380), `richText` (page 392), and `richValue` (page 392) properties, and the Annotation Object `richContents` (page 37) property.

Example

This example changes the keystroke to upper case, alternately colors the text blue and red, and switches underlining off and on.

```
// Custom Keystroke event for text rich field.
var span = event.richChange;
for ( var i=0; i<span.length; i++)
{
    span[i].text = span[i].text.toUpperCase();
```

```
        span[i].underline = !span[i].underline;
        span[i].textColor = (span[i].underline) ? color.blue :\
            color.red;
    }
    event.richChange = span;
```

richChangeEx

6.0			

This property is only defined for rich text fields. It mirrors the behavior of the
event.changeEx (page 327) property for text fields. Its value is an array of
Span Objects (page 601) that specify both the text entered into the field and
the formatting. Keystrokes are represented as single member arrays, while
rich text pasted into a field is represented as an array of arbitrary length.

If event.fieldFull (page 329) is true, richChangeEx is set to the entire
rich formatted text string the user attempted to enter and
event.richChange (page 331) is the rich formatted text string cropped to
what fits within the field. Use event.changeEx (page 327) (and
event.change, page 327) to handle (plain) text fields.

Type: Array of Span Objects   Access: R/W   Events: Keystroke

Related objects and properties are event.richChange
(page 331),event.richValue (page 333), the Span Object (page 601), the
Field Object defaultStyle (page 380), richText (page 392), and
richValue (page 392) properties, and the Annotation Object
richContents (page 37) property.

Example

If the text field is filled up by the user, allow additional text by setting the
field to scroll.

```
if ( event.fieldFull )
{
    app.alert("You've filled the given space with text,"
    + " and as a result, you've lost some text. I'll set the
field to"
    + " scroll horizontally, and paste in the rest of your"
    + " missing text.");
    // reset field to lose focus
    this.resetForm([event.target.name]);
    event.target.doNotScroll = false;        // make changes
    if ( event.target.richText )
        event.richChange = event.richChangeEx
    else
        event.change = event.changeEx;
}
```

See also event.fieldFull (page 329).

richValue

6.0			

This property mirrors the `richValue` (page 392) property of the Field Object and the `event.value` (page 398) property for each event.

Type: Array of Span Objects   *Access: R/W*   *Events:* `Keystroke`

Related objects and properties are the Span Object (page 601), the Field Object properties `defaultStyle` (page 380), `richText` (page 392), `richValue` (page 392), `event.richChange` (page 331), `event.richChangeEx` (page 332), and the Annotation Object `richContents` (page 37) property.

Example

This example turns all bold text into red underlined text.

```
// Custom Format event for a rich text field.
var spans = event.richValue;
for ( var i = 0; i < spans.length; i++ )
{
   if( spans[i].fontWeight >= 700 )
   {
       spans[i].textColor = color.red;
       spans[i].fontWeight = 400; // change to default weight
       spans[i].underline = true;
   }
}
event.richValue = spans;
```

selEnd

3.01			

The ending position of the current text selection during a keystroke event.

Type: Integer   *Access: R/W*

Example

This function merges the last change (of a text field) with the uncommitted change. The function uses both `selEnd` and `selStart` (page 334).

```
function AFMergeChange(event)
{
   var prefix, postfix;
   var value = event.value;

   if(event.willCommit) return event.value;
   if(event.selStart >= 0)
      prefix = value.substring(0, event.selStart);
```

```
        else prefix = "";
        if(event.selEnd >= 0 && event.selEnd <= value.length)
            postfix = value.substring(event.selEnd, value.length);
        else postfix = "";
        return prefix + event.change + postfix;
    }
```

selStart

The starting position of the current text selection during a keystroke event.

Type: Integer   *Access: R/W*

Example

See the example following `selEnd` (page 333).

shift

`true` if the shift key is down during a particular event, `false` otherwise.

Type: Boolean   *Access: R*

Example

The following is a mouse-up button action:
```
if (event.shift)
    this.gotoNamedDest("dest2");
else
    this.gotoNamedDest("dest1");
```

source

The Field Object (page 371) that triggered the calculation event. This object is usually different from the `target` (page 334) of the event, which is the field that is being calculated.

Type: object   *Access: R*

target

The target object that triggered the event. In all mouse, focus, blur, calculate, validate, and format events, it is the Field Object (page 371) that triggered

---

Adobe® Acrobat® Official JavaScript Reference

the event. In other events, such as page open and close, it is the Document Object (page 188) or `this` Object (page 631).

Type: object   *Access: R*

targetName

5.0			

Tries to return the name of the JavaScript being executed. Can be used for debugging purposes to help identify the code causing exceptions to be thrown. Common values of `targetName` include:

- The folder-level script file name for `App/Init` (page 314) events
- The document-level script name for `Doc/Open` (page 315) events
- The PDF file name being processed for `Batch/Exec` (page 314) events
- The field name for `Field` events
- The menu item name for `Menu/Exec` (page 321) events.
- The screen annotation name for `Screen` events (multimedia events).

When an exception is thrown, `targetName` is reported if there is an identifiable name.

Type: String   *Access: R*

Example

In this example, the first line of the folder-level JavaScript file `conserve.js` has an error in it. When the viewer starts, an exception is thrown and the message reveals the source of the problem.

```
MissingArgError: Missing required argument.
App.alert:1:Folder-Level:App:conserve.js
===> Parameter cMsg.
```

type

5.0			

The type of the current event. The type and `name` (page 330) together uniquely identify the event. Valid types are:

```
Batch     External
Console   Bookmark
App       Link
Doc       Field
Page      Menu
```

Type: String   *Access: R*

value

3.01			

This property has different meanings for different `field` events:

- For the `Field/Validate` (page 320) event, it is the value that the field contains when it is committed. For a combo box, it is the face value, not the export value (see changeEx, page 327).

  For example, the following JavaScript verifies that the field value is between zero and 100:

  ```
  if (event.value < 0 || event.value > 100) {
      app.beep(0);
      app.alert("Invalid value for field " + event.target.name);
      event.rc = false;
  }
  ```

- For a `Field/Calculate` (page 317) event, JavaScript should set this property. It is the value that the field should take upon completion of the event.

  For example, the following JavaScript sets the calculated value of the field to the value of the SubTotal field plus tax.

  ```
  var f = this.getField("SubTotal");
  event.value = f.value * 1.0725;
  ```

- For a `Field/Format` (page 318) event, JavaScript should set this property. It is the value used when generating the appearance for the field. By default, it contains the value that the user has committed. For a combo box, this is the face value, not the export value (see changeEx, page 327, for the export value).

  For example, the following JavaScript formats the field as a currency type of field.

  ```
  event.value = util.printf("$%.2f", event.value);
  ```

- For a `Field/Keystroke` (page 318) event, it is the current value of the field. If modifying a text field, for example, this is the text in the text field before the keystroke is applied.

- For `Field/Blur` (page 316) and `Field/Focus` (page 317) events, it is the current value of the field. During these two events, `event.value` is read only. That is, the field value cannot be changed by setting `event.value`.

  Beginning with Acrobat 5.0, for a list box that allows multiple selections (see `field.multipleSelection`, page 387), the following behavior occurs. If the field value is an array (that is, multiple items are selected), `event.value` returns an empty string when getting, and does not accept setting.

Type: various   *Access: R/W*

willCommit

3.01			

Verifies the current keystroke event before the data is committed. It can be used to check target form field values to verify, for example, whether character data was entered instead of numeric data. JavaScript sets this property to `true` after the last `keystroke` event and before the field is validated.

Type: Boolean   *Access: R*

Example

This example shows the structure of a keystroke event.

```
var value = event.value
if (event.willCommit)
    // Final value checking.
else
    // Keystroke-level checking.
```

EventListener Object

This object is a collection of multimedia event methods with optional local data. Event method names begin with `on` or `after`, followed by the event name, for example, `onPause` or `afterPause`. When an event is dispatched, matching `on` event methods are called immediately and matching `after` event methods are called a short while later, at the next idle time.

`on` event methods have certain restrictions:

- An `on` event method for a MediaPlayer Object (page 448) cannot call any of that MediaPlayer's methods, nor can it call any other Acrobat methods that may indirectly cause a method of the MediaPlayer to be called. For example, an `on` method must not close the document, save it, change the active page, change the focus, or anything else that may eventually call a method of the MediaPlayer.

- `on` event methods cannot be reentered.

`after` event methods do not have these restrictions and therefore are more versatile for most purposes. Use an `on` event method only when the event must be processed synchronously, such as an `onGetRect` (page 353) method.

Inside an event method, `this` is the EventListener object. The document is available in `event.media.doc` and the event target (MediaPlayer or ScreenAnnot) is in `event.target`.

`Events.add` (page 358) installs EventListener objects for dispatching, `Events.dispatch` (page 359) dispatches an event to the matching event methods, and `Events.remove` (page 361) removes EventListener objects from the dispatch table.

Example

```
// Create a simple MediaEvents object
var events = new app.media.Events
({
    // Called immediately during a Play event:
    onPlay: function() { console.println( "onPlay" ); },

    // Called during idle time after the Play event:
    afterPlay: function() { console.println( "afterPlay" ); },
});
var player = app.media.createPlayer({events: events});
player.events.add({
    afterPlay: function( e ) {
        app.alert("Playback started, doc.URL = "
            + e.media.doc.URL );
    }
});
player.open();
```

EventListener Methods

The events listed here are specific to multimedia.

In addition to these events, a screen annotation may receive the standard events used elsewhere in Acrobat (Destroy, Mouse Up, Mouse Down, Mouse Enter, Mouse Exit, Page Open, Page Close, Page Visible, Page Invisible, Focus, and Blur). See the event Object (page 314) for details on those events.

afterBlur

6.0			

The Blur event is triggered when a MediaPlayer or screen annotation loses the keyboard focus after having it. See also onBlur (page 349) (the difference between on and after event methods are explained in "EventListener Object" on page 338).

Parameters

oMediaEvent	An event Object (page 314) that is automatically passed to this EventListener.

Returns

Nothing

Example

The following script is executed as a Rendition action. The user clicks the screen annotation to open but not play the movie clip. Clicking outside the screen annotation (a Blur event) plays the movie. Clicking the screen annotation (a Focus event) while the movie is playing pauses the movie. To continue, the user clicks outside the screen annotation again.

```
var playerEvents = new app.media.Events
({
    afterBlur: function () { player.play(); },
    afterFocus: function () { player.pause(); }
});
var settings = { autoPlay: false };
var args = { settings: settings, events: playerEvents};
var player = app.media.openPlayer(args);
```

See also afterFocus (page 343).

afterClose

6.0			

The Close event is triggered when a MediaPlayer is closed for any reason. See also `onClose` (page 349) (the difference between `on` and `after` event methods are explained in "EventListener Object" on page 338).

To start another media player from the Close event, be sure to test `doc.media.canPlay` (page 302) first to make sure playback is allowed. For example, playback may not be allowed because the document is closing.

The `event` Object (page 314) for a Close event includes these properties in addition to the standard event properties:

`media.closeReason`	Why the player was closed, from `app.media.closeReason` (page 116).
`media.hadFocus`	Did the player have the focus when it was closed?

When a player closes while it has the focus, it first receives a Blur event and then the Close event. In the Close event, `media.hadFocus` indicates whether the player had the focus before closing.

When the `afterClose` event method is called, the MediaPlayer has already been deleted and its JavaScript object is dead.

Parameters

`oMediaEvent`	An `event` Object (page 314) that is automatically passed to this EventListener.

Returns

Nothing

Example

See `onClose` (page 349) for a representative example.

afterDestroy

6.0			

The Destroy event is triggered when a screen annotation is destroyed.

When the `afterDestroy` event method is called, the screen annotation has already been deleted from the document and its JavaScript object is dead.

See also `onDestroy` (page 350) (the difference between `on` and `after` event methods are explained in "EventListener Object" on page 338).

Parameters

`oMediaEvent`	An `event` Object (page 314) that is automatically passed to this EventListener.

Returns

Nothing

afterDone

6.0			

The Done event is triggered when media playback reaches the end of media.

See also `onDone` (page 351) (the difference between `on` and `after` event methods are explained in "EventListener Object" on page 338).

Parameters

`oMediaEvent`	An `event` Object (page 314) that is automatically passed to this EventListener.

Returns

Nothing

afterError

6.0			

The Error event is triggered when an error occurs in a MediaPlayer. See also `onError` (page 351) (the difference between `on` and `after` event methods are explained in "EventListener Object" on page 338).

The `event` object for an Error event includes these properties in addition to the standard `event` properties:

`media.code`	Status code value
`media.serious`	True for serious errors, false for warnings
`media.text`	Error message text

Parameters

oMediaEvent	An event Object (page 314) that is automatically passed to this EventListener.

Returns

Nothing

afterEscape

6.0			

The Escape event is triggered when the user presses the Escape key while a MediaPlayer is open and has the keyboard focus. A MediaPlayer may receive an Escape event before it receives the Ready event.

See also onEscape (page 352) (the difference between on and after event methods are explained in "EventListener Object" on page 338).

Parameters

oMediaEvent	An event Object (page 314) that is automatically passed to this EventListener.

Returns

Nothing

afterEveryEvent

6.0			

If an Events Object (page 358) contains an onEveryEvent (page 352) or afterEveryEvent property, its EventListener methods are called for every event, not just a specific one. (The difference between on and after event methods are explained in "EventListener Object" on page 338).

The EventListener functions in an onEveryEvent (page 352) or afterEveryEvent property are called before any listener functions that name the specific event.

Parameters

oMediaEvent	An event Object (page 314) that is automatically passed to this EventListener.

Returns

Nothing

Example

```
var events = new app.media.Events(
{
   // This is called immediately during every event:
   onEveryEvent: function( e )
   { console.println( 'onEveryEvent, event = ' + e.name ); },

   // This is called during a Play event, after onEveryEvent
is
   // called:
   onPlay: function() { console.println( "onPlay" ); },

   // This is called for every event, but later during idle
time:
   afterEveryEvent: function( e )
   { console.println( "afterEveryEvent, event = " + e.name );
},

   // This is called during idle time after a Play event,
   // and after afterEveryEvent is called:
   afterPlay: function() { console.println( "afterPlay" ); },
});
```

afterFocus

6.0			

The Focus event is triggered when a MediaPlayer or screen annotation gets the keyboard focus. See also onFocus (page 353) (the difference between on and after event methods are explained in "EventListener Object" on page 338).

Parameters

oMediaEvent	An event Object (page 314) that is automatically passed to this EventListener.

Returns

Nothing

Example

See afterBlur (page 339) for an example of usage.

---

afterPause

The Pause event is triggered when media playback pauses, either because of user interaction or when the pause (page 455) method is called. See also onPause (page 354) (the difference between on and after event methods are explained in "EventListener Object" on page 338).

Parameters

oMediaEvent	An event Object (page 314) that is automatically passed to this EventListener.

Returns

Nothing

afterPlay

The Play event is triggered when media playback starts or resumes, either because of user interaction or when the play (page 456) method is called. See also onPlay (page 355) (the difference between on and after event methods are explained in "EventListener Object" on page 338).

Parameters

oMediaEventg	An event Object (page 314) that is automatically passed to this EventListener.

Returns

Nothing

afterReady

6.0			

The Ready event is triggered when a newly-created MediaPlayer is ready for use. See also onReady (page 355) (the difference between on and after event methods are explained in "EventListener Object" on page 338).

Most methods of a MediaPlayer Object (page 448) cannot be called until the Ready event is triggered.

Parameters

oMediaEvent	An event Object (page 314) that is automatically passed to this EventListener.

Returns

Nothing.

See afterScript (page 346), Markers.get (page 444), and the MediaOffset Object (page 446).

Example

This (document-level) script plays multiple media clips. For each screen annotation, a media (OpenPlayer) player is opened. When it is ready, the afterReady script signals this fact to Multiplayer.

```
// Parameters: doc, page, rendition/annot name, mulitPlayer
instance
function OnePlayer( doc, page, name, multiPlayer )
{
    var player = app.media.openPlayer({
        annot: doc.media.getAnnot(
            { nPage: page, cAnnotTitle: name }),
        rendition: doc.media.getRendition( name ),
        settings: { autoPlay: false },
        events: {
            afterReady: function( e ) {
                multiPlayer.afterReady( player );
            },
        }
    });
    return player;
}
// Parameters: doc, page, list of rendition/annot names
function MultiPlayer( doc, page )
{
    var nPlayersCueing = 0;  // number of players cueing up
    var players = [];  // the SinglePlayers

    this.afterReady = function( player ) {
        if( ! player.didAfterReady ) {
            player.didAfterReady = true;
            nPlayersCueing--;
            if( nPlayersCueing == 0 ) this.play();
        }
    }
    this.play = function() {
        for( var i = 0;  i < players.length;  i++ )
players[i].play();
    }
```

```
            for( var i = 2;  i < arguments.length;  i++ ) {
                players[i-2] = new
        OnePlayer(doc,page,arguments[i],this );
                nPlayersCueing++;
            }
        }
```

Playing multiple media clips is accomplished by executing the code

```
var myMultiPlayer = new MultiPlayer( this, 0, "Clip1",
    "Clip2" );
```

from, for example, a mouse-up action of a form button.

See `afterScript` for another example of `afterReady`.

afterScript

6.0			

The Script event is triggered when a script trigger is encountered in the media during playback. See also `onScript` (page 355) (the difference between `on` and `after` event methods are explained in "EventListener Object" on page 338).

The `event` Object (page 314) for a Script event includes these properties in addition to the standard `event` properties:

`media.command`	Command name
`media.param`	Command parameter string

These two strings can contain any values that the media clip provides. They do not necessarily contain executable JavaScript code and it is up to the `onScript` or `afterScript` EventListener to interpret them.

Parameters

`oMediaEvent`	An `event` Object (page 314) that is automatically passed to this EventListener.

Returns

Nothing

Example

The following is part of a complete example presented after `MediaPlayer.seek` (page 456). The media is an audio clip (`.wma`) of (famous) quotations, which supports markers and scripts. The `afterReady` listener counts the number of markers, one at the beginning of each

---

quotation. At the end of each quotation, there is also a embedded command script. The `afterScript` listener watches for these commands and if it is a `pause` command, it pauses the player.

```
var nMarkers=0;
var events = new app.media.Events;
events.add({
    // count the number of quotes in this audio clip,
    // save as nMarkers
    afterReady: function() {
        var g = player.markers;
        while ( (index =  g.get( { index: nMarkers } ) )  != null
)
            nMarkers++;
    },
    // Each quote should be followed by a script, if the command
    //is to pause, then pause the player.
    afterScript: function( e ) {
        if ( e.media.command == "pause" ) player.pause();
    }
});
var player = app.media.openPlayer({
    rendition: this.media.getRendition( "myQuotes" ),
    settings: { autoPlay: false },
    events: events
});
```

afterSeek

6.0			

The Seek event is triggered when a MediaPlayer is finished seeking to a playback offset as a result of a `seek` (page 456) call. See also `onSeek` (page 356) (the difference between `on` and `after` event methods are explained in "EventListener Object" on page 338).

Not all media players trigger Seek events.

Parameters

oMediaEvent	An event Object (page 314) that is automatically passed to this EventListener.

Returns

Nothing

afterStatus

6.0			

The Status event is triggered on various changes of status that a MediaPlayer reports. See also `onStatus` (page 357) (the difference between `on` and `after` event methods are explained in "EventListener Object" on page 338).

The `event` Object (page 314) for a Status event includes these properties in addition to the standard `event` properties:

`media.code`	Status code value, defined in `app.media.status` (page 120)
`media.text`	Status message text

The following values are used only by some media players and only when `media.code == app.media.status.buffering`. They are zero otherwise.

`media.progress`	Progress value from 0 to media.total
`media.total`	Maximum progress value

Parameters

oMediaEvent	An `event` Object (page 314) that is automatically passed to this EventListener.

Returns

Nothing

Example

The following code would monitor the status of the player, as executed from a Rendition event associated with a screen annotation.

```
var events = new app.media.Events
events.add({
   afterStatus: function ( e ) {
      console.println( "Status code " + e.media.code +
      ", description: " + e.media.text);
   }
});
app.media.openPlayer({ events: events });
```

afterStop

6.0			

The Stop event is triggered when media playback stops, either because of user interaction or when the `stop` (page 458) method is called. See also

---

onStop (page 357) (the difference between on and after event methods are explained in "EventListener Object" on page 338).

Parameters

oMediaEvent	An event Object (page 314) that is automatically passed to this EventListener.

Returns

Nothing

onBlur

6.0			

The Blur event is triggered when a MediaPlayer or screen annotation loses the keyboard focus after having it. See also afterBlur (page 339) (the difference between on and after event methods are explained in "EventListener Object" on page 338).

Parameters

oMediaEvent	An event Object (page 314) that is automatically passed to this EventListener.

Returns

Nothing

onClose

6.0			

The Close event is triggered when a MediaPlayer is closed for any reason. See also afterClose (page 340) (the difference between on and after event methods are explained in "EventListener Object" on page 338).

To start another media player from the Close event, be sure to test doc.media.canPlay (page 302) first to make sure playback is allowed. For example, playback may not be allowed because the document is closing.

The event object for a Close event includes these properties in addition to the standard event properties:

media.closeReason	Why the player was closed, from app.media.closeReason (page 116)?
media.hadFocus	Did the player have the focus when it was closed?

When a player closes while it has the focus, it first receives a Blur event and then the Close event. In the Close event, `media.hadFocus` indicates whether the player had the focus before closing.

When the afterClose event method is called, the MediaPlayer has already been deleted and its JavaScript object is dead.

Parameters

oMediaEvent	An event Object (page 314) that is automatically passed to this EventListener.

Returns

Nothing

Example

This script gets information about why the media clip closed, executed from a Rendition action. See `app.media.closeReason` (page 116).

```
var playerEvents = new app.media.Events({
    onClose: function (e) {
        var eReason, r = app.media.closeReason;
        switch ( e.media.closeReason )
        {
            case r.general: eReason = "general"; break;
            case r.error: eReason = "error"; break;
            case r.done: eReason = "done"; break;
            case r.stop: eReason = "stop"; break;
            case r.play: eReason = "play"; break;
            case r.uiGeneral: eReason = "uiGeneral"; break;
            case r.uiScreen: eReason = "uiScreen"; break;
            case r.uiEdit: eReason = "uiEdit"; break;
            case r.docClose: eReason = "Close"; break;
            case r.docSave: eReason = "docSave"; break;
            case r.docChange: eReason = "docChange"; break;
        }
        console.println("Closing...The reason is  " + eReason
);
    }
});
app.media.openPlayer({ events: playerEvents });
```

onDestroy

6.0			

The Destroy event is triggered when a screen annotation is destroyed. See also `afterDestroy` (page 340) (the difference between on and after event methods are explained in "EventListener Object" on page 338).

Adobe® Acrobat® Official JavaScript Reference

Parameters

oMediaEvent	An event Object (page 314) that is automatically passed to this EventListener.

Returns

Nothing

onDone

6.0			

The Done event is triggered when media playback reaches the end of media. See also afterDone (page 341) (the difference between on and after event methods are explained in "EventListener Object" on page 338).

Parameters

oMediaEvent	An event Object (page 314) that is automatically passed to this EventListener.

Returns

Nothing

onError

6.0			

The Error event is triggered when an error occurs in a MediaPlayer. See also afterError (page 341) (the difference between on and after event methods are explained in "EventListener Object" on page 338).

The event object for an Error event includes these properties in addition to the standard event properties:

media.code	Status code value
media.serious	true for serious errors, false for warnings
media.text	Error message text

Parameters

oMediaEvent	An event Object (page 314) that is automatically passed to this EventListener.

Returns

Nothing

onEscape

6.0			

The Escape event is triggered when the user presses the Escape key while a MediaPlayer is open and has the keyboard focus. A MediaPlayer may receive an Escape event before it receives the Ready event.

See also `afterEscape` (page 342) (the difference between `on` and `after` event methods are explained in "EventListener Object" on page 338).

Parameters

oMediaEvent	An `event` Object (page 314) that is automatically passed to this EventListener.

Returns

Nothing

onEveryEvent

6.0			

If an `event` Object (page 314) contains an `onEveryEvent` or `afterEveryEvent` property, its EventListener methods are called for every event, not just a specific one.

The EventListener methods in an `onEveryEvent` or `afterEveryEvent` (page 342) property are called before any listener functions that name the specific event. (The difference between `on` and `after` event methods are explained in "EventListener Object" on page 338).

Parameters

oMediaEvent	An `event` Object (page 314) that is automatically passed to this EventListener.

Returns

Nothing

onFocus

6.0			

The Focus event is triggered when a MediaPlayer or screen annotation gets the keyboard focus. See also `afterFocus` (page 343) (the difference between `on` and `after` event methods are explained in "EventListener Object" on page 338).

Parameters

oMediaEvent	An `event` Object (page 314) that is automatically passed to this EventListener.

Returns

Nothing

onGetRect

6.0			

The GetRect event is triggered whenever the multimedia plug-in needs to get the display rectangle for a docked MediaPlayer.

The `event` object for a GetRect event includes this property in addition to the standard `event` properties:

media.rect	Player rectangle, an array of four numbers in device space

The `onGetRect` method must set this property in the `oMediaEvent` before returning.

Note: Although you can write an `afterGetRect` listener, there is no useful purpose for it. If it returns a `rect` property, it will be ignored. The `onGetRect` listener is where the `rect` property must be set.

Parameters

oMediaEvent	An `event` Object (page 314) that is automatically passed to this EventListener.

Returns

Nothing

Example

Page 0 has a series of (thumbnail-size) ScreenAnnots and page 1 is a blank page. Put the viewer into continuous facing mode so that both pages are seen side-by-side. Below is a typical Rendition action or mouse-up button JavaScript action.

```
var rendition = this.media.getRendition("Clip1");
var settings = rendition.getPlaySettings();
var annot = this.media.getAnnot({
nPage:0,cAnnotTitle:"ScreenClip1" });
var player = app.media.openPlayer({
    rendition: rendition,
    annot: annot,
    settings: { windowType: app.media.windowType.docked },
    events:
    {
        onGetRect: function (e) {
            var width = e.media.rect[2] - e.media.rect[0];
            var height = e.media.rect[3] - e.media.rect[1];
            width *= 3; // triple width and height
            height *= 3;
            e.media.rect[0] = 36; // move left, upper to
            e.media.rect[1] = 36; // upper left-hand corner
            e.media.rect[2] = e.media.rect[0]+width;
            e.media.rect[3] = e.media.rect[1]+height;
            return e.media.rect; // return this
        }
    }
});
player.page = 1; // show on page 1, this triggers an onGetRect
event.
```

See `MediaPlayer.page` (page 451) and `MediaPlayer.triggerGetRect` (page 459) for a variation on this same example.

onPause

6.0			

The Pause event is triggered when media playback pauses, either because of user interaction or when the `play` (page 456) method is called. See also `afterPause` (page 344) (the difference between `on` and `after` event methods are explained in "EventListener Object" on page 338).

Parameters

oMediaEvent	An `event` Object (page 314) that is automatically passed to this EventListener.

Returns

Nothing

onPlay

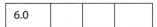

The Play event is triggered when media playback starts or resumes, either because of user interaction or when the `pause` (page 455) method is called. See also `afterPlay` (page 344) (the difference between `on` and `after` event methods are explained in "EventListener Object" on page 338).

Parameters

oMediaEvent	An `event` Object (page 314) that is automatically passed to this EventListener.

Returns

Nothing

onReady

The Ready event is triggered when a newly-created MediaPlayer is ready for use. Most methods of a MediaPlayer Object (page 448) cannot be called until the Ready event is triggered. See also `afterReady` (page 344) (the difference between `on` and `after` event methods are explained in "EventListener Object" on page 338).

Parameters

oMediaEvent	An `event` Object (page 314) that is automatically passed to this EventListener.

Returns

Nothing

onScript

6.0

The Script event is triggered when a script trigger is encountered in the media during playback. See also `afterScript` (page 346) (the difference between `on` and `after` event methods are explained in "EventListener Object" on page 338).

The `event` object for a Script event includes these properties in addition to the standard `event` properties:

`media.command`	Command name
`media.param`	Command parameter string

These two strings can contain any values that the media clip provides. They do not necessarily contain executable JavaScript code and it is up to the `onScript` or `afterScript` EventListener to interpret them.

Parameters

oMediaEvent	An `event` Object (page 314) that is automatically passed to this EventListener.

Returns

Nothing

onSeek

6.0			

The Seek event is triggered when a MediaPlayer is finished seeking to a playback offset as a result of a `seek (page 456)` call. Not all media players trigger Seek events.

See also `afterSeek` (page 347) (the difference between `on` and `after` event methods are explained in "EventListener Object" on page 338).

Parameters

oMediaEvent	An `event` Object (page 314) that is automatically passed to this EventListener.

Returns

Nothing

onStatus

6.0			

The Status event is triggered on various changes of status that a MediaPlayer reports. See also `afterStatus` (page 348) (the difference between `on` and `after` event methods are explained in "EventListener Object" on page 338).

The `event` Object (page 314) for a Status event includes these properties in addition to the standard `event` properties:

`media.code`	Status code value, defined in `app.media.status` (page 120)
`media.text`	Status message text

The following values are used only by some media players, and only when `media.code == app.media.status.buffering`. They are zero otherwise.

`media.progress`	Progress value from 0 to media.total
`media.total`	Maximum progress value

Parameters

oMediaEvent	An `event` Object (page 314) that is automatically passed to this EventListener.

Returns

Nothing

onStop

6.0			

The Stop event is triggered when media playback stops, either because of user interaction or when the `stop` (page 458) method is called.

See also `afterStop` (page 348) (the difference between `on` and `after` event methods are explained in "EventListener Object" on page 338).

Parameters

oMediaEvent	An `event` Object (page 314) that is automatically passed to this EventListener.

Returns

Nothing

Events Object

A multimedia Events object is a collection of EventListener Objects (page 338). The events property of a MediaPlayer Object (page 448) or a ScreenAnnot Object (page 533) is an Events object.

The constructor for an Events object is app.media.Events.

Example

This following is executed as a rendition action.

```
console.println("Ready to play \"" +
event.action.rendition.uiName
    +"\" from screen annot \"" + event.targetName + "\".");
// Create a simple app.media.Events object
var events = new app.media.Events({
    // The Event object is passed as a parameter to all event
    // listeners, this is a the parameter "e" below/
    // Called immediately during a Play event:
    onPlay: function( e ) { console.println( "onPlay: media.id
= "
        + e.media.id ); },
    // Called during idle time after the Play event:
    afterPlay: function() { console.println( "afterPlay" ); },
});
var player = app.media.openPlayer({ events: events });
```

Events Methods

add

6.0			

Adds any number of EventListener Objects (page 338) to the dispatch table for this Events Object. Any previous listeners are preserved and when an event is triggered, all matching listener methods are called.

The standard event dispatcher first calls any onEveryEvent (page 352) methods in the order they were added, then calls any on events for the specific event being dispatched, also in the order they were added. Finally, it sets a very short timer (one millisecond) to call any after events. When that timer is triggered, the after events are called in the same order described for on events.

See the description of on and after events in the introductory paragraphs to EventListener Object (page 338).

Note: If you try to add the same EventListener twice, the second attempt is ignored.

If you add an EventListener from inside an event method, the new listener's methods will be called as part of the dispatching for the current event.

Parameters

Any number of parameters, each one an EventListener Object (page 338).

Returns

Nothing

Example

```
// Add an EventListener for the onPlay event, here, player is a
// MediaPlayer object.
player.events.add
({
    onPlay: function() { console.println( "onPlay" ); }
});
```

See also remove (page 361).

dispatch

6.0			

When a MediaPlayer triggers an event, the Multimedia plug-in creates an event Object (page 314) and calls MediaPlayer.events.dispatch(event). Similarly, a ScreenAnnot calls ScreenAnnot.events.dispatch(event).

The dispatch method is the only part of the event dispatching system that the Acrobat Multimedia plug-in calls directly. You can substitute your own, entirely different event dispatching system by providing your own MediaPlayer.events object with its own dispatch method.

The dispatch method is responsible for calling each of the EventListeners associated with the event, as identified by oMediaEvent.name. In most cases, a PDF file will not provide its own dispatch method but will use the standard event dispatching system.

Parameters

oMediaEvent	An event Object (page 314).

Returns

Nothing.

If you write your own `dispatch` method, note that `oMediaEvent.name` may contain spaces. The standard `dispatch` method makes a copy of `oMediaEvent.name` in `oMediaEvent.media.id` with the spaces removed, to allow the name to be used directly as part of a JavaScript event method name.

Also, if you write your own `dispatch` method, it will be called synchronously when each event occurs, and any processing you do will be subject to the same limitations as described for on event methods (see EventListener Object, page 338). In particular, the method cannot make any calls to a MediaPlayer Object (page 448) nor do anything that can indirectly cause a MediaPlayer method to be called.

The `dispatch` method is not usually called directly from JavaScript code, although it can be.

Example

```
// Create a new media player with a custom event dispatcher.
// This is an advanced technique that would rarely be used in
// typical PDF JavaScript.
var player = doc.media.newPlayer(
{
    events:
    {
        dispatch: function( e )
        {
            console.println( 'events.dispatch' + e.toSource() );
        }
    }
});
// Synthesize and dispatch a Script event, as if one had been
// encountered while the media was playing. With the standard
// event dispatcher, this will call any and all event
// listeners that have been added for this event.
// With the custom dispatcher above, it will log a message
// to the console.
var event = new Event;
event.name = "Script";
event.media = { command: "test", param: "value" };
player.events.dispatch( event );
```

remove

6.0			

The method removes one or more EventListeners that were previously added with `Events.add` (page 358). If you use an object literal directly in `Events.add`, you will not be able to remove that listener using `Media.remove` because there is no way to pass a reference to the same object. To be able to remove an EventListener, you must pass it to the `add` (page 358) method in a variable instead of as an object literal, so that you can pass the same variable to `remove`, as in the example below.

The `remove` method can be called from inside an event method to remove any EventListener, even the listener that the current event method is part of. The current event method continues executing, but no other event methods in the same EventListener object will be called.

Parameters

Any number of EventListener Objects (page 338).

Returns

Nothing

Example

Assume `player` is a MediaPlayer object.

```
var listener = { afterStop: function() {
app.alert("Stopped!"); } }
player.events.add( listener );       // add listener
.....
player.events.remove( listener );   // later, remove it
```

FDF Object

6.0		☯	

This object corresponds to a PDF-encoded data exchange file. Typically, FDF files contain forms data that is exported from a PDF file. However, FDF files can also be used as general purpose data files and it is for this latter purpose that the FDF object exists.

(Security ☯): All methods and properties marked with ☯ in their quickbar are available only during batch, console, application initialization, and menu events. See "Privileged versus Non-privileged Context" on page 8 for details.

FDF Properties

deleteOption

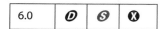

6.0	𝓓	☯	✕

Indicates whether the FDF file should be automatically deleted after it is processed. This value may or may not be used, depending on the content of the FDF file and how it is processed. It is used for embedded files beginning in Acrobat 6.0. Allowed values are

0 (default): Acrobat will automatically delete the FDF file after processing

1: Acrobat will not delete the FDF file after processing (however, a web or email browser may still delete the file).

2: Acrobat will prompt the user to determine whether to delete the FDF file after processing (however, a web or email browser may still delete the file).

Type: Integer   *Access: R/W*

isSigned

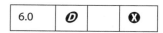

6.0	𝓓		✕

Returns

true if the FDF data file is signed.

Type: Boolean   *Access: R*

Example

See if the fdf is signed.

```
var fdf = app.openFDF("/C/temp/myDoc.fdf");
console.println( "It is "+ fdf.isSigned
    + " that this FDF is signed");
fdf.close();
```

See a more complete example following `signatureSign` (page 368).

numEmbeddedFiles

The number of files embedded in the FDF file. If the `FDF` object is a valid FDF file, no exceptions will be thrown.

A file may be embedded in an FDF file with the `addEmbeddedFile` (page 364) method.

Type: Integer   *Access: R*

Example

Create a new FDF object, embed a PDF doc, save the FDF, open the FDF again, and count the number of embedded files.

```
var fdf = app.newFDF();
fdf.addEmbeddedFile("/C/myPDFs/myDoc.pdf");
fdf.save("/c/temp/myDocWrapper.fdf");
fdf = app.openFDF("/c/temp/myDocWrapper.fdf");
console.println("The number of embedded files = "
    + fdf.numEmbeddedFiles);
fdf.close();
```

FDF Methods

addContact

Adds a contact to the FDF file.

Parameters

oUserEntity	A UserEntity Object (page 181) that list the contact to be added to the FDF file.

Returns

Throws an exception on failure.

Example

```
var oEntity={firstName:"Fred", lastName:"Smith",
fullName:"Fred Smith"};
var f = app.newFDF();
f.addContact( oEntity );
f.save( "/c/temp/FredCert.fdf" );
```

addEmbeddedFile

Add the specified file to the end of the array of embedded files in the FDF file. Anyone opening the FDF file will be instructed to save the embedded file or files according to nSaveOption. If the embedded file is a PDF file, it is opened and displayed. If the embedded file is an FDF file, the file is opened for processing.

FDF files containing embedded files have been supported beginning with Acrobat 4.05. An example use for embedding PDF files is when these files are hosted on an HTTP server and the user should click to download and save the PDF file, rather than viewing the file in the browser. There is no relationship between these embedded files and files that are associated with forms data that is stored in an FDF file.

Parameters

cDIPath	(optional) A device-independent absolute path to a file on the user's hard drive. If not specified, the user is prompted to locate a file.
nSaveOption	(optional) Specifies how the embedded file will be presented to the user opening this FDF file, where the file will be saved, and whether the file will be deleted after it is saved. Values are: ● 0: The file will be automatically saved to the Acrobat document folder. ● 1 (the default): The user will be prompted for a file name to which to save the embedded file. ● 2: Should not be used. ● 3: The file will be automatically saved as a temporary file and deleted during cleanup (when Acrobat is closed). In Acrobat 4.05 through 5.05, for values of 0 and 3, the user is prompted for the location of the save folder if they have not already set this value. For all values of nSaveOption, if the file is a PDF or FDF file, it is automatically opened by Acrobat after it is saved.

Returns

Throws an exception if this operation could not be completed, otherwise returns the number of embedded files that are now in the FDF file.

Example

Create a new FDF, embed a PDF doc, then save.

```
var fdf = app.newFDF();
fdf.addEmbeddedFile("/C/myPDFs/myDoc.pdf");
fdf.save("/c/temp/myDocs.fdf");
```

addRequest

Adds a request to the FDF file. There can be only one request in an FDF file. If the FDF file already contains a request, it is replaced with this new request.

Parameters

cType	What is being requested. Currently the only valid value is the string "CMS", which is a request for contact information.
cReturnAddress	The return address string for the request. This must begin with `mailto:`, `http:` or `https:` and be of the form `"http://www.acme.com/cgi.pl"` or `"mailto:jdoe@adobe.com"`.
cName	(optional) The name of the person or organization that has generated the request.

Returns

Throws an exception if there is an error.

Example

```
var f = app.newFDF();
f.addRequest( "CMS", "http://www.acme.com/cgi.pl", \
    "Acme Corp" );
f.save( "/c/tmp/request.fdf" );
```

close

Immediately closes the FDF file.

Parameters

None

Returns

Throws an exception if there is an error.

See the FDF Object `save` (page 367) method, which also closes an FDF file.

Example

See example following the `addEmbeddedFile` (page 364) method.

mail

Saves the FDF Object (page 362) as a temporary FDF file and mails this file as an attachment to all recipients, with or without user interaction. The temporary file is deleted after it is no longer needed.

See also `app.mailGetAddrs` (page 92), `app.mailMsg` (page 93), the Document Object methods `mailDoc` (page 268) and `mailForm` (page 270) ,and the Report Object method `mail` (page 527).

Note: On Windows, the client computer must have its default mail program configured to be MAPI enabled to use this method.

Parameters

`bUI`	(optional) Specifies whether to display a user interface. If `true` (the default), the rest of the parameters are used to seed a compose-new-message window that is displayed to the user. If `false`, the `cTo` parameter is required and all others are optional.
`cTo`	(optional) A semicolon-separated list of recipients for the message.
`cCc`	(optional) A semicolon-separated list of CC recipients for the message.
`cBcc`	(optional) A semicolon-separated list of BCC recipients for the message.
`cSubject`	(optional) The subject of the message. The length limit is 64 KB.
`cMsg`	(optional) The content of the message. The length limit is 64 KB.

Returns

Throws an exception if there is an error.

Example

```
var fdf = app.openFDF( "/c/temp/myDoc.fdf" );
```

Adobe® Acrobat® Official JavaScript Reference

```
/* This opens the compose new message window */
fdf.mail();

/* This will send out the mail with the attached FDF file to
fun1@fun.com and fun2@fun.com */
fdf.mail( false, "fun1@fun.com", "fun2@fun.com", "",
   "This is the subject", "This is the body.");
```

save

| 6.0 |  |

Save the FDF Object (page 362) as a file. A save will always occur. The file is closed when it is saved and the FDF object no longer contains a valid object reference.

See the `close` (page 365) method, which also closes a FDF file.

Parameters

cDIPath	The device-independent path of the file to be saved.
	Note: (Security ): cDIPath must be a safe path (see "Safe Path" on page 8) and must have an extension of .fdf.

Returns

Throws an exception if there is an error.

Example

Create a new FDF, embed a PDF doc, then save.

```
var fdf = app.newFDF()
fdf.addEmbeddedFile("/C/myPDFs/myDoc.pdf");
fdf.save("/c/temp/myDocs.fdf");
```

signatureClear

| 6.0 | |

If the FDF Object (page 362) is signed, clears the signature and returns `true` if successful. Does nothing if the FDF object is not signed. Does not save the file.

Parameters

None

Returns

`true` on success.

---

signatureSign

6.0	*D*	*S*	*X*

Sign the FDF Object (page 362) with the specified security object. FDF objects can be signed only once. The FDF object is signed in memory and is not automatically saved as a file to disk. Call `save` (page 367) to save the FDF object after it is signed. Call `signatureClear` (page 367) to clear FDF signatures.

Parameters

oSig	The SecurityHandler Object (page 557) that is to be used to sign. Security objects normally require initialization before they can be used for signing. Check the documentation for your security handler to see if it is able to sign FDF files. The `signFDF` (page 561) property of the SecurityHandler object will indicate whether a particular security object is capable of signing FDF files.
oInfo	(optional) A SignatureInfo Object (page 570) containing the writable properties of the signature.
nUI	(optional) The type of dialog box to show when signing. Values are: 0: Show no dialog box. 1: Show a simplified dialog box with no editable fields (fields can be provided in `oInfo`). 2: Show a more elaborate dialog box that includes editable fields for reason, location, and contact information. The default is 0.
cUISignTitle	(optional) The title to use for the sign dialog box. It is used only if `nUI` is non-zero.
cUISelectMsg	(optional) A message to display when a user must select a resource for signing, such as selecting a credential. It is used only when `nUI` is non-zero.

Returns

`true` if the signature was applied successfully, `false` otherwise.

Example

Open existing FDF data file and sign.

```
var eng = security.getHandler( "Adobe.PPKLite" );
eng.login("myPassword" ,"/c/test/Acme.pfx");
var myFDF = app.openFDF( "/c/temp/myData.fdf" );
if( !myFDF.isSigned ) {
```

```
myFDF.signatureSign({
    oSig: eng,
    nUI: 1,
    cUISignTitle: "Sign Embedded File FDF",
    cUISelectMsg: "Please select a Digital ID to use to "
        + "sign your embedded file FDF."
});
myFDF.save( "/c/temp/myData.fdf" );
};
```

signatureValidate

6.0			⊗

Validate the signature of an FDF Object (page 362) and return a
SignatureInfo Object (page 570) specifying the properties of the signature.

Parameters

oSig	(optional) The security handler to be used to validate the signature. Can be either a SecurityHandler Object (page 557) or a generic object with the following properties:
	• oSecHdlr: The SecurityHandler Object to use to validate this signature.
	• bAltSecHdlr: A Boolean. If true, an alternate security handler, selected based on user preference settings, may be used to validate the signature. The default is false, meaning that the security handler returned by the signature's handlerName property is used to validate the signature. This parameter is not used if oSecHdlr is provided.
	If oSig is not supplied, the security handler returned by the signature's handlerName property is used to validate the signature.
bUI	(optional) If true, allow the UI to be shown, if necessary, when validating the data file. The UI may be used to select a validation handler, if none is specified.

Returns

A SignatureInfo Object (page 570). The signature status is described in
status property.

Example

```
fdf = app.openFDF("/c/temp/myDoc.fdf");
eng = security.getHandler( "Adobe.PPKLite" );
if (fdf.isSigned)
{
   var oSigInfo = fdf.signatureValidate({
       oSig: eng,
       bUI: true
   });
   console.println("Signature Status: " + oSigInfo.status);
   console.println("Description: " + oSigInfo.statusText);
} else {
   console.println("FDF not signed");
}
```

Field Object

This object represents an Acrobat form field (that is, a field created using the Acrobat form tool or the Document Object addField, page 211, method). In the same manner that a form author can modify an existing field's properties, such as the border color or font, the JavaScript user can use the Field object to perform the same modifications.

Before a field can be accessed, it must be bound to a JavaScript variable through a method provided by the Document Object (page 188). More than one variable may be bound to a field by modifying the field's object properties or accessing its methods. This affects all variables bound to that field.

```
var f = this.getField("Total");
```

This example allows the script to manipulate the form field "Total" by means of the variable f.

Fields can be arranged hierarchically within a document. For example, form fields with names like "FirstName" and "LastName" are called *flat names* and there is no association between them. By changing the field names, a hierarchy of fields within the document can be created.

For example, "Name.First" and "Name.Last" forms a tree of fields. The period (".") separator in Acrobat forms denotes a hierarchy shift. "Name" in these fields is the parent; "First" and "Last" are the children. Also, the field "Name" is an *internal* field because it has no visible appearance. "First" and "Last" are *terminal* fields that appear on the page.

Acrobat form fields that share the same name also share the same value. Terminal fields can have different presentations of that data. For example, they can appear on different pages, be rotated differently, or have a different font or background color, but they have the same value. Therefore, if the value of one presentation of a terminal field is modified, all others with the same name are updated automatically.

Each presentation of a terminal field is referred to as a *widget*. An individual widget does not have a name but is identified by index (0-based) within its terminal field. The index is determined by the order in which the individual widgets of this field were created (and is unaffected by tab-order).

You can determine the index for a specific widget by using the **Fields** navigation tab in Acrobat. The index is the number that follows the '#' sign in the field name shown. (In Acrobat 6.0 or later, the widget index is displayed only if the field has more than one widget.) You can double-click an entry in the **Fields** panel to go to the corresponding widget in the document.

Alternatively, if you select a field in the document, the corresponding entry in the **Fields** panel is highlighted.

Beginning with Acrobat 6.0, `getField` (page 248) can be used to retrieve the Field Object of one individual widget of a field. This notation consists of appending a "." (a dot) followed by the widget index to the field name passed. When this approach is used, the Field Object returned by `getField` encapsulates only one individual widget. You can use the Field Objects returned this way anywhere you would use a Field Object returned by passing the unaltered field name. However, the set of nodes that are affected may vary, as shown in the following table.

Action	Field Object that Represents All Widgets	Field Object that Represents One Specific Widget
Get a widget property	Gets the property of widget # 0.	Gets the property of the widget.
Set a widget property	Sets the property of all widgets that are children of that field. (The `rect` property and the `setFocus` method are exceptions that apply to widget # 0. See example below.)	Sets the property of the widget.
Get a field property	Gets the property of the field.	Gets the property of the parent field.
Set a field property	Sets the property of the field.	Sets the property of the parent field.

The following example changes the `rect` property of the second radio button (the first would have index 0) of the field "my radio".

```
var f = this.getField("my radio.1");
f.rect = [360, 677, 392, 646];
```

Field versus Widget Attributes

Some properties of the Field Object, such as `value`, apply to all widgets that are children of that field. Other properties, such as `rect`, are specific to individual widgets.

The following field properties and methods affect field-level attributes:

```
calcOrderIndex, charLimit, comb, currentValueIndices,
defaultValue, doNotScroll, doNotSpellCheck, delay, doc,
editable, exportValues, fileSelect, multiline,
multipleSelection, name, numItems, page, password, readonly,
required, submitName, type, userName, value, valueAsString,
clearItems, browseForFileToSubmit, deleteItemAt, getItemAt,
```

```
insertItemAt, setAction, setItems, signatureInfo,
signatureSign, and signatureValidate.
```

The following field properties and methods affect widget-level attributes:

```
alignment, borderStyle, buttonAlignX, buttonAlignY,
buttonPosition, buttonScaleHow, buttonScaleWhen, display,
fillColor, hidden, highlight, lineWidth, print, rect, strokeColor,
style, textColor, textFont, textSize, buttonGetCaption,
buttonGetIcon, buttonImportIcon, buttonSetCaption,
buttonSetIcon, checkThisBox, defaultIsChecked, isBoxChecked,
isDefaultChecked, setAction, and setFocus.
```

Note: The `setAction` method can apply at the field or widget level, depending on the event. The `Keystroke`, `Validate`, `Calculate`, and `Format` events apply to fields. The `MouseUp`, `MouseDown`, `MouseEnter`, `MouseExit`, `OnFocus`, and `OnBlur` events apply to widgets.

Note: The `checkThisBox`, `defaultIsChecked`, `isBoxChecked`, and `isDefaultChecked` methods take a widget index, `nWidget`, as a parameter. If you invoke these methods on a Field Object `f` that represents one specific widget, the `nWidget` parameter is optional (and is ignored if passed) and the method acts on the specific widget encapsulated by `f`.

Field Properties

In general, field properties correspond to those stored in field and annotation dictionaries in the PDF document (see section 8.4.1, "Annotation Dictionaries," and section the *PDF Reference*).

Some property values are stored in the PDF document as names (see section 3.2.4 on name objects in the *PDF Reference*), while others are stored as strings (see section 3.2.3 on string objects in the *PDF Reference*). For a property that is stored as a name, there is a 127-character limit on the length of the string.

Examples of properties that have a 127-character limit include `value` and `defaultValue` for check boxes and radio buttons. The *PDF Reference* documents all Annotation properties as well as how they are stored.

alignment

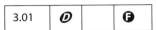

3.01	*D*		*F*	

Controls how the text is laid out within the text field. Values are

```
left
center
right
```

Type: String   *Access: R/W*   *Fields:* text

Example

```
var f = this.getField("MyText");
f.alignment = "center";
```

borderStyle

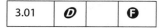

The border style for a field. Valid border styles are

```
solid
dashed
beveled
inset
underline
```

The border style determines how the border for the rectangle is drawn. The border object is a static convenience constant that defines all the border styles of a field, as shown in the following table:

Type	Keyword	Description
solid	border.s	Strokes the entire perimeter of the rectangle with a solid line.
beveled	border.b	Equivalent to the solid style with an additional beveled (pushed-out appearance) border applied inside the solid border.
dashed	border.d	Strokes the perimeter with a dashed line.
inset	border.i	Equivalent to the solid style with an additional inset (pushed-in appearance) border applied inside the solid border.
underline	border.u	Strokes the bottom portion of the rectangle's perimeter.

Type: String   *Access: R/W*   *Fields: all*

Example

The following example shows how to set the border style of a field to solid:

```
var f = this.getField("MyField");
f.borderStyle = border.s; /* border.s evaluates to "solid" */
```

buttonAlignX

Controls how space is distributed from the left of the button face with respect to the icon. It is expressed as a percentage between 0 and 100, inclusive. The default value is 50.

Adobe® Acrobat® Official JavaScript Reference

If the icon is scaled anamorphically (which results in no space differences), this property is not used.

Type: Integer   *Access: R/W*   *Fields:* button

buttonAlignY

Controls how unused space is distributed from the bottom of the button face with respect to the icon. It is expressed as a percentage between 0 and 100, inclusive. The default value is 50.

If the icon is scaled anamorphically (which results in no space differences), this property is not used.

Type: Integer   *Access: R/W*   *Fields:* button

Example

This example is an elevator animation. The field "myElevator" is a button form field that has small width and large height. An icon is imported as the appearance face.

```
function MoveIt()
{
    if ( f.buttonAlignY == 0 ) {
        f.buttonAlignY++;
        run.dir = true;
        return;
    }
    if ( f.buttonAlignY == 100 ) {
        f.buttonAlignY--;
        run.dir = false;
        return;
    }
    if (run.dir) f.buttonAlignY++;
    else f.buttonAlignY--;
}
var f = this.getField("myElevator");
f.buttonAlignY=0;
run = app.setInterval("MoveIt()", 100);
run.dir=true;
toprun = app.setTimeOut(
    "app.clearInterval(run); \
    app.clearTimeOut(toprun)", 2*20000+100);
```

buttonFitBounds

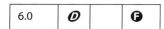

| 6.0 | *D* | | **F** |

If `true`, the extent to which the icon may be scaled is set to the bounds of the button field. The additional icon placement properties are still used to scale and position the icon within the button face.

In previous versions of Acrobat, the width of the field border was always taken into consideration when scaling an icon to fit a button face, even when no border color was specified. Setting this property to `true` when a border color has been specified for the button will cause an exception to be raised.

Type: Boolean　　　*Access: R/W*　　*Fields:* `button`

buttonPosition

| 5.0 | *D* | | **F** |

Controls how the text and the icon of the button are positioned with respect to each other within the button face. The convenience `position` object defines all of the valid alternatives:

Icon/Text Placement	Keyword
Text Only	`position.textOnly`
Icon Only	`position.iconOnly`
Icon top, Text bottom	`position.iconTextV`
Text top, Icon bottom	`position.textIconV`
Icon left, Text right	`position.iconTextH`
Text left, Icon right	`position.textIconH`
Text in Icon (overlaid)	`position.overlay`

Type: Integer　　　*Access: R/W*　　*Fields:* `button`

buttonScaleHow

5.0	*D*		**F**

Controls how the icon is scaled (if necessary) to fit inside the button face. The convenience `scaleHow` object defines all of the valid alternatives:

How is Icon Scaled	Keyword
Proportionally	`scaleHow.proportional`
Non-proportionally	`scaleHow.anamorphic`

Type: Integer   *Access: R/W*   *Fields:* `button`

buttonScaleWhen

5.0	*D*		**F**

Controls when an icon is scaled to fit inside the button face. The convenience `scaleWhen` object defines all of the valid alternatives:

When is Icon Scaled	Keyword
Always	`scaleWhen.always`
Never	`scaleWhen.never`
If icon is too big	`scaleWhen.tooBig`
If icon is too small	`scaleWhen.tooSmall`

Type: Integer   *Access: R/W*   *Fields:* `button`

calcOrderIndex

3.01	*D*		**F**

Changes the calculation order of fields in the document. When a computable `text` or combo box field is added to a document, the field's name is appended to the calculation order array. The calculation order array determines in what order the fields are calculated. The `calcOrderIndex` property works similarly to the **Calculate** tab used by the Acrobat Form tool.

Type: Integer   *Access: R/W*   *Fields:* `combobox, text`

Example

```
var a = this.getField("newItem");
var b = this.getField("oldItem");
a.calcOrderIndex = b.calcOrderIndex + 1;
```

In this example, the "newItem" field was added after the "oldItem" field. The script changes the `calcOrderIndex` property of the "newItem" field so that it is calculated before the "oldItem" field.

charLimit

Limits the number of characters that a user can type into a text field.

See `event.fieldFull` (page 329) to detect when the maximum number of characters is reached.

Type: Integer   *Access: R/W*   *Fields:* `text`

Example

Set a limit on the number of characters that can be typed into a field.

```
var f = this.getField("myText");
f.charLimit = 20;
```

comb

If set to `true`, the field background is drawn as series of boxes (one for each character in the value of the field) and each character of the content is drawn within those boxes. The number of boxes drawn is determined from the `charLimit` (page 378) property.

It applies only to text fields. The setter will also raise if any of the following field properties are also set `multiline` (page 387), `password` (page 389), and `fileSelect` (page 385). A side-effect of setting this property is that the `doNotScroll` (page 382) property is also set.

Type: Boolean   *Access: R/W*   *Fields:* `text`

Example

Create a comb field in the upper left corner of a newly created document.

```
var myDoc = app.newDoc();                    // create a blank doc
var Bbox = myDoc.getPageBox("Crop");         // get crop box
var inch = 72;

// add a text field at the top of the document
var f = myDoc.addField("Name.Last", "text", 0,
    [ inch, Bbox[1]-inch, 3*inch, Bbox[1]- inch - 14 ] );
// add some attributes to this text field
f.strokeColor = color.black;
f.textColor = color.blue;
```

```
f.fillColor = ["RGB",1,0.66,0.75];

f.comb = true;        // declare this is a comb field
f.charLimit = 10;     // Max number of characters
```

commitOnSelChange

6.0	*Ⓓ*		Ⓕ

Controls whether a field value is committed after a selection change:

- If `true`, the field value is committed immediately when the selection is made.
- If `false`, the user can change the selection multiple times without committing the field value. The value is committed only when the field loses focus, that is, when the user clicks outside the field.

Type: Boolean   *Access: R/W*   *Fields:* `combobox`, `listbox`

currentValueIndices

5.0	*Ⓓ*		Ⓕ

Reads and writes single or multiple values of a list box or combo box.

Read

Returns the options-array indices of the strings that are the value of a list box or combo box field. These indices are 0-based. If the value of the field is a single string, it returns an integer. Otherwise, it returns an array of integers sorted in ascending order. If the current value of the field is not a member of the set of offered choices (as could happen in the case of an editable combo box) it returns -1.

Write

Sets the value of a list box or combo box. It accepts a single integer or array of integers as an argument. To set a single string as the value, pass an integer that is the 0-based index of that string in the options array. Note that in the case of an editable combo box, if the desired value is not a member of the set of offered choices, you must set the `value` (page 398) instead. Except for this case, `currentValueIndices` is the preferred way to set the value of a list box or combo box.

To set a multiple selection for a list box that allows it, pass an array as argument to this property, containing the indices (sorted in ascending order) of those strings in the options array. This is the only way to invoke multiple selections for a list box from JavaScript. The ability for a list box to support multiple selections can be set through multipleSelection (page 387).

Related methods and properties include numItems (page 388), getItemAt (page 407), insertItemAt (page 409), deleteItemAt (page 406), and setItems (page 412).

Type: Integer | Array   *Access: R/W*   *Fields:* combobox, listbox

Example (Read)

The script below is a mouse-up action of a button. The script gets the current value of a list box.

```
var f = this.getField("myList");
var a = f.currentValueIndices;
if (typeof a == "number") // a single selection
   console.println("Selection: " + f.getItemAt(a, false));
else {              // multiple selections
   console.println("Selection:");
   for (var i = 0; i < a.length; i ++)
       console.println("   " + f.getItemAt(a[i], false));
}
```

Example (Write)

The following code, selects the second and fourth (0-based index values, 1 and 3, respectively) in a list box.

```
var f = this.getField("myList");
f.currentValueIndices = [1,3];
```

defaultStyle

6.0	*Ⓓ*		Ⓕ

This property defines the default style attributes for the form field. If the user clicks into an empty field and begins entering text without changing properties using the property toolbar, these are the properties that will be used. This property is a single Span Object (page 601) without a text (page 603) property. Some of the properties in the default style span mirror the properties of the Field Object (page 371). Changing these properties also modifies the defaultStyle property for the field and vice versa.

The following table details the properties of the Field Object that are also in the default style and any differences between their values.

Field Properties	defaultStyle (Span Properties)	Description
alignment (page 373)	alignment (page 601)	The alignment property has the same values for both the default style and the Field Object.
textFont (page 396)	fontFamily (page 601) fontStyle (page 602) fontWeight (page 602)	The value of this field property is a complete font name that represents the font family, weight, and style. In the default style property, each property is represented separately. If an exact match for the font properties specified in the default style cannot be found, a similar font will be used or synthesized.
textColor (page 395)	textColor (page 603)	The textColor property has the same values for both the default style and the Field Object.
textSize (page 397)	textSize (page 604)	The textSize property has the same values for both the default style and the Field Object.

Note: When a field is empty, defaultStyle is the style used for newly entered text. If a field already contains text when defaultStyle is changed, the text will not pick up any changes to defaultStyle. Newly entered text uses the attributes of the text it is inserted into (or specified with the toolbar).

When pasting rich text into a field, unspecified attributes in the pasted rich text are filled with those from defaultStyle.

Superscript and Subscript are ignored in defaultStyle.

Type: Span Object   *Access: R/W*   *Fields:* rich text

Example

Change the default style for a text field.

```
var style = this.getField("Text1").defaultStyle;
style.textColor = color.red;
style.textSize = 18;

// if Courier Std is not found on the user's system,
// use a monospace
style.fontFamily = ["Courier Std", "monospace" ];

this.getField("Text1").defaultStyle = style;
```

defaultValue

The default value of a field—that is, the value that the field is set to when the form is reset. For combo boxes and list boxes, either an export or a user value can be used to set the default. A conflict can occur, for example, when the field has an export value and a user value with the same value but these apply to different items in the list. In such cases, the export value is matched against first.

Type: String   *Access: R/W*   *Fields: all except* button, signature

Example

```
var f = this.getField("Name");
f.defaultValue = "Enter your name here.";
```

doNotScroll

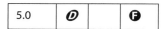

If true, the text field does not scroll and the user, therefore, is limited by the rectangular region designed for the field. Setting this property to true or false corresponds to checking or unchecking the **Scroll long text** field in the **Options** tab of the field.

Type: Boolean   *Access: R/W*   *Fields:* text

doNotSpellCheck

If true, spell checking is not performed on this editable text field. Setting this property to true or false corresponds to unchecking or checking the **Check spelling** attribute in the **Options** tab of the **Field Properties** dialog box.

Type: Boolean   *Access: R/W*   *Fields:* combobox *(editable),* text

delay

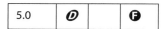

Delays the redrawing of a field's appearance. It is generally used to buffer a series of changes to the properties of the field before requesting that the field regenerate its appearance. Setting the property to true forces the field to wait until delay is set to false. The update of its appearance then takes place, redrawing the field with its latest settings.

There is a corresponding Document Object `delay` (page 192) flag if changes are being made to many fields at once.

Type: Boolean   *Access: R/W*   *Fields: all*

Example

This example changes the appearance of a check box. It sets `delay` to `true`, makes changes, and sets `delay` to `false`.

```
// Get the myCheckBox field
var f = this.getField("myCheckBox");
// set the delay and change the fields properties
// to beveled edge and medium thickness line.
f.delay = true;
f.borderStyle = border.b;
...                    // a number of other changes
f.strokeWidth = 2;
f.delay = false;       // force the changes now
```

display

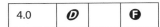

Controls whether the field is hidden or visible on screen and in print. Values are:

Effect	Keyword
Field is visible on screen and in print	`display.visible`
Field is hidden on screen and in print	`display.hidden`
Field is visible on screen but does not print	`display.noPrint`
Field is hidden on screen but prints	`display.noView`

This property supersedes the older `hidden` (page 386) and `print` (page 390) properties.

Type: Integer   *Access: R/W*   *Fields: all*

Example

```
// Set the display property
var f = getField("myField");
f.display = display.noPrint;

// Test whether field is hidden on screen and in print
if (f.display == display.hidden) console.println("hidden");
```

doc

3.01			

Returns the Document Object (page 188) of the document to which the field belongs.

Type: object   *Access: R*   *Fields: all*

editable

3.01	*D*		*F*

Controls whether a combo box is editable. If `true`, the user can type in a selection. If `false`, the user must choose one of the provided selections.

Type: Boolean   *Access: R/W*   *Fields:* `combobox`

Example

```
var f = this.getField("myComboBox");
f.editable = true;
```

exportValues

5.0	*D*		*F*

An array of strings representing the export values for the field. The array has as many elements as there are annotations in the field. The elements are mapped to the annotations in the order of creation (unaffected by tab-order).

For radio button fields, this property is required to make the field work properly as a group. The button that is checked at any time gives its value to the field as a whole.

For check box fields, unless an export value is specified, " Yes" (or the corresponding localized string) is the default when the field is checked. "Off" is the default when the field is unchecked (the same as for a radio button field when none of its buttons are checked).

Type: Array   *Access: R/W*   *Fields:* `checkbox, radiobutton`

Example

This example creates a radio button field and sets its export values.

```
var d = 40;
var f = this.addField("myRadio","radiobutton",0, [200, 510, 210, 500]);
this.addField("myRadio","radiobutton",0, [200+d, 510-d, 210+d, 500-d]);
this.addField("myRadio","radiobutton",0, [200, 510-2*d, 210, 500-2*d]);
this.addField("myRadio","radiobutton",0, [200-d, 510-d, 210-d, 500-d]);
```

```
f.strokeColor = color.black;
// now give each radio field an export value
f.exportValues = ["North", "East", "South", "West"];
```

fileSelect

If `true`, sets the file-select flag in the **Options** tab of the text field (**Field is Used for File Selection**). This indicates that the value of the field represents a pathname of a file whose contents may be submitted with the form.

The pathname may be entered directly into the field by the user, or the user can browse for the file. (See "browseForFileToSubmit" on page 399.)

Note: The file select flag is mutually exclusive with the `multiline` (page 387), `charLimit` (page 378), `password` (page 389), and `defaultValue` (page 382) properties. Also, on the Macintosh platform, when setting the file select flag, the field gets treated as read-only. Therefore, the user must browse for the file to enter into the field. (See browseForFileToSubmit, page 399.)

(Security *S*): This property can only be set during batch, menu, or console events. See "Privileged versus Non-privileged Context" on page 8 for details. The `event` Object (page 314) contains a discussion of Acrobat JavaScript events.

Type: Boolean   *Access: R/W*   *Fields:* `text`

fillColor

Specifies the background color for a field. The background color is used to fill the rectangle of the field. Values are defined by using `transparent`, `gray`, `RGB` or `CMYK` color. See "Color Arrays" on page 156 for information on defining color arrays and how values are used with this property.

In older versions of this specification, this property was named `bgColor`. The use of `bgColor` is now discouraged, although it is still valid for backward compatibility.

Type: Array   *Access: R/W*   *Fields: all*

Example

This code changes the background color of a text field. If the current color is red, it changes to blue, otherwise it changes to yellow.

```
var f = this.getField("myField");
if (color.equal(f.fillColor, color.red))
    f.fillColor = color.blue;
else
    f.fillColor = color.yellow;
```

hidden

Note: This property has been superseded by the `display` (page 383) property and its use is discouraged.

If the value is `false`, the field is visible to the user; if `true`, the field is invisible. The default value is `false`.

Type: Boolean   *Access: R/W*   *Fields: all*

highlight

| 3.01 | ⓓ | | ⓕ |

Defines how a button reacts when a user clicks it. The four highlight modes supported are:

`none`: No visual indication that the button has been clicked.

`invert`: The region encompassing the button's rectangle inverts momentarily.

`push`: The down face for the button (if any) is displayed momentarily.

`outline`: The border of the rectangleinverts momentarily.

The convenience `highlight` object defines each state, as follows:

Type	Keyword
none	highlight.n
invert	highlight.i
push	highlight.p
outline	highlight.o

Type: String   *Access: R/W*   *Fields:* `button`

Example

The following example sets the `highlight` property of a button to "invert".

```
// set the highlight mode on button to invert
var f = this.getField("myButton");
f.highlight = highlight.i;
```

lineWidth

4.0	*D*		**F**

Specifies the thickness of the border when stroking the perimeter of a field's rectangle. If the stroke color is transparent, this parameter has no effect except in the case of a beveled border. Values are:

0: none

1: thin

2: medium

3: thick

In older versions of this specification, this property was `borderWidth`. The use of `borderWidth` is now discouraged, although it is still valid for backward compatibility.

The default value for `lineWidth` is 1 (thin). Any integer value can be used; however, values beyond 5 may distort the field's appearance.

Type: Integer   *Access: R/W*   *Fields: all*

Example

```
// Change the border width of the Text Box to medium thickness
f.lineWidth = 2
```

multiline

3.01	*D*		**F**

Controls how text is wrapped within the field. If `false` (the default), the text field can be a single line only. If `true`, multiple lines are allowed and they wrap to field boundaries.

Type: Boolean   *Access: R/W*   *Fields: `text`*

Example

See "Example 1" on page 249 following the Document Object getField method.

multipleSelection

5.0	*D*		**F**

If `true`, indicates that a list box allows a multiple selection of items.

See also `type` (page 335), `value` (page 398), and `currentValueIndices` (page 379).

Type: Boolean   *Access: R/W*   *Fields:* `listbox`

name

3.01			

This property returns the fully qualified field name of the field as a string object.

Beginning with Acrobat 6.0, if the Field Object (page 371) represents one individual widget, the returned name includes an appended '.' followed by the widget index.

Type: String   *Access: R*   *Fields: all*

Example

Get a Field Object and write the `name` of the field to the console.

```
var f = this.getField("myField");

// displays "myField" in console window
console.println(f.name);
```

numItems

3.01			

The number of items in a combo box or list box.

Type: Integer   *Access: R*   *Fields:* `combobox`, `listbox`

Example

Get the number of items in a list box.

```
var f = this.getField("myList");
console.println("There are " + f.numItems
    + " in this list box");
```

Face names and values of a combo box or list box can be accessed through the `getItemAt` (page 407) method. See that method for an additional example of `numItems`.

---

page

5.0			

The page number or an array of page numbers of a field. If the field has only one appearance in the document, the page property returns an integer representing the 0-based page number of the page on which the field appears. If the field has multiple appearances, it returns an array of integers, each member of which is a 0-based page number of an appearance of the field. The order in which the page numbers appear in the array is determined by the order in which the individual widgets of this field were created (and is unaffected by tab-order). If an appearance of the field is on a hidden template page, page returns a value of -1 for that appearance.

Type: Integer | Array   *Access: R*   *Fields: all*

Example 1

```
var f = this.getField("myField");
if (typeof f.page == "number")
    console.println("This field only occurs once on page "
        + f.page);
else
    console.println("This field occurs " + f.page.length
        + " times);
```

Example 2 (Acrobat 6.0)

The page property can be used to get the number of widgets associated with a field name. This example gets the number of radio buttons in a radio button field.

```
var f = this.getField("myRadio");
if ( typeof f.page == "object" )
    console.println("There are " + f.page.length
        + " radios in this field.");
```

password

3.01	*Ⓓ*		Ⓕ

Specifies whether the field should display asterisks when data is entered in the field. (Upon submission, the actual data entered is sent.) If this property is true, data in the field is not saved when the document is saved to disk.

Type: Boolean   *Access: R/W*   *Fields: text*

---

print

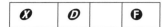

Note: This property has been superseded by the `display` (page 383) property and its use is discouraged.

If `true`, the field appears when the user prints the document. If `false`, the field does not appear when printing. This property can be used to hide control buttons and other fields that are not useful on the printed page.

Type: Boolean   *Access: R/W*   *Fields: all*

radiosInUnison

If `false`, even if a group of radio buttons have the same name and export value, they behave in a mutually exclusive fashion, like HTML radio buttons. The default for new radio buttons is `false`.

If `true`, if a group of radio buttons have the same name and export value, they turn on and off in unison, as in Acrobat 4.0.

Type: Boolean   *Access: R/W*   *Fields: `radiobutton`*

readonly

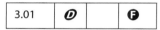

The read-only characteristic of a field. If a field is read-only, the user can see the field but cannot change it.

Type: Boolean   *Access: R/W*   *Fields: all*

Example

Get a field and make it read-only.

```
var f = this.getField("myTextField");
f.value = "You can't change this message!";
f.readonly = true;
```

rect

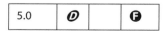

An array of four numbers in rotated user space that specify the size and placement of the form field. These four numbers are the coordinates of the bounding rectangle and are listed in the following order: upper-left *x*, upper-left *y*, lower-right *x* and lower-right *y*.

Note: The Annotation Object (page 19) also has a rect property. However, the coordinates are not in rotated user space and they are in a different order than in the Field Object (page 371) `rect` property.

Type: Array   *Access: R/W*   *Fields: all*

Example 1

Lay out a 2-inch-wide text field just to the right of the field "myText".

```
var f = this.getField("myText"); // get the Field Object
var myRect = f.rect;  // and get its rectangle

// make needed coordinate adjustments for new field
myRect[0] = f.rect[2];       // the ulx for new = lrx for old
myRect[2] += 2 * 72;         // move two inches for lry
f = this.addField("myNextText", "text",
    this.pageNum, myRect);
f.strokeColor = color.black;
```

Example 2

Move an existing button field 10 points to the right.

```
var b = this.getField("myButton");
var aRect = b.rect; // make a copy of b.rect
aRect[0] += 10;  // increment first x coordinate by 10
aRect[2] += 10;  // increment second x coordinate by 10
b.rect = aRect;  // update the value of b.rect
```

required

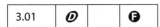

Specifies whether a field requires a value. If `true`, the field's value must be non-`null` when the user clicks a submit button that causes the value of the field to be posted. If the field value is `null`, the user receives a warning message and the submit does not occur.

Type: Boolean   *Access: R/W*   *Fields: all except* button

Example

Make "myField" into a required field.

```
var f = this.getField("myField");
f.required = true;
```

richText

If `true`, the field allows rich text formatting. The default is `false`.

Type: Boolean   *Access: R/W*   *Fields:* `text`

Related objects and properties are `richValue` (page 392), `defaultStyle` (page 380), **event**.`richValue` (page 333), `event.richChange` (page 331), `event.richChangeEx` (page 332), the Annotation Object `richContents` (page 37) property, and the Span Object (page 601).

Example 1

Get a Field Object and set it for rich text formatting.

```
var f = this.getField("Text1");
f.richText = true;
```

See "Example 2" on page 393 following richValue for a more complete example.

Example 2

Count the number of rich text fields in the document.

```
var count = 0;
for ( var i = 0; i < this.numFields; i++)
{
    var fname = this.getNthFieldName(i);
    var f = this.getField(fname);
    if ( f.type == "text" && f.richText ) count++
}
console.println("There are a total of "+ count
    + " rich text fields.");
```

richValue

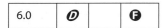

This property specifies the text contents and formatting of a rich text field. For field types other than rich text, this property is `undefined`. The rich text contents are represented as an array of Span Objects (page 601) containing the text contents and formatting of the field.

Type: Array of Span Objects   *Access: R/W*   *Fields: rich text*

Related objects and properties are `richText` (page 392), `defaultStyle` (page 380), `event.richValue` (page 333), `event.richChange` (page 331), `event.richChangeEx` (page 332), the Annotation Object `richContents` (page 37) property, and the Span Object (page 601).

Example 1

This example turns all bold text into red underlined text.

```
var f = this.getField("Text1");
var spans = f.richValue;
for ( var i = 0; i < spans.length; i++ )
{
    if( spans[i].fontWeight >= 700 )
    {
        spans[i].textColor = color.red;
        spans[i].underline = true;
    }
}
f.richValue = spans;
```

Example 2

This example creates a text field, marks it for rich text formatting, and inserts rich text.

```
var myDoc = app.newDoc();          // create a blank doc
var Bbox = myDoc.getPageBox("Crop");  // get crop box
var inch = 72;

// add a text field at the top of the document
var f = myDoc.addField("Text1", "text", 0,
    [72, Bbox[1]-inch, Bbox[2]-inch, Bbox[1]-2*inch ] );
// add some attributes to this text field
f.strokeColor = color.black;
f.richText = true;                 // rich text
f.multiline = true;                // multiline

// now build up an array of Span objects
var spans = new Array();
spans[0] = new Object();
spans[0].text = "Attention:\r";
spans[0].textColor = color.blue;
spans[0].textSize = 18;

spans[1] = new Object();
spans[1].text = "Adobe Acrobat 6.0\r";
spans[1].textColor = color.red;
spans[1].textSize = 20;
spans[1].alignment = "center";

spans[2] = new Object();
spans[2].text = "will soon be here!";
spans[2].textColor = color.green;
spans[2].fontStyle = "italic";
spans[2].underline = true;
spans[2].alignment = "right";

// now give the rich field a rich value
f.richValue = spans;
```

rotation

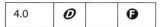

The rotation of a widget in counterclockwise increments. Valid values are 0, 90, 180, and 270.

Type: Integer　　　　*Access: R/W*　　*Fields: all*

Example

Create a rotated text field on each page and fill it with text.

```
for ( var i=0; i < this.numPages; i++) {
    var f = this.addField("myRotatedText"+i,"text",i,
        [6, 6+72, 18, 6]);
    f.rotation = 90; f.value = "Confidential";
    f.textColor = color.red; f.readonly = true;
}
```

strokeColor

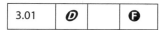

Specifies the stroke color for a field that is used to stroke the rectangle of the field with a line as large as the line width. Values are defined by using transparent, gray, RGB or CMYK color. See "Color Arrays" on page 156 for information on defining color arrays and how values are used with this property.

In older versions of this specification, this property was borderColor. The use of borderColor is now discouraged, although it is still valid for backward compatibility.

Type: Array　　　　*Access: R/W*　　*Fields: all*

Example

Change the stroke color of each text field in the document to red.

```
for ( var i=0; i < this.numFields; i++) {
    var fname = this.getNthFieldName(i);
    var f = this.getField(fname);
    if ( f.type == "text" ) f.strokeColor = color.red;
}
```

style

Allows the user to set the glyph style of a check box or radio button. The glyph style is the graphic used to indicate that the item has been selected.

The style values are associated with keywords as follows:

Style	Keyword
check	`style.ch`
cross	`style.cr`
diamond	`style.di`
circle	`style.ci`
star	`style.st`
square	`style.sq`

Type: String   *Access: R/W*   *Fields:* `checkbox`, `radiobutton`

Example

This example sets the glyph style to circle.

```
var f = this.getField("myCheckbox");
f.style = style.ci;
```

submitName

If nonempty, used during form submission instead of `name` (page 388). Only applicable if submitting in HTML format (that is, URLencoded).

Type: String   *Access: R/W*   *Fields: all*

textColor

The foreground color of a field. It represents the text color for text, button, or list box fields and the check color for check box or radio button fields. Values are defined the same as the `fillColor` (page 385). See "Color Arrays" on page 156 for information on defining color arrays and how values are set and used with this property.

In older versions of this specification, this property was `fgColor`. The use of `fgColor` is now discouraged, although it is still valid for backward compatibility.

Note: An exception is thrown if a transparent color space is used to set `textColor`.

Type: Array   *Access: R/W*   *Fields: all*

Example

This example sets the foreground color to red.

```
var f = this.getField("myField");
f.textColor = color.red;
```

textFont

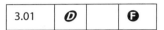

The font that is used when laying out text in a text field, combo box, list box or button. Valid fonts are defined as properties of the `font` Object (page 396). Beginning with Acrobat 5.0, arbitrary fonts can also be used. See "Use of arbitrary fonts" on page 396.

Type: String   *Access: R/W*   *Fields:* `button`, `combobox`, `listbox`, `text`

font Object

Text Font	Keyword
Times-Roman	`font.Times`
Times-Bold	`font.TimesB`
Times-Italic	`font.TimesI`
Times-BoldItalic	`font.TimesBI`
Helvetica	`font.Helv`
Helvetica-Bold	`font.HelvB`
Helvetica-Oblique	`font.HelvI`
Helvetica-BoldOblique	`font.HelvBI`
Courier	`font.Cour`
Courier-Bold	`font.CourB`
Courier-Oblique	`font.CourI`
Courier-BoldOblique	`font.CourBI`
Symbol	`font.Symbol`
ZapfDingbats	`font.ZapfD`

Use of arbitrary fonts

Beginning with Acrobat 5.0, an arbitrary font can be used when laying out a text field, combo box, list box or button by setting the value of `textFont` to the **PDSysFont font name, as returned by PDSysFontGetName**. (See the *Acrobat and PDF Library API Reference*.)

To find the **PDSysFont font name** of a font:

1. Create a text field in a PDF document. Using the UI, set the text font for this field to the desired font.

2. Open the JavaScript Debugger Console and execute the script
   ```
   this.getField("Text1").textFont
   ```
   The above code assumes the name of the field is `Text1`.

3. The string returned to the console is the font name needed to programmatically set the text font.

Example

This example sets the font to Helvetica.
```
var f = this.getField("myField");
f.textFont = font.Helv;
```

Example (Acrobat 5.0)

Set the font of "myField" to Viva-Regular.
```
var f = this.getField("myField");
f.textFont = "Viva-Regular";
```

textSize

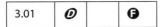

Specifies the text size (in points) to be used in all controls. In check box and radio button fields, the text size determines the size of the check. Valid text sizes range from 0 to 32767, inclusive. A value of zero means the largest point size that allows all text data to fit in the field's rectangle.

Type: Number　　　*Access: R/W*　　*Fields: all*

Example

Set the text size of "myField" to 28 points.
```
this.getField("myField").textSize = 28;
```

type

Returns the type of the field as a string. Valid types are:
```
button
```

```
checkbox
combobox
listbox
radiobutton
signature
text
```

Type: String   *Access: R*   *Fields: all*

Example

Count the number of text fields in the document.

```
var count = 0;
for ( var i=0; i<this.numFields; i++) {
    var fname = this.getNthFieldName(i);
    if ( this.getField(fname).type == "text" ) count++;
}
console.println("There are " + count + " text fields.");
```

userName

The user name (short description string) of the field. It is intended to be used as tooltip text whenever the cursor enters a field. It can also be used as a user-friendly name, instead of the field name, when generating error messages.

Type: String   *Access: R/W*   *Fields: all*

Example

Add a tooltip to a button field.

```
var f = this.getField("mySubmit");
f.userName = "Press this button to submit your data.";
```

value

The value of the field data that the user has entered. Depending on the `type` (page 397) of the field, may be a String, Date, or Number. Typically, the `value` is used to create calculated fields.

Beginning with Acrobat 6.0, if a field contains rich text formatting, modifying this property will discard the formatting and regenerate the field value and appearance using the `defaultStyle` (page 380) and plain text value. To modify the field value and maintain formatting use the `richValue` (page 392) property.

Note: For signature fields, if the field has been signed, a non-`null` string is returned as the value.

For Acrobat 5.0 or later, if the field is a list box that accepts multiple selections (see multipleSelection, page 387), you can pass an array to set the `value` of the field, and `value` returns an array for a list box with multiple values currently selected.

The `currentValueIndices` (page 379) of a list box that has multiple selections is the preferred and most efficient way to get and set the value of this type of field.

See also `valueAsString` (page 399) and `event.type` (page 335).

Type: various   *Access: R/W*   *Fields: all except* `button`

Example

In this example, the `value` of the field being calculated is set to the sum of the "Oil" and "Filter" fields and multiplied by the state sales tax.

```
var oil = this.getField("Oil");
var filter = this.getField("Filter");
event.value = (oil.value + filter.value) * 1.0825;
```

valueAsString

5.0	*D*		

Returns the value of a field as a JavaScript string.

It differs from `value` (page 398), which attempts to convert the contents of a field contents to an accepted format. For example, for a field with a value of "020", `value` returns the integer 20, while `valueAsString` returns the string "020".

Type: String   *Access: R*   *Fields: all except* `button`

Field Methods

browseForFileToSubmit

5.0	*D*		

If invoked on a text field for which the `fileSelect` (page 385) flag is set (checked), opens a standard file-selection dialog box. The path entered through the dialog box is automatically assigned as the value of the text field.

If invoked on a text field in which the `fileSelect` (page 385) flag is clear (unchecked), an exception is thrown.

Parameters

None

Returns

Nothing

Example

The following code references a text field with the file select flag checked. It is a mouse-up action of a button field.

```
var f = this.getField("resumeField");
f.browseForFileToSubmit();
```

buttonGetCaption

5.0			

Gets the caption associated with a button.

Use buttonSetCaption (page 402) to set the caption.

Parameters

nFace	(optional) If specified, gets a caption of the given type: 0: (default) normal caption 1: down caption 2: rollover caption

Returns

The caption string associated with the button.

Example

This example places pointing arrows to the left and right of the caption on a button field with icon and text.

```
// a mouse enter event
event.target.buttonSetCaption("=> "
    + event.target.buttonGetCaption()
    +" <=");

// a mouse exit event
var str = event.target.buttonGetCaption();
str = str.replace(/=> | <=/g, "");
event.target.buttonSetCaption(str);
```

The same effect can be created by having the same icon for rollover and the same text, with the arrows inserted, for the rollover caption. This approach

---

would be slower and cause the icon to flicker. The above code gives a very fast and smooth rollover effect because only the caption is changed, not the icon.

buttonGetIcon

5.0			

Gets the Icon Object (page 434) of a specified type associated with a button.

See also the `buttonSetIcon` (page 403) method for assigning an icon to a button.

Parameters

`nFace`	(optional) If specified, gets an icon of the given type:
	0: (default) normal icon
	1: down icon
	2: rollover icon

Returns

The Icon Object (page 434).

Example

```
// Swap two button icons.
var f = this.getField("Button1");
var g = this.getField("Button2");
var temp = f.buttonGetIcon();
f.buttonSetIcon(g.buttonGetIcon());
g.buttonSetIcon(temp);
```

See also `buttonSetIcon` (page 403) and `buttonImportIcon` (page 401).

buttonImportIcon

3.01			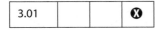

Imports the appearance of a button from another PDF file. If neither optional parameter is passed, the user is prompted to select a file.

See also `buttonGetIcon` (page 401), `buttonSetIcon` (page 403), `addIcon` (page 212), `getIcon` (page 249), `importIcon` (page 263), and `removeIcon` (page 276).

Parameters

`cPath`	(optional, Acrobat 5.0) The device-independent pathname for the file. Beginning with Acrobat 6.0, Acrobat first attempts to open `cPath` as a PDF file. On failure, Acrobat tries to convert the file to PDF from one of the known graphics formats (BMP, GIF, JPEG, PCX, PNG, TIFF) and then import the converted file as a button icon.
`nPage`	(optional, Acrobat 5.0) The 0-based page number from the file to turn into an icon. The default is 0.

Returns

An integer, as follows:

1: The user canceled the dialog

0: No error

-1: The selected file could not be opened

-2: The selected page was invalid

Example (Acrobat 5.0)

It is assumed that we are connected to an employee information database. We communicate with the database using the ADBC Object (page 10) and related objects. An employee's record is requested and three columns are utilized, *FirstName*, *SecondName*, and *Picture*. The *Picture* column, from the database, contains a device-independent path to the employee's picture, stored in PDF format. The script might look like this:

```
var f = this.getField("myPicture");
f.buttonSetCaption(row.FirstName.value + " "
    + row.LastName.value);
if (f.buttonImportIcon(row.Picture.value) != 0)
    f.buttonImportIcon("/F/employee/pdfs/NoPicture.pdf");
```

The button field "myPicture" has been set to display both icon and caption. The employee's first and last names are concatenated to form the caption for the picture. Note that if there is an error in retrieving the icon, a substitute icon can be imported.

buttonSetCaption

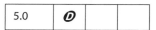

5.0	*D*		

Sets the caption associated with a button.

Use `buttonGetCaption` (page 400) to get the current caption.

See `buttonAlignX` (page 374) , `buttonAlignY` (page 375), `buttonFitBounds` (page 376), `buttonPosition` (page 376), `buttonScaleHow` (page 377), and `buttonScaleWhen` (page 377) for details on how the icon and caption are placed on the button face.

Parameters

cCaption	The caption associated with the button.
nFace	(optional) If specified, sets a caption of the given type: 0: (default) normal caption 1: down caption 2: rollover caption

Returns

Nothing

Example

```
var f = this.getField("myButton");
f.buttonSetCaption("Hello");
```

buttonSetIcon

5.0	*Ø*		

Sets the icon associated with a button.

See `buttonAlignX` (page 374) , `buttonAlignY` (page 375), `buttonFitBounds` (page 376), `buttonPosition` (page 376), `buttonScaleHow` (page 377), and `buttonScaleWhen` (page 377) for details on how the icon and caption are placed on the button face.

Use either `buttonGetIcon` (page 401) or `doc.getIcon` (page 249) to get an Icon Object (page 434) that can be used for the `oIcon` parameter of this method.

Parameters

oIcon	The Icon Object (page 434) associated with the button.
nFace	(optional) If specified, sets an icon of the given type: 0: (default) normal icon 1: down icon 2: rollover icon

Returns

Nothing

Example

This example takes every named icon in the document and creates a list box using the names. Selecting an item in the list box sets the icon with that name as the button face of the field "myPictures". What follows is the mouse-up action of the button field "myButton".

```
var f = this.getField("myButton")
var aRect = f.rect;
aRect[0] = f.rect[2];          // place list box relative to
the
aRect[2] = f.rect[2] + 144;  // position of "myButton"
var myIcons = new Array();
var l = addField("myIconList", "combobox", 0, aRect);
l.textSize = 14;
l.strokeColor = color.black;
for (var i = 0; i < this.icons.length; i++)
    myIcons[i] = this.icons[i].name;
l.setItems(myIcons);
l.setAction("Keystroke",
    'if (!event.willCommit) {\r\t'
    + 'var f = this.getField("myPictures");\r\t'
    + 'var i = this.getIcon(event.change);\r\t'
    + 'f.buttonSetIcon(i);\r'
    + '}');
```

The named icons themselves can be imported into the document through an interactive scheme, such as the example given in addIcon (page 212) or through a batch sequence.

See also buttonGetCaption (page 400) for a more extensive example.

checkThisBox

Checks or unchecks the specified widget.

Only check boxes can be unchecked. A radio button cannot be unchecked using this method, but if its default state is unchecked (see defaultIsChecked, page 406), it can be reset to the unchecked state using the resetForm (page 281) method of the Document Object (page 188).

Note: For a set of radio buttons that do not have duplicate export values, you can set the value (page 398) to the export value of the individual widget that should be checked (or pass an empty string if none should be).

Parameters

nWidget	The 0-based index of an individual check box or radio button widget for this field. The index is determined by the order in which the individual widgets of this field were created (and is unaffected by tab-order). Every entry in the **Fields** panel has a suffix giving this index; for example, MyField #0.
bCheckIt	(optional) Specifies whether the widget should be checked. The default is `true`.

Returns

Nothing

Example

Check a check box:

```
// check the box "ChkBox"
var f = this.getField("ChkBox");
f.checkThisBox(0,true);
```

clearItems

Clears all the values in a list box or combo box.

Related methods and properties include `numItems` (page 388), `getItemAt` (page 407), `deleteItemAt` (page 406), `currentValueIndices` (page 379), `insertItemAt` (page 409), and `setItems` (page 412).

Parameters

None

Returns

Nothing

Example

Clear the field "myList" of all items.

```
this.getField("myList").clearItems();
```

defaultIsChecked

5.0			

Sets the specified widget to be checked or unchecked by default.

Note: For a set of radio buttons that do not have duplicate export values, you can set the defaultValue (page 382) to the export value of the individual widget that should be checked by default (or pass an empty string if none should be).

Parameters

nWidget	The 0-based index of an individual radio button or check box widget for this field. The index is determined by the order in which the individual widgets of this field were created (and is unaffected by tab-order). Every entry in the **Fields** panel has a suffix giving this index (for example, MyField #0).
bIsDefaultChecked	(optional) If true (the default), the widget should be checked by default (for example, when the field gets reset). If false, it should be unchecked by default.

Returns

true on success.

Example

Change the default of "ChkBox" to checked, then reset the field to reflect the default value.

```
var f = this.getField("ChkBox");
f.defaultIsChecked(0,true);
this.resetForm(["ChkBox"]);
```

deleteItemAt

4.0	*⍟*		**⑤**

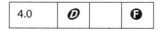

Deletes an item in a combo box or a list box.

For a list box, if the current selection is deleted, the field no longer has a current selection. If this method is invoked again on the same field and no parameter is specified, unexpected behavior can result because there is no current selection to delete. Therefore, it is important to make a new selection (such as by using the currentValueIndices method, page 379) for the method to behave as documented.

Parameters

nIdx	(optional) The 0-based index of the item in the list to delete. If not specified, the currently selected item is deleted.

Returns

Nothing

Example

Delete the current item in the list, then select the top item in the list.

```
var a = this.getField("MyListBox");
a.deleteItemAt();// delete current item, and...
a.currentValueIndices = 0;// select top item in list
```

getArray

3.01			

Gets the array of terminal child fields (that is, fields that can have a value) for this Field Object (page 371), the parent field.

Parameters

None

Returns

An array of Field Objects (page 371)

Example

This example makes a calculation of the values of the child fields of the parent field.

```
// f has 3 children: f.v1, f.v2, f.v3
var f = this.getField("f");
var a = f.getArray();
var v = 0.0;
for (j =0; j < a.length; j++) v += a[j].value;
// v contains the sum of all the children of field "f"
```

getItemAt

3.01			

Gets the internal value of an item in a combo box or a list box.

The number of items in a list can be obtained from `numItems` (page 388). See also `insertItemAt` (page 409), `deleteItemAt` (page 406), `clearItems` (page 405), `currentValueIndices` (page 379), and `setItems` (page 412).

Parameters

nIdx	The 0-based index of the item in the list or -1 for the last item in the list.
bExportValue	(optional, Acrobat 5.0) Specifies whether to return an export value: • If `true` (the default), if the item has an export value, it is returned. If there is no export value, the item name is returned. • If `false`, the method returns the item name.

Returns

The export value or name of the specified item.

Example

In the two examples that follow, assume there are three items on "myList": "First", with an export value of 1; "Second", with an export value of 2; and "Third", with no export value.

```
// returns value of first item in list, which is 1
var f = this.getField("myList");
var v = f.getItemAt(0);
```

The following example shows the use of the second optional parameter. By setting it to `false`, the item name (face value) can be obtained, even if there is an export value.

```
for (var i=0; i < f.numItems; i++)
    console.println(f.getItemAt(i,true) + ":  "
        + f.getItemAt(i,false));
```

The output to the console reads:

```
1:      First
2:      Second
Third:  Third
```

getLock

Gets a Lock Object (page 414), a generic object that contains the lock properties of a signature field.

See also `setLock` (page 413).

Parameters

None

Returns

The Lock Object (page 414) for the field.

insertItemAt

Inserts a new item into a combo box or a list box.

Related methods and properties include `numItems` (page 388), `getItemAt` (page 407), `deleteItemAt` (page 406), `clearItems` (page 405), `currentValueIndices` (page 379), and `setItems` (page 412).

Parameters

cName	The item name that will appear in the form.
cExport	(optional) The export value of the field when this item is selected. If not provided, the cName is used as the export value.
nIdx	(optional) The index in the list at which to insert the item. If 0 (the default), the new item is inserted at the top of the list. If –1, the new item is inserted at the end of the list.

Returns

Nothing

Example

```
var l = this.getField("myList");
l.insertItemAt("sam", "s", 0);
/* inserts sam to top of list l */
```

isBoxChecked

Determines whether the specified widget is checked.

Note: For a set of radio buttons that do not have duplicate export values, you can get the `value` (page 398), which is equal to the export value of the individual widget that is currently checked (or returns an empty string, if none is).

Parameters

`nWidget`	The 0-based index of an individual radio button or check box widget for this field. The index is determined by the order in which the individual widgets of this field were created (and is unaffected by tab-order).
	Every entry in the **Fields** panel has a suffix giving this index, for example, MyField #0.

Returns

`true` if the specified widget is currently checked, `false` otherwise.

Example

```
var f = this.getField("ChkBox");
if(f.isBoxChecked(0))
  app.alert("The Box is Checked");
else
  app.alert("The Box is not Checked");
```

isDefaultChecked

5.0			

Determines whether the specified widget is checked by default (for example, when the field gets reset).

Note: For a set of radio buttons that do not have duplicate export values, you can get the `defaultValue` (page 382), which is equal to the export value of the individual widget that is checked by default (or returns an empty string, if none is).

Parameters

`nWidget`	The 0-based index of an individual radio button or check box widget for this field. The index is determined by the order in which the individual widgets of this field were created (and is unaffected by tab-order).
	Every entry in the **Fields** panel has a suffix giving this index, for example, MyField #0.

Returns

`true` if the specified widget is checked by default, `false` otherwise.

Example

```
var f = this.getField("ChkBox");
if (f.isDefaultChecked(0))
   app.alert("The Default: Checked");
else
   app.alert("The Default: Unchecked");
```

setAction

Sets the JavaScript action of the field for a given trigger.

Related methods are the Bookmark Object setAction (page 145) method and the Document Object methods setAction (page 285), addRequirement (page 215), and setPageAction (page 288).

Note: This method will overwrite any action already defined for the chosen trigger.

Parameters

cTrigger	A string that sets the trigger for the action. Values are: MouseUp MouseDown MouseEnter MouseExit OnFocus OnBlur Keystroke Validate Calculate Format For a list box, use the Keystroke trigger for the Selection Change event.
cScript	The JavaScript code to be executed when the trigger is activated.

Returns

Nothing

Example

This example sets up a button field with a mouse-up action.

```
var f = this.addField("actionField", "button", 0 ,
   [20, 100, 100, 20]);
f.setAction("MouseUp", "app.beep(0);");
f.delay = true;
   f.fillColor = color.ltGray;
   f.buttonSetCaption("Beep");
   f.borderStyle = border.b;
```

```
        f.lineWidth = 3;
        f.strokeColor = color.red;
        f.highlight = highlight.p;
    f.delay = false;
```

setFocus

4.05			

Sets the keyboard focus to this field. This can involve changing the page that the user is currently on or causing the view to scroll to a new position in the document. This method brings the document the field resides in to the front, if it is not already there.

See also bringToFront (page 224).

Parameters

None

Returns

Nothing

Example

Search for a certain open document, then focus in on the field of interest. This script uses app.activeDocs (page 49), which requires the disclosed (page 193) property of the documents to be true, or the script to be run during console, batch, or menu events.

```
var d = app.activeDocs;
for (var i = 0; i < d.length; i++) {
    if (d[i].info.Title == "Response Document") {
        d[i].getField("name").value="Enter your name here: "
        // also brings the doc to front.
        d[i].getField("name").setFocus();
        break;
    }
}
```

setItems

4.0	 *D*		*F*

Sets the list of items for a combo box or a list box.

Related methods and properties include numItems (page 388), getItemAt (page 407), deleteItemAt (page 406), currentValueIndices (page 379), and clearItems (page 405).

Parameters

oArray	An array in which each element is either an object convertible to a string or another array:

- For an element that can be converted to a string, the user and export values for the list item are equal to the string.
- For an element that is an array, the array must have two subelements convertible to strings, where the first is the user value and the second is the export value.

Returns

Nothing

Examples

```
var l = this.getField("ListBox");
l.setItems(["One", "Two", "Three"]);

var c = this.getField("StateBox");
c.setItems([["California", "CA"],["Massachusetts", "MA"],
    ["Arizona", "AZ"]]);

var c = this.getField("NumberBox");
c.setItems(["1", 2, 3, ["PI", Math.PI]]);
```

setLock

Controls which fields are to be locked when a signature is applied to this signature field. No modifications can be made to locked fields. If the signature is cleared, all fields that were locked become unlocked. The property settings can be obtained using getLock (page 408).

Note: (Security ☺): The method can be executed during a batch, application initialization, console, or menu events. See "Privileged versus Non-privileged Context" on page 8 for details.

This method cannot be applied to a field that is in a document that is already signed.

Parameters

oLock	A Lock Object (page 414) containing the lock properties.

Returns

true if successful, otherwise false or throws an exception.

Lock Object

A generic JavaScript object containing lock properties. This object is passed to `setLock` (page 413) and returned by `getLock` (page 408) for a signature field. It contains the following properties.

Property	Type	Access	Description
action	String	R/W	The language-independent name of the action. Values are: `All`: All fields in the document are to be locked. `Include`: Only the fields specified in fields are to be locked. `Exclude`: All fields except those specified in fields are to be locked.
fields	Array of Strings	R/W	An array of strings containing the field names. Required if the value of action is `Include` or `Exclude`.

signatureGetModifications

7.0			

Returns an object containing information on modifications that have been made to the document after the signature field was signed. The information includes only the difference between the current and signed state of the document. Transient objects, such as objects added after the signature but then subsequently deleted, are not reported.

Parameters

None

Returns

An object containing modification information. The object has the following properties:

Property	Type	Description
formFieldsCreated	Array of Field Objects	Array of form fields created after signing.
formFieldsDeleted	Array of Generic Objects	Array of form fields deleted after signing. Each generic object in the array is a string of the form `name : type`.
formFieldsFilledIn	Array of Field Objects	Array of form fields filled in after signing.
formFieldsModified	Array of Field Objects	Array of form fields modified after signing. In this context, form field fill-in does not constitute modification.

Property	Type	Description
annotsCreated	Array of Annotation Objects	Array of annotations created after signing. If the annotation is transient (for example, a dynamically created pop-up), the corresponding element of the array is a string of the form author : name : type.
annotsDeleted	Array of Generic Objects	Array of annotations deleted after signing. Each generic object in the array is of the form author : name : type.
annotsModified	Array of Annotation Objects	Array of annotations modified after signing. If the annotation is transient (for example, a dynamically created pop-up), the corresponding element of the array is a string of the form author : name : type.
numPagesCreated	Integer	Number of pages added after signing.
numPagesDeleted	Integer	Number of pages deleted after signing.
numPagesModified	Integer	Number of pages whose content has been modified after signing (add/delete/modify of annotations/form fields are not considered as page modification for this purpose).
spawnedPagesCreated	Array of Strings	List of pages spawned after signing. For each spawned page, the name of the source template is provided.
spawnedPagesDeleted	Array of Strings	List of spawned pages deleted after signing. For each spawned page, the name of the source template is provided.
spawnedPagesModified	Array of Strings	List of spawned pages modified after signing. For each spawned page, the name of the source template is provided.

Example

This example writes modification information back to the console.

```
var sigField = this.getField( "mySignature" );
var sigMods = sigField.signatureGetModifications();

var formFieldsCreated = sigMods.formFieldsCreated;
for( var i = 0; i < formFieldsCreated.length; i++ )
    console.println( formFieldsCreated[i].name );

var formFieldsDeleted = sigMods.formFieldsDeleted;
for( var i = 0; i < formFieldsDeleted.length; i++ )
    console.println( formFieldsDeleted[i].name );

var formFieldsFilledIn = sigMods.formFieldsFilledIn;
for( var i = 0; i < formFieldsFilledIn.length; i++ )
    console.println( formFieldsFilledIn[i].name );
```

```
var formFieldsModified = sigMods.formFieldsModified;
for( var i = 0; i < formFieldsModified.length; i++ )
   console.println( formFieldsModified[i].name );

var spawnedPages = sigMods.spawnedPagesCreated;
for( var i = 0; i < spawnedPages.length; i++ )
   console.println( spawnedPages[i] );

console.println( sigMods.numPagesDeleted );
```

signatureGetSeedValue

6.0			

Returns a SeedValue Object (page 418) that contains the seed value properties of a signature field. Seed values are used to control properties of the signature, including the signature appearance, reasons for signing, and the person.

See `signatureSetSeedValue` (page 418).

Parameters

None

Returns

A SeedValue Object (page 418).

Example

Access the seed value for a signature field.

```
var f = this.getField( "sig0" );
var seedValue = f.signatureGetSeedValue();
// displays the seed value filter and flags
console.println( "Filter name:" + seedValue.filter);
console.println( "Flags:" + seedValue.flags);
// displays the certificate seed value constraints
var certSpec = seedValue.certspec;
console.println( "Issuer:" + certspec.issuer);
```

signatureInfo

5.0			

Returns a SignatureInfo Object (page 570) that contains the properties of the signature. The object is a snapshot of the signature at the time that this method is called. A security handler may specify additional properties that are specific to the security handler.

Note: (Security ☯): There are no restrictions on when this method can be called. However, the specified security handler, `oSig`, may not always be available. See the `security.getHandler` (page 553) method for details.

Some properties of a signature handler, for example, `certificates` (a property of the SignatureInfo Object, page 570), may return a `null` value until the signature is validated. Therefore, `signatureInfo` should be called again after `signatureValidate` (page 423).

Parameters

`oSig`	(optional) The SecurityHandler Object (page 557) to use to retrieve the signature properties. If not specified, the security handler is determined by the user preferences. (It is usually the handler that was used to create the signature.)

Returns

A SignatureInfo Object (page 570) that contains the properties of the signature. This type of object is also used when signing signature fields, signing FDF objects, or with the FDF Object `signatureValidate` (page 369) method.

Example

This example shows how to access SignatureInfo Object (page 570) properties.

```
// get all info
var f = getField( "Signature1" );
f.signatureValidate();
var s = f.signatureInfo();
console.println( "Signature Attributes:" );
for(i in s) console.println( i + " = " + s[i] );

// get particular info
var f = this.getField("Signature1");
// uses the ppklite sig handler
var Info = f.signatureInfo();
// some standard signatureInfo properties
console.println("name = " + Info.name);
console.println("reason = " + Info.reason);
console.println("date = " + Info.date);

// additional signatureInfo properties from PPKLite
console.println("contact info = " + Info.contactInfo);

// get the certificate; first (and only) one
var certificate = Info.certificates[0];

// common name of the signer
```

```
console.println("subjectCN = " + certificate.subjectCN);
console.println("serialNumber = " +
certificate.serialNumber);

// Display some information about this the distinguished
// name of signer
console.println("subjectDN.cn = " +
certificate.subjectDN.cn);
console.println("subjectDN.o = " + certificate.subjectDN.o);
```

signatureSetSeedValue

Sets properties that are used when signing signature fields. The properties are stored in the signature field and are not altered when the field is signed, the signature is cleared, or when `resetForm` (page 281) is called. Use `signatureGetSeedValue` (page 416) to obtain the property settings.

Note: (Security 🕗): The method can be executed during a batch, application initialization, console, or menu events. See "Privileged versus Non-privileged Context" on page 8 for details.

Seed values cannot be set for author signatures. Author signatures are signatures with a SignatureInfo Object (page 570) `mdp` property value of `allowNone`, `default`, or `defaultAndComments`.

Not allowed in Adobe Reader.

Parameters

oSigSeedValue	A SeedValue Object (page 418) containing the signature seed value properties.

Returns

Nothing

SeedValue Object

A generic JavaScript object, passed to `signatureSetSeedValue` (page 418) and returned by `signatureGetSeedValue` (page 416), which represents a signature seed value. It has the following properties:

Property	Type	Access	Description
certspec	object	R/W	A seed value CertificateSpecifier Object (page 420).
filter	String	R/W	The language-independent name of the security handler to be used when signing.

Property	Type	Access	Description
flags	Number	R/W	A set of bit flags controlling which of the following properties of this object are required. The value is the logical OR of the following values, which are set if the corresponding property is required: 1: filter 2: subFilter 4: version 8: reasons If this field is not present, all properties are optional.
legalAttestations	Array of Strings	R/W	(Acrobat 7.0) A list of legal attestations that the user can use when creating an MDP signature.
mdp	String	R/W	(Acrobat 7.0) The Modification Detection and Prevention (MDP) setting to use when signing the field. Values are unique identifiers, described in the table titled "Modification Detection and Prevention (MDP) Values" on page 578. Note that allowAll results in MDP not being used for the signature, resulting in this not being an author signature, but rather a user signature.
reasons	Array of Strings	R/W	A list of reasons that the user is allowed to use when signing.
subFilter	Array of Strings	R/W	An array of acceptable formats to use for the signature. Refer to the Signature Info object's subFilter property for a list of known formats.
timeStampspec	Object	R/W	(Acrobat 7.0) A Seed Value timeStamp Specifier Object (page 420).
version	Number	R/W	The minimum version of the signature format dictionary that is required when signing.

CertificateSpecifier Object

This generic JavaScript object contains the certificate specifier properties of a signature seed value. Used in the `certSpec` property of the SeedValue Object (page 418). This object contains the following properties:

Property	Type	Access	Description
subject	Array of Certificate Objects	R/W	Array of Certificate Objects (page 149) that are acceptable for signing. **Note:** If specified, the signing certificate must be an exact match with one of the certificates in this array.
issuer	Array of Certificate Objects	R/W	Array of Certificate Objects (page 149) that are acceptable for signing. **Note:** If specified, the signing certificate must be issued by a certificate that is an exact match with one of the certificates in this array.
oid	Array of Strings	R/W	Array of strings that contain Policy OIDs that must be present in the signing certificate. This property is only applicable if the `issuer` property is present.
url	String	R/W	A URL that can be used to enroll for a new credential if a matching credential is not found.
flags	Number	R/W	A set of bit flags controlling which of the following properties of this object are required. The value is the logical OR of the following values, which are set if the corresponding property is required: 1: `subject` 2: `issuer` 4: `oid` If this field is not present, all properties are optional.

Seed Value timeStamp Specifier Object

The properties of the seed value timeStamp specifier object are as follows:

Property	Type	Access	Description
url	String	R/W	URL of the timeStamp server providing RFC 3161 compliant timeStamp.
flags	Number	R/W	A bit flag controlling whether the time stamp is required (1) or not required (0). The default is 0.

Example 1

Sets the signing handler as PPKMS and the format as "adbe.pkcs7.sha1".

```
var f = this.getField( "sig0" );

f.signatureSetSeedValue( {
    filter: "Adobe.PPKMS",
    subFilter: ["adbe.pkcs7.sha1"],
    flags: 0x03 } );
```

Example 2

Sets the signing handler as PPKLite and the issuer of the signer's certificate as caCert. Both are mandatory seed values and signing will fail if either of constraint is not met.

```
var caCert = security.importFromFile("Certificate",
"/C/CA.cer");
f.signatureSetSeedValue({
    filter: "Adobe.PPKLite",
    certspec: {
        issuer: [caCert],
        url: "http://www.ca.com/enroll.html",
        flags : 0x02
    },
    flags: 0x01
});
```

signatureSign

5.0	*D*	*S*	*G*

Signs the field with the specified security handler. See also `security.getHandler (page 553)` and `securityHandler.login (page 562)`.

Note: (Security *S*) This method can only be executed during batch, console, menu, or application initialization events. See "Privileged versus Non-privileged Context" on page 8 for details. The `event` Object (page 314) contains a discussion of Acrobat JavaScript events.

Signature fields cannot be signed if they are already signed. Use `resetForm` (page 281) to clear signature fields.

Parameters

oSig	Specifies the SecurityHandler Object (page 557) to be used for signing. Throws an exception if the specified handler does not support signing operations. Some security handlers require that the user be logged in before signing can occur. If oSig is not specified, this method selects a handler based on user preferences or by prompting the user if bUI is true.
oInfo	(optional) A SignatureInfo Object (page 570) specifying the writable properties of the signature. See also signatureInfo (page 416).
cDIPath	(optional) The device-independent path to the file to save to following the application of the signature. If not specified, the file is saved back to its original location.
bUI	(optional, Acrobat 6.0) A Boolean specifying whether the security handler should show the user interface when signing. If true, oInfo, and cDIPath are used as default values in the signing dialog boxes. If false (the default), the signing occurs without a user interface.
cLegalAttest	(optional, Acrobat 6.0) A string that can be provided when creating an author signature. Author signatures are signatures where the mdp property of the SignatureInfo Object (page 570) has a value other than allowAll. When creating an author signature, the document is scanned for legal warnings and these warnings are embedded in the document. A caller can determine what legal warnings are found by first calling the Document Object getLegalWarnings (page 250) method. If warnings are to be embedded, an author may provide an attestation as to why these warnings are being applied to a document.

Returns

true if the signature was applied successfully, false otherwise.

Example 1

The following example signs the "Signature" field with the PPKLite signature handler:

```
var myEngine = security.getHandler( "Adobe.PPKLite" );
myEngine.login( "dps017", "/c/profile/dps.pfx" );
var f = this.getField("Signature");

// Sign the field
f.signatureSign( myEngine,
    { password: "dps017",  // provide password
      location: "San Jose, CA",   // ... see note below
```

```
            reason: "I am approving this document",
            contactInfo: "dpsmith@adobe.com",
            appearance: "Fancy"} );
```

Note: In the above example, a password was provided. This may or may not
have been necessary depending whether the `Password Timeout`
had expired. The `Password Timeout` can be set programmatically by
`securityHandler.setPasswordTimeout` (page 568).

Example 2

This example signs an author signature field

```
var myEngine = security.getHandler( "Adobe.PPKLite" );
myEngine.login( "dps017", "/c/profile/dps.pfx" );

var f = this.getField( "AuthorSigFieldName" );
var s = { reason: "I am the author of this document",
        mdp: "allowNone" };
f.signatureSign({
    oSig: myEngine,
    oInfo: s,
    bUI: false,
    cLegalAttest: "Fonts are not embedded to reduce file size"
});
```

signatureValidate

5.0	_Ⓓ_		

Validates and returns the validity status of the signature in a signature field.
This routine can be computationally expensive and take a significant amount
of time depending on the signature handler used to sign the signature.

Note: There are no restrictions on when this method can be called.
However, the parameter `oSig` is not always available. See
`security.getHandler` (page 553) for details.

Parameters

oSig	(optional) The security handler to be used to validate the signature. Its value is either a SecurityHandler Object (page 557) or a SignatureParameters Object (page 424). If this handler is not specified, the method uses the security handler returned by the signature's `handlerName` property.
bUI	(optional, Acrobat 6.0) If `true`, allows the UI to be shown when validating, if necessary. The UI may be used to select a validation handler if none is specified. The default is `false`.

Returns

The validity status of the signature. Validity values are:

-1: Not a signature field

0: Signature is blank

1: Unknown status

2: Signature is invalid

3: Signature of document is valid, identity of signer could not be verified

4: Signature of document is valid and identity of signer is valid.

See the `status` and `statusText` properties of the SignatureInfo Object (page 570).

SignatureParameters Object

A generic object with the following properties that specify which security handlers are to be used for validation by `signatureValidate` (page 423):

Property	Description
oSecHdlr	The security handler object to use to validate this signature.
bAltSecHdlr	If `true`, an alternate security handler, selected based on user preference settings, may be used to validate the signature. The default is `false`, which means that the security handler returned by the signature's `handlerName` property is used to validate the signature. This parameter is not used if `oSecHdlr` is provided.

Example

```
var f = this.getField("Signature1") // get signature field
var status = f.signatureValidate();
var sigInfo = f.signatureInfo();
if ( status < 3 )
    var msg = "Signature not valid! " + sigInfo.statusText;
else
    var msg = "Signature valid! " + sigInfo.statusText;
app.alert(msg);
```

FullScreen Object

5.0	*Ⓟ*		

The interface to fullscreen (presentation mode) preferences and properties. To acquire a `fullScreen` object, use `app.fs` (page 52).

FullScreen Properties

backgroundColor

The background color of the screen in full screen mode. See "Color Arrays" on page 156 for details.

Type: Color Array   *Access: R/W*

Example

```
app.fs.backgroundColor = color.ltGray;
```

clickAdvances

Specifies whether a mouse click anywhere on the page causes the page to advance.

Type: Boolean   *Access: R/W*

cursor

Determines the behavior of the pointer in full screen mode. The convenience `cursor` object defines all the valid cursor behaviors:

Cursor Behavior	Keyword
Always hidden	`cursor.hidden`
Hidden after delay	`cursor.delay`
Visible	`cursor.visible`

Type: Number   *Access: R/W*

Example

```
app.fs.cursor = cursor.visible;
```

defaultTransition

The default transition to use when advancing pages in full screen mode. Use `transitions (page 427)` to obtain list of valid transition names supported by the viewer.

"No Transition" is equivalent to `app.fs.defaultTransition = "";`

Type: String   *Access: R/W*

Example

Put the document into presentation mode.

```
app.fs.defaultTransition = "WipeDown";
app.fs.isFullScreen = true;
```

escapeExits

A Boolean specifying the escape key can be used to exit full screen mode.

Type: Boolean   *Access: R/W*

isFullScreen

If `true`, the viewer is in fullscreen mode rather than regular viewing mode, which is possible only if one or more documents are open for viewing.

Note: A PDF document being viewed from within a web browser cannot be put into fullscreen mode.

Type: Boolean   *Access: R/W*

Example

```
app.fs.isFullScreen = true;
```

In the above example, the viewer is set to fullscreen mode. If `isFullScreen` was previously `false`, the default viewing mode would be set. (The default viewing mode is defined as the original mode the Acrobat application was in before full screen mode was initiated.)

loop

Specifies whether the document will loop around to the beginning of the document in response to a page advance (whether generated by mouse click, keyboard, or timer) in full screen mode.

Type: Boolean   *Access: R/W*

timeDelay

The default number of seconds before the page automatically advances in full screen mode. See `useTimer` (page 427) to activate or deactivate automatic page turning.

Type: Number   *Access: R/W*

Example

```
app.fs.timeDelay = 5;      // delay 5 seconds
app.fs.useTimer = true;    // activate automatic page turning
app.fs.usePageTiming = true; // allow page override
app.fs.isFullScreen = true;  // go into fullscreen
```

transitions

An array of strings representing valid transition names implemented in the viewer. No Transition is equivalent to setting defaultTransition (page 425) to the empty string:

```
app.fs.defaultTransition = "";
```

Type: Array   *Access: R*

Example

This script produces a listing of the currently supported transition names.

```
console.println("[" + app.fs.transitions + "]");
```

usePageTiming

Specifies whether automatic page turning will respect the values specified for individual pages in full screen mode. Set transition properties of individual pages using setPageTransitions (page 292).

Type: Boolean   *Access: R/W*

useTimer

Specifies whether automatic page turning is enabled in full screen mode. Use timeDelay (page 426) to set the default time interval before proceeding to the next page.

Type: Boolean   *Access: R/W*

global Object

This is a static JavaScript object that allows you to share data between documents and to have data be persistent across sessions. Such data is called *persistent global data*. Global data-sharing and notification across documents is done through a subscription mechanism, which allows you to monitor global data variables and report their value changes across documents.

Creating Global Properties

You can specify global data by adding properties to the global object. The property type can be a String, a Boolean, or a Number.

For example, to add a variable called `radius` and to allow all document scripts to have access to this variable, the script defines the property:

```
global.radius = 8;
```

The global variable `radius` is now known across documents throughout the current viewer session. Suppose two files, `A.pdf` and `B.pdf`, are open and the global declaration is made in `A.pdf`. From within either file (`A.pdf` *or* `B.pdf`), you can calculate the volume of a sphere using `global.radius`:

```
var V = (4/3) * Math.PI * Math.pow(global.radius, 3);
```

In either file, you obtain the same result, 2144.66058. If the value of `global.radius` changes and the script is executed again, the value of `V` changes accordingly.

Deleting Global Properties

To delete a variable or a property from the `global` object, use the `delete` operator to remove the defined property. Information on the reserved JavaScript keyword `delete` can be found in the JavaScript 1.5 documentation (see "References" on page 2).

For example, to remove the `global.radius` property, call the following script:

```
delete global.radius
```

global Methods

setPersistent

3.01	*P*		

Controls whether a specified variable is persistent across invocations of Acrobat.

Persistent global data only applies to variables of type Boolean, Number, or String. Acrobat 6.0 places a 2-4 KB limit for the maximum size of the global persistent variables. Any data added to the string after this limit is dropped.

Persistent global variables are stored upon application exit in the `glob.js` file located in the user's folder for folder-level JavaScripts and re-loaded at application start. There is a 2-4 KB limit on the size of this file, for Acrobat 6.0 or later.

It is recommended that developers use a naming convention when specifying persistent global variables. For example, you can give your variables the form `myCompany_variableName`. This prevents collisions with other persistent global variable names throughout the documents.

Parameters

`cVariable`	The variable (global property) for which to set persistence.
`bPersist`	If `true`, the property will exist across Acrobat viewer sessions. If `false` (the default) the property will be accessible across documents but not across the Acrobat viewer sessions.

Returns

Nothing

Example

For example, to make the `radius` property persistent and accessible for other documents you can use:

```
global.radius = 8;    // declare radius to be global
global.setPersistent("radius", true);// now say it's
persistent
```

The volume calculation, defined above, will now yield the same result across viewer sessions, or until the value of `global.radius` is changed.

subscribe

5.0			

Allows you to automatically update fields when the value of a global variable changes. If the specified property cVariable is changed, even in another document, the specified function fCallback is called. Multiple subscribers are allowed for a published property.

Parameters

cVariable	The global property.
fCallback	The function to call when the property is changed.

Returns

Nothing

Example

In this example, there are two files, setRadius.pdf and calcVolume.pdf, open in Acrobat or Adobe Reader:

- setRadius.pdf has a single button with the code

```
global.radius = 2;
```

- calcVolume.pdf has a document-level JavaScript named subscribe:

```
// In the Advanced > JavaScripts > Document JavaScripts
global.subscribe("radius", RadiusChanged);
function RadiusChanged(x)    // callback function
{
    var V = (4/3) * Math.PI * Math.pow(x,3);
    this.getField("MyVolume").value = V;
                            // put value in text field
}
```

- With both files open, clicking on the button in setRadius.pdf immediately gives an update in the text field "MyVolume" in calcVolume.pdf of 33.51032 (as determined by global.radius =2.

The syntax of the callback function is as follows:

```
function fCallback(newval) {
// newval is the new value of the global variable you
// have subscribed to.
    < code to process the new value of the global variable >
}
```

HostContainer Object

This object manages communication between a PDF document and a corresponding host container that the document is contained within, such as an HTML page. The host container for a document is specified by the Document Object hostContainer (page 196) property.

The Embedded PDF Object (page 308) provides the corresponding API for the object model of the container application.

HostContainer Properties

messageHandler

7.0.5			

A notification object that is called if a script in the host container calls the postMessage (page 433) method. This object may expose the following methods and properties:

Method/Property	Description
onMessage	(Optional) A method that is called in response to postMessage (page 433). The message is delivered asynchronously. The method is passed a single array parameter containing the array that was passed to postMessage.
onError	(Optional) A method that is called in response to an error. The method is passed an Error Object (page 311) and an array of strings corresponding to the message that caused the error.
	The name (page 312) property of the Error Object is set to one of these:
	• "MessageGeneralError": A general error occurred.
	• "MessageNotAllowedError": The operation failed for security reasons.
	If an error occurs and this property is undefined, the error will not be delivered (unlike messages, errors are not queued).

Method/Property	Description
onDisclose	A required method that is called to determine whether the host application is permitted to send messages to the document. This allows the PDF document author to control the conditions under which messaging can occur for security reaons. The method should be set during the Doc/Open (page 315) event. The method is passed two parameters: • cURL: The URL indicating the location of the host container (for example, the URL of an HTML page using an <OBJECT> tag). • cDocumentURL: The URL of the PDF document that disclosure is being checked for. If the method returns true, the host container is permitted to post messages to the message handler.
allowDeliverWhileDocIsModal	A Boolean indicating whether messages and errors will be delivered while the document is in a modal state. By default (false), messages and errors are queued and not delivered to the onMessage and onError handlers if the application is currently displaying a modal dialog. The app.isModal (page 198) property can be used to detect this case.

Note: Instead of specifying a method, onDisclose may specify the value HostContainerDisclosurePolicy.SameOriginPolicy, which means that the document will be disclosed to the host container if they both originate from the same location. In this case, the origination is determined by the scheme, server, and port. The scheme must be http, https, or ftp for the document to be disclosed.

When these methods are invoked, the this Object (page 631) will be the messageHandler instance that the method is being called on.

Other methods and properties can be added to messageHandler provided that they do not begin with on.

If messageHandler is set to null or an object without an onMessage method, messages sent by postMessage (page 433) are queued until the property is set to a valid messageHandler instance.

Messages are guaranteed to be delivered in the order in which they are posted and errors are guaranteed to be delivered in the order in which they occurred. However, there is no correspondence between the delivery order of messages and errors.

Exceptions thrown from within the handler methods will be discarded. If an exception is thrown from within onDisclose, the function will be treated as a failure. Messages and errors will not be delivered while inside an onMessage / onError / onDisclose handler.

Adobe® Acrobat® Official JavaScript Reference

Type: Object   *Access: R/W*

Example

```
this.hostContainer.messageHandler =
{
   onMessage: function(aMessage)
   {
       for(var i = 0; i < aMessage.length; i++)
       console.println("Recv'd Msg[ " + i + "]: " +
aMessage[i]);
   },
   onError: function(error, aMessage)
   { },
   onDisclose:
HostContainerDisclosurePolicy.SameOriginPolicy
};
```

HostContainer Methods

postMessage

7.0.5			

Sends a message asynchronously to the message handler for the host container of the PDF document. For this message to be delivered, the host container (for example, an <OBJECT> element in an HTML page) must have registered for notification by setting its messageHandler (page 431) property. The message is passed to the onMessage method of the messageHandler (page 431).

The messages are submitted to a queue until they are delivered. If the queue exceeds a maximum number of messages, a parameter error is thrown until some of the messages in the queue have been delivered.

Parameters

aMessage	An array of one or more strings that are passed to the onMessage method of the messageHandler (page 431) property.

Returns

Nothing

Example

```
var aMessage = ["MyMessageName", "Message Body"];
this.hostContainer.postMessage(aMessage);
```

Icon Object

This generic JavaScript object is an opaque representation of a Form XObject appearance stored in the Document Object `icons` (page 196) property. It is used with Field Objects of type `button`. The `icon` object contains the following property:

Property	Type	Access	Description
name	string	R	The name of the icon. An icon has a name if it exists in the document-level named icons tree.

Icon Stream Object

This generic JavaScript object represents an icon stream. It is used by `app.addToolButton` (page 62) and `collab.addStateModel` (page 153). It has the following properties:

Property	Description
read(nBytes)	A function that takes the number of bytes to read and returns a hex-encoded string. The data should be the icon representation as 32 bits per pixel with 4 channels (ARGB) or 8 bits per channel with the channels interleaved. If the icon has multiple layers, the function may return the pixels for the topmost layer, followed by the next layer behind it, and so on.
width	The icon width in pixels.
height	The icon height in pixels.

The `util.iconStreamFromIcon` (page 639) method can be used to convert an Icon Object (page 434) to an Icon Stream Object.

identity Object

| 5.0 | | 𝕊 | |

This is a static object that identifies the current user of the application.

Note: (Security 𝕊): `identity` object properties are only accessible during batch, console, menu, and application initialization events to protect the privacy of the user. See "Privileged versus Non-privileged Context" on page 8 for details.

identity Properties

corporation

The corporation name that the user has entered in the Identity preferences panel.

Type: String   *Access: R/W*

email

The email address that the user has entered in the Identity preferences panel.

Type: String   *Access: R/W*

loginName

The login name as registered by the operating system.

Type: String   *Access: R*

name

The user name that the user entered in the Identity preferences panel.

Type: String   *Access: R/W*

Example

The following can be executed in the console, or, perhaps, a folder-level JavaScript.

```
console.println("Your name is " + identity.name);
console.println("Your e-mail is " + identity.email);
```

Index Object

5.0			

An object that represents a Catalog-generated index. It is non-creatable and returned by various methods of the search Object (page 538) and catalog Object (page 146). You use this object to perform various indexing operations using Catalog. You can find the status of the index with a search.

Index Properties

available

Specifies whether the index is available for selection and searching. An index may be unavailable if a network connection is down or a CD-ROM is not inserted, or if the index administrator has brought the index down for maintenance purposes.

Type: Boolean   *Access: R*

name

The name of the index as specified by the index administrator at indexing time.

See `search.indexes` (page 540), which returns an array of the Index objects currently accessed by the search engine.

Type: String   *Access: R*

Example

This example enumerates all of the indexes and writes their names to the console.

```
for (var i = 0; i < search.indexes.length; i++) {
    console.println("Index[" + i + "] = " +
search.indexes[i].name);
}
```

path

The device-dependent path where the index resides. See Section 3.10.1, "File Specification Strings", in the *PDF Reference* for exact syntax of the path.

Type: String   *Access: R*

selected

Specifies whether the index participates in the search. If `true`, the index is searched as part of the query. If `false` it is not searched. Setting or unsetting this property is equivalent to checking the selection status in the index list dialog box.

Type: Boolean   *Access: R/W*

Index Methods

build

Builds the index associated with the Index object using the Catalog plug-in. This method does not build a new index.

The index is built at the same location as the index file. If the index already exists, the included directories are scanned again for changes and the index is updated. If the index does not exist, a new index can be defined and built through the user interface.

The index build is started immediately if Catalog is idle. Otherwise, it gets queued with Catalog.

Note: (Security , Acrobat 7.0) This method can only be executed during batch or console events. See "Privileged versus Non-privileged Context" on page 8 for details. The `event` Object (page 314) contains a discussion of Acrobat JavaScript events.

Parameters

cExpr	(optional) An expression to be evaluated after the build operation on the index is complete. The default is no expression. See "JavaScript Actions" in section 8.6.4 in the *PDF Reference* for more details.
bRebuildAll	(optional) If `true`, a clean build is performed. The index is first deleted and then built. The default is `false`.

Returns

A CatalogJob Object (page 148) that can be used to check the job parameters and status.

Example

```
/* Building an index */
if (typeof catalog != "undefined")  {
   var idx = catalog.getIndex("/c/mydocuments/index.pdx");
   var job = idx.build("Done()", true);
   console.println("Status : ", job.status);
}
```

Link Object

This object is used to set and get the properties and to set the JavaScript action of a link.

Link objects can be obtained from the Document Object methods `addLink` (page 213) or `getLinks` (page 251). (See also `removeLinks` on page 277.)

Link Properties

borderColor

The border color of a Link object. See "Color Arrays" on page 156 for information on defining color arrays and how colors are used with this property.

Type: Array   *Access: R/W*

borderWidth

The border width of the Link object.

Type: Integer   *Access: R/W*

highlightMode

The visual effect to be used when the mouse button is pressed or held down inside an active area of a link. The valid values are:

```
None
Invert (the default)
Outline
Push
```

Type: String   *Access: R/W*

rect

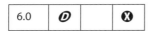

The rectangle in which the link is located on the page. Contains an array of four numbers, the coordinates in rotated user space of the bounding

---

rectangle, listed in the following order: upper-left *x*, upper-left *y*, lower-right *x* and lower-right *y*.

Type: Array   *Access: R/W*

Link Methods

setAction

Sets the specified JavaScript action for the MouseUp trigger for the Link object.

Note: This method will overwrite any action already defined for this link.

Parameters

cScript	The JavaScript action to use.

Returns

Nothing

Marker Object

A Marker object represents a named location in a media clip that identifies a particular time or frame number, similar to a track on an audio CD or a chapter on a DVD. Markers are defined by the media clip itself.

A Marker object can be obtained from the `Markers.get` (page 444) method.

Marker Properties

frame

A frame number, where 0 represents the beginning of media. For most players, markers have either a frame or a time value, but not both.

Type: Number   *Access: R*

index

An arbitrary index number assigned to this marker. Markers have sequential index numbers beginning with 0, but these index numbers may not be in the same order that the markers appear in the media.

Type: Number   *Access: R*

name

The name of this marker. Each marker in a media clip has a unique name.

Type: String   *Access: R*

Example

Get a marker by its index, then print the name of the marker to the console.

```
// assume player is a MediaPlayer object
var markers = player.markers;
// get marker with index of 2
var markers = g.get( { index: 2 } );
console.println( "The marker with index of " + markers.index
    +", has a name of " + index.name );
```

time

6.0			

A time in seconds, where 0 represents the beginning of media. For most players, markers have either a frame or a time value, but not both.

Type: Number   *Access: R*

Example

Get a named marker, then print the time in seconds from the beginning of the media, of that marker.

```
// assume player is a MediaPlayer object
var markers = player.markers;
// get marker with name of "Chapter 1"
var markers = g.get( { name: "Chapter 1" } );
console.println( "The named marker \"Chapter 1\",
    occurs at time " + markers.time);
```

Markers Object

The `markers` (page 451) property of a MediaPlayer is a Markers object that represents all of the markers found in the media clip currently loaded into the player. A marker is a named location in a media clip that identifies a particular time or frame number, similar to a track on an audio CD or a chapter on a DVD. Markers are defined by the media clip.

The constructor is `app.media.Markers`.

Markers Properties

player

6.0			

The MediaPlayer Object (page 448) that this Markers object belongs to.

Type: MediaPlayer Object   *Access: R*

Markers Methods

get

6.0			

Looks up a marker by name, index number, time in seconds, or frame number and returns the Marker Object (page 442) representing the requested marker. The object parameter should contain either a name, index, time, or frame property. A marker name can also be passed in directly as a string.

If a time or frame is passed in, the nearest marker at or before that time or frame is returned. If the time or frame is before any markers in the media, null is returned.

Parameters

An object or string representing the name, index number, time in seconds, or the frame number of the marker. The object parameter should contain either a name, index, time, or frame property. A marker name can also be passed in directly as a string.

Returns

Marker Object (page 442) or `null`

Marker index numbers are assigned sequentially starting with 0. They are not necessarily in order by time or frame. In particular, note that these are not the same values that Windows Media Player uses for marker numbers. To find all of the available markers in a media clip, call `MediaPlayer.markers.get` in a loop starting with `{index: 0}` and incrementing the number until `get` returns `null`.

Example

This example counts the number of markers on the media clip.

```
var index, i =  0;
// assume player is a MediaPlayer object.
var m = player.markers;
while ( (index = m.get ( { index: i } ) ) != null ) i++;
console.println("There are " + i + " markers.");
```

Example

```
// Get a marker by name, two different ways
var marker = player.markers.get ( "My Marker" );
var marker = player.markers.get ({ name: "My Marker" });
// Get a marker by index
var marker = player.markers.get ({ index: 1 });
// Get a marker by time
var marker = player.markers.get ({ time: 17.5 });
// Get a marker by frame
var marker = player.markers.get ({ frame: 43 });
```

MediaOffset Object

A MediaOffset represents a position in a MediaClip, specified by time or frame count. The position can be absolute (that is, relative to the beginning of the media) or relative to a named marker.

The MediaOffset object can have the properties specified below, or it can simply be a number, which is interpreted as {time: number}.

Some media formats (such as QuickTime) are time-based and others (such as Flash) are frame-based. A MediaOffset that specifies a time or frame must match the media format in use. If both time and frame are specified, the results are undefined. The incorrect one may be ignored, or a JavaScript exception may be thrown.

The MediaOffset object is used by MediaPlayer.seek (page 456), MediaPlayer.where (page 460), MediaSettings.endAt (page 466), and MediaSettings.startAt (page 472).

MediaOffset Properties

frame

A frame number. If the marker property is also present, this frame number is relative to the specified marker and may be positive, negative, or zero. Otherwise, it is relative to the beginning of media and may not be negative. Note that {frame: 0} represents the beginning of media.

Type: Number   *Access: R/W*

marker

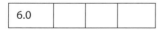

The name of a specific marker in the media.

Type: String   *Access: R/W*

time

A time in seconds, or Infinity. If the marker property is also present, this time is relative to the specified marker and is a nonnegative value, but not Infinity. Otherwise, the time is relative to the beginning of media and

---

must not be negative. Note that the offset { time: 0 } represents the beginning of media.

Type: Number   *Access: R/W*

Example

These are examples of absolute and relative offsets.

```
{ time: 5.4 } // offset 5.4 seconds from the beginning of media
{ marker: "Chapter 1", time: 17 } // 17 seconds after "Chapter
1"
```

These offsets can be used by the `MediaPlayer.seek` (page 456) method.

```
// assume player is a MediaPlayer object
player.seek({ time: 5.4 });
player.seek({ marker: "Chapter 1", time: 17 });
```

MediaPlayer Object

A MediaPlayer object represents an instance of a multimedia player such as QuickTime, Windows Media Player, or others. Its `settings` and `events` properties let you manipulate the player from JavaScript code and handle events that the player triggers. MediaPlayer is not part of a PDF file; it is a transient object created in memory when needed.

MediaPlayer Properties

annot

A reference to the screen annotation associated with a MediaPlayer. This property exists only for a MediaPlayer object that is connected to a screen annotation. The property is set by app.media.`addStockEvents` (page 122) or by methods that call `addStockEvents` indirectly, such as `app.media.openPlayer` (page 136).

Type: ScreenAnnot Object　　　　　*Access: R/W*

defaultSize

A read-only object containing the width and height of the MediaPlayer's MediaClip:

```
{ width: number, height: number }
```

If the media player is unable to provide this value, it is `undefined`.

Type: Object　　　　*Access: R*

doc

A reference to the Document Object (page 188) that owns the MediaPlayer.

Type: Object　　　　*Access: R*

events

6.0			

An Events Object (page 358) containing the EventListeners that are attached to a MediaPlayer. See Events Object (page 358) for details.

Type: Events Object   *Access: R/W*

Example

Create a media player, then modify the events of that player. The script is executed as a Rendition action with an associated rendition.

```
var events = new app.media.Events;
var player = app.media.createPlayer();
player.events.add({
    onReady: function() {
        console.println("The player is ready"); }
});
player.open();
```

hasFocus

6.0			

A Boolean that is `true` if the media player is open and has the keyboard focus.

Type: Boolean   *Access: R*

id

6.0			

The player ID for the player software that this player is using. It is `undefined` if the player has not been opened. This player ID is the same value that is found in `PlayerInfo.id` (page 489) for the media player software that implements this player.

Type: Boolean   *Access: R*

Example

Print the player ID to the console.

```
// assume args has been defined
var player = app.media.openPlayer( args )
console.println("player.id = " + player.id);
// in the console, this script could possibly print...
player.id = vnd.adobe.swname:ADBE_MCI
```

innerRect

A rectangle array representing the player's inner rectangle. As with other such arrays in Acrobat JavaScript, the coordinates are in the order [left, top, right, bottom]. The rectangle does not include a window title or other such gadgets around the edges of the player, but it does include the player controller, if present. It is undefined if the player is not open.

For a docked media player, this rectangle is in device space and is read-only (it throws an exception if you try to set it). Instead, use `triggerGetRect` (page 459) to cause a docked player to be resized. For a floating media player, the rectangle is in screen coordinates and is writable, but the user's security settings may override a value you set here. For example, if you try to move a floating media player offscreen, it may be forced back on-screen. This will not throw an exception. You can read this property after writing it to see if your value was overridden.

Type: Array   *Access: R/W*

See also `outerRect` (page 451).

isOpen

A Boolean that is `true` if the media player is currently open. Use `MediaPlayer.open` (page 454) and `MediaPlayer.close` (page 453) to open or close a player.

Type: Boolean   *Access: R*

isPlaying

A Boolean that is `true` if the media is currently playing. It is `false` if the player is not open, or if the media is paused, stopped, fast forwarding or rewinding, or in any other state.

Type: Boolean   *Access: R*

markers

6.0			

A collection of all the markers available for the current media.

See Markers Object (page 444) for details of this property.

Type: Markers Object   Access: R

Example

See "Example 2" on page 457 for an illustration of usage.

outerRect

6.0			

A rectangle array representing the player's outer rectangle. As with other such arrays in Acrobat JavaScript, the coordinates are in the order [left, top, right, bottom]. This rectangle includes any player controller, window title, and other such gadgets around the edges of the player. It is `undefined` if the player is not open.

For a docked media player, this rectangle is in device space and is read-only. It will throw an exception if you try to set it. Instead, use `MediaPlayer.triggerGetRect` (page 459) to cause a docked player to be resized. For a floating media player, the rectangle is in screen coordinates and is writable, but the user's security settings may override a value you set here. For example, if you try to move a floating media player offscreen, it may be forced back on-screen. This will not throw an exception. You can read this property after writing it to see if your value was overridden.

Type: Array   Access: R or R/W

See also `innerRect` (page 450).

page

6.0			

The page number in which a docked media player appears. It is `undefined` for players that are not docked. A docked media player can be moved to another page by changing its `page` property, which triggers a GetRect (see onGetRect, page 353) event.

Type: Number   Access: R/W

Example

Play a media clip on page 1 (base zero). The placement of the media player on page 1 is the same as the screen annotation on page 0.

```
var player = app.media.openPlayer({
    rendition: this.media.getRendition( "myClip" ),
    annot: this.media.getAnnot({
        nPage:0, cAnnotTitle:"myScreen" }),
    settings: { windowType: app.media.windowType.docked }
});
player.page = 1;
```

See onGetRect (page 353) and triggerGetRect (page 459) for variations on this same example.

settings

6.0			

Includes all of the settings that are used to create a MediaPlayer. See MediaSettings Object (page 464) for a complete list.

Note: In Acrobat 6.0, changing a property in MediaPlayer.settings after the player has been created has no effect. This may be changed in a future release to make these settings live. For compatibility with current and future releases, avoid changing any settings properties while a player is open.

Type: MediaSettings Object   *Access: R/W*

uiSize

6.0			

An array containing the size of the controller of the player for each edge of the player, in the same order as a window rectangle: [left, top, right, bottom]. Each of these values is normally a positive value or zero. These values do not include window gadgets such as title bars.

This property is not available until the Ready event is triggerd (see onReady, page 355, and afterReady, page 344). Unlike most MediaPlayer properties, it is permissible to read it during an on event method such as onReady.

Type: Array   *Access: R*

Example

Get the uiSize of the player. This code is executed as a Rendition action event.

```
var args = {
    events: {
        onReady: function () {
            console.println("uiSize = " + player.uiSize );
        }
    }
};
var player = app.media.openPlayer(args);
```

visible

6.0			

A Boolean controlling whether the player is visible. Unlike
`MediaPlayer.settings.visible` (page 473), this property takes effect
immediately. If the player is not open, reading this property returns
`undefined` and setting it throws an exception.

Setting this property may trigger events. For example, if the player is visible
and has the focus, making it invisible triggers a Blur event.

Type: Boolean   *Access: R/W*

Example

Play the audio *only* of a video clip

```
// assume a definition of args
var player = app.media.openPlayer(args);
player.visible = false;
```

MediaPlayer Methods

close

6.0			

Closes the media player if it is open. Does nothing (and is not an error) if the
player is closed.

The `eReason` parameter should be a value from the
`app.media.closeReason` (page 116) enumeration. This value is passed
through to the `event.media.closeReason` property for the Close event
(see `onClose` on page 349 and `afterClose` on page 340) that the `close`
method is triggered.

If the player has the keyboard focus, a Blur event (`onBlur`,
page 349/`afterBlur`, page 339) is triggered before the Close event. Other
events, such as Status (`onStatus`, page 357/`afterStatus`, page 348) and

Stop (`onStop`, page 357/`afterStop`, page 348), may also be triggered depending on the particular media player.

Parameters

eReason	eReason is a value from the `app.media.closeReason` (page 116) enumeration.

Returns

Nothing

open

6.0			

Attempts to open the media player as specified by `MediaPlayer.settings` (page 452). If the player is already open, an exception is thrown. If the player was previously opened and then closed, `open` may be called to open the player again. This uses the same JavaScript object as before but opens a new instance of the actual media player. In this case, for example, the new player does not remember the playback position from the old player.

For a docked player, a GetRect event (onGetRect, page 353) is triggered when the player is opened.

If `MediaPlayer.settings.autoPlay` (page 464) is `true` (which it is by default), playback begins and a Play event (`onPlay`, page 355/`afterPlay`, page 344) is triggered.

The `open` method may result in a security prompt dialog box, depending on the user's settings. It may also result in events being triggered in objects such as other media players and screen annotations. For example, if another media player has the keyboard focus, it will receive a Blur event (`onBlur`, page 349/`afterBlur`, page 339).

If `bAllowSecurityUI` is `false`, the `open` method never displays a security prompt, but returns a failure code instead.

For a media player in a floating window, additional security checks are made against the user's settings. For example, the user may specify that title bars are required on all floating player windows. If `MediaPlayer.settings.floating` (page 467) contains options that the user does not allow, `bAllowFloatOptionsFallback` controls what happens. If it is `false`, playback is disallowed and an error code is returned. If it is `true`, the options in `MediaPlayer.settings.floating` are changed as needed to conform to the user's security settings and `open` proceeds with those changed settings.

The return value is an object that currently contains one property, `code`, which is a result code from the `app.media.openCode` `(page 118)` enumeration. If your PDF is opened in a future version of Acrobat, there may be additional properties in this object, or a code value added in that future version. Be sure to handle any such values gracefully.

Parameters

`bAllowSecurityUI`	(optional) The default is `true`. See the description of this parameter given above.
`bAllowFloatOptionsFallback`	(optional) The default is `true`. See the description of this parameter given above.

Returns

An object with a `code` property

Example

See "Example 1" on page 128 for an example of usage.

pause

6.0			

Pauses playback of the current media and triggers a Pause event ("onPause" on page 354/"afterPause" on page 344). The Pause event may occur during the `pause` call or afterward, depending on the player.

The `pause` method has no effect if the media is already paused or stopped, or if playback has not yet started or has completed. Not every media player and media format supports `pause`. In particular, most streaming formats do not support `pause`. Players may either throw an exception or silently ignore `pause` in these cases.

Parameters

None

Returns

Nothing

Example

See "Example 2" on page 457 for an example of usage.

play

6.0			

Starts playback of the current media and triggers a Play event ("onPlay" on page 355/"afterPlay" on page 344). The Play event may occur during the `play` call or afterward, depending on the player.

If the media is already playing, it continues playing and no event is triggered. If it is paused, rewinding, or fast forwarding, it resumes playback at the current position. If it is stopped, either at the beginning or end of media, playback starts from the beginning.

Parameters

None

Returns

Nothing

Example

See "Example 2" on page 457 for an example of usage.

seek

6.0			

Sets the current media's playback location to the position described by the MediaOffset Object (page 446) contained in `oMediaOffset`.

If the media is playing, it continues playing at the new location. If the media is paused, it moves to the new location and remains paused there. If the media is stopped, the result will vary depending on the player.

Media players handle seek errors in different ways. Some ignore the error and others throw a JavaScript exception.

Most, but not all, media players trigger a Seek event ("onSeek" on page 356/"afterSeek" on page 347) when a seek is completed.

The seek operation may take place during the execution of the `seek` method or later, depending on the player. If `seek` returns before the seek operation is completed and you call another player method before the seek is completed, the results will vary depending on the player.

Parameters

oMediaOffset	A MediaOffset Object (page 446), the properties of which indicate the playback location to be set.

Returns

Nothing

Example 1

```
// Rewind the media clip
player.seek({ time: 0 });

// Play starting from marker "First"
player.seek({ marker: "First" });

// Play starting five seconds after marker "One"
player.seek({ marker: "One", time: 5 });
```

Example 2

The following script randomly plays (famous) quotations. The media is an audio clip (.wma) of famous quotations, which does support markers and scripts. The afterReady listener counts the number of markers, one at the beginning of each quotation. At the end of each quotation, there is also an embedded command script. The afterScript listener watches for these commands and if it is a "pause" command, it pauses the player.

```
var nMarkers=0;
var events = new app.media.Events;
events.add({
    // count the number of quotes in this audio clip,
    //save as nMarkers
    afterReady: function()
    {
        var g = player.markers;
        while ( (index = g.get( { index: nMarkers } ) ) != null )
            nMarkers++;
    },
    // Each quote should be followed by a script, if the command
    // is to pause, then pause the player.
    afterScript: function( e ) {
        if ( e.media.command == "pause" ) player.pause();
    }
});
var player = app.media.openPlayer({
    rendition: this.media.getRendition( "myQuotes" ),
    settings: { autoPlay: false },
    events: events
});
// randomly choose a quotation
function randomQuote() {
```

```
var randomMarker, randomMarkerName;
console.println("nMarkers = " + nMarkers);
// randomly choose an integer between 1 and
// nMarkers, inclusive
randomMarker = Math.floor(Math.random() * 100) % ( nMarkers )
    + 1;
// indicate what quotation we are playing
this.getField("Quote").value = "Playing quote "
    + randomMarker;
// The marker names are "quote 1", "quote 2", "quote 3", etc.
randomMarkerName = "quote " + randomMarker;
// see the marker with the name randomMarkerName
player.seek( { marker: randomMarkerName } );
player.play();
}
```

Action is initiated by the mouse-up button action such as

```
try { randomQuote() } catch(e) {}
```

setFocus

Sets the keyboard focus to the media player and triggers a Focus event ("onFocus" on page 353/"afterFocus" on page 343). If another player or PDF object has the focus, that object receives a Blur event ("onBlur" on page 349/"afterBlur" on page 339). If the media player already has the focus, nothing happens. If the player is not open or not visible, an exception is thrown.

Parameters

None

Returns

Nothing

Example

See "Example 1" on page 128 for an example of usage.

stop

Stops playback of the current media, if it is playing or paused, and triggers a Stop event ("onStop" on page 357/"afterStop" on page 348). The Stop event may occur during execution of the `stop` method or afterward, depending on the player. Does nothing if the media is not playing or paused.

Throws an exception if the player is not open.

After playback stops, the player sets the media position to either the beginning or end of media, depending on the player. If `MediaPlayer.play` (page 456) is called after this, playback starts at the beginning of media.

Parameters

None

Returns

Nothing

triggerGetRect

6.0			

Triggers a GetRect event (see "onGetRect" on page 353) to cause a docked media player to be resized.

Parameters

None

Returns

Nothing

Example

This example is similar to the one that follows `onGetRect` (page 353). Page 0 has a series of (thumbnail-size) ScreenAnnots. Below is a typical Rendition action or mouse-up button JavaScript action, when the action is executed, the media clip is resized and played.

```
var rendition = this.media.getRendition("Clip1");
var annot = this.media.getAnnot({
nPage:0,cAnnotTitle:"ScreenClip1" });
var player = app.media.openPlayer({
    rendition: rendition,
    annot: annot,
    settings: { windowType: app.media.windowType.docked },
    events: {
        onGetRect: function (e) {
            var width = e.media.rect[2] - e.media.rect[0];
            var height = e.media.rect[3] - e.media.rect[1];
            width *= 3; // triple width and height
            height *= 3;
            e.media.rect[0] = 36; // move left,upper to
            e.media.rect[1] = 36; // upper left-hand corner
            e.media.rect[2] = e.media.rect[0]+width;
```

```
                    e.media.rect[3] = e.media.rect[1]+height;
                    return e.media.rect; // return this
                }
            }
        });
        player.triggerGetRect(); // trigger the onGetRec event
```

where

6.0			

Reports the current media's playback location in a MediaOffset Object (page 446). This object contains either a time or frame property, depending on the media player and media type.

Throws an exception if the player is not open or if the player does not support where.

Parameters

None

Returns

MediaOffset Object (page 446)

Example

```
// What is the playback location in seconds?
// This code assumes that the player supports where() using
time.
var where = player.where();
var seconds = where.time;
// What chapter (marker) are we in?
var marker = player.markers.get({ time: seconds });
var name = marker ? marker.name : "no marker";
```

MediaReject Object

A MediaReject provides information about a Rendition that was rejected by a `Rendition.select` (page 523) call. It includes a reference to the original Rendition along with the reason why it was rejected. In a MediaSelection Object (page 462) returned by `select` (page 523), `MediaSelection.rejects` (page 463) is an array of MediaReject objects.

MediaReject Properties

rendition

A reference to the Rendition that was rejected in a `select` (page 523) call.

Type: Rendition Object   Access: R

Example

Get a list of rejected renditions. The script is executed as a Rendition action.

```
selection = event.action.rendition.select(true);
for ( var i=0; i<selection.rejects.length; i++)
    console.println("Rejected Renditions: "
        + selection.rejects[i].rendition.uiName);

// now play the first available rendition.
console.println( "Preparing to play " +
selection.rendition.uiName);
var settings = selection.rendition.getPlaySettings();
var args = {
    rendition: selection.rendition,
    annot: this.media.getAnnot({ nPage: 0,
        cAnnotTitle: "myScreen" }),
    settings: settings
};
app.media.openPlayer(args);
```

MediaSelection Object

The `Rendition.select` (page 523) method returns a MediaSelection object that can be used to create a MediaSettings Object (page 464) for playback.

MediaSelection Properties

selectContext

A value that can be used to write a loop that calls `Rendition.select` (page 523) repeatedly to do a customized selection based on any criteria that you can test in JavaScript code.

Type: Object   *Access: R*

Example

```
function MyTestSelection( selection )
{
    // This function should test the selection as you wish
    // and return true to use it or false to reject it and
    // try another one.
}
function MyGetSelection( rendition )
{
    var selection;
    for( selection = rendition.select(); selection;
        selection = rendition.select
            ({ oContext: selection.selectContext }))
    {
        if( MyTestSelection( selection ) )
            break;
    }
    return selection;
}
```

players

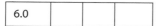

An array of strings identifying the media players that may be used to play `MediaSelection.rendition` (page 463). Both the players and rendition properties are `null` if no playable rendition is found.

Type: Array of String   *Access: R*

Example

Get a list of the players that will play the selected rendition. The code below assumes execution as a Rendition action.

```
var selection = event.action.rendition.select();
for ( var o in selection.players )
    console.println( selection.players[o].id );
```

rejects

6.0			

An array of MediaReject Objects (page 461). These are the Renditions that were rejected by the `Rendition.select` (page 523) call that returned this MediaSelection. See MediaReject Object (page 461) for details.

Type: Array of MediaReject Objects   *Access: R*

Example

See "Example" on page 461.

rendition

6.0			

The selected rendition, or `null` if none was playable.

Type: Rendition Object   *Access: R*

Example

Get the name of the selected rendition. This script is executed from a Rendition action event.

```
var selection = event.action.rendition.select();
console.println( "Preparing to play " +
selection.rendition.uiName);
```

MediaSettings Object

A MediaSettings object contains settings required to create and open a MediaPlayer. It is the value of the `settings` (page 452) property of the MediaPlayer Object. Many of these settings have default values, but some are required depending on the type of player being opened and depending on other settings. See the notes for each MediaSettings property for details.

Acrobat and the various media players will attempt to use these settings, but there is no guarantee that they will all be honored. (For example, very few players honor the `palindrome` setting, page 470.)

MediaSettings Properties

autoPlay

Specifies whether the media clip should begin playing automatically after the player is opened. If you set `autoPlay` to `false`, use `MediaPlayer.play` (page 456) to begin playback. The default value is `true`.

Type: Boolean   *Access: R/W*

Example

See the examples following `afterReady` (page 344) and `players` (page 470).

baseURL

The base URL to be used to resolve any relative URLs used in the media clip, for example, if the media opens a web page. There is no default value; if baseURL is not specified, the interpretation of a relative URL will vary depending the media player, but in most cases will not work.

Type: String   *Access: R/W*

bgColor

The background color for the media player window. The array may be in any of the color array formats supported by Acrobat JavaScript.

If bgColor is not specified, the default value depends on the window type:

- Docked: Whit
- Floating: The window background color specified in the operating system control panel
- Full Screen: The full screen background color specified in the user's Acrobat preferences

Type: Color Array   *Access: R/W*

Example

```
// Red background
settings.bgColor = [ "RGB", 1, 0, 0 ];
```

bgOpacity

6.0			

The background opacity for the media player window. The value may range from 0.0 (fully transparent) to 1.0 (fully opaque). The default value is 1.0.

Type: Number   *Access: R/W*

data

6.0			

An object, often referred to as a *MediaData object*, that a media player can use to read its media clip data, whether from an external file or embedded in the PDF. The contents of this object are not directly usable from JavaScript.

This object can be obtained from `app.media.getAltTextData` (page 129), `app.media.getURLData` (page 133), or indirectly by `Rendition.getPlaySettings` (page 522). The `data` object may be bound to the rendition's document, so it may become unavailable if the document is closed.

Type: Object   *Access: R*

Example

See the examples that follow `app.media.getURLData` (page 133).

duration

6.0			

The amount of time in seconds that playback will take. If not specified, the default is to play the entire media, or the amount of time between the

---

startAt (page 472) and endAt (page 466) points if either of those is specified.

Note that the duration may be longer than the entire media length or the difference between the startAt and endAt points. In that case, playback continues to the end of media or to the endAt point and then playback pauses at that location until the duration elapses.

Type: Number   *Access: R/W*

Example

Play a floating window with infinite duration. The playback location (from the UI) of the rendition is a floating window. The code below is executed from a form button. The floating window remains open after the player has reached the end of the media. To avoid stacked floating windows, the player is closed before reopening it.

If this script is executed from a Rendition action, the rendition can be specified through the UI and closing the player would not be necessary.

```
var rendition = this.media.getRendition("Clip");
if ( player && player.isOpen )
    try { player.close(app.media.closeReason.done);
        } catch(e) {};
var player = app.media.openPlayer({
    rendition: rendition,
    settings: { duration: Infinity }
});
```

endAt

6.0			

The ending time or frame for playback. This may be an absolute time or frame value, or a marker name, or a marker plus a time or frame, as described under MediaOffset Object (page 446). Playback ends at the specified time or frame, or as close to that point as the media player is able to stop. If endAt is not specified, the default value is the end of media.

See also startAt (page 472).

Type: MediaOffset Object   *Access: R/W*

Example

The following script plays an audio clip beginning 3 seconds into the media to 8 seconds into the media.

```
var player = app.media.openPlayer({
        rendition: this.media.getRendition( "myAudio" ),
        doc: this,
```

```
            settings: {
                startAt: 3,
                endAt: 8
            }
        });
```

floating

6.0			

An object containing properties (listed below) that define the location and style of a floating window.

This object is ignored unless `MediaSettings.windowType` (page 473) has a value of `app.media.windowType.floating` (page 121).

Defaults are used for all the floating settings if they are not specified.

Property	Type	Description
`align`	Number	Specifies how the floating window is to be positioned relative to the window specified by the over property. The value of `align` is one of the values of `app.media.align` (page 115).
`over`	Number	Specifies what window the floating window is to be aligned relative to. The value of `over` is one of the values of `app.media.over` (page 118).
`canResize`	Number	Specifies whether the floating window may be resized by the user. The value of `canResize` is one of the values of `app.media.canResize` (page 116).
`hasClose`	Boolean	If `true`, the floating window should have a close window control button.
`hasTitle`	Boolean	If `true`, a title should be displayed in the title bar.
`title`	String	This title to be displayed if `hasTitle` is `true`.
`ifOffScreen`	Number	Specifies what action should be taken if the floating window is positioned totally or partially offscreen. The value of ifOffScreen is one of the values of `app.media.ifOffScreen` (page 117).
`rect`	Array of four Numbers	An array of screen coordinates specifying the location and size of the floating window. Required if `width` and `height` are not given.
`width`	Number	The width of the floating window. Required if `rect` is not given.
`height`	Number	The height of the floating window. Required if `rect` is not given.

Type: Object   *Access: R*

Example

```
var rendition = this.media.getRendition( "myClip" );
var floating = {
    align: app.media.align.topCenter,
    over: app.media.over.appWindow,
    canResize: app.media.canResize.no,
    hasClose: true,
    hasTitle: true,
    title: rendition.altText,
    ifOffScreen: app.media.ifOffScreen.forceOnScreen,
    width: 400,
    height: 300
};
var player = app.media.openPlayer({
    rendition: rendition,
    settings: {
        windowType: app.media.windowType.floating,
        floating: floating
    }
});
```

layout

6.0			

A value chosen from the `app.media.layout` (page 117) enumeration, which defines whether and how the content should be resized to fit the window. The default value varies with different media players.

Type: Number   *Access: R/W*

monitor

6.0			

For a full screen media player, this property determines which display monitor will be used for playback. This may be either a Monitor Object (page 475) or a Monitors Object (page 477). If it is an array, the first element (which is a Monitor object) is used.

Type: Monitor or Monitors object   *Access: R/W*

Note: Only the `rect` property `MediaSettings.monitor.rect` (page 476) (in the case of a Monitor object) or `MediaSettings.monitor[0].rect` (page 476) (for a Monitors object) is used for playback.

See `monitorType` (below) for a discussion of the relationship between the `monitor` and `monitorType` properties.

Example

Play a media clip in full screen from a form button.

```
var player = app.media.openPlayer({
    rendition: this.media.getRendition("Clip"),
    settings: {
        monitor: app.monitors.primary(),
        windowType: app.media.windowType.fullScreen,
    }
});
```

Note: The user trust manager settings must allow fullscreen play back.

monitorType

6.0			

An `app.media.monitorType` value that represents the type of monitor to be selected for playback for a floating or full screen window.

Note the difference between the `monitor` and `monitorType` properties :

- `monitor` (page 468) specifies a specific monitor on the current system by defining its rectangle.
- `monitorType` specifies a general category of monitor based on attributes such as primary, secondary, and best color depth.

A PDF file that does not use JavaScript cannot specify a particular monitor, but it can specify a monitor type. When `monitorType` is specified in a call to `app.media.createPlayer` (page 126) or `app.media.openPlayer` (page 136), JavaScript code gets the list of monitors available on the system and uses `monitorType` to select one of the monitors for playback. The monitor rectangle is then used when `MediaPlayer.open` (page 454) is called to select the monitor.

Type: Number   *Access: R/W*

Example

Play a media clip in full screen on a monitor with the best color depth.

```
var player = app.media.openPlayer({
    rendition: this.media.getRendition("Clip"),
    settings: {
        monitorType: app.media.monitorType.bestColor,
        windowType: app.media.windowType.fullScreen,
    }
});
```

page

For a docked media player, this property is the number of the page on which the player should be docked. For other types of media players, this property is ignored.

Type: Number   *Access: R/W*

See also `MediaPlayer.page` (page 451).

palindrome

If this property is `true`, the media plays once normally and then plays in reverse back to the beginning. If `repeat` (page 471) is specified, this forward-and-reverse playback repeats that many times. Each complete forward and reverse playback counts as one repeat.

The default value is `false`.

Type: Boolean   *Access: R/W*

Note: Most media players do not support palindrome and ignore this setting.

Example

Use QuickTime, which supports palindrome, to view the media clip.

```
var playerList =
    app.media.getPlayers().select({ id: /quicktime/i });
var settings = { players: playerList, palindrome: true };
var player = app.media.openPlayer({ settings: settings });
```

The above code should be run within a Rendition action event with an associated rendition.

players

An array of objects that represent the media players that can be used to play this rendition. JavaScript code does not usually access this array directly but passes it through from `Rendition.select` (page 523) to the `settings` (page 452) object for `app.media.createPlayer` (page 126).

Type: Players or Array of String   *Access: R/W*

Example

List the available players that can play this rendition. This script is run as a Rendition action with associated rendition.

```
var player = app.media.openPlayer({ settings: {autoPlay:
false} });
console.println("players: " +
player.settings.players.toSource() );

// Sample output to the console:
players: [{id:"vnd.adobe.swname:ADBE_MCI", rank:0},
{id:"vnd.adobe.swname:AAPL_QuickTime", rank:0},
{id:"vnd.adobe.swname:RNWK_RealPlayer", rank:0},
{id:"vnd.adobe.swname:MSFT_WindowsMediaPlayer", rank:0}]
```

rate

A number that specifies the playback rate. The default value is 1, which means normal playback. Other values are relative to normal speed. For example, .5 is half speed, 2 is double speed, and -1 is normal speed in reverse.

Many players and media types are limited in the values they support for rate and will choose the closest playback rate that they support.

Type: Number   *Access: R/W*

Example

Play a media clip at doublespeed. This script is executed as a Rendition action.

```
var player = app.media.createPlayer();
player.settings.rate = 2;
player.open();
```

repeat

The number of times the media playback should automatically repeat. The default of value of 1 causes the media to be played once.

Many players support only integer values for repeat, but some allow non-integer values such as 1.5. A value of `Infinity` plays the media clip continuously.

The default value is 1.

Type: Number   *Access: R/W*

Example

Play a media clip from a Rendition action continuously.

```
var player =
    app.media.openPlayer({settings: { repeat: Infinity } });
```

showUI

A Boolean that specifies whether the controls of the media player should be visible or not.

The default value is `false`.

Type: Boolean   *Access: R/W*

Example

Show the controls of the media player. This script is executed as a Rendition action.

```
var player = app.media.createPlayer();
player.settings.showUI = true;
player.open();
```

or

```
app.media.openPlayer( {settings: {showUI: true} });
```

startAt

Defines the starting time or frame for playback. This may be an absolute time or frame value, or a marker name, or a marker plus a time or frame, as described under MediaOffset. Playback starts at the specified time or frame, or as close to that point as the media player is able to stop. If startAt is not specified, the default value is the beginning of media.

Type: MediaOffset Object   *Access: R/W*

See also `endAt` (page 466).

Example

See the example that follows `endAt` (page 466).

visible

6.0			

A Boolean that specifies whether the player should be visible.

The default value is `true`.

Type: Boolean   *Access: R/W*

Example

Set a docked media clip to play audio only. Script is executed as a Rendition action.

```
var args = {
    settings: {
        visible: false,
        windowType: app.media.windowType.docked
    }
};
app.media.openPlayer( args );
```

See also `MediaPlayer.visible` (page 453).

volume

6.0			

Specifies the playback volume. A value of 0 is muted, a value of 100 is normal (full) volume; values in between are intermediate volumes. Future media players may allow values greater than 100 to indicate louder than normal volume, but none currently do.

The default value is 100.

Type: Number   *Access: R/W*

windowType

6.0			

A value, chosen from the `app.media.windowType` (page 121) enumeration, that defines what type of window the MediaPlayer should be created in.

If you use the low-level function `doc.media.newPlayer` (page 306), the default value for `windowType` is `app.media.windowType.docked` (page 121).

- If an `annot` is provided (see the description of the PlayerArgs Object, page 127), the default is `app.media.windowType.docked`.
- If a `settings.floating` object is provided (see the description of the PlayerArgs Object, page 127), the default is `app.media.windowType.floating`.
- Otherwise, the default is undefined.

Type: Number   *Access: R/W*

Example

The script below creates media players with different window types. Script is executed as a Rendition action, so the selection of the specification of the rendition is not needed.

```
// Docked player that will be played in the associated
ScreenAnnot
app.media.openPlayer({
    settings: { windowType: app.media.windowType.docked }
});
// Play in full screen mode, see also monitor and monitorType
app.media.openPlayer({
    settings: { windowType: app.media.windowType.fullScreen }
});
// Show media clip in a floating window, also, see the floating
property
var args = {
    settings: {
        windowType: app.media.windowType.floating,
        floating: {
            title: "A. C. Robat",
            width: 352,
            height: 240,
        }
    }
};
app.media.openPlayer( args );
```

Monitor Object

A Monitor object represents an individual display monitor. A Monitor object can be obtained from `app.media.monitors` (page 54), which returns an array of all monitors connected to the system. `app.media.monitors` is a Monitors Object (page 477) so the methods of the Monitors object can be used to select or filter out monitors from a multiple monitor system based on different criteria. See the Monitors object for details.

The Monitor object and the Monitors Object (page 477) are used in the MediaSettings `monitor` (page 468) property.

Monitor Properties

colorDepth

The color depth of the monitor; that is, the number of bits per pixel.

Type: Number   *Access: R*

Example

Get the primary monitor and check its color depth. The `Monitors.primary` (page 482) method is use to select the primary monitor.

```
var monitors = app.monitors.primary();
console.println( "Color depth of primary monitor is "
   + monitors[0].colorDepth );
```

isPrimary

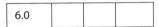

A Boolean that is `true` for the primary monitor, `false` for all other monitors.

Type: Boolean   *Access: R*

Example

Get the widest monitor and determine if it is the primary monitor.

```
var monitors = app.monitors.widest();
var isIsNot = (monitors[0].isPrimary) ? "is" : "is not";
console.println("The widest monitor "+isIsNot+"
   the primary monitor.");
```

rect

6.0			

A rectangle specifying the boundaries of the monitor in virtual desktop coordinates:

- The origin of the virtual desktop is the top left corner of the primary monitor. Therefore, the primary monitor's bounds are always in the form [0, 0, right, bottom].
- Secondary monitors may have positive or negative values in their bounds arrays, depending on where they are positioned relative to the primary monitor.

Type: Rectangle   *Access: R*

workRect

6.0			

A rectangle representing a monitor's workspace boundaries in virtual desktop coordinates. See `rect` (page 476) for information about these coordinates.

The workspace is the area of a monitor that is normally used for applications, omitting any items such as docked toolbars or taskbars. For example, running Windows on a single 800x600 display, `rect` is [0, 0, 800, 600]. With a standard Windows taskbar 30 pixels high and always visible at the bottom of the screen, `workRect` is [0, 0, 800, 570].

Type: Rectangle   *Access: R*

Monitors Object

A Monitors object is equivalent to a read-only array of Monitor Objects (page 475), each one representing a single monitor. Elements can be accessed using the usual array notation and the `length` property.

The `app.monitors` (page 54) property returns a Monitors object that includes every monitor connected to the user's system. JavaScript code can loop through this array to get information about the available monitors and select one for a full screen or pop-up media player.

Note: The Monitors object returned by `app.monitors` (page 54) is unsorted the monitors are not listed in any particular order.

The Monitors object has a number of filter methods that select one or more monitors based on various criteria. All of the monitor selection options provided in the PDF file format are implemented as calls to these filter methods.

None of the filter methods modify the original Monitors object. They each return a new Monitors object, which normally contains one or more Monitor objects. If a single monitor matches the filtering criterion better than any other, the result Monitors object contains that monitor. If more than one monitor satisfies the filtering criterion equally (for example, for the `bestColor` (page 478) method, if more than one monitor has the same greatest color depth), the result contains all of those monitors.

Several of the filter methods have an optional minimum or required parameter. If this parameter is specified and no monitor meets that minimum requirement, the result Monitors object is empty. Otherwise, the result always contains at least one monitor if the original Monitors object was not empty.

Wherever a filter method refers to height, width, or area, the dimensions are in pixels.

Example

```
var monitors = app.monitors;
for ( var i = 0; i< monitors.length; i++)
console.println("monitors["+i+"].colorDepth =
"+monitors[i].colorDepth);
```

`Monitors.length` contains the number of elements in the Monitors object. For the Monitors object returned by `app.monitors` (page 54), this is the number of monitors in the user's system. For a Monitors object returned by one of the filter methods, this number may be smaller.

Monitors Methods

bestColor

Returns a copy of the Monitors Object (page 477), filtered to include the monitor or monitors with the greatest color depth.

If nMinColor is specified, returns an empty Monitors array if the best color depth is less than nMinColor.

Parameters

nMinColor	(optional) The minimal color depth required for the monitor.

Returns

A Monitors Object (page 477)

Example

```
var monitors = app.monitors.bestColor(32);
if (monitors.length == 0 )
   console.println("Cannot find the required monitor.");
else
   console.println("Found at least one monitor.");
```

bestFit

6.0			

Returns a copy of the Monitors Object (page 477), filtered to include only the smallest monitor or monitors with at least the specified nWidth and nHeight in pixels.

Parameters

nWidth	Minimum width of the best fit monitor.
nHeight	Minimum height of the best fit monitor.
bRequire	(optional) Specifies what to return if no monitors have at least the specified width and height. If true, the method returns an empty Monitors array. If false or omitted, a Monitors array containing the largest monitor or monitors is returned.

Returns

A Monitors Object (page 477)

---

desktop

6.0			

Creates a new Monitors Object (page 477) containing one Monitor Object (page 475) that represents the entire virtual desktop. The `rect` (page 476) property is the union of every `rect` in the original Monitors object, the `workRect` (page 476) property is the union of every `workRect` in the original Monitors object, and `colorDepth` (page 475) is the minimum `colorDepth` value found in the original Monitors object.

Parameters

None

Returns

A Monitors Object (page 477)

Note: The `desktop` method is normally called directly on a Monitors object returned by `app.monitors` (page 54). If that Monitors object is first filtered by any of its other methods, the `desktop` method does the same calculations listed above with that subset of the monitors.

document

6.0			

Returns a copy of the Monitors Object (page 477), filtered to include the monitor or monitors that display the greatest amount of the document, as specified by the Document Object (page 188) parameter `doc`.

If the document does not appear on any of the monitors in the original Monitors object, the method returns an empty Monitors array if `bRequire` is `true` or a Monitors array containing at least one arbitrarily chosen monitor from the original array if `bRequire` is `false` or omitted.

Parameters

`doc`	The Document Object (page 188) of the document
`bRequire`	(optional) A Boolean. See the description above.

Returns

A Monitors Object (page 477)

filter

6.0			

Returns a copy of the Monitors Object (page 477), filtered by calling a ranker function for each monitor in the list. The ranker function takes a Monitor parameter and returns a numeric rank. The return value from `filter` is a Monitors array containing the monitors that had the highest rank (either a single monitor, or more than one if there was a tie).

Parameters

fnRanker	A (ranker) function that takes a Monitor parameter and returns a numeric rank
nMinRank	(optional) If `nMinRank` is undefined, `filter` always includes at least one monitor from the original list (unless the original list was empty). If `nMinRank` is specified, `filter` returns an empty Monitors array if no monitors had at least that rank according to the ranker function.

Returns

A Monitors Object (page 477)

Note: Most of the other Monitors filtering functions are implemented as `filter` calls.

Example

This script implements `Monitors.bestColor( minColor)`. It returns a Monitors object containing the monitor or monitors that have the greatest color depth. If `minColor` is specified, returns an empty Monitors array if the best color depth is less than `minColor`.

```
bestColor: function( minColor )
{
    return this.filter(
        function( m ) { return m.colorDepth; }, minColor );
}
```

largest

6.0			

Returns a copy of the Monitors Object (page 477), filtered to include the monitor or monitors with the greatest area in pixels.

Parameters

nMinArea	(optional) If the optional parameter nMinArea, a number, is specified, largest() returns an empty Monitors array if that greatest area is less than that value.

Returns

A Monitors Object (page 477)

leastOverlap

6.0			

Returns a copy of the Monitors Object (page 477), filtered to include the monitor or monitors that contain the smallest amount of the rectangle, as specified by the rect parameter.

Parameters

rect	A rectangle, an array of four numbers in screen coordinates.
maxOverlapArea	(optional) If maxOverlapArea is specified, the result Monitors array contains only those monitors that contain at least that much area of the rectangle, or an empty Monitors array if no monitors contain that much area of the rectangle.

Returns

A Monitors Object (page 477)

mostOverlap

6.0			

Returns a copy of the Monitors Object (page 477), filtered to include the monitor or monitors that contain the largest amount of the rectangle, as specified by the rect parameter.

If there is no monitor with at least that much overlapping area, the method returns an empty Monitors array if minOverlapArea is specified, or a Monitors array containing at least one arbitrarily chosen monitor from the original array if minOverlapArea is omitted.

Parameters

rect	A rectangle, an array of four numbers in screen coordinates.
minOverlapArea	(optional) A Boolean; see description above.

Returns

A Monitors Object (page 477)

nonDocument

6.0			

Returns a copy of the Monitors Object (page 477), filtered to include the monitor or monitors that display none of, or the least amount of, the document.

Parameters

doc	The Document Object (page 188) of the target document
bRequire	(optional) bRequire is a Boolean that determines the return value when there is no monitor that is completely clear of the document. If true, nonDocument returns an empty, or if false or omitted, nonDocument returns a Monitors array containing at least one arbitrarily chosen monitor from the original Monitors array.

Returns

A Monitors Object (page 477)

primary

6.0			

Returns a copy of the Monitors Object (page 477), filtered by removing all secondary monitors, leaving only the primary monitor if it was present in the original list.

If the primary monitor was not present in the original list, returns a Monitors array containing at least one arbitrarily chosen monitor from the original list.

Parameters

None

Returns

A Monitors Object (page 477)

Example

Get the primary monitor and check its color depth.

```
var monitors = app.monitors.primary();
// recall that each element in a monitors object is a monitor
// object, this code uses monitor.colorDepth
console.println( "Color depth of primary monitor is "
    + monitors[0].colorDepth );
```

secondary

Returns a copy of the Monitors Object (page 477), filtered by removing the primary monitor, returning only secondary monitors.

If the original Monitors object contained only the primary monitor and no secondary monitors, returns the original list.

Parameters

None

Returns

A Monitors Object (page 477)

select

6.0

Returns a copy of the Monitors Object (page 477), filtered according nMonitor, a monitor selection value as used in PDF and enumerated in app.media.monitorType (page 117).

The doc is required when nMonitor is app.media.monitorType.document or app.media.monitorType.nonDocument and ignored for all other nMonitor values.

These selection values correspond directly to the various Monitors filter methods. select calls the corresponding filter method and then, in most cases, also filters with primary (page 482) as a tie-breaker in case more than one monitor matches the main filter.

Parameters

`nMonitor`	The monitor type, a number from `app.media.monitorType` (page 117).
`doc`	A Document Object (page 188). The parameter is required if `nMonitor` is either `app.media.monitorType.document` (page 117) or `app.media.monitorType.nonDocument`, ignored otherwise.

Returns

A Monitors Object (page 477)

Example

```
// These two calls are equivalent:
settings.monitor =
app.monitors().select( app.media.monitorType.document, doc );
settings.monitor = app.monitors().document(doc).primary();
```

tallest

6.0			

Returns a copy of the Monitors Object (page 477), filtered to include only the monitor or monitors with the greatest height in pixels.

Parameters

`nMinHeight`	(optional) If `nMinHeight` is specified and no monitor has at least that height, the return value is an empty Monitors array.

Returns

A Monitors Object (page 477)

widest

6.0			

Returns a copy of the Monitors Object (page 477), filtered to include only the monitor or monitors with the greatest width in pixels.

Parameters

`nMinWidth`	(optional) If nMinWidth is specified and no monitor has at least that width, the return value is an empty Monitors array.

Returns

A Monitors Object (page 477)

Adobe® Acrobat® Official JavaScript Reference

OCG Object

An OCG object represents an *optional content group* in a PDF file. Content in the file can belong to one or more optional content groups. Content belonging to one or more OCGs is referred to as op*tional content* and its visibility is determined by the states (**ON** or **OFF**) of the OCGs to which it belongs. In the simplest case, optional content belongs to a single OCG, with the content being visible when the OCG is on and hidden when the OCG is off. More advanced visibility behavior can be achieved by using multiple OCGs and different visibility mappings.

Use the Document Object `getOCGs` (page 253) method to get an array of OCG objects for a PDF document.

The Document Object methods `addWatermarkFromFile` (page 218) and `addWatermarkFromText` (page 221) add watermarks in an OCG.

See the *PDF Reference*, Section 4.10, for additional details on optional content groups.

OCG Properties

constants

7.0			

Each instance of an OCG object inherits this property, which is a wrapper object for holding various constant values.

intents Object

An OCG's intent array can contain arbitrary strings, but those contained in this object are the only ones recognized by Acrobat.

Property	Description
design	Designates a design intent in an OCG object.
view	Designates a view intent in an OCG object.

states Object

The `states` object is used to set the initial state of the OCG (see initState, page 486).

Property	Description
on	Designates an OCG state of **ON**.
off	Designates an OCG state of **OFF**.

initState

This property is used to determine whether this OCG is on or off by default. See the `states` Object (page 486) for possible values.

Type: Boolean   *Access: R/W (Adobe Reader: R only)*

Example

Set an initial state of an OCG to off.

```
var ocgs = this.getOCGs();
ocgs[0].initState.constants.states.off;
```

locked

This property is used to determine whether this OCG is locked. If an OCG is locked, its on/off state cannot be toggled through the UI.

Type: Boolean   *Access: R/W (Adobe Reader: R only)*

name

The text string seen in the UI for this OCG. It can be used to identify OCGs, although it is not necessarily unique.

Note: In Acrobat 6.0, the `name` is read-only; for Acrobat 7.0, it is read/write.

Type: String   *Access: R/W (Adobe Reader: R only)*

Example

```
/* Toggle the Watermark OCG */
function ToggleWatermark(doc)
{
    var ocgArray = doc.getOCGs();
```

```
            for (var i=0; i < ocgArray.length; i++) {
                if (ocgArray[i].name == "Watermark") {
                    ocgArray[i].state = !ocgArray[i].state;
                }
            }
        }
```

state

6.0			

Represents the current on/off state of this OCG.

Type: Boolean   *Access: R/W*

Example

Turn on all the OCGs in the given document.

```
function TurnOnOCGsForDoc(doc)
{
    var ocgArray = doc.getOCGs();
    for (var i=0; i < ocgArray.length; i++)
        ocgArray[i].state = true;
}
```

OCG Methods

getIntent

7.0			

Returns this OCG's intent array.

An OCG will affect the visibility of content only if it has `onstants.intents.view` as an intent.

See also `setIntent` (page 488) and the `intents` Object (page 485).

Parameters

None

Returns

An array of strings. See `constants.intents` for possible values.

setAction

6.0			

Registers a JavaScript expression to be evaluated after every state change for this OCG.

Note: This method will overwrite any action already defined for this OCG.

Parameters

cExpr	The expression to be evaluated after the OCG state changes.

Returns

Nothing

Example

```
/* Beep when the given ocg is changed */
function BeepOnChange(ocg)
{
    ocg.setAction("app.beep()");
}
```

setIntent

7.0	𝒟		𝗫

Sets this OCG's intent array. An OCG should only affect the visibility of content if this array contains `constants.intents.view`. See the `intents` Object (page 485) for possible values.

See also `getIntent` (page 487) and the `intents` Object (page 485).

Parameters

aIntentArray	An array of strings to be used as this OCG's intent array.

Returns

Nothing

Example

Set the intent of all OCGs in the document to both View and Design.

```
var ocgs = this.getOCGs();
for (i=0; i < ocgs.length; i++) {
    ocgs[i].setIntent( [ocgs[i].constants.intents.view,
    ocgs[i].constants.intents.design]);
}
```

Adobe® Acrobat® Official JavaScript Reference

PlayerInfo Object

A PlayerInfo object represents a media player that is available for media playback. The `app.media.getPlayers` (page 131) method returns a PlayerInfoList Object (page 496), which is a collection of PlayerInfo objects.

PlayerInfo Properties

id

Represents a media player plug-in and associated media player. This string is not localized and is not intended for display to the user. This string may be used in the `MediaPlayer.settings.players` (page 452) array when creating a MediaPlayer, and it is also found in the `MediaPlayer.id` (page 449) property after opening a player.

Type: String   *Access: R*

Example

List player information for all media players that play "video/mpeg".

```
var playerInfoList = app.media.getPlayers("video/mpeg");

for ( var i=0; i < playerInfoList.length; i++) {
    console.println("id: " + playerInfoList[i].id)
    console.println("name: " + playerInfoList[i].name)
    console.println("version: " + playerInfoList[i].version)
}
```

mimeTypes

An array of strings listing the MIME types that this media player supports.

Type: Array of String   *Access: R*

Example

```
var qtinfo =
    app.media.getPlayers().select({id: /quicktime/i })[0];
console.println( qtinfo.mimeTypes );
```

---

name

The name of the media player. This string is localized according to the current language as found in app.language. It is suitable for display in list boxes and the like, but not for direct comparisons in JavaScript code.

Type: String   *Access: R*

version

A string containing the version number of the media player. For most players, it is the version number of the underlying media player that is installed on the user's system. This string is in dotted decimal format, for example, 7.4.030.1170 .

Type: String   *Access: R*

PlayerInfo Methods

canPlay

Checks to see if the media player can be used for playback, taking the user's security settings into account.

If the parameter bRejectPlayerPrompt is true, the method returns false if using this player would result in a security prompt. Otherwise the method returns true if playback is allowed either with or without a security prompt. (This method itself never triggers a security prompt, but a later attempt to create a media player may.)

Parameters

oDoc	A Document Object (page 188).
bRejectPlayerPrompt	A Boolean value whose default is false. If true, the method returns false if using this player would result in a security prompt. If false, the method returns true if playback is allowed either with or without a security prompt.

Returns

Boolean

canUseData

6.0			

Tells whether the player can use the specified data, as passed by its parameter oData, for playback. Returns `true` if the data can be used for playback and `false` otherwise.

Parameters

oData	A MediaData object (see `MediaSettings.data`, page 465, for a description of this object). This object is obtained in several ways, from `app.media.getAltTextData` (page 129), `app.media.getURLData` (page 133), or indirectly by `Rendition.getPlaySettings` (page 522).

Returns

Boolean

honors

7.0			

Asks a player plug-in whether it can honor all of the settings, methods, and events listed in the `args` parameter. The answer is not guaranteed to be correct, but is a best guess without opening a media player. For example, if `args.URL` is provided, the scheme (such as `"http://"`) is checked, but `honors` does not try to actually open the URL.

Note: Compatibility: `honors` is supported only on Acrobat 7.0 and above. The Acrobat SDK provides JavaScript source code that can be copied into a PDF to provide compatibility with both Acrobat 6.0 and Acrobat 7.0. This code uses hard-coded tests for Acrobat 6.0 and calls `honors` on newer versions of Acrobat. See the `playerHonors` Function (page 495) for details.

`honors` and the HonorsArgs Object (page 493) are similar to the **MH** ("must honor") entries in the PDF format, some of which can be set in the **Playback Requirements** panel of the **Rendition Settings** for a multimedia rendition. The `honors` method provides a way to choose a player that meets playback requirements dynamically in JavaScript code instead of statically in the PDF file.

Parameters

args	The HonorsArgs Object (page 493) to be tested. The HonorsArgs Object is very similar to the parameter, PlayerArgs Object (page 127), used by the `app.media.openPlayer` method. In fact, any PlayerArgs object can be used as an HonorsArgs. HonorsArgs also allows a few other options that are used only with `honors`.

Returns

A Boolean whose value is `true` if the player plug-in can honor everything in the `args` object.

Example

Play a media clip using a player that supports specific features.

```
function playWithRequirements( args )
{
    var plugins = app.media.getPlayers( args.mimeType )
    if( plugins )
    {
        for (var plugin in plugins)
        {
            if( plugin.honors(args) )
            {
                args.players = [plugin];
                return app.media.openPlayer( args );
            }
        }
    }
}
```

Play using a media player that has these capabilities for an AVI file on an http URL: It can turn off autoplay, supports the pause method, the seek method and startAt setting using a marker+time offset, and supports the Ready and Close events.

```
playWithRequirements({
    mimeType: 'video/avi',
    URL: 'http://www.foo.com/bar.avi',
    settings:
    {
        autoPlay: false,
        startAt: { marker: 'test', time: 1 },
    },
    methods:
    {
        pause:[],
        seek[ { marker: 'test', time: 1 } ],
    },
    events:
    {
```

```
                    afterReady: doAfterReady( e ),
                    onClose: doOnClose( e ),
                },
        } );
```

HonorsArgs Object

The HonorsArgs object lists settings, methods, and events that are used in a call to the `honors` (page 491) method of the PlayerInfo Object (page 489) or the `playerHonors` Function (page 495) . In this discussion, `PlayerInfo.honors` refers to both.

Any PlayerArgs Object (page 127) (as used in a call to `app.media.openPlayer`) may be used as an HonorsArgs object, or an HonorsArgs object can be created to be used in a `PlayerInfo.honors` call.

If the same object is used in `app.media.openPlayer` and `PlayerInfo.honors`, be aware that the two functions interpret unknown `args` differently. `app.media.openPlayer` ignores settings or events that it does not know about, but `PlayerInfo.honors` returns `false` if there are any settings, methods, or events it does not recognize.

For example, { `settings: { upsideDown: true }` } would be allowed in an `app.media.openPlayer` call. There is no such setting as "upsideDown", so the setting is ignored. But in a call to `PlayerInfo.honors`, this unknown setting return `false`.

Below is a complete list of the properties allowed in the HonorsArgs object. This illustration is loosely in the form of a JavaScript object literal, but it shows the type or description of each property instead of an actual property value:

```
args =
{
    mimeType: string,
    URL: string,
    settings:
    {
        autoPlay: boolean,
        baseURL: string,
        bgColor: Acrobat color array,
        duration: number,
        endAt: MediaOffset,
        layout: number,
        palindrome: boolean,
        rate: number,
        repeat: number,
        showUI: boolean,
        startAt: MediaOffset,
        visible: boolean,
        volume: number,
    },
    methods:
```

```
{
   pause: [],
   play: [],
   seek: [ MediaOffset ],
   stop: [],
   where: [],
},
events:
{
   Done: anything, onDone: anything, afterDone: anything,
   Error: anything, onError: anything, afterError: anything,
   Escape: anything, onEscape: anything, afterEscape: anything,
   Pause: anything, onPause: anything, afterPause: anything,
   Play: anything, onPlay: anything, afterPlay: anything,
   Ready: anything, onReady: anything, afterReady: anything,
   Script: anything, onScript: anything, afterScript: anything,
   Seek: anything, onSeek: anything, afterSeek: anything,
   Status: anything, onStatus: anything, afterStatus: anything,
   Stop: anything, onStop: anything, afterStop: anything,
},
}
```

Additional comments on the above listing.

- The mimeType, URL, and settings properties are identical to the corresponding properties in PlayerArgs. The mimeType property is required; the honors method does not try to determine the MIME type from the URL's file extension. URL can be a real URL or a fictitious one, as long as it is in the correct URL format. See MediaSettings Object (page 464) for a description of these properties.

- The methods property lists the MediaPlayer methods that the player must support for the given MIME type. The value of each methods property is an array containing the arguments that would be passed into a call to that method. In Acrobat 7.0, the only player method that has any arguments is seek, which takes a single MediaOffset argument. See MediaPlayer Object (page 448) for a description of these properties.

  If you use the same object as a PlayerArgs and an HonorsArgs, it can have a methods property, even though a PlayerArgs normally does not have that property. Anywhere a PlayerArgs is used, the unknown property is ignored.

- The events property lists the events that the player must support. As shown above, each event can be named with the on or after prefix or no prefix. All three mean the same thing. If a player supports a particular on event, it always supports the corresponding after event (because the after events are generated in the same way for all players). See EventListener Object (page 338) for a description of these properties.

  The notation anything means literally that: in the HonorsArgs, these values are just placeholders. So, the events object from a PlayerArgs works in an HonorsArgs:

```
events:
{
    afterReady: doAfterReady( e ),
    onClose: doOnClose( e ),
},
```

Or, if you are creating an HonorsArgs, you can simplify the notation as follows:

```
events: { Ready: true, Close: true },
```

playerHonors Function

This function is provided as JavaScript source code that can be copied into a PDF file as a document script. It performs the same tests as the honors method in Acrobat 7.0, but it works on Acrobat 6.0 as well.

When running on Acrobat 6.0, playerHonors uses hard-coded tests that match the capabilities of the media players shipped with Acrobat 6.0.

When running on Acrobat 7.0 and later, playerHonors calls honors.

Parameters

doc	A Document Object (page 188).
info	A PlayerInfo Object (page 489).
args	The HonorsArgs Object (page 493) to be tested.

Returns

A Boolean whose value is true if the player plug-in can honor everything in the args object.

Example

This example is the same as shown for the honors (page 491) method of the PlayerInfo Object (page 489), but using the playerHonors JavaScript function. This works on both Acrobat 6.0 and 7.0, provided a copy of the playerHonors source code is placed into the target PDF.

```
function playWithRequirements( args ) {
    var plugins = app.media.getPlayers( 'video/avi' )
    if( plugins ) {
        for (var plugin in plugins) {
            if( playerHonors( doc, plugin, args ) ) {
                args.players = [plugin];
                return app.media.openPlayer( args );
            }
        }
    }
}
```

PlayerInfoList Object

This object is equivalent to an array of PlayerInfo Objects (page 489). The individual elements (the PlayerInfo Objects) can be accessed using the usual array notation. The number of elements can be obtained from the `length` property.

This object is returned by the `app.media.getPlayers` (page 131) method. It has one method, `select` (page 523), which can be used to filter the list using any of the properties in a PlayerInfo.

When a media player is created using `app.media.createPlayer` (page 126), the `settings.players` property of the PlayerArgs Object (page 127) passed to the method may contain a PlayerInfoList. The created player is restricted to those in the list.

PlayerInfoList Methods

select

Returns a copy of the PlayerInfoList, filtered to include only the players that match selection criteria. If no players match, an empty array is returned.

Parameters

object	(optional) An object that contains any of the properties id, name, or version. The values of these properties may be strings or regular expressions. Specified properties are required to match. Omitted properties can match any player.

Returns

PlayerInfoList Object (page 496)

Example 1

Use QuickTime to view the media clip.

```
var playerList =
    app.media.getPlayers().select({ id: /quicktime/i });
// QuickTime supports palindrome, so let's try it.
var settings = { players: playerList, palindrome: true };
var player = app.media.openPlayer({ settings: settings });
```

Example 2

Choose the Flash player by using a pattern match on its player ID.

```
var player = app.media.createPlayer();
player.settings.players = app.media.getPlayers().select({
id:/flash/i});
player.open();
```

PlugIn Object

5.0			

This object gives access to information about the plug-in it represents. A PlugIn object is obtained using `app.plugIns` (page 55).

PlugIn Properties

certified

If `true`, the plug-in is certified by Adobe. Certified plug-ins have undergone extensive testing to ensure that breaches in application and document security do not occur. The user can configure the viewer to only load certified plug-ins.

Type: Boolean   *Access: R*

Example

Get the number of uncertified plug-ins.

```
var j=0; aPlugins = app.plugIns;
for (var i=0; i < aPlugins.length; i++)
    if (!aPlugins[i].certified) j++;
console.println("Report: There are "+j
    +" uncertified plug-ins loaded.");
```

loaded

If `true`, the plug-in was loaded.

Type: Boolean   *Access: R*

name

The name of the plug-in.

Type: String   *Access: R*

Example

```
// get array of PlugIn Objects
var aPlugins = app.plugIns;
// get number of plug-ins
var nPlugins = aPlugins.length;
// enumerate names of all plug-ins
for (var i = 0; i < nPlugins; i++)
    console.println("Plugin \#" + i + " is "
        + aPlugins[i].name);
```

path

The device-independent path to the plug-in.

Type: String   *Access: R*

version

The version number of the plug-in. The integer part of the version number indicates the major version, and the decimal part indicates the minor and update versions. For example, 5.11 would indicate that the plug-in has major version 5, minor version 1, and update version 1.

Type: Number   *Access: R*

PrintParams Object

This is a generic object that controls printing parameters that affect any document printed using JavaScript. Changing this object does not change the user preferences or make any permanent changes to the document.

In Acrobat 6.0, the Document Object `print` (page 273) method takes a PrintParams object as its argument. You can obtain a PrintParams object from the Document Object `getPrintParams` (page 258) method. The returned object can then be modified.

Many of the PrintParams properties take integer constants as values, which you can access using the `constants` (page 501) property. For example:

```
// get the printParams object of the default printer
var pp = this.getPrintParams();
// set some properties
pp.interactive = pp.constants.interactionLevel.automatic;
pp.colorOverride = pp.colorOverrides.mono;
// print
this.print(pp);
```

The `constants` (page 501) properties are all integers allowing read access only.

PrintParams Properties

binaryOK

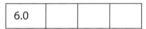

`true` if a binary channel to the printer is supported. The default is `true`.

Type: Boolean   *Access: R/W*

bitmapDPI

The dots per inch (DPI) to use when producing bitmaps or rasterizing transparency. Valid range is 1 to 9600. If the document protections specify a maximum printing resolution, the lower of the two values is used. The default is 300. Illegal values are treated as 300. See also `gradientDPI` (page 506).

Type: Integer   *Access: R/W*

colorOverride

6.0			

Specifies whether to use color override. Values are the properties of the constants `colorOverrides` Object (page 501). Illegal values are treated as `auto`, the default value.

Note: This property is supported on the Windows platform only.

colorOverrides Object

Property	Description
auto	Let Acrobat decide color overrides.
gray	Force color to grayscale.
mono	Force color to monochrome.

Type: Integer constant   Access: R/W

Example

```
var pp = this.getPrintParams();
pp.colorOverride = pp.constants.colorOverrides.mono;
this.print(pp);
```

colorProfile

The color profile to use. A list of available color spaces can be obtained from `printColorProfiles` (page 55). The default is "Printer/PostScript Color Management".

Type: String   Access: R/W

constants

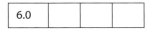

Each instance of a PrintParams object inherits this property, which is a wrapper that holds various constant values. The values are all integers allowing read access only. They are used as option values of some of the other properties of the PrintParams object, and their values are listed with the properties to which they apply.

Constant Object	Contains Constant Values for this Property
colorOverrides	colorOverride (page 501)
fontPolicies	fontPolicy (page 505)
handling	pageHandling (page 510)
interactionLevel	interactive (page 506)
nUpPageOrders	nUpPageOrder (page 509)
printContents	printContent (page 511)
flagValues	flags (page 503)
rasterFlagValues	rasterFlags (page 513)
subsets	pageSubset (page 511)
tileMarks	tileMark (page 515)
usages	usePrinterCRD (page 516) useT1Conversion (page 516)

Type: object   *Access: R*

downloadFarEastFonts

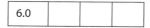

If `true` (the default), send Far East fonts to the printer if needed. Set this property to `false` if the printer has Far East fonts but incorrectly reports that it needs them.

Type: Boolean   *Access: R/W*

fileName

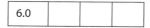

The device-independent pathname for a file name to be used instead of sending the print job to the printer (Print to File). The pathname may be relative to the location of the current document. When printing to a file, if the interaction level (see interactive, page 506) is set to `full`, it is lowered to `automatic`.

The default value is the empty string (no file name).

Note: Printing to a file produces output suitable for the printer, for example, Postscript or GDI commands.

Note: When printerName (page 512) is an empty string and fileName (page 502) is specified, the current document is saved as a PostScript file.

Type: String   *Access: R/W*

Example

```
var pp = this.getPrintParams();
pp.fileName = "/c/print/myDoc.prn";
this.print(pp);
```

Example 2

Save the current document as a PostScript file.

```
var pp = this.getPrintParams();
pp.fileName = "/c/temp/myDoc.ps";
pp.printerName = "";
this.print(pp);
```

firstPage

The first page number of the document to print. The number is 0-based. The first page of any document is 0, regardless of page number labels. The default value is 0, and values that are out of the document's page range are treated as 0.

See also lastPage (page 507).

Type: Integer   *Access: R/W*

Example

```
var pp = this.getPrintParams();
pp.firstPage = 0;
pp.lastPage = 9;
this.print(pp);
```

flags

A bit field of flags to control printing. These flags can be set or cleared using bitwise operations through the constants flagValues Object (page 504).

Zero or more flags can be set; unsupported flags are ignored. The flags default to those set by user preferences.

---

flagValues Object

Where **⊗** appears in the **Reader** column, the property is not available for any version of Adobe Reader.

Property	Reader	Description
applyOverPrint	⊗	Do overprint preview when printing. Turn off if overprinting is natively supported.
applySoftProofSettings	⊗	Use the soft proofing settings before doing color management.
applyWorkingColorSpaces	⊗	Apply working color spaces when printing.
emitHalftones	⊗	Emit the halftones specified in the document.
emitPostScriptXObjects	⊗	PostScript only, do include PostScript XObjects' content in output.
emitFormsAsPSForms	⊗	Converts Form XObjects to PS forms. The default is off.
maxJP2KRes	⊗	Use the maximum resolution of JPeg2000 images instead of the best matching resolution.
setPageSize		Enable setPageSize. Choose the paper tray by the PDF page size.
suppressBG	⊗	Do not emit the BlackGeneration in the document.
suppressCenter		Do not center the page.
suppressCJKFontSubst	⊗	Suppress CJK Font Substitution on Printer—does not apply when kAVEmitFontAllFonts is used.
suppressCropClip		Do not emit the cropbox page clip.
suppressRotate		Do not rotate the page.
suppressTransfer	⊗	Do not emit the transfer functions in the document.
suppressUCR	⊗	Do not emit UnderColorRemovals in the document.
useTrapAnnots	⊗	Print TrapNet and PrinterMark annotations, even if the print setting is "document only".
usePrintersMarks	Ⓟ	Print PrinterMark annotations, even if the print setting is "document only".

Type: Integer   *Access: R/W*

Example 1

Check the **Apply Proof Settings** check box Output options in the Advanced Printing Setup dialog box.

```
pp = getPrintParams();
fv = pp.constants.flagValues;
// or pp.flags |= fv.applySoftProofSettings;;
pp.flags = pp.flags | fv.applySoftProofSettings;
this.print(pp);
```

Example 2

Uncheck **Auto-Rotate and Center** (checked by default) in the Print dialog box.

```
pp = getPrintParams();
fv = pp.constants.flagValues;
pp.flags |= (fv.suppressCenter | fv.suppressRotate);
this.print(pp);
```

Example 3

Check **Emit Undercolor Removal/Black Generation** check box of the PostScript Options in the Advanced Printing Setup dialog box.

```
pp = getPrintParams();
fv = pp.constants.flagValues;
pp.flags &= ~(fv.suppressBG | fv.suppressUCR)
this.print(pp)
```

fontPolicy

6.0			

Sets the font policy. The value of the `fontpolicy` property is set through the constants `fontPolicies` Object (page 505). The default is `pageRange`.

Type: Integer   *Access: R/W*

fontPolicies Object

Property	Description
everyPage	Emit needed fonts before every page and free all fonts after each page. This produces the largest, slowest print jobs, but requires the least amount of memory from the printer.
jobStart	Emit needed fonts at the beginning of the print job and free them at the end of the print job. This produces the smallest, fastest print jobs, but requires the most memory from the printer.

Property	Description
pageRange	(Default) Emit fonts before the first page that uses them and free them after the last page that uses them. This also produces the smallest and fastest print jobs and can use less memory. However, the print job must be printed as produced because of page ordering. **Note:** pageRange can be a good compromise between speed and memory. However, do not use it if the PostScript pages will be programmatically reordered afterwards.

gradientDPI

6.0			**⊗**

The dots per inch to use when rasterizing gradients. This value can generally be set lower than bitmapDPI (page 500) because it affects areas to which the eye is less sensitive. It must be set from 1 to 9600. Illegal values are treated as 150. If the document protections specify a maximum printing resolution, the lower of the two values will be used. The default value is 150.

Type: Integer   *Access: R/W*

interactive

6.0			

Specifies the level of interaction between the user and the print job. The value of this property is set through the constants InteractionLevel Object (page 507). The default is full.

(Security ⊘, Acrobat 7.0) Non-interactive printing can only be executed during batch, console, and menu events. Printing is made non-interactive by setting bUI to false when calling the Document object print method or by setting the interactive (page 506) property to silent, for example,

```
var pp = this.getPrintParams();
pp.interactive =
pp.constants.interactionLevel.silent;
```

Outside of batch, console, and menu events, the values of bUI and of interactive (page 506) are ignored, and a print dialog box will always be presented.

Note:

See also "Privileged versus Non-privileged Context" on page 8.

Type: Integer   *Access: R/W*

InteractionLevel Object

Property	Description
automatic	No print dialog is displayed. During printing, a progress monitor and cancel dialog box is displayed and removed automatically when printing is complete.
full	Displays the print dialog box, allowing the user to change print settings and requiring the user to press OK to continue. During printing, a progress monitor and cancel dialog box is displayed and removed automatically when printing is complete.
silent	No print dialog box is displayed. No progress or cancel dialog box is displayed. Even error messages are not displayed.

Example

```
var pp = this.getPrintParams();
pp.interactive = pp.constants.interactionLevel.automatic;
pp.printerName = "Adobe PDF";
this.print(pp);
```

lastPage

6.0			

The last 0-based page number of the document to print. The term "0-based" means the first page of any document is 0, regardless of page number labels. If the value is less than firstPage (page 503) or outside the legal range of the document, this reverts to the default value. The default value is the number of pages in the document less one.

Type: Integer　　　*Access: R/W*

See firstPage (page 503) for an example.

nUpAutoRotate

7.0			

A Boolean that if true, automatically rotates each page to match the page orientation to the available paper area during Multiple Pages Per Sheet printing. The default is false, but nUpAutoRotate obeys the print settings.

Multiple Pages Per Sheet is obtained by setting pageHandling (page 510) to nUp.

Type: Boolean　　　*Access: R/W*

nUpNumPagesH

7.0			

When printing Multiple Pages Per Sheet, `nUpNumPagesH` sets is the number of pages to be laid out in the horizontal direction. The default is 2, but `nUpNumPagesH` obeys the print settings.

Multiple Pages Per Sheet is obtained by setting `pageHandling` (page 510) to `nUp`.

Type: Integer   *Access: R/W*

Example

Perform Multiple Pages Per Sheet printing on this document, set up parameters, and print.

```
pp = this.getPrintParams();
pp.pageHandling = pp.constants.handling.nUp;
pp.nUpPageOrders = pp.constants.nUpPageOrders.Vertical;
pp.nUpNumPagesH = 3;
pp.nUpNumPagesV = 3;
pp.nUpPageBorder=true;
pp.nUpAutoRotate=true;
this.print(pp);
```

nUpNumPagesV

7.0			

When printing Multiple Pages Per Sheet, `nUpNumPagesV` is the number of pages to be laid out in the vertical direction. The default is 2, but `nUpNumPagesV` obeys the print settings.

Multiple Pages Per Sheet is obtained by setting `pageHandling` (page 510) to `nUp`.

Type: Integer   *Access: R/W*

See `nUpNumPagesH` (page 508) for an example.

nUpPageBorder

7.0			

A Boolean that if `true`, draws and prints a page boundary around each of the pages during Multiple Pages Per Sheet printing. The default is `false`, but `nUpPageBorder` obeys the print settings.

Multiple Pages Per Sheet is obtained by setting `pageHandling` (page 510) to nUp.

Type: Boolean   *Access: R/W*

See `nUpNumPagesH` (page 508) for an example.

nUpPageOrder

7.0			

When printing multiple pages per sheet, the `nUpPageOrder` property determines how the multiple pages are laid out on the sheet. The value of the `nUpPageOrder` property is set through the constants `nUpPageOrders Object` (page 509). The default is `Horizontal`, but `nUpPageOrder` obeys the print settings.

Multiple Pages Per Sheet is obtained by setting `pageHandling` (page 510) to nUp.

Type: Integer   *Access: R/W*

nUpPageOrders Object

Property	Description
Horizontal	Pages are placed from left to right, from top to bottom.
HorizontalReversed	Pages are placed from right to left, from top to bottom.
Vertical	Pages are placed from top to bottom, from left to right.
VerticalReversed	Pages are placed from top to bottom, from right to left.

Example

Perform Multiple Pages Per Sheet printing on this document, set the parameters, and print.

```
pp = this.getPrintParams();
pp.pageHandling = pp.constants.handling.nUp;
pp.nUpPageOrders = pp.constants.nUpPageOrders.Horizontal;
pp.nUpNumPagesH = 2;
pp.nUpNumPagesV = 2;
pp.nUpPageBorder=true;
this.print(pp);
```

pageHandling

6.0			

Takes one of four values specified by the constants `handling` Object (page 510). If set to an illegal value, it is treated as `shrink`. The default is `shrink`.

Type: Integer   *Access: R/W*

handling Object

Property	Reader	Description
`none`		No page scaling is applied.
`fit`		Pages are enlarged or shrunk to fit the printer's paper.
`shrink`		Small pages are printed small, and large pages are shrunk to fit on the printer's paper.
`tileAll`	⊗	All pages are printed using tiling settings. This can be used to turn a normal-sized page into a poster by setting the `tileScale` (page 515) property greater than 1.
`tileLarge`	⊗	Small or normal pages are printed in the original size and large pages are printed on multiple sheets of paper.
`nUp`		(Acrobat 7.0) Pages are rescaled to print multiple pages on each printer page. Properties related to Multiple Pages Per Sheet printing are `nUpAutoRotate` (page 507), `nUpNumPagesH` (page 508), `nUpNumPagesV` (page 508), `nUpPageBorder` (page 508), and `nUpPageOrder` (page 509).

Example 1

```
var pp = this.getPrintParams();
pp.pageHandling = pp.constants.handling.shrink;
this.print(pp);
```

Example 2

Perform Multiple Pages Per Sheet printing on this document, set the parameters and print.

```
pp = this.getPrintParams();
pp.pageHandling = pp.constants.handling.nUp;
pp.nUpPageOrders = pp.constants.nUpPageOrders.Horizontal;
pp.nUpNumPagesH = 2;
pp.nUpNumPagesV = 2;
pp.nUpPageBorder=true;
this.print(pp);
```

pageSubset

6.0			

Select even, odd, or all the pages to print. The value of `pageSubset` is set through the constants `subsets` Object (page 511). The default is `all`.

Type: Integer   *Access: R/W*

subsets Object

Property	Description
all	Print all pages in the page range.
even	Print only the even pages. Page labels are ignored, and the document is treated as if it were numbered 1 through n, the number of pages.
odd	Print only the odd pages.

Example

```
var pp = this.getPrintParams();
pp.pageSubset = pp.constants.subsets.even;
this.print(pp);
```

printAsImage

6.0			

Set to `true` to send pages as large bitmaps. This can be slow and more jagged looking but can work around problems with a printer's PostScript interpreter. Set `bitmapDPI` (page 500) to increase or decrease the resolution of the bitmap. If interaction (see interactive, page 506) is `full`, the user's printer preferences for `printAsImage` will be used. The default is `false`.

Type: Boolean   *Access: R/W*

printContent

6.0			

Sets the contents of the print job. The value of the `printContent` property is set through the constants `printContents` Object (page 512). The default is `doc`.

Type: Integer   *Access: R/W*

printContents Object

Property	Description
doc	Print the document contents, not comments.
docAndComments	Print the document contents and comments.
formFieldsOnly	Print the contents of form fields only. Useful for printing onto pre-preprinted forms.

Example

```
var pp = this.getPrintParams();
pp.interactive = pp.constants.interactionLevel.silent;
pp.printContent = pp.constants.printContents.formFieldsOnly;
this.print(pp);
```

printerName

6.0			

The name of the destination printer. This property is a Windows-only feature. Currently, the destination printer cannot be set through this property on the Macintosh.

By default, printerName is set to the name of the default printer. If you set printerName to an empty string, the default printer is used. When printerName is an empty string and fileName (page 502) is a nonempty string, the current document is saved as a PostScript file. See **Example 2** below.

See also app.printerNames (page 56).

Type: String   *Access: R/W*

Example 1

```
var pp = this.getPrintParams();
pp.printerName = "hp officejet d series";
this.print(pp);
```

Example 2

Save the current document as a PostScript file.

```
var pp = this.getPrintParams();
pp.fileName = "/c/temp/myDoc.ps";
pp.printerName = "";
this.print(pp);
```

psLevel

Level of PostScript that is emitted to PostScript printers. Level 0 indicates to use the PostScript level of the printer. Level 1 is not supported. In addition to 0, current legal values of psLevel are 2 and 3. If the printer only supports PostScript level 1, printAsImage (page 511) is set to true. Illegal values are treated as 3. The default value for psLevel is 3.

Type: Integer   *Access: R/W*

rasterFlags

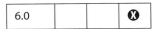

A bit field of flags. These flags can be set or cleared using bitwise operations through the constants rasterFlagValues Object (page 513). The default is set by user preferences.

Type: Integer   *Access: R/W*

rasterFlagValues Object

Property	Reader	Description
textToOutline	✖	Text converted to outlines can become thicker (especially noticeable on small fonts). If text is mixed into artwork with transparency, it may be converted to outline during flattening, resulting in inconsistency with text that is not mixed into artwork. In this case, turning on this option ensures that all text looks consistent.
strokesToOutline	✖	Strokes converted to outlines can become thicker (especially noticeable on thin strokes). If strokes are mixed into artwork with transparency, they may be converted to outlines during flattening, resulting in inconsistency with strokes that are not mixed into artwork. In this case, turning on this option ensures that all strokes look consistent.

Property	Reader	Description
allowComplexClip	Ⓧ	This option ensures that the boundaries between vector artwork and rasterized artwork fall closely along object paths. Selecting this option reduces stitching artifacts that result when part of an object is flattened while another part of the object remains in vector form. However, selecting this option may result in paths that are too complex for the printer to handle.
preserveOverprint	Ⓧ	Select this option if you are printing separations and the document contains overprinted objects. Selecting this option generally preserves overprint for objects that are not involved in transparency and therefore improves performance. This option has no effect when printing composite. Turning it off might result in more consistent output because all overprinting will be flattened, whether or not it is involved in transparency.

Example 1

Check the "Convert All Text to Outlines" check box in the Transparency Flattening option of the Advanced Print Setup.

```
pp = getPrintParams();
rf = pp.constants.rasterFlagValues;
pp.rasterFlags |= rf.textToOutline;
this.print(pp);
```

Example 2

Uncheck "Complex Clip Regions" (checked by default) in the Transparency Flattening option of the Advanced Print Setup.

```
pp = getPrintParams();
rf = pp.constants.rasterFlagValues;
pp.rasterFlags = pp.rasterFlags & ~rf.allowComplexClip;
// or pp.rasterFlags &= ~rf.allowComplexClip;
this.print(pp);
```

reversePages

6.0			

Set to `true` to print pages in reverse order (last to first). The default value is `false`.

Type: Boolean   *Access: R/W*

tileLabel

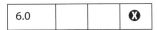

Label each page of tiled output. Labeled pages indicate row and column, file name, and print date. The default is `false`.

Type: Boolean   *Access: R/W*

tileMark

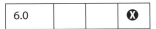

Tile marks indicate where to cut the page and where overlap occurs. The value is set through the constants `tileMarks` Object (page 515). If set to an illegal value, it is treated as `none`. The default is `none`.

Type: Integer   *Access: R/W*

tileMarks Object

Property	Description
none	No tile marks
west	Western style tile marks
east	Eastern style tile marks

tileOverlap

The number of points that tiled pages have in common. Value must be between 0 and 144. Illegal values are treated as 0. The default value is 0.

Type: Integer   *Access: R/W*

tileScale

The amount that tiled pages are scaled. Pages that are not tiled are unaffected by this value. The default is unscaled (1.0). Larger values increase the size of the printout (for example, 2.0 is twice as large, a value of 0.5 is half as large). The value of `tileScale` must be between 0.01 and 99.99. Illegal values are treated as 1.0, which is the default value.

Type: Number   *Access: R/W*

transparencyLevel

An integer value from 1 to 100 indicates how hard Acrobat tries to preserve high-level drawing operators. A value of 1 indicates complete rasterization of the image, which results in poor image quality but high speeds. A value of 100 indicates as much should be preserved as possible, but can result in slow print speeds. If set to an illegal value, 75 is used. When rasterizing, the `bitmapDPI` (page 500) and `gradientDPI` (page 506) values are used. The default value is 75.

Type: Integer   *Access: R/W*

usePrinterCRD

Takes one of three values. The value is set through the constants `usages` Object (page 516). See also `usePrinterCRD` (page 516); the two properties use the same values, but the interpretations are different.

Type: Integer   *Access: R/W*

usages Object

Property	Description
`auto`	Let Acrobat decide whether the printer Color Rendering Dictionary (CRD) should be used. Acrobat maintains a list of a handful of printers that have incorrect CRDs. Illegal values are treated as `auto`. The default is `auto`.
`use`	Use the printer's CRD.
`noUse`	Do not use the printer's CRD.

useT1Conversion

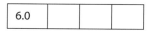

Takes one of three values. The value of the `useT1Conversion` property is set through the constants `usages` Object (page 516). See also `usePrinterCRD` (page 516); the two properties use the same values, but the interpretations are different.

Note: This property is supported on Windows platforms only.

Type: Integer   *Access: R/W*

This property uses the usages Object (page 516) values as follows.

Property	Description
auto	Let Acrobat decide whether to disable converting Type 1 fonts to more efficient printer representations (for example, TrueType). Acrobat maintains a list of a handful of printers that have problems with these fonts. Illegal values are treated as auto. The default is auto.
use	Allow conversion of Type 1 fonts even if the printer is known to have problems with alternative font representations.
noUse	Never convert Type 1 fonts to more efficient representations.

RDN Object

This generic object represents a Relative Distinguished Name. It is used by securityHandler.`newUser` (page 566) and the certificate.`issuerDN` (page 149) and `subjectDN` `(page 150)` properties.

It has the following properties.

Property	Type	Access	Description
c	String	R	Country or Region. Must be a two-character upper case ISO 3166 standard string (for example, "US")
cn	String	R	Common name (for example, "John Smith")
o	String	R	Organization name (for example, "Adobe Systems Incorporated")
ou	String	R	Organizational unit (for example, "Acrobat Engineering")
e	String	R	Email address (for example, "jsmith@adobe.com")

ReadStream Object

A ReadStream object is an object literal that represents a stream of data. It contains a method to allow reading data the stream.

Method	Parameters	Returns	Description
read	nBytes	String	The read method takes the number of bytes to read and returns a hex-encoded string with the data from the stream. The read method is a destructive operation on the stream and returns a zero length string to indicate the end of the stream.

Rendition Object

A Rendition contains information needed to play a media clip, including embedded media data (or a URL) and playback settings. It corresponds to a Rendition in the Acrobat authoring user interface.

A Rendition is a base type for either a MediaRendition or a MediaSelector. A function that accepts a Rendition can take either of these two types. The properties and methods described in this section are available for both MediaRendition and MediaSelector. Use the `type` (page 521) property to distinguish between MediaRendition and MediaSelector.

Rendition Properties

altText

The alternate text string for the rendition (an empty string if no alternate text was specified). This property is available only if the `type` (page 521) of the `rendition` is `app.media.renditionType.media` (page 120) (a MediaRendition).

Type: String   *Access: R*

Example

Get the `altText` of a rendition.

```
this.media.getRendition("myClip").altText;
```

See the examples that follow `app.media.getAltTextSettings` (page 129).

doc

A reference to the document that contains the Rendition.

Type: Document Object   Access: R

fileName

If the media is embedded, this property returns an empty string. Otherwise it returns the file name or URL of the media. This property is available only if the `type` (page 521) of the `rendition` is `app.media.renditionType.media` (page 120).

Type: String   *Access: R*

type

6.0			

An `app.media.renditionType` (page 120) value indicating the type of rendition.

Currently, there are two types: MediaRendition and RenditionList:

- When `Rendition.type` is equal to `app.media.renditionType.media`, the Rendition is a MediaRendition. A MediaRendition is an individual Rendition, as it appears in the Settings tab of the Multimedia Properties dialog box.

- When `Rendition.type` is equal to `app.media.renditionType.selector`, the Rendition is a RenditionList. A RenditionList is an array of MediaRendition. The list is the one that appears in the Settings tab of the Multimedia Properties dialog box.

Future versions of Acrobat may add more `renditionType` values, so JavaScript code should not assume that only the existing `app.media.renditionType` values may be encountered.

Type: Number   *Access: R*

uiName

6.0			

The name of the Rendition, as found in the **N** entry in its dictionary in the PDF file.

Type: String   *Access: R*

Example

The following is executed as a Rendition action.

```
console.println("Preparing to play \""
    + event.action.rendition.uiName + "\"");
```

See the `event` Object (page 314) for a description of `event.action.rendition`.

Rendition Methods

getPlaySettings

6.0			

Creates and returns a MediaSettings Object (page 464) that can be used to create a MediaPlayer object.

This method is available only for a MediaRendition.

Parameters

bGetData	(optional) A Boolean. If `true`, the MediaSettings object returns the MediaData (See `MediaSettings.data`, page 465).

Returns

A MediaSettings Object (page 464)

Note: `app.media.getAltTextSettings` (page 129) calls `getPlaySettings(false)` to obtain the correct settings to display alternate text.

This MediaSettings object includes these properties:

```
autoPlay
baseURL (if specified in rendition)
bgColor
bgOpacity
data (if bGetData is true)
duration
endAt
layout
monitorType
palindrome
showUI
rate
repeat
startAt
visible
volume
windowType
```

In the current version of Acrobat, all of these properties are present in the settings object (except as noted above). `null` is used when values such as `startAt` (page 472) are unspecified. This may change in the future to return only those values that are actually specified, with defaults assumed for the rest.

Example

```
// Get the MediaSettings for this Rendition
var settings = myRendition.getPlaySettings();
if( settings.startAt !== null ) // Do NOT use this strict
comparison!
...
if( settings.startAt ) // This is OK
...
```

See `app.media.getAltTextSettings` (page 129) and
`app.media.openPlayer` (page 136) for examples of usage.

select

6.0			

Selects a media player to play a MediaRendition or a RenditionSelector. If the Rendition is a RenditionSelector, `select` examines every MediaRenditon contained within and selects the most suitable one. (See "type" on page 521 for a description of RenditionSelector and MediaRendition.)

The return value is a MediaSelection Object (page 462) that can be used to create a MediaSettings Object (page 464). This object can then be used to create a MediaPlayer Object (page 448).

Parameters

bWantRejects	(optional) If bWantRejects is true, the rejects (page 463) property of the resulting MediaSelection will contain information about media players that were rejected during the selection process.
oContext	(optional) oContext is a MediaSelection.selectContext (page 462) value from a previous Rendition.select call. This parameter allows you to write a loop that calls Rendition.select repeatedly until you find a media player that satisfies any selection criteria that you want to test in JavaScript code.

Returns

A MediaSelection Object (page 462)

Example 1

Get a usable MediaSelection for this Rendition.

```
var selection = rendition.select();
```

Example 2

Get the name of the selected rendition. This script is executed from a Rendition action event.

```
var selection = event.action.rendition.select();
console.println( "Preparing to play " +
selection.rendition.uiName);
```

testCriteria

6.0			

Tests the Rendition against any criteria that are specified in the PDF file, such as minimum bandwidth, and returns a Boolean indicating whether the Rendition satisfied all of those criteria.

Parameters

None

Returns

Boolean

Report Object

The Report object allows the user to programmatically generate PDF documents suitable for reporting with JavaScript. Use the `writeText` (page 530) constructor to create a `Report` object; for example,

```
var rep = new Report();
```

The properties and methods can then be used to write and format a report.

Report Properties

absIndent

Controls the absolute indentation level. It is desirable to use the `indent` (page 527) and `outdent` (page 529) methods whenever possible, because they correctly handle indentation overflows.

If a report is indented past the middle of the page, the effective indent is set to the middle. Note that `divide` (page 527) indicates that it has been indented too far.

Type: Number   *Access: R/W*

color

Controls the color of any text and any divisions written into the report.

Text is written to the report with `writeText` (page 530) and divisions (horizontal rules) are written using `divide` (page 527).

Type: Color   *Access: R/W*

Example

```
var rep = new Report();
rep.size = 1.2;
rep.color = color.blue;
rep.writeText("Hello World!");
```

size

Controls the size of any text created by `writeText` (page 530) It is a multiplier. Text size is determined by multiplying the `size` property by the default size for the given style.

Type: Number   *Access: R/W*

Example

Write a "Hello World!" document.

```
var rep = new Report();
rep.size = 1.2;
rep.writeText("Hello World!");
```

style

This property controls the style of the text font for the text created by `writeText` (page 530). Values of `style` are

```
DefaultNoteText
NoteTitle
```

Type: String   *Access: R/W*

Example

```
var rep = new Report();
rep.size = 1.2;
rep.style = "DefaultNoteText";
rep.writeText("Hello World!");
rep.open("My Report");
```

Report Methods

breakPage

Ends the current page and begins a new one.

Parameters

None

Returns

Nothing

divide

Writes a horizontal rule across the page at the current location with the given width. The rule goes from the current indent level to the rightmost edge of the bounding box. If the indent level is past the middle of the bounding box, the rule shows this.

Parameters

nWidth	(optional) The horizontal rule width to use.

Returns

Nothing

indent

Increments the current indentation mark by nPoints or the default amount. If a report is indented past the middle of the page, the effective indent is set to the middle. Note that divide (page 527) makes a mark to indicate whether it has been indented too far.

See writeText (page 530) for an example of usage.

Parameters

nPoints	(optional) The number of points to increment the indentation mark.

Returns

Nothing

mail

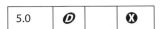

Ends report generation and mails the report.

See also `mailGetAddrs` (page 92), `app.mailMsg` (page 93), the Document Object `mailForm` (page 270) method, and the FDF Object `mail` (page 366) method.

Parameters

bUI	(optional) Specifies whether to display a user interface. If `true` (the default), the rest of the parameters are used to seed the compose-new-message window that is displayed to the user. If `false`, the cTo parameter is required and all others are optional.
cTo	(optional) A semicolon-separated list of recipients for the message.
cCc	(optional) A semicolon-separated list of CC recipients for the message.
cBcc	(optional) A semicolon-separated list of BCC recipients for the message.
cSubject	(optional) The subject of the message. The length limit is 64 KB.
cMsg	(optional) The content of the message. The length limit is 64 KB.

Returns

Nothing

open

Ends report generation, opens the report in Acrobat and returns a Document Object (page 188) that can be used to perform additional processing of the report.

Parameters

cTitle	The report title.

Returns

A Document Object (page 188)

Example

```
var docRep = rep.open("myreport.pdf");
docRep.info.Title = "End of the month report: August 2000";
docRep.info.Subject =
    "Summary of comments at the August meeting";
```

See `writeText` (page 530) for a more complete example.

outdent

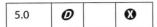

The opposite of indent; that is, decrements the current indentation mark by `nPoints` or the default amount.

See `writeText` (page 530) for an example of usage.

Parameters

nPoints	(optional) The number of points to decrement the indentation mark.

Returns

Nothing

Report

A constructor. Creates a new Report Object (page 525) with the given media and bounding boxes (values are defined in points or 1/72 of an inch). Defaults to a 8.5 x 11 inch media box and a bounding box that is indented 0.5 inches on all sides from the media box.

Parameters

aMedia	(optional) The media type.
aBBox	(optional) The bounding box size.

Returns

A Report Object (page 525)

save

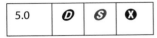

Ends report generation and saves the report to the specified path.

Note: (Security ◎): This method can only be executed during batch or console events. See "Privileged versus Non-privileged Context" on page 8 for details. The `event` Object (page 314) contains a discussion of Acrobat JavaScript events.

Parameters

cDIPath	The device-independent path.
cFS	(optional) The file system. The only value for cFS is "CHTTP". In this case, the cDIPath parameter should be an URL. This parameter is only relevant if the web server supports WebDAV.

Returns

Nothing

Example 1

```
rep.save("/c/myReports/myreport.pdf");
```

Example 2

```
rep.save({
    cDIPath:
"http://www.mycompany.com/reports/WebDAV/myreport.pdf",
    cFS:"CHTTP"}
);
```

writeText

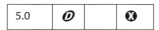

| 5.0 | *D* | | *X* |

Writes out a block of text to the report. Every call is guaranteed to begin on a new line at the current indentation mark. Correctly wraps Roman, CJK, and WGL4 text.

Parameters

String	The block of text to use.

Example

```
// Get the comments in this document, and sort by author
this.syncAnnotScan();
annots = this.getAnnots({nSortBy: ANSB_Author});

// open a new report
var rep = new Report();

rep.size = 1.2;
rep.color = color.blue;
rep.writeText("Summary of Comments: By Author");
rep.color = color.black;
rep.writeText(" ");
rep.writeText("Number of Comments: " + annots.length);
rep.writeText(" ");
```

```
var msg = "\200 page %s: \"%s\"";
var theAuthor = annots[0].author;
rep.writeText(theAuthor);
rep.indent(20);
for (var i=0; i < annots.length; i++) {
    if (theAuthor != annots[i].author) {
        theAuthor = annots[i].author;
        rep.writeText(" ");
        rep.outdent(20);
        rep.writeText(theAuthor);
        rep.indent(20);
    }
rep.writeText(util.printf(msg, 1
    + annots[i].page, annots[i].contents));
}

// now open the report
var docRep = rep.open("myreport.pdf");
docRep.info.Title = "End of the month report: August 2000";
docRep.info.Subject =
    "Summary of comments at the August meeting";
```

Row Object

This generic JavaScript object contains the data from every column in a row. It is returned by the Statement Object `getRow` (page 621) method. It contains the following properties:

Property	Type	Access	Description
`columnArray`	Array	R	An array of Column Objects (page 159). It is equivalent to what the Statement Object `getColumnArray` (page 620) method would return if called on the same Statement Object at the same time that this `row` object was created.
column properties	any	R	There is a property corresponding to each column selected by the query, containing the data for that row in that column.

ScreenAnnot Object

A ScreenAnnot object represents a screen annotation, which is a rectangular area within a PDF document viewed on the display screen. A ScreenAnnot may have Renditions and RenditionActions associated with it for multimedia playback.

ScreenAnnot Properties

altText

The alternate text string for the annotation (an empty string if no alternate text was specified).

Type: String   *Access: R*

Example

Get an annotation and write its `altText` to the debug console.

```
var annot =
    this.media.getAnnot({ nPage:0, cAnnotTitle: "myScreen" });
console.println( "annot.altText = " + annot.altText );
```

alwaysShowFocus

Normally, a screen annotation shows and hides a focus rectangle to indicate whether it has the keyboard focus. If this property is `true`, the focus rectangle is displayed by the screen annotation even if it does not have the focus. This is used for docked media playback, so that the focus rectangle of the annotation can remain visible even though the media player actually has the keyboard focus.

This property is not saved in the PDF file. If you change it, the change affects the current session only.

Type: Boolean   *Access: R/W*

display

Same as the Field Object (page 371) `display` property.

This property is not saved in the PDF file. If you change it, the change affects the current session only.

Type: Integer   *Access: R/W*

Example

Hide the annotation.

```
var annot =
    this.media.getAnnot({ nPage:0, cAnnotTitle: "myScreen" });
annot.display = display.hidden;
```

doc

A reference to the document that contains the screen annotation.

Type: Document Object   *Access: R*

events

An Events Object (page 358) containing the EventListeners that are attached to a screen annotation.

This property is not saved in the PDF file. If you change it, the change affects the current session only.

Type: Events Object   *Access: R/W*

Example

Create a simple focus EventListener.

```
var annot =
    this.media.getAnnot({ nPage:0, cAnnotTitle: "myScreen" });
var myFocusEvent = {
    onFocus: function () {
        console.println("Focusing...");
    }
};
annot.events.add( myFocusEvent );
```

This EventListener can be removed at a later time by executing the following code.

```
annot.events.remove( myFocusEvent );
```

extFocusRect

6.0			

When a screen annotation draws a focus rectangle, the rectangle normally encloses only the screen annotation itself. If extFocusRect is specified, the screen annotation takes the union of its normal rectangle and extFocusRect, and it uses the resulting rectangle to draw the focus rectangle.

This property is not saved in the PDF file. If you change it, the change affects the current session only.

Type: Array of 4 Numbers   *Access: R/W*

innerDeviceRect

6.0			

This property and outerDeviceRect (page 536) define the interior and exterior rectangles of the screen annotation as it appears in the current page view.

Type: Array of 4 Numbers   *Access: R*

Example

Get the innerDeviceRect.

```
annot =
    this.media.getAnnot({ nPage:0, cAnnotTitle: "myScreen" });
console.println("annot.innerDeviceRect = "
    + annot.innerDeviceRect.toSource() );
```

noTrigger

6.0			

If true, the screen annotation cannot be triggered through the Acrobat user interface. Typically, clicking on a screen annotation starts playback of a media player. This property suppresses this.

This property is not saved in the PDF file. If you change it, the change affects the current session only.

Type: Boolean   *Access: R/W*

Example

Use form buttons to control the media clip, so turn off interaction with the annotation.

```
annot =
    this.media.getAnnot({ nPage:0, cAnnotTitle: "myScreen" });
annot.noTrigger = true;
```

outerDeviceRect

This property and `innerDeviceRect` (page 535) define the interior and exterior rectangles of the screen annotation as it appears in the current page view.

Type: Array of 4 Numbers   *Access: R*

page

The page number of the PDF file in which the screen annotation is located.

Type: Number   *Access: R*

player

A reference to the MediaPlayer associated with a screen annotation. This property exists only for a ScreenAnnot Object (page 533) that is connected to a MediaPlayer. The property is set by `MediaPlayer.open` (page 454) or by methods that call `open` indirectly, such as `app.media.openPlayer` (page 136).

Type: ScreenAnnot   *Access: R/W*

rect

The rectangle of the screen annotation in default user coordinates. Changing this property dirties the PDF file, and the new setting will be saved if the PDF file is saved. The `innerDeviceRect` (page 535) and `outerDeviceRect` (page 536) properties are also updated to reflect the new rectangle.

Type: Array of 4 Numbers   *Access: R/W*

Example

Adjust the position of the annotation slightly.

```
var annot =
    this.media.getAnnot({ nPage:0, cAnnotTitle: "myScreen" });
```

```
var aRect = annot.rect;
aRect[0] += 10;
aRect[2] += 10;
annot.rect = aRect;
```

ScreenAnnot Methods

hasFocus

6.0

Tells whether the screen annotation currently has the keyboard focus.

Parameters

None

Returns

Boolean

setFocus

6.0

Sets the keyboard focus to the screen annotation. The focus is set synchronously (before `setFocus` returns) if it is safe to do so. If it is unsafe to set the focus synchronously (for example, when the property is changed within an on event method), `bAllowAsync` determines what happens:

- If `true`, the focus will be set asynchronously during idle time.
- If `false` or omitted, the focus remains unchanged.

The return value is `true` if the operation was performed synchronously, or `false` if it was deferred to be performed asynchronously.

Parameters

bAllowAsync	(optional) A Boolean that determines the behavior of `setFocus` when it is not safe to set the focus synchronously. If `true`, the focus will be set asynchronously during idle time. If `false` or omitted, the focus remains unchanged. The default is `false`.

Returns

Boolean

search Object

The `search` object is a static object that accesses the functionality provided by the Acrobat Search plug-in. This plug-in must be installed to interface with the `search` object (see "available" on page 538).

See also the Index Object (page 437), which is returned by some of the methods of the `search` object.

The results for `query` (page 544) calls are displayed in the Find dialog of Acrobat.

Note: Acrobat 7.0 indexes are incompatible with the search engines of Acrobat 5.0 and earlier versions.

In Acrobat 7.0, searching indexes created by versions of Acrobat 5.0 and earlier is not possible on the Macintosh platform.

search Properties

attachments

7.0			

Determines whether any PDF file attachments should be searched along with the base document. The default is `false`.

This property is ignored on the Macintosh platform when searching a document from within the Safari web browser. As a result, attachments are not searched inside Safari.

Type: Boolean   *Access: R/W*

available

5.0			

Returns `true` if the Search plug-in is loaded and query capabilities are possible. A script author should check this Boolean before performing a query or other `search` object manipulation.

Type: Boolean   *Access: R*

Example

Make sure the `search` object exists and is available.

```
if (typeof search != "undefined" && search.available) {
    search.query("Cucumber");
}
```

bookmarks

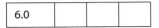

Specifies whether bookmarks are searched for the query. The default is
`false`.

Type: Boolean   *Access: R/W*

docInfo

Specifies whether the document information is searched for the query. The
default is `false`.

Type: Boolean   *Access: R/W*

docText

Specifies whether the document text is searched for the query. The default is
`true`.

Type: Boolean   *Access: R/W*

docXMP

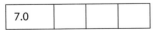

Specifies whether document-level XMP metadata is searched for the query.
The default is `false`.

Type: Boolean   *Access: R/W*

ignoreAccents

Specifies whether accents and diacriticals are ignored while searching the
query term. The default is `false`.

Type: Boolean   *Access: R/W*

ignoreAsianCharacterWidth

6.0			

Specifies whether the Kana characters in the document exactly match the search query. The default is `false`.

Type: Boolean   *Access: R/W*

indexes

5.0			

An array of all of the Index Objects (page 437) currently accessible by the search engine.

Note: (Security , Acrobat 7.0) This property can only be accessed during batch or console events. See "Privileged versus Non-privileged Context" on page 8 for details. The `event` Object (page 314) contains a discussion of Acrobat JavaScript events.

Type: Array   *Access: R*

Example

Enumerate all of the indexes and dump their names.

```
for (var i = 0; i < search.indexes.length; i++) {
    console.println("Index[" + i
        + "]=", search.indexes[i].name);
}
```

jpegExif

6.0			

Specifies whether EXIF data associated with JPEG images in the PDF is searched. The default is `false`.

Type: Boolean   *Access: R/W*

legacySearch

6.0			

Returns `true` if the `Search5.api` plug-in is loaded. This plug-in provides the capability to search indexes generated by Acrobat Catalog in Acrobat 5.0 and earlier versions. See the sections in Acrobat Help pertaining to searching such indexes.

Type: Boolean   *Access: R*

markup

6.0			

Specifies whether markup (annotations) are searched for the query. The default is `false`.

Type: Boolean   *Access: R/W*

matchCase

5.0			

Specifies whether the search query is case sensitive. The default is `false`.

Type: Boolean   *Access: R/W*

matchWholeWord

6.0			

Specifies whether search finds only occurrences of complete words that are specified in the query. For example, when this option is set to `true`, if you search for the word "stick", the words "tick" and "sticky" will not be highlighted. The default is `false`.

Type: Boolean   *Access: R/W*

maxDocs

5.0			

The maximum number of documents that will be returned as part of the search query. The default is 100 documents.

Type: Integer   *Access: R/W*

objectMetadata

7.0			

This property determines whether object-level metadata should be searched. This is the same data that is visible from the Acrobat 7.0 **Tools > Object Data > Object Data Tool** menu item.

The default is `false`.

Type: Boolean   *Access: R/W*

proximity

5.0			

Specifies whether the search query will reflect the proximity of words in the results ranking when performing the search that contains *AND* Boolean clauses. The default is `false`. See the sections in the Acrobat Online Guide pertaining to Search capabilities for a more thorough discussion of proximity.

Type: Boolean   *Access: R/W*

proximityRange

7.0			

The range of proximity search in number of words. This property will be used only if the property `proximity` (page 542) is set to `true`. See the sections in the Acrobat Online Guide pertaining to Search capabilities for a more thorough discussion of proximity.

The default is 900 words. The value of this parameter can be any non-zero positive integer.

Type: Integer   *Access: R/W*

refine

5.0			

Specifies whether the search query will take the results of the previous query and refine the results based on the next query. The default is `false`. See the sections in the Acrobat Online Guide pertaining to Search capabilities for a more thorough discussion of refining queries.

Type: Boolean   *Access: R/W*

soundex

Note: Beginning with Acrobat 6.0, the use of this property is discouraged. It has a value of `false` and access is restricted to read only.

Specifies whether the search query will take the sound of words (for example, MacMillan, McMillan, McMilon) into account when performing the search. The default is `false`. See the sections in the Acrobat Online Guide pertaining to Search capabilities for a more thorough discussion of soundex.

Type: Boolean   *Access: R*

stem

Specifies whether the search query will take the stemming of words (for example, run, runs, running) into account when performing the search. The default is `false`. See the sections in the Acrobat Online Guide pertaining to Search capabilities for a more thorough discussion of stemming.

Type: Boolean   *Access: R/W*

thesaurus

Note: Beginning with Acrobat 6.0, the use of this property is discouraged. This property has a value of `false` and access is restricted to read only.

Specifies whether the search query will find similar words. For example, searching for "embellish" might yield "enhanced", "gracefully", or "beautiful". The default is `false`.

Type: Boolean   *Access: R*

wordMatching

Table: | 6.0 | | | |

How individual words in the query will be matched to words in the document. Values are:

```
MatchPhrase
MatchAllWords
MatchAnyWord
BooleanQuery (default)
```

This property is relevant only when a query has more than one word. The `BooleanQuery` option is ignored when searching active document.

Type: String   *Access: R/W*

search Methods

addIndex

5.0	*P*		

Adds the specified index to the list of searchable indexes.

Parameters

cDIPath	A device-independent path to an index file on the user's hard drive.
bSelect	(optional) Specifies whether the index should be selected for searching.

Returns

An Index Object (page 437)

Example

Adds the standard help index for Acrobat to the index list:

```
search.addIndex("/c/program files/adobe/acrobat 5.0/help/exchhelp.pdx",
    true);
```

getIndexForPath

5.0			

Searches the index list and returns the Index Object (page 437) whose path corresponds to the specified path.

Parameters

cDIPath	A device-independent path to an index file on the user's hard drive.

Returns

The Index Object (page 437) whose path corresponds to the specified path.

query

5.0			

Searches the specified document or index for the specified text. Properties associated with the search object (such as matchCase, matchWholeWord, stem) may affect the result.

Parameters

cQuery	The text for which to search.
cWhere	(optional) Specifies where the text should be searched. Values are: ActiveDoc Folder Index ActiveIndexes *(default)*
cDPIPath	(optional) A device-independent path to a folder or Catalog index on the user's computer. When cWhere is Folder or Index, this parameter is required.

Returns

Nothing

Examples

Search for the word "Acrobat".

cWhere	Query
ActiveIndexes	search.query("Acrobat"); // "ActiveIndexes" is the default. search.query("Acrobat", "ActiveIndexes");
ActiveDoc	search.query("Acrobat", "ActiveDoc");

Folder	search.query("Acrobat","Folder","/c/myDocuments");
	search.query("Acrobat","Folder",app.getPath("user","documents"));
	search.query("Acrobat", "Folder", "//myserver/myDocuments");

Index	search.query("Acrobat", "Index", "/c/Myfiles/public/index.pdx");

removeIndex

5.0	ⓟ		

Removes the specified Index Object (page 437) from the index list.

Parameters

index	The Index Object (page 437) to remove from the index list.

Returns

Nothing

security Object

5.0		🝚	Ⓧ

The `security` object is a static JavaScript object that exposes security-related PDF functions such as encryption and digital signatures. Security functions are performed using a SecurityHandler Object (page 557), which is obtained from the `security` object using the `getHandler` (page 553) method.

Note: (Security 🝚): The `security` object is available without restriction, including in Adobe Reader. The methods and properties of the `security` object can only be executed during batch, console or application initialization events including in Adobe Reader, except where otherwise stated. See also "Privileged versus Non-privileged Context" on page 8. The `event` Object (page 314) contains a discussion of Acrobat JavaScript events.

security Constants

Several convenience strings are defined the `security` object, beginning with Acrobat 7.0. The constants are held as properties of the wrapper objects listed below.

HandlerName Object

These are constants used when determining which handler to use.

Property	Type	Access	Description
StandardHandler	String	R	This value can be specified in the `handler` property for a SecurityPolicy Object (page 569) that is based on the Standard (password-based) security handler.
PPKLiteHandler	String	R	This value can be specified in the `handler` property for a SecurityPolicy Object (page 569) that is based on the PPKLite (certificate-based) security handler. This value can also be passed to `security.getHandler` (page 553) to create a new security context.
APSHandler	String	R	This the value specified in the `handler` property for a SecurityPolicy Object (page 569) that is based on the Adobe Policy Server security handler. This value can also be passed to `security.getHandler` (page 553) to create a new security context.

Adobe® Acrobat® Official JavaScript Reference

Example

The constant (string) `security.StandardHandler` is used to specify the `handler` property of the SecurityPolicy Object (page 569).

```
security.getHandler(security.PPKLiteHandler, true);
```

EncryptTarget Object

These constants are used when determining what data a policy is encrypting. They can be used in the `target` property of the SecurityPolicy Object (page 569).

Property	Type	Access	Description
EncryptTargetDocument	String	R	The Security Policy encrypts the entire document when applied.
EncryptTargetAttachments	String	R	The Security Policy encrypts only the file attachments embedded within the document. This means the document can be opened, but attachments cannot be opened without providing the correct security authentication. It is used for eEnvelope workflows.

Example

```
var filterOptions = { target:
security.EncryptTargetAttachments };
security.chooseSecurityPolicy( { oOptions: filterOptions } );
```

security Properties

handlers

An array containing the language-independent names of the available security handlers that can be used for encryption or signatures.

See also `getSecurityPolicies` (page 554).

The following information applies to different versions of Acrobat:

- Beginning with Acrobat 6.0, access to this property is unrestricted, to allow querying to see which handlers are available.

- In Acrobat 6.0, this call returned three handlers, Adobe.PPKLite, Adobe.PPKMS, and Adobe.AAB. Starting with Acrobat 7.0, all the functionality provided by Adobe.PPKMS has been rolled into Adobe.PPKLite, and Adobe.PPKMS is no longer available as a separate handler.

- Beginning with Acrobat 7.0, a new handler is available, Adobe.APS. This handler is used for authentication prior to calling any of the methods `encryptUsingPolicy` (page 232), `getSecurityPolicies` (page 554), or `chooseSecurityPolicy` (page 551). It has no other valid usage currently.

- Beginning with Acrobat 7.0, `security` Constants (see page 546) are defined for each of the handlers. (Adobe.AAB is an exception. No constant was added because this handler will probably be deprecated in the near future.) These constants should be used when creating a new handler instance with `getHandler` (page 553) or comparing against the handlers list.

Type: Array   *Access: R*

Example

Get the list of security handlers available on this system:

```
for ( var i=0; i < security.handlers.length; i++ )
    console.println(security.handlers[i])
```

The output to the console might be

```
Adobe.APS
Adobe.PPKLite
Adobe.PPKMS
Adobe.AAB
```

validateSignaturesOnOpen

Gets or sets the user-level preference that causes signatures to be automatically validated when a document is opened.

Note: (Security 🔵) : The property can be used to get in all situations, but can only set new values during batch, console, application initialization and menu events. See "Privileged versus Non-privileged Context" on page 8 for details.

Type: Boolean   *Access: R/W*

security Methods

chooseRecipientsDialog

6.0		𝒮	ⓧ

Opens a dialog box that allows a user to choose a list of recipients. Returns an array of generic Group objects that can be used when encrypting documents or data using either `encryptForRecipients` (page 230) or `addRecipientListCryptFilter` (page 214) methods of the Document Object.

Note: Can be executed only during console, menu, or application initialization events. See "Privileged versus Non-privileged Context" on page 8 for details.

Parameters

oOptions	A DisplayOptions Object (page 549) containing the parameters for the display options.

Returns

An array of Group Objects (page 231).

See the Document Object `encryptForRecipients` (page 230) method for a description of the Group Object.

DisplayOptions Object

It contains the following properties:

Property	Description
bAllowPermGroups	Controls whether permissions can be set for entries in the recipient list. Default value is `true`.
bPlaintextMetadata	If this property is specified, a check box is displayed to allow a user to select whether metadata is plaintext or encrypted. Its default value is the value of this property (`true` or `false`). If this property is not specified, the check box is not shown.
cTitle	The title to be displayed in the dialog box. The default is "Choose Recipients".
cNote	A note to be displayed in the dialog box. The default is to not show any note.
bAllowImportFromFile	Specifies whether the option is displayed that allows a user to import recipients from a file. The default value is `true`.

Property	Description
bRequireEncryptionCert	If true, recipients will be required to include an encryption certificate. The default value is true.
bRequireEmail	If true, recipients will be required to include an email address. The default value is false.
bUserCert	If true, the user will be prompted to provide his or her own certificate so that he or she can be included in the list of recipients. Setting this flag to true results in a prompt but does not require that the user provide a certificate.

Example 1

Retrieve groups with permissions

```
var oOptions = {
   bAllowPermGroups: true,
   bPlaintextMetadata: false,
   cTitle: "Encrypt and Email",
   cNote: "Select recipients",
   bAllowImportFromFile: false,
   bRequireEncryptionCert: true,
   bRequireEmail: true
};
var groupArray = security.chooseRecipientsDialog( oOptions );
console.println("Full name = "
   + groupArray[0].userEntities[0].fullName);
```

Example 2

Get a list of recipients for which to encrypt data and email the document.

```
var oOptions = { bAllowPermGroups: false,
   cNote: "Select the list of recipients. "
   + "Each person must have both an email address and a
certificate.",
   bRequireEmail: true,
   bUserCert: true
};
var oGroups = security.chooseRecipientsDialog( oOptions );
// Display the list of recipients in an alert
// Build an email "to" mailList
var numCerts = oGroups[0].userEntities.length;
var cMsg =
   "The document will be encrypted for the following:\n";
var mailList = new Array;
for( var g=0; g<numCerts; ++g )
{
   var ue = oGroups[0].userEntities[g];
   var oCert = ue.defaultEncryptCert;
   if( oCert == null )
       oCert = ue.certificates[0];
   cMsg += oCert.subjectCN + ", " + ue.email + "\n";
```

```
var oRDN = oCert.subjectDN;
if( ue.email )
{
    mailList[g] = ue.email;
}
else
    if ( oRDN.e )
    {
        mailList[g] = oRDN.e;
    }
}
var result = app.alert( cMsg );
```

Example 3

List all the entries in an array of groups.

```
var  groups = security.chooseRecipientsDialog( oOptions );
for( g in groups ) {
    console.println( "Group No. " + g );
    // Permissions
    var perms = groups[g].permissions;
    console.println( "Permissions:" );
    for(p in perms) console.println( p + " = "
        + eval("perms." +p));
    // User Entities
    for( u in groups[i].userEntities ) {
    var user = groups[g].userEntities[u];
    console.println( "User No. " + u );
    for(i in user) console.println( i + " = "
        + eval("user." +i));
    }
}
```

chooseSecurityPolicy

Displays a dialog box to allow a user to choose from a list of security policies, filtered according to the options.

Note: (Security  Can be executed only during batch, console, menu, or application initialization events. See "Privileged versus Non-privileged Context" on page 8 for details. This method will display UI.

Parameters

oOptions	(optional) A SecurityPolicyOptions Object (page 554) containing the parameters used for filtering the list of security policies returned. If not specified, all policies found are displayed.

Returns

Returns a single SecurityPolicy Object (page 569) or `null` if the user canceled the selection.

Example

In this example a policy is chosen and the name is displayed.

```
var options = { cHandler: security.APSHandler };
var policy = security.chooseSecurityPolicy( options );
console.println("The policy chosen was: " + policy.name);
```

`security.APSHandler` is one of the security Constants (see "Document Object" on page 188).

exportToFile

Exports a Certificate Object (page 149) to a local disk as a raw certificate file.

Note: (Security ⑤): Data being written must be data for a valid certificate; arbitrary data types cannot be written. This method will not overwrite an existing file.

See also `security.importFromFile` (page 555).

Parameters

`oObject`	The Certificate Object (page 149) that is to be exported to disk.
`cDIPath`	The device-independent save path.
	Note: (Security ⑤): The parameter `cDIPath` must be a safe path (see "Safe Path" on page 8) and must end with the extension `.cer`.

Returns

The path of the file that was written, if successful.

Example

```
var outPath = security.exportToFile(oCert, "/c/outCert.cer");
```

getHandler

5.0		⊘	

Obtains a SecurityHandler Object (page 557). The caller can create as many new engines as desired and each call to `getHandler` creates a new engine. However, there is only one UI engine.

Note: (Security ⊘): This method is available from batch, console, app initialization and menu events. See "Privileged versus Non-privileged Context" on page 8 for details.

Backward Compatibility Note: Because Adobe.PPKMS is no longer available as a separate handler starting with Acrobat 7.0, invoking `getHandler` with `cName` as "Adobe.PPKMS" returns the engine associated with Adobe.PPKLite handler.

Parameters

cName	The language-independent name of the security handler, as returned by the `handlers` (page 547) property.
	(Acrobat 7.0) Beginning with Acrobat 7.0, constant strings are defined for each of the valid handlers. See `security` Constants (page 546), in particular the HandlerName Object (page 546).
bUIEngine	(optional) If `true`, the method returns the existing security handler instance that is associated with the Acrobat user interface (so that, for example, a user can log in through the user interface). If `false` (the default), returns a new engine.

Returns

The SecurityHandler Object (page 557) specified by `cName`. If the handler is not present, returns a `null` object.

Example

This code selects the *Adobe.PPKLite SecurityHandler*.

```
// validate signatures on open
security.validateSignaturesOnOpen = true;

// list all available signature handlers
var a = security.handlers;
for (var i = 0; i < a.length; i++)
   console.println("a["+i+"] = "+a[i]);

// use "Adobe.PPKLite" handler engine for the UI
var ppklite = security.getHandler(
   security.PPKLiteHandler, true);
```

```
// login
ppklite.login("dps017", "/C/profiles/DPSmith.pfx");
```

See also the example following `signatureSign` (page 421) for a continuation of this example.

getSecurityPolicies

Returns the list of security policies currently available, filtered according to the options specified. The master list of security policies will be updated prior to filtering. The default SecurityHandler Objects (page 557) are used to retrieve the latest policies. If no policies are available or none meet the filtering restrictions, `null` will be returned.

Note: You may be able to retrieve more policies by calling `login` on the default SecurityHandler objects before calling this function.

(Security ◉) Can be executed only during console or application initialization events. Not available in Adobe Reader.

Parameters

bUI	(optional) A flag controlling whether UI can be displayed. Default value is `false`.
oOptions	(optional) A SecurityPolicyOptions Object (page 554) containing the parameters used for filtering the list of security policies returned. If not specified, all policies found are returned.

Returns

An array of SecurityPolicy Objects (page 569) or `null`.

SecurityPolicyOptions Object

The SecurityPolicyOptions object has the following properties:

Property	Description
bFavorites	If not passed, policies are not filtered based on whether a policy is a Favorite. If `true`, only policies that are Favorites are returned. If `false`, only policies that are not Favorites are returned.

Property	Description
cHandler	If not passed, policies are not filtered based on security filter. If defined, only policies that match the specified security filter are returned. The valid values are defined in security Constants (page 546) (see the HandlerName Object, page 546). Only a single value can be passed.
cTarget	If not defined, policies are not filtered based on the target. If defined, only policies that match the specified target are returned. The valid values are defined in the EncryptTarget Object (page 547) of security Constants (page 546) ("EncryptTarget Object" on page 547). Only a single value can be passed.

Example 1

Retrieve the list of favorite PPKLite policies and display the names. This example uses security.PPKLiteHandler (see security Constants, page 546).

```
var options = { bFavorites:true,
cHandler:security.PPKLiteHandler };
var policyArray =
    security.getSecurityPolicies( { oOptions: options } );
for( var i = 0; i < policyArray.length; i++)
    console.println( policyArray[i].name );
```

Example 2

Force the login, retrieve the list of APS policies, and display the names. This example uses security.APSHandler (see security Constants, page 546).

```
var aps = security.getHandler( security.APSHandler, true );
aps.login();
var options = { cHandler: security.APSHandler };
var policyArray = security.getSecurityPolicies({
    bUI: true,
    oOptions: options
});
for(var i = 0; i < policyArray.length; i++)
    console.println( policyArray[i].name );
```

importFromFile

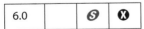

Reads a raw data file and returns the data as an object with a type specified by cType. The file being imported must be a valid certificate.

A related method is security.exportToFile (page 552).

Parameters

cType	The type of object to be returned by this method. The only supported type is "Certificate".
cDIPath	(optional) When bUI is false, this parameter is required and specifies the device-independent path to the file to be opened. If bUI is true, this is the seed path used in the open dialog box.
bUI	(optional) true if the user should be prompted to select the file that is to be imported. The default is false.
cMsg	(optional) If bUI is true, the title to use in the open dialog box. If cMsg is not specified, the default title is used.

Returns

A Certificate Object (page 149)

Example

```
var oMyCert = security.importFromFile("Certificate",
"/c/myCert.cer");
```

SecurityHandler Object

SecurityHandler objects are used to access security handler capabilities such as signatures, encryption, and directories. Different security handlers have different properties and methods. This section documents the full set of properties and methods that security objects may have. Individual SecurityHandler objects may or may not implement these properties and methods.

SecurityHandler objects can be obtained using the `security.getHandler` (page 553) method.

The JavaScript interface for Adobe.PPKLite signatures was introduced in Acrobat 5.0, and the remainder of the JavaScript interface was introduced in Acrobat 6.0. Prior to Acrobat 6.0, there was no support in Acrobat to enable JavaScript in third-party security handlers.

Not all security handlers are JavaScript-enabled. Not all JavaScript enabled handlers are enabled for all security operations. Third-party public key security handlers may support JavaScript, but only if they use the new *PubSec* programming interface that was introduced in Acrobat 6.0.

JavaScript enabled handlers provided by Adobe include:

- The Adobe.PPKLite security handler supports signatures and encryption. On the Windows operating system, it provides directory access through the Microsoft Active Directory Scripting Interface (ADSI).
- The Adobe.AAB security handler provides a local address book and support for directory operations.

Note: The Standard security handler, used for password encryption of documents, is not JavaScript-enabled in general. However, starting with Acrobat 7.0, encryption using Standard security is possible using predefined policies. See `encryptUsingPolicy` (page 232) for more details.

Also starting with Acrobat 7.0, the Adobe.APS handler can be used for encryption with the `encryptUsingPolicy` (page 232) method. This handler also makes a directory available through the directory services, but because no certificates are returned from this directory, it is of limited general use.

Note: (Security ☯): SecurityHandler objects can only be created using the security Object `getHandler` (page 553) method. This method is available only for batch, console, application initialization and menu events (see "Privileged versus Non-privileged Context" on page 8 for details) and is available in Adobe Reader.

SecurityHandler Properties

appearances

An array containing the language-dependent names of the available user-configured appearances for the specified security handler. Appearances are used to create the on-page visual representation of a signature when signing a signature field. The name of an appearance can be specified as a signature info object property when signing a signature field using the Field Object `signatureSign` (page 421) method.

Acrobat provides a standard signature appearance module that is used by Adobe signature plug-ins and that can also be used by third-party signature plug-ins. This standard signature appearance module is preconfigured with one appearance and can be configured by users to contain more appearances. The name of the one pre-configured appearance, called *Standard Text* in the user interface, is not returned by this property.

If a security handler does not support selection of appearances, this property will return null.

Type: Array   *Access: R*

digitalIDs

The certificates that are associated with the currently selected digital IDs for this security handler.

Type: Object   *Access: R*

The return value is a generic object with the following properties:

Property	Type	Version	Description
oEndUserSignCert	Certificate Object (page 149)	6.0	The certificate that is associated with the currently selected digital IDs that is to be used by this SecurityHandler object when signing. The property is undefined if there is no current selection.
oEndUserCryptCert	Certificate Object (page 149)	6.0	The certificate that is associated with the currently selected digital IDs that is to be used when encrypting a document with this SecurityHandler object. The property is undefined if there is no current selection.

Property	Type	Version	Description
certs	Array of Certificate Objects (page 149)	6.0	An array of certificates corresponding to the list of all digital IDs that are available for this SecurityHandler object.
stores	Array of Strings	6.0	An array of strings, one for every Certificate Object, identifying the store where the digital ID is stored. The string values are up to the security handler. For *Adobe.PPKLite* the valid values are 'PKCS12' and 'MSCAPI'.

The Adobe.PPKLite security handler returns all currently available digital IDs present in Password-protected digital ID files (both PKCS#12 and APF) and, on Windows, IDs present in the Windows (MSCAPI) store.

Both `oEndUserSignCert` and `oEndUserCryptCert` properties can be set using the user-interface. `oEndUserSignCert` can also be set using the `login` (page 562) method. This means that `oEndUserCryptCert` will only be returned when using a Security Handler object that is obtained using the `getHandler` (page 553) method with `bUIEngine` set to `true`.

Example

```
var sh = security.getHandler( "Adobe.PPKMS", true );
var ids = sh.digitalIDs;
var oCert = ids.oEndUserSignCert;
security.exportToFile( oCert, "/c/MySigningCert.cer" );
```

directories

An array of the available Directory Objects (page 184) for this Security Handler. New Directory Objects can be created using the `newDirectory` (page 566) method.

Type: Array *Access: R*

directoryHandlers

An array containing the language-independent names of the available directory handlers for the specified security handler. For example, the Adobe.PPKMS security handler has a directory handler named Adobe.PPKMS.ADSI that supports queries using the *Microsoft Active Directory Script Interface* (ADSI). Valid directory handler names are required when activating a new Directory Object (page 184) using its `info` (page 184) property.

Type: Array   *Access: R*

isLoggedIn

Returns `true` if currently logged into this SecurityHandler Object (page 557). See the `login (page 562)` method.

Different security handlers will have their own rules for determining the value of this property. The *Adobe.PPKLite* handler will return `true` if a user is logged in to a profile file (also called credential file, implemented as a PKCS#12 file). Adobe.PPKMS will always return `true`.

Type: Boolean   *Access: R*

Example

```
var ppklite = security.getHandler("Adobe.PPKLite", true);
console.println( "Is logged in = " + ppklite.isLoggedIn ); //
false
ppklite.login( "dps017", "/C/signatures/DPSmith.pfx");
console.println( "Is logged in = " + ppklite.isLoggedIn ); //
true
```

loginName

The name associated with the actively selected signing digital ID for the security handler. This may require that the `login (page 562)` method be called to select a signing credential. The return value is `null` if a signing credential is not selected or if the security handler does not support this property.

Type: String   *Access: R*

loginPath

The device-independent path to the user's profile file used to login to the security handler. The return value is null if no one is logged in, if the security handler does not support this property, or if this property is irrelevant for the currently logged in user.

Type: String   *Access: R*

name

5.0

The language-independent name of the security handler. Example values for the Default Certificate, Windows Certificate, and Entrust Security Handlers are *Adobe.PPKLite*, Adobe.PPKMS, and *Entrust.PPKEF*. All security handlers must support this property.

Type: String   *Access: R*

signAuthor

6.0

Specifies whether the security handler is capable of generating certified documents. A certified document is signed with both a byte-range signature and an object signature. Object signatures, which are generated by traversing the document's object tree, are used to detect and prevent modifications to a document. See the mdp property of the SignatureInfo Object (page 570) for details regarding modification detection and prevention (MDP) settings.

Type: Boolean   *Access: R*

signFDF

6.0

Indicates that the security handler is capable of signing FDF files.

Type: Boolean   *Access: R*

signInvisible

5.0

Specifies whether the security handler is capable of generating invisible signatures.

Type: Boolean   *Access: R*

signValidate

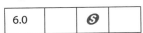

6.0

Indicates whether the security handler is capable of validating signatures.

Type: Boolean   *Access: R*

signVisible

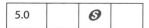

Specifies whether the security handler is capable of generating visible signatures.

Type: Boolean   *Access: R*

uiName

The language-dependent string for the security handler. This string is suitable for user interfaces. All security handlers must support this property.

Type: String   *Access: R*

SecurityHandler Methods

login

Provides a mechanism by which digital IDs can be accessed and selected for a particular Security Handler. Through the user interface, a default digital ID can be selected that persists either eternally or for as long as the application is running. If such a selection has been made through the UI, it might not be necessary to log into a Security Handler prior to using the digital ID.

Parameters tend to be specific to a particular handler. The behavior for Adobe.PPKLite and Adobe.PPKMS handlers is specified below.

The parameters `cPassword` and `cDIPath` are provided for backward compatibility, or they can be included as properties of the `oParams` object. This latter method is the preferred calling convention beginning in Acrobat 6.0.

See also `logout` (page 565), `newUser` (page 566), and `loginName` (page 560).

Parameters

cPassword	(optional, Acrobat 5.0) The password necessary to access the password-protected digital ID. This parameter is supported by Adobe.PPKLite for accessing digital ID files and PKCS#11 devices.
cDIPath	(optional, Acrobat 5.0) A device-independent path to the password-protected digital ID file or a PKCS#11 library. This parameter is supported by Adobe.PPKLite.
oParams	(optional, Acrobat 6.0) A LoginParameters Object (page 563) with parameters that are specific to a particular SecurityHandler Object (page 557). The common fields in this object are described below. These fields include the cDIPath and cPassword values, thus allowing the parameter list to be expressed in different ways.
bUI	(optional, Acrobat 6.0) Set to true if the user interface should be used to log the user in. This attribute should be supported by all security handlers that support this method.

Returns

Returns true if the login succeeded, false otherwise.

LoginParameters Object

This generic JavaScript object contains parameters for the login (page 562) method. It has the following properties:

Property	Type	Version	Description
cDIPath	String	5.0	The path to a file that contains the digital ID or a PKCS#11 library. Supported by Adobe.PPKLite security handler.
cPassword	String	6.0	A password that is used to authenticate the user. This password may used to access a password-protected digital ID file or a PKCS#11 device. Supported by Adobe.PPKLite security handler. Note that Acrobat does not guarantee that this password is obfuscated in memory.
cPFX	String	7.0	(optional) A hex-encoded PFX to log into. If this parameter is specified, it takes precedence over cDIPath. **Note:** This parameter is only used internally.Currently, there is no way to retrieve a hex encoded PFX file through JavaScript.

Property	Type	Version	Description
oEndUserSignCert	generic object	6.0	Selects a digital ID for the purpose of performing end-user signing. The value of this property is a Certificate Object (page 149) (or a generic object with the same property names as a Certificate Object), which defines the certificate that is being selected.
			It may not be necessary to call this method for a particular handler. For example, if logged in to a PKCS#12 file containing one signing digital ID with Adobe.PPKLite, a signing credential does not need to be selected. All security handlers must be able to process the binary and SHA1Hash properties of this object. This object can be empty if bUI is true.
cMsg	String	6.0	A message to display in the login dialog, if bUI is true.
cURI	String	7.0	URI used to connect to a server. Only supported by the Adobe.APS handler.
cUserId	String	7.0	User name used when connecting to a server. Only supported by the Adobe.APS handler.
cDomain	String	7.0	Domain name used when connecting to a server. Only supported by the Adobe.APS handler.
iSlotID	Integer	7.0	Specifies the slot ID of a PKCS#11 device to log into. This parameter is supported by the Adobe.PPKLite handler only.
cTokenLabel	String	7.0	Specifies the token label of a PKCS#11 device to log into. This parameter is supported by the Adobe.PPKLite handler only.

Example 1

```
// Use "Adobe.PPKLite" Security Handler Object for the UI
var ppklite = security.getHandler( security.PPKLiteHandler,
    true );
var oParams = { cPassword: "dps017", cDIPath: "/C/DPSmith.pfx"
}
ppklite.login( oParams );
<..... make a signature field and sign it ......>
ppklite.logout();

// PPKLite - Use UI to select a credential,
// when already logged in
ppklite.login(
{ oParams:
    { oEndUserSignCert: {},
      cMsg: "Select your Digital ID" },
      bUI : true
} );
```

```
// PPKLite - Login and select signing credential
var oCert = { SHA1Hash: "00000000" };
ppklite.login(
{ oParams:
    { cDIPath: "/C/test/DPSmith.pfx",
      cPassword: "dps017",
      oEndUserSignCert: oCert,
        cMsg: "Select your Digital ID"
    },
  bUI : true
});
```

Example 2

```
// Use "Adobe.PPKMS" Security Handler Object
var ppkms = security.getHandler( "Adobe.PPKMS" );

// Select credential to use when signing
var oCert = myCerts[0];
ppkms.login( { oParams: { oEndUserSignCert: oCert } } );
```

Example 3

Use the Adobe.APS SecurityHandler Object. This example uses
security.APSHandler, see security Constants (page 546).

```
var aps = security.getHandler( security.APSHandler, true );
var oParams = { cUserName: "acrobat", cPassword: "adobedon" };
aps.login( oParams );
<... encrypt a document using this handle and a policy id ...>
aps.logout();
```

See signatureSign (page 421) for details on signing a PDF document.

logout

5.0			

Logs out for the SecurityHandler Object (page 557). This method is used by
Adobe.PPKLite, not by *Adobe.PPKMS*.

Also see the login (page 562) method.

Parameters

None

Returns

Beginning in Acrobat 6.0, returns `true` if the logout succeeded, `false` otherwise. Previous Acrobat releases did not generate a return value.

newDirectory

Returns a new Directory Object (page 184). This object must be activated using its `info` (page 184) property before it is marked for persistence and can be used for searches. Existing directory objects can be discovered using the `directories` (page 559) property.

Parameters

None

Returns

A new Directory Object (page 184)

newUser

Supports enrollment with Adobe.PPKLite and Adobe.PPKMS security handlers by creating a new self-sign credential.

Note: (Security ⑤): This method will not allow the user to overwrite an existing file.

Parameters

`cPassword`	(optional) The password necessary to access the password-protected digital ID file. This parameter is ignored by Adobe.PPKMS.
`cDIPath`	(optional) The device-independent path to the password-protected digital ID file. This parameter is ignored by Adobe.PPKMS.
	Note: (Security ⑤): Beginning with Acrobat 6.0, the parameter `cDIPath` must be a safe path (see "Safe Path" on page 8) and end with the extension `.pfx`.

oRDN	(optional) The relative distinguished name (RDN) as an RDN Object (page 518) containing the issuer or subject name for a certificate. The only required field is `cn`. If the country `c` is provided, it must be two characters, using the ISO 3166 standard (for example, "US").
oCPS	(optional, Acrobat 6.0) A generic object containing certificate policy information that will be embedded in the Certificate Policy extension of the certificate. The object has these properties: ● `oid` is required and indicates the certificate policy object identifier. ● `url` (optional) is a URL that points to detailed information about the policy under which the certificate has been issued ● `notice` (optional) is an abridged version of the information, embedded in the certificate.
bUI	(optional, Acrobat 6.0) If `true`, the user interface can be used to enroll. This parameter is supported by all security handlers that support this method.
cStore	(optional, Acrobat 7.0) A string identifying the store where the generated credential has to be stored. For the Adobe.PPKLite security handler, the valid store identifiers are "PKCS12" and "MSCAPI". If this parameter is omitted and `cDIPath` is provided, the generated credential is stored in a PKCS#12 file, else it is stored in the CAPI store.

Returns

`true` if successful, throws an exception if not successful.

Example

```
// Create a new PPKLite self-sign credential (Acrobat 5.0 syntax)
var ppklite = security.getHandler(security.PPKLiteHandler);
var oRDN = { cn: "Fred NewUser", c: "US" };
var oCPS = {oid: "1.2.3.4.5",
   url: "http://www.myca.com/mycps.html",
   notice: "This is a self generated certificate, hence the "
      + "recipient must verify it's authenticity through an out "
      + "of band mechansism" };
ppklite.newUser( "testtest", "/d/temp/FredNewUser.pfx",
   oRDN, oCPS);

// Alternate generic object syntax, allowing additional parameters
var oParams = {
   cPassword : "myPassword",
   cDIPath : "/d/temp/FredNewUser.pfx",
   oRDN : oRDN,
   oCPS : oCPS,
   bUI : false
};
```

```
ppklite.newUser( oParams );

// Use a certificate from an existing signed, field
//to create the RDN
var f = this.getField( "mySignature" );
f.signatureValidate();
var sigInfo = f.signatureInfo();
var certs = sigInfo.certificates;
var oSubjectDN = certs[0].subjectDN;

ppklite.newUser({
    cPassword: "dps017",
    cDIPath: "/c/temp/DPSmith.pfx",
    oRDN: oSubjectDN
});
```

setPasswordTimeout

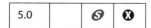

Sets the number of seconds after which password should expire between signatures. This method is only supported by the Adobe.PPKLite security handler. For this handler the default timeout value for a new user is 0 (password always required).

Parameters

cPassword	The password needed to set the timeout value.
iTimeout	The timeout value, in seconds. Set to 0 for always expire (that is, password always required). Set to 0x7FFFFFFF for never expire.

Returns

Throws an exception if the user has not logged in to the Adobe.PPKLite security handler, or unsuccessful for any other reason.

Example

This example logs in to the *PPKLite* security handler and sets the password timeout to 30 seconds. If the password timeout has expired—30 seconds in this example—the signer must provide a password. The password is not necessary if the password has not timed out.

```
var ppklite= security.getHandler( "Adobe.PPKLite" );
ppklite.login( "dps017", "/d/profiles/DPSmith.pfx" );
ppklite.setPasswordTimeout( "dps017", 30 );
```

SecurityPolicy Object

The Security Policy object represents a group of security settings used to apply encryption to a document. It is acquired as the return value of both getSecurityPolicies (page 554) and chooseSecurityPolicy (page 551).

SecurityPolicy Properties

Property	Type	Access	Description
policyID	String	R	A generated string that uniquely identifies the Security Policy. It is not intended to be human-readable. This may be set to a known policy ID on a newly created SecurityPolicy object to force any method using this policy to retrieve the correct security settings before applying the policy.
name	String	R	The policy name used in the UI. It may be localized.
description	String	R	The policy description used in the UI. It may be localized.
handler	String	R	An enumerated value representing the security handler implementing this Security Policy. The possible values are defined in the HandlerName Object in security Constants (page 546).
target	String	R	An enumeration value representing the target data to be encrypted. The possible values are defined in the EncryptTarget Object (page 547) in security Constants.

SignatureInfo Object

A generic JavaScript object that contains the properties of a digital signature. Some properties are supported by all handlers, and additional properties can be supported.

The SignatureInfo object is returned by the Field Object (page 371) methods `signatureValidate` (page 369) and `signatureInfo` (page 416) and is passed to the FDF Object methods `signatureSign` (page 368) and `signatureValidate` (page 369).

Writable properties can be specified when signing the object.

SignatureInfo Properties

All handlers define the following properties.

SignatureInfo Object Properties				
Property	Type	Access	Version	Description
buildInfo	Object	R	6.0	An object containing software build and version information for the signature. The format of this object is described in the technical note *PDF Signature Build Dictionary Specification* on the Adobe Solutions Network website.
date	Date object	R	5.0	The date and time that the signature was created, returned as a JavaScript Date object.
dateTrusted	Boolean	R	7.0	A Boolean that indicates whether the date is from a trusted source. If this value is not present, the date should be assumed to be from an untrusted source (for example, the signer's computer system time).
handlerName	String	R	5.0	The language-independent name of the security handler that was specified as the **Filter** attribute in the signature dictionary. It is usually the name of the security handler that created the signature, but can also be the name of the security handler that the creator wants to be used when validating the signature.
handlerUserName	String	R	5.0	The language-dependent name corresponding to the security handler specified by `handlerName`. It is available onlywhen the named security handler is available.

SignatureInfo Object Properties

Property	Type	Access	Version	Description
handlerUIName	String	R	5.0	The language-dependent name corresponding to the security handler specified by handlerName. It is available only when the named security handler is available.
location	String	R/W	5.0	Optional user-specified location when signing. It can be a physical location (such as a city) or hostname.
mdp	String	R/W	6.0	The Modification Detection and Prevention (MDP) setting that was used to sign the field or FDF Object (page 362) being read, or the MDP setting to use when signing. Values are: allowNone allowAll default defaultAndComments See "Modification Detection and Prevention (MDP) Values" on page 578 for details. The value of allowAll, the default, means that MDP is not used for the signature, resulting in this not being an author signature.
name	String	R	5.0	Name of the user that created the signature.
numFieldsAltered	Number	R	5.0 only	Deprecated. The number of fields altered between the previous signature and this signature. Used only for signature fields. Beginning in Acrobat 7.0, the functionality offered by the Field Object method signatureGetModifications (page 414) should be used instead.
numFieldsFilledIn	Number	R	5.0 only	Deprecated. The number of fields filled-in between the previous signature and this signature. Used only for signature fields. Beginning in Acrobat 7.0, the functionality offered by the Field Object method signatureGetModifications (page 414) should be used instead.
numPagesAltered	Number	R	5.0 only	Deprecated. The number of pages altered between the previous signature and this signature. Used only for signature fields. Beginning in Acrobat 7.0, the functionality offered by signatureGetModifications (page 414) should be used instead.

SignatureInfo Object Properties

Property	Type	Access	Version	Description
numRevisions	Number	R	5.0	The number of revisions in the document. Used only for signature fields.
reason	String	R/W	5.0	The user-specified reason for signing.
revision	Number	R	5.0	The signature revision to which this signature field corresponds. Used only for signature fields.
sigValue	String	R	7.0	Raw bytes of the signature, as a hex encoded string.
status	Number	R	5.0	The validity status of the signature, computed during the last call to signatureValidate (page 423). See the return codes of the status property in the table "status and idValidity Properties" on page 575.
statusText	String	R	5.0	The language-dependent text string, suitable for user display, denoting the signature validity status, computed during the last call to the signatureValidate (page 423).
subFilter	String	R/W	6.0	The format to use when signing. Consult the *PDF Reference* for a complete list of supported values. The known values used for public key signatures include adbe.pkcs7.sha1, adbe.pkcs7.detached, and adbe.x509.rsa_sha1. It is important that the caller know that a particular signature handler can support this format.
timeStamp	String	W	7.0	The URL of the server for time-stamping the signature. The only schemes and transport protocols supported for fetching time stamps are http or https. This property is write-only. If the signature is timestamped, during verification the property dateTrusted will be set to true (provided the timestamp signature is trusted) and the verifyDate and the signing date will be the same.
verifyDate	Date object	R	7.0	The date and time that the signature was verified (if the signature has been verified), returned as a JavaScript Date object.

SignatureInfo Object Properties

Property	Type	Access	Version	Description
verifyHandler Name	String	R	6.0	The language-independent name of the security handler that was used to validate this signature. This will be `null` if the signature has not been validated (that is, if the `status` property has a value of 1).
verifyHandler UIName	String	R	6.0	The language-dependent name corresponding to the security handler specified by `verifyHandlerName`. This will be null if the signature has not been validated, that is, if the `status` property has a value of 1).

SignatureInfo Object Public Key Security Handler Properties

Public key security handlers may define the following additional properties:

SignatureInfo Object Public Key Security Handler Properties

Property	Type	Access	Version	Description
appearance	String	W	5.0	The name of the user-configured appearance to use when signing this field. PPKLite and PPKMS use the standard appearance handler. In this situation, the appearance names can be found in the signature appearance configuration dialog box of the Security user preferences. The default, when not specified, is to use the Standard Text appearance. Used only for visible signature fields.
certificates	Array	R	5.0	Array containing a hierarchy of certificates that identify the signer. The first element in the array is the signer's certificate. Subsequent elements include the chain of certificates up to the certificate authority that issued the signer's certificate. For self-signed certificates this array will contain only one entry.
contactInfo	String	R/W	5.0	The user-specified contact information for determining trust. For example, it can be a telephone number that recipients of a document can use to contact the author. This is not recommended as a scalable solution for establishing trust.
byteRange	Array	R	6.0	An array of numbers indicating the bytes that are covered by this signature.

SignatureInfo Object Public Key Security Handler Properties				
Property	**Type**	**Access**	**Version**	**Description**
docValidity	Number	R	6.0	The validity status of the document byte range digest portion of the signature, computed during the last call to `signatureValidate` (page 423). All PDF document signature field signatures include a byte range digest. See "Validity Values" on page 576 for details of the return codes.
idPrivValidity	Number	R	6.0	The validity of the identity of the signer. This value is specific to the handler. See "Private Validity Values" on page 576 for values supported by the Adobe.PPKLite and Adobe.PPKMS handlers. This value is 0 unless the signature has been validated, that is, if the `status` property has a value of 1.
idValidity	Number	R	6.0	The validity of the identity of the signer as number. See the return codes of the `idValidity` property in the table "status and idValidity Properties" on page 575.
objValidity	Number	R	6.0	The validity status of the object digest portion of the signature, computed during the last call to `signatureValidate` (page 423). For PDF documents, signature field author signatures and document-level application rights signatures include object digests. All FDF files are signed using object digests. See "Validity Values" on page 576 for details of the return codes.
revInfo	Object	R	7.0	A generic object containing two properties, `CRL` and `OCSP`. These properties are arrays of hex-encoded strings, where each string contains the raw bytes of the revocation information that was used to carry out revocation checking of a certificate. For `CRL`, the strings represent CRLs. For `OCSP`, the strings represents OCSP responses. These properties are populated only if the application preference to populate them is turned on, because this data can potentially get very large.

SignatureInfo Object Public Key Security Handler Properties				
Property	Type	Access	Version	Description
trustFlags	Number	R	6.0	The bits in this number indicate what the signer is trusted for. The value is valid only when the value of the status property is 4. These trust settings are derived from trust setting in the recipient's trust database, for example, the Acrobat Address Book (Adobe.AAB). Bit assignments are: ● 1- trusted for signatures ● 2- trusted for certifying documents ● 3- trusted for dynamic content such as multimedia ● 4- Adobe internal use ● 5- the JavaScript in the PDF file is trusted to operate outside the normal PDF restrictions
password	String	W	5.0	Password required as authentication when accessing a private key that is to be used for signing. This may or may not be required, dependent on the policies of the security handler.

status and idValidity Properties

The following table list the codes returned by the SignatureInfo Object, `status` and `idValidity` properties.

Status Code	Description
-1	Not a signature field.
0	Signature is blank or unsigned.
1	Unknown status. This occurs if the signature has not yet been validated. This can occur if the document has not completed downloading over a network connection.
2	Signature is invalid.
3	Signature is valid but the identity of the signer could not be verified.
4	Signature is valid and the identity of the signer is valid.

Validity Values

The following codes are returned by the `docValidity` and `objValidity` properties. (See "SignatureInfo Object Public Key Security Handler Properties" on page 573). They provide a finer granularity of the validity of the signature than the `status` property.

Validity Values	
Status Code	**Description**
`kDSSigValUnknown`	Validity not yet determined.
`kDSSigValUnknownTrouble`	Validity could not be determined because of errors encountered during the validation process.
`kDSSigValUnknownBytesNotReady`	Validity could not be determined because all bytes are not available, for example, when viewing a file in a web browser. Even when bytes are not immediately available, this value may not be returned if the underlying implementation blocks when bytes are not ready. Adobe makes no commitment regarding whether validation checks will block or not block. However, the implementation in Acrobat 6.0 will block when validating `docValidity` and not block when validating `objValidity`.
`kDSSigValInvalidTrouble`	Validity for this digest was not computed because there were errors in the formatting or information contained in this signature. There is sufficient evidence to conclude that the signature is invalid.
`kDSSigValInvalidTrouble`	The validity for this digest is not used (for example, no document validity if no byte range).
`kDSSigValJustSigned`	The signature was just signed, so it is implicitly valid.
`kDSSigValFalse`	The digest or validity is invalid.
`kDSSigValTrue`	The digest or validity is valid.

Private Validity Values

Verification of the validity of the signer's identity is specific to the handler that is being used to validate the identity. This value may contain useful information regarding an identity. The identity is returned in the `idPrivValidity` property. Values for Adobe.PPKMS and Adobe.PPKLite security handlers are shown here. This value is also mapped to an `idValidity` value that is common across all handlers.

Private Validity Values			
Status Code	**idValidity Mapping**	**Security Handler**	**Description**
`kIdUnknown`	1 (unknown)	PPKMS, PPKLite	Validity not yet determined.
`kIdTrouble`	1 (unknown)	PPKMS, PPKLite	Could not determine validity because of errors, for example, internal errors, or could not build the chain, or could not check basic policy.
`kIdInvalid`	2 (invalid)	PPKMS, PPKLite	Certificate is invalid: not time nested, invalid signature, invalid/unsupported constraints, invalid extensions, chain is cyclic.
`kIdNotTimeValid`	2 (invalid)	PPKMS, PPKLite	Certificate is outside its time window (too early or too late).
`kIdRevoked`	2 (invalid)	PPKMS	Certificate has been revoked.
`kIdUntrustedRoot`	1 (unknown)	PPKMS, PPKLite	Certificate has an untrusted root certificate.
`kIdBrokenChain`	2 (invalid)	PPKMS, PPKLite	Could not build a certificate chain up to a self-signed root certificate.
`kIdPathLenConstraint`	2 (invalid)	PPKLite	Certificate chain has exceeded the specified length restriction. The restriction was specified in Basic Constraints extension of one of the certificates in the chain.
`kIdCriticalExtension`	1 (unknown)	PPKMS	One of the certificates in the chain has an unrecognized critical extension.
`kIdJustSigned`	4 (valid)	PPKMS, PPKLite	Just signed by user (similar to kIdIsSelf)
`kIdAssumedValid`	3 (idunknown)	PPKMS	Certificate is valid to a trusted root, but revocation could not be checked and was not required.
`kIdIsSelf`	4 (valid)	PPKMS, PPKLite	Certificate is my credential (no further checking was done).
`kIdValid`	4 (valid)	PPKMS, PPKLite	Certificate is valid to a trusted root (in the Windows or Acrobat Address Book).
`kIdRevocationUnknown`	?	PPKMS, PPKLite	Certificate is valid to a trusted root, but revocation could not be checked and was required by the user.

Modification Detection and Prevention (MDP) Values

Modification detection and prevention (MDP) settings control which changes are allowed to occur in a document before the signature becomes invalid. Changes are recorded outside of the byte range, for signature fields, and can include changes that have been incrementally saved as part of the document or changes that have occurred in memory between the time that a document is opened and when the signature is validated. MDP settings may only be applied to the first signature in a document. Use of MDP will result in an author signature. MDP has one of the following four values:

- `allowAll`: Allow all changes to a document without any of these changes invalidating the signature. This results in MDP not being used for the signature. This was the behavior for Acrobat 4.0 through 5.1.

- `allowNone`: Do not allow any changes to the document without invalidating the signature. Note that this will also lock down the author's signature.

- `default`: Allow form field fill-in if form fields are present in the document. Otherwise, do not allow any changes to the document without invalidating the signature.

- `defaultAndComments`: Allow form field fill-in if form fields are present in the document and allow annotations (comments) to be added, deleted or modified. Otherwise, do not allow any changes to the document without invalidating the signature. Note that annotations can be used to obscure portions of a document and thereby affect the visual presentation of the document.

SOAP Object

The SOAP object allows remote procedure calls to be made to, or sends an XML Message to, a remote server from JavaScript.

The SOAP 1.1 protocol (see http://www.w3.org/TR/SOAP/) is used to marshall JavaScript parameters to a remote procedure call (either synchronously or asynchronously) and to unmarshall the result as a JavaScript object. The SOAP object also has the ability to communicate with web services, described by the Web Services Description Language (WSDL—see http://www.w3.org/TR/wsdl).

Note: The SOAP methods `connect` (page 579), `request` (page 587), and `response` (page 595) are available only for documents open in Acrobat Professional and Standard and for documents with Form Export Rights(**F**) open in Adobe Reader 6.0 or later.

SOAP Properties

wireDump

6.0			

If `true`, synchronous SOAP requests will cause the XML Request and Response to be dumped to the JavaScript Console. This is useful for debugging SOAP problems.

Type: Boolean   *Access: R/W*

SOAP Methods

connect

6.0			**F**

Converts the URL of a WSDL document (cURL) to a JavaScript object with callable methods corresponding to the web service.

The parameters to the method calls and the return values obey the rules specified for the `SOAP.request` (page 587) method.

Parameters

cURL	The URL of a WSDL document. It must be an HTTP or HTTPS URL.

Returns

A WSDL Service Proxy object with a JavaScript method corresponding to each operation in the WSDL document provided at the URL. The parameters required for the method depend on the WSDL operation you are calling and how the operation encodes its parameters:

- If the WSDL operation is using the SOAP RPC encoding (as described in Section 7 of the SOAP 1.1 Specification), the arguments to the service method are the same as the parameter order in the WSDL document.

- If the WSDL service is using the SOAP document/literal encoding, the function will have a single argument indicating the request message. The argument may be a JavaScript object literal describing the message or it may be either a string or a ReadStream Object (page 519) with an XML fragment describing the message. The return value of the service method will correspond to the return value of the WSDL operation.

The JavaScript function objects corresponding to each web service method use the following properties if they are set. The default is for none of the properties to be set.

Property	Description
asyncHandler	Indicates that the web service method should be performed asynchronously. The property corresponds to the oAsync parameter of SOAP.request (page 587).
requestHeader	Indicates that the web service method should include a SOAP Header in the request. The property corresponds to the oReqHeader parameter of SOAP.request (page 587).
responseHeader	Indicates that the web service method should return a SOAP Header from the response. The property corresponds to the oRespHeader parameter of SOAP.request (page 587).
authenticator	Indicates how authentication should be handled for the web service method. The property corresponds to the oAuthenticate parameter of SOAP.request (page 587).

Exceptions

SOAP Faults cause a SOAPError exception to be thrown. If there is a problem at the networking level, such as an unavailable endpoint, a NetworkError is thrown. See the request (page 587) method for more information.

Adobe® Acrobat® Official JavaScript Reference

Example

A service WSDL Document URL is needed. These can be obtained from the "Round 2 Interop Services - using SOAP 1.2" section at the following URL: http://www.whitemesa.com/interop.htm.

```
var cURL = <get a URL for this service from
        http://www.whitemesa.com/interop.htm>;

// Connect to the test service
var service = SOAP.connect(cURL);

// Print out the methods this service supports to the console
for(var i in service) console.println(i);

var cTestString = "This is my test string";

// Call the echoString service--it is an RPC Encoded method
var result = service.echoString(cTestString);

// This should be the same as cTestString
console.println(result + " == " + cTestString);

// Call the echoInteger service -- JavaScript doesn't
// support integers so we make our own integer object.
var oTestInt =
{
    soapType: "xsd:int",
    soapValue: "10"
};
var result = service.echoInteger(oTestInt);

// This should be the same as oTestInt.soapValue
console.println(result + " == " + oTestInt.soapValue);
```

This produces the following output:

```
echoBase64
echoBoolean
echoDate
echoDecimal
echoFloat
echoFloatArray
echoHexBinary
echoInteger
echoIntegerArray
echoPolyMorph
echoPolyMorphArray
echoPolyMorphStruct
echoString
echoStringArray
echoStruct
echoStructArray
echoVoid
This is my test string == This is my test string
10 == 10
```

querySentices

7.0		✒	

Locate network services that have published themselves using DNS Service Discovery (DNS-SD). This method can locate services that have registered using Multicast DNS (mDNS) for location on a local networking link or through unicast DNS for location within an enterprise. The results of service location are always returned asynchronously and the query continues (with notification as services become available or unavailable) until it is stopped.

The result of querying for services is a set of service names that can be bound when needed by calling `resolveService`.

Services can either use a third-party mDNS responder to be located in the local network link or register themselves in a DNS server (either statically or dynamically) to be located within an enterprise networking environment.

Parameters

cType	The DNS SRV Service Name to search for. Some possible examples are: • `"http"`: Locate web servers • `"ftp"`: Locate FTP servers See the DNS SRV Service Name Registry for more examples
oAsync	A notification object that is notified when services are located on the network or when services that had previously been reported are removed. The notification methods are not called until the `queryServices` method returns and are called during idle processing. The oAsync parameter should implement the following methods: • `addServices`: This method is called when available services matching the query are located. The parameter is an array of Service Description Objects (page 583) for the services that have been added. • `removeServices`: This method is called when services that had previously been introduced by calling the `addServices` notification method are no longer available. The parameter is an array of Service Description Objects (page 583) for the services that have been removed. **Note:** In Acrobat 7.0, only services located through mDNS (that is, in the "local." domain) are updated dynamically.

aDomains	(optional) An array of domains that the query should be made for. The only valid domains are:

- `ServiceDiscovery.local`: Search for services in the local networking link using Multicast DNS (mDNS). This is useful for finding network services in an *ad hoc* networking environment, but network services will only be located within the scope of the current network router.
- `ServiceDiscovery.DNS`: Search for services in the default DNS domain using unicast DNS. This is useful for locating network services in the context of a DNS server, but typically requires IS assistance to register a service and is less dynamic.

Returns

A service query object that manages the duration of the query. The query will continue until one of the following conditions is met:

- The service query object returned from `queryServices` is garbage collected.
- The `stop` method of the service query object returned from `queryServices` is called.

Method	Description
stop	Causes the query to terminate. This method can be called from a notification callback but the operation will not stop until idle processing time.

Exceptions

Standard Acrobat exceptions.

Service Description Object

The service description object passed to `addServices` and `removeServices` have the following properties:

Property	Description
name	The Unicode display name of the service.
domain	The DNS domain in which the service was located. If the service was located in the local networking link, the domain name will be "local".
type	The DNS SRV Service Name of the service that was located – this will be the same as the `cType` parameter passed to `queryServices`. This can be useful when the same notification callback is being used for multiple queries.

Example

This example code will produce different output depending on where it is run.

```
var oNotifications =
{
  addServices: function(services)
  {
    for(var i = 0; i < services.length; i++)
    console.println("ADD: "+ services[i].name + " in domain "
        + services[i].domain);
  }
  removeServices: function(services)
  {
    for(var i = 0; i < services.length; i++)
    console.println("DEL: " + services[i].name + " in
domain "
        + services[i].domain);
  }
};
SOAP.queryServices({
  cType:"http",
  oAsync:oNotifications,
  aDomains:[ServiceDiscovery.local, ServiceDiscovery.DNS]
});
```

The output depends on the current network environment; if there are no services advertised by DNS Service Discovery, the example will produce no output. The following is a representative output:

```
ADD: My Web Server in domain local.
ADD: Joe's Web Server in domain local.
ADD: Example.org Web Server in domain example.org.
```

resolveService

Allows a service name to be bound to a network address and port in order for a connection to be made. The connection information is returned asynchronously and should be treated as temporary since the network location of a service may change over time (for example, if a DHCP lease expires or if a service moves to a new server).

Parameters

cType	The DNS SRV Service Name to resolve.
cDomain	The domain that the service was located in.
cService	The service name to resolve.
oAsync	An object that will be called when the service is resolved. See "Additional Notes on the oAsync Parameter" on page 585.

Returns

A service query object that manages the duration of the resolve. The resolve will continue until one of the following conditions is met:

- The service query object returned from resolveService is garbage collected.
- The resolve method of the oAsync object is called indicating that the operation completed (either by resolving the service, error, or a timeout).
- The stop method of the service query object returned from resolveService is called.

Method	Description
stop	Causes the resolve to terminate. This method can be called from a notification callback but the operation will not stop until idle time.

Exceptions

Standard Acrobat Exceptions.

Additional Notes on the oAsync Parameter

The oAsync object is a notification object that will be called when the service is resolved. The notification methods will not be called until the resolveService method returns and are called during idle processing. The oAsync parameter should implement the following method:

Method	Description
resolve	This method is called with two parameters (nStatus and oInfo) when the service is resolved or if it cannot be resolved. The parameter nStatus is the state indicating if the service could be resolved (see below). If the service was successfully resolved, the oInfo object, an instance of the ServiceInfo object (see below), specifies the connection information.

The `nStatus` parameter passed to the resolve method can have one of the following values:

Value	Description
0	The service was successfully resolved.
1	The service timed out before being resolved. The default timeout in Acrobat 7 is 60 seconds.
-1	There was an networking error trying to resolve the service.

The `ServiceInfo` object passed to the resolve method has the following properties:

Property	Description
target	The IP address or DNS name of the machine supplying the service.
port	The port on the machine supplying the service.
info	An object with name - value pairs that the service has supplied. For example, in the case of an HTTP service, the path property will contain the path on the webservice so that the service URL would be `http://<target>:<port>/<info["path"]>)`.

Example

This example code will produce different output depending on where it is run. If there are no services advertised by DNS Service Discovery, this example will produce no output.

```
var oNotifications =
{
    resolve: function(status, info)
    {
        if(status == 0)
            console.println("RESOLVE: http://"
                + info.target + ":" + info.port + "/"
                + info.info.path);
        else console.println("ERROR: " + status);
    }
};
SOAP.resolveService({
    cType: "http",
    cDomain: "local.",
    cService: "Joe's Web Server",
    oAsync: oNotifications
});
```

The output depends on the current network environment – the following is a representative output:

```
RESOLVE: http://127.0.0.1:80/index.html
```

request

6.0			

Initiates a remote procedure call (RPC) or sends an XML message to a SOAP HTTP endpoint. The method either waits for the endpoint to reply (synchronous processing) or calls a method on the notification object (asynchronous processing).

Parameters

cURL	The URL for a SOAP HTTP Endpoint. The URL method must be one of :
	• http—Connect to a server at a URI on a port. For example, http://serverName:portNumber/URI
	• https—Connect to a secured (SSL) server at a URI on a port. For example, https://serverName:portNumber/URI
oRequest	An object that specifies the remote procedure name and parameters or the XML message to send.
	See "Additional Notes on the oRequest Parameter" on page 590.
oAsync	(optional) An object that specifies that the method invocation will occur asychronously. The default is for the request to be made synchronously. The object has been modified in Acrobat 7.0.
	(Acrobat 6.0) The oAsync object literal must have a function called response that will be called with two parameters (oResult and cURI) when the response returns. oResult is the same result object that would have been returned from the request call if it was called synchronously. cURI is the URI of the endpoint that the request was made to.
	(Acrobat 7.0) The oAsync object response callback has the following parameters:
	• response: The response object from the SOAP request.
	• uri: The URI that the SOAP request was made to.
	• exception: An exception object (see the exceptions below) if there was an error, null otherwise.
	• header: A response SOAP header (see the description of the oRespHeader parameter) or null if there are no response headers.
cAction	(optional) In SOAP 1.1, this parameter is passed as the SOAPAction header. In SOAP 1.2, this parameter is passed as the action parameter in the Content-Type header.
	The default is for the action to be an empty string.
	The SOAPAction is a URN written to an HTTP header used by firewalls and servers to filter SOAP requests. The WSDL file for the SOAP service or the SOAP service description will usually describe the SOAPAction header required (if any).
bEncoded	(optional) Encoded the request using the SOAP Encoding described in the SOAP Specification. Otherwise, the literal encoding is used.
	The default is true.

cNamespace	(optional) A namespace for the message schema when the request does not use the SOAP Encoding.
	The default is to omit the schema declaration.
oReqHeader	(optional, Acrobat 7.0) An object that specifies a SOAP header to be included with the request. The default is to send a request with only a SOAP Body.
	The object is specified in the same way as the `oRequest` object except for two additional properties that can be specified in the request description:
	• `soapActor`: The recipient (or actor specified as a URI) that the SOAP header should be processed by. The default is that the header will be processed by the first recipient to process the request.
	• `soapMustUnderstand`: A Boolean indicating that the request body cannot be interpreted if this header type is not understood by the recipient. The default is that understanding the header is optional.
oRespHeader	(optional, Acrobat 7.0) An object that will be populated with the SOAP headers returned when the method completes if the function is being called synchronously (the header will be passed to the `oAsync` callback method otherwise).
	The default is for the headers to not be returned.
	See the description of the `cResponseStyle` parameter for the object format.
cVersion	(optional, Acrobat 7.0) The version of the SOAP protocol to use when generating the XML Message – either 1.1 or 1.2.
	The default is to use "SOAPVersion.version_1_1".
oAuthenticate	(optional, Acrobat 7.0) An object that specifies how to handle HTTP authentication or credentials to use for Web Service Security. The default is to present a user interface to the user to handle HTTP authentication challenges for BASIC and DIGEST authentication modes. The `oAuthenticate` object can have the following properties:
	• `Username`: A string containing the username to use for authentication.
	• `Password`: A string containing the authentication credential to use.
	• `UsePlatformAuth`: A Boolean indicating that platform authentication should be used. If platform authentication is enabled, the `Username` and `Password` are ignored and the underlying platform networking code is used. This may cause an authentication UI to be shown to the user and/or the credentials of the currently logged in user to be used. The default is `false` and is only supported on the Windows platform.

cResponseStyle	(optional, Acrobat 7.0) An enumerated type indicating how the return value (in the case of the SOAP Body) and the oRespHeader object (in the case of a SOAP header) will be structured: ● SOAPMessageStyle.JS (Default): The response will be an object describing the SOAP Body (or SOAP Header) of the returned message (this is the result that Acrobat 6.0 produced). This is recommended when using the SOAP encoding for the request but is not ideal when using the literal encoding – using the XML or Message style is better. ● SOAPMessageStyle.XML: The response will be a stream object containing the SOAP Body (or SOAP Header) as an XMLfragment. If there are any attachments associated with the response, the Stream object will have an object property oAttachments. The object keys are the unique names for the attachment parts and the value must be a Stream object containing the attachment contents. ● SOAPMessageStyle.Message: The response will be an object describing the SOAP Body (or SOAP Header) corresponding to the XML Message. This differs from the JavaScript response style in the following ways: XML Elements are returned as an array of objects rather than an object to maintain order and allow elements with the same name. XML Attributes are preserved using the soapAttributes property. Namespaces are processed and returned in the soapName and soapQName properties. The content of an element is in the soapValue property.
cRequestStyle	(optional, Acrobat 7.0.5) Allows the interpretation of oRequest to be altered. The following values are permitted: ● SOAPRequestStyle.SOAP (the default): The request is made using the SOAP messaging model. ● SOAPRequestStyle.RawPost: The oRequest parameter is used as the request body for an HTTP Post. oRequest must be a ReadStream Object (page 519). If this method is called within the context of a document, the document must be open in the browser. Additionally, the origination URL of the document (scheme, server, and port) must match the origination of the cURL parameter. The response is a ReadStream Object with the response from the request.
cContentType	(optional, Acrobat 7.0.5) Allows the HTTP content-type header to be specified. The default is to use the SOAP messaging HTTP content-type.

Returns

A response object if the method was called synchronously (that is, there is no oAsync parameter) or nothing if the method was called asynchronously. See the description of cResponseStyle above for the object description.

The SOAP types in the result are mapped to JavaScript types as follows:

SOAP Type	JavaScript Type
xsd:string	String
xsd:integer	Number
xsd:float	Number
xsd:dateTime	Date
xsd:boolean	Boolean
xsd:hexBinary	ReadStream Object (page 519)
xsd:base64Binary	ReadStream Object
SOAP-ENC:base64	ReadStream Object
SOAP-ENC:Array	Array
No Type Information	String

Exceptions

SOAPError is thrown when the SOAP endpoint returns a SOAPFault. The SOAPError Exception object has the following properties:

Property	Description
faultCode	A string indicating the SOAP Fault Code for this fault.
faultActor	A string indicating the SOAP Actor that generated the fault.
faultDetail	A string indicating detail associated with the fault.

NetworkError is thrown when there is a failure from the underlying HTTPtransport layer or in obtaining a Network connection. The NetworkError Exception object has the property statusCode, which is an HTTP Status code or –1 if the Network connection could not be made.

Standard Acrobat exceptions can also be thrown.

Note: If the method was called asynchronously, the exception object may be passed to the response callback method.

Additional Notes on the oRequest Parameter

The oRequest parameter is an object literal that specifies the remote procedure name and the parameters to call. The object literal uses the fully qualified method name of the remote procedure as the key. The namespace should be separated from the method name by a colon.

For example, if the namespace for the method is
`http://mydomain/methods` and the method name is `echoString`, the fully
qualified name would be `http://mydomain/methods:echoString`. The
value of this key is an object literal, each key is a parameter of the method,
and the value of each key is the value of the corresponding parameter of the
method. For example:

```
oRequest: {
    "http://soapinterop.org/:echoString":{inputString: "Echo!"}
}
```

When passing parameters to a remote procedure, JavaScript types are
bound to SOAP types automatically as listed in the table:

JavaScript Type	SOAP Type
String	xsd:string
Number	xsd:float
Date	xsd:dateTime
Boolean	xsd:boolean
ReadStream Object	SOAP-ENC:base64
Array	SOAP-ENC:Array
Other	No type information

Note: The `xsd` namespace refers to the XML Schema Datatypes namespace
`http://www.w3.org/2001/XMLSchema`. The `SOAP-ENC` namespace
refers to the SOAP Encoding namespace
`http://schemas.xmlsoap.org/soap/encoding/`.

The `oRequest` object supports the following properties:

Property	Description
soapType	The SOAP type that will be used for the value when generating the SOAP message. It is useful when a datatype is needed other than the automatic datatype binding described above. The type should be namespace qualified using the `<namespace>:<type>` notation, for example `http://mydomain/types:myType` However, the `xsd` (XMLSchema Datatypes), `xsi` (XMLSchema Instance), and SOAP-ENC (SOAP Encoding) namespaces are implicitly defined in the SOAP message, so the `soapType` can use them, as in `xsd:int` for the XMLSchema Datatype Integer type.

Property	Description
soapValue	(Acrobat 6.0) The value that will be used when generating the SOAP message. It can be a string or a ReadStream Object (page 519). soapValue is passed unescaped (that is, not XML Entity escaped). For example, "<" is not converted to "<" in the XML Message. Consequently, soapValue can be a raw XML fragment that will be passed to the XML Message.

(Acrobat 7.0) soapValue can now also be an array of nodes that are an ordered set of children of the node in the request message. |
| soapName | The element name that will be used when generating the SOAP message instead of the key name in the object literal.

For example, integers are not supported in JavaScript, but an integer parameter to a SOAP method can be constructed as follows:

```
var oIntParameter = {
    soapType: "xsd:int",
    soapValue: "1"
};
```

Later, the oRequest parameter for the SOAP.request method might be this:

```
oRequest: {
    "http://soapinterop.org/:echoInteger":
        { inputInteger: oIntParameter }
}
```

Example 1 (page 593) that follows the description of the SOAP.request shows this technique. |
| soapAttributes | (Acrobat 7.0) An object specifiying XML attributes to be included when building the element corresponding to the request node. The object keys are the attribute names and the corresponding value is the attribute value. |
| soapQName | (Acrobat 7.0) An object specifying the namespace qualified name (QName) of the request node. For example, in the element <ns:local xmlns:ns="urn:example.org">, the element name is a QName consisting of a local name ("local") and a namespace ("urn:example.org").

This object has two properties:

• localName: A string indicating the local name of the QName.
• nameSpace: A string indicating the namespace of the QName. |
| soapAttachment | (Acrobat 7.0) A Boolean indicating that the soapValue contents of the node should be encoded as an attachment according to the SwA specification. The soapValue *must* be a stream if the corresponding soapAttachment property is true, otherwise an exception will be thrown. |
| soapParamOrder | (Acrobat 7.0) An array indicating the order in which RPC parameters should be sent to the server. The array is a set of strings with the parameter names. This value is only applicable when bEncoding is true. |

Example 1

A service WSDL Document URL is needed. It can be obtained from the "Round 2 Interop Services - using SOAP 1.2" section at the following URL: http://www.whitemesa.com/interop.htm.

```
var cURL = <get a URL for this service from
      http://www.whitemesa.com/interop.htm>;

var cTestString = "This is my test string";

// Call the echoString SOAP method -- it is an RPC Encoded method
var response = SOAP.request(
{
   cURL: cURL,
   oRequest: {
      "http://soapinterop.org/:echoString": {
         inputString: cTestString
      }
   },
   cAction: "http://soapinterop.org/"
});

var result =
response["http://soapinterop.org/:echoStringResponse"]["return"];

// This should be the same as cTestString
console.println(result + " == " + cTestString);

// Call the echoInteger SOAP method -- JavaScript doesn't support
// integers so we make our own integer object.
var oTestInt =
{
   soapType: "xsd:int",
   soapValue: "10"
};

var response = SOAP.request(
{
   cURL: cURL,
   oRequest: {
      "http://soapinterop.org/:echoInteger": {
         inputInteger: oTestInt
      }
   },
   cAction: "http://soapinterop.org/"
});

var result =
response["http://soapinterop.org/:echoIntegerResponse"]["return"];

// This should be the same as oTestInt.soapValue
console.println(result + " == " + oTestInt.soapValue);
```

This produces the following output:

```
This is my test string == This is my test string
10 == 10
```

Example 2

This example sets a SOAP Header and gets it back.

```
var cURL = <URL of a Service>;
var NS = "http://adobe.com/FEAT/:";
var oHeader = {};
oHeader[NS + "testSession"] =
{
    soapType: "xsd:string",
    soapValue: "Header Test String"
};
var oResultHeader = {};
var oRequest = {};
oRequest[NS + "echoHeader"] = {};
var response = SOAP.request(
{
    cURL: cURL,
    oRequest: oRequest,
    cAction: "http://soapinterop.org/",
    oReqHeader: oHeader,
    oRespHeader: oResultHeader
});
```

Example 3

This example uses HTTP Authentication.

```
var oAuthenticator =
{
    Username: "myUserName",
    Password: "myPassword"
};
var response = SOAP.request(
{
    cURL: cURL,
    oRequest: {
        "http://soapinterop.org/:echoString":
        {
            inputString: cTestString
        }
    },
    cAction: "http://soapinterop.org/",
    oAuthenticate: oAuthenticator
});
```

response

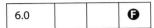

6.0			**F**

Initiates a remote procedure call (RPC) or sends an XML message to a SOAP HTTP endpoint without waiting for a reply.

Parameters

cURL	The URL for a SOAP HTTP Endpoint. The URL method must be one of these: • http—Connect to a server at a URI on a port. For example, http://serverName:portNumber/URI • https—Connect to a secured (SSL) server at a URI on a port. For example, https://serverName:portNumber/URI See the cURL parameter of SOAP.request (page 587).
oRequest	An object that specifies the remote procedure name and parameters or the XML message to send. See the oRequest parameter of SOAP.request (page 587).
cAction	(optional) The SOAP Action header for this request as specified by the SOAP Specification. The default is for the SOAP Action to be empty. See the cAction parameter of SOAP.request (page 587).
bEncoded	(optional) A Boolean specifying whether the request was encoded using the SOAP Encoding described in the SOAP Specification. The default is true.
cNamespace	(optional) A namespace for the message schema when the request does not use the SOAP Encoding (the bEncoded flag is false). The default is to have no namespace.
oReqHeader	(optional, Acrobat 7.0) An object that specifies a SOAP header to be included with the request. The default is to send a request with only a SOAP Body. See the oReqHeader parameter of SOAP.request (page 587).
cVersion	(optional, Acrobat 7.0) The version of the SOAP protocol to use. The default is to use "SOAPVersion.version_1_1". See the cVersion parameter of SOAP.request (page 587).
oAuthenticate	(optional, Acrobat 7.0) An object that specifies the type of authentication scheme to use and to provide credentials. The default is for an interactive UI to be displayed if HTTP authentication is encountered. See the oAuthenticate parameter of SOAP.request (page 587).

cRequestStyle	(optional, Acrobat 7.0.5) Same as cRequestStyle for SOAP.request (page 587), except that there is no response from the server.
cContentType	(optional, Acrobat 7.0.5) Same as cContentType for SOAP.request (page 587), except that there is no response from the server.

Returns

Boolean

Exceptions

If there is a problem at the networking level, such as an unavailable endpoint, a NetworkError will be thrown.

Example

See the "Example 1" on page 593 that follows the SOAP.request (page 587) method.

streamDecode

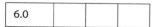

Allows the oStream object to be decoded with the specified encoding type, cEncoder. It returns a decoded ReadStream Object (page 519). Typically, it is used to access data returned as part of a SOAP method that was encoded in Base64 or hex encoding.

Parameters

oStream	A stream object to be decoded with the specified encoding type.
cEncoder	Permissible values for this string are "hex" (hex-encoded) and "base64" (Base 64-encoded).

Returns

ReadStream Object (page 519)

streamDigest

7.0			

Allows the oStream object to be digested with the specified encoding type, cEncoder. It returns a ReadStream Object (page 519) containing the computed digest of the oStream. Typically, this is used to compute a digest

---

to validate the integrity of the original data stream or as part of an authentication scheme for a web service.

Parameters

oStream	A stream object to compute the digest of, using the specified message digest algorithm.
cEncoder	The digest algorithm to use. The cEncoder parameter must be one of the following values:

- StreamDigest.MD5: Digest the content using the MD5 Digest Algorithm (see RFC 1321).
- StreamDigest.SHA1: Digest the content using the SHA-1 Digest Algorithm (see RFC 3174).

Returns

A ReadStream Object (page 519) with the binary digest of the stream. To be used as a string, the result must be converted to a text format such as Base64 or hex using SOAP.streamEncode.

Example

```
var srcStm = SOAP.streamFromString("This is a string I want to
digest");
var digest = SOAP.streamDigest(srcStm, StreamDigest.SHA1);
```

streamEncode

6.0			

This function allows the oStream object to be encoded with the specified encoding type, cEncoder. It returns a ReadStream Object (page 519) that will have the appropriate encoding applied. Typically, this is used to pass data as part of a SOAP method when it must be encoded in Base 64 or hex encoding.

Parameters

oStream	A stream object to be encoded with the specified encoding type.
cEncoder	Permissible values for this string are "hex" (for hex-encoded) and "base64" (base 64-encoded).

Returns

.

streamFromString

6.0			

This function converts a string to a ReadStream Object (page 519). Typically, this is used to pass data as part of a SOAP method.

Parameters

cString	The string to be converted.

Returns

ReadStream Object (page 519)

stringFromStream

6.0			

This function converts a ReadStream Object (page 519) to a string. Typically, this is used to examine the contents of a stream object returned as part of a response to a SOAP method.

Parameters

oStream	The ReadStream Object (page 519) to be converted.

Returns

String

Sound Object

5.0			

This object represents a sound that is stored in the document. The array of all Sound objects can be obtained from the Document Object `sounds` (page 206) property. See also Document Object methods `getSound` (page 258), `importSound` (page 265), and `deleteSound` (page 229).

Sound Properties

name

The name associated with this Sound object.

Type: String   *Access: R*

Example

```
console.println("Dumping all sound objects in this document.");
var s = this.sounds;
for (var i = 0; i < this.sounds.length; i++)
    console.println("Sound[" + i + "]=" + s[i].name);
```

Sound Methods

pause

Pauses the currently playing sound. If the sound is already paused, the sound play is resumed.

Parameters

None

Returns

Nothing

play

Plays the sound asynchronously.

Parameters

None

Returns

Nothing

stop

Stops the currently playing sound.

Parameters

None

Returns

Nothing

Span Object

| 6.0 | | | |

This object represents a length of text and its associated properties in a rich text form field or annotation. A rich text value consists of an array of span objects representing the text and formatting.

Note: Span objects are a copy of the rich text value of the field or annotation. To modify and reset the rich text value to update the field, use the Field Object `richValue` (page 392) property , or the Annotation Object property `richContents` (page 37), and the `event` Object (page 314) properties `richValue` (page 333), `richChange` (page 331), and `richChangeEx` (page 332).

Span Properties

alignment

The horizontal alignment of the text. Alignment for a line of text is determined by the first span on the line. The values of `alignment` are

```
left
center
right
```

The default value is `left`.

Type: String   *Access: R/W*

The example following `superscript` (page 603) uses `alignment`.

fontFamily

The font family used to draw the text. It is an array of family names to be searched for in order. The first entry in the array is the font name of the font to use. The second entry is an optional generic family name to use if an exact match of the first font is not found. The generic family names are

```
symbol, serif, sans-serif, cursive, monospace, fantasy
```

The default generic family name is `sans-serif`.

Type: Array   *Access: R/W*

Example

Set the `defaultStyle` (page 380) font family for a rich text field.

```
f = this.getField("Text1");
style = f.defaultStyle;
```

```
// if Courier Std is not found on the user's system,
// use a monospace
style.fontFamily = ["Courier Std", "monospace" ];
f.defaultStyle = style;
```

fontStretch

Specifies the normal, condensed or extended face from a font family to be used to draw the text. The values of `fontStretch` are

`ultra-condensed, extra-condensed, condensed, semi-condensed, normal, semi-expanded, expanded, extra-expanded, ultra-expanded`

The default value is `normal`.

Type: String   *Access: R/W*

fontStyle

Specifies the text is drawn with an italic or oblique font.

`italic`
`normal`

The default is `normal`.

Type: String   *Access: R/W*

fontWeight

The weight of the font used to draw the text. For the purposes of comparison, normal is anything under 700 and bold is greater than or equal to 700. The values of `fontWeight` are

`100,200,300,400,500,600,700,800,900`

The default value is 400.

Type: Number   *Access: R/W*

strikethrough

If `strikethrough` is `true`, the text is drawn with a strikethrough. The default is `false`.

Type: Boolean   *Access: R/W*

subscript

Specifies the text is subscript. If `true`, subscript text is drawn with a reduced point size and a lowered baseline. The default is `false`.

Type: Boolean   *Access: R/W*

---

superscript

Specifies the text is superscript. If `true`, superscript text is drawn with a
reduced point size and a raised baseline. The default is `false`.

Type: Boolean   *Access: R/W*

Example

Write rich text to a rich text field using various properties. See the Field
Object `richValue` (page 392) property for more details and examples.

```
var f = this.getField("myRichField");

// need an array to hold the Span objects
var spans = new Array();

// each Span object is an object, so we must create one
spans[0] = new Object();
spans[0].alignment = "center";
spans[0].text = "The answer is x";

spans[1] = new Object();
spans[1].text = "2/3";
spans[1].superscript = true;

spans[2] = new Object();
spans[2].superscript = false;
spans[2].text = ".  ";

spans[3] = new Object();
spans[3].underline = true;
spans[3].text = "Did you get it right?";
spans[3].fontStyle = "italic";
spans[3].textColor = color.red;

// now assign our array of Span objects to the field using
// field.richValue
f.richValue = spans;
```

text

The text within the span.

Type: String   *Access: R/W*

The example following `superscript` (page 603) uses `text`.

textColor

A color array representing the RGB color to be used to draw the text (see the
`color Object` (page 156)). The default color is black.

Type: Color Array   *Access: R/W*

The example following superscript (page 603) uses textColor.

textSize

The point size of the text. The value of textSize can be any number between 0 and 32767, inclusive. A text size of zero means to use the largest point size that will allow all text data to fit in the field's rectangle.

The default text size is 12.0.

Type: Number   *Access: R/W*

The example following the Field Object richValue (page 392) property uses textSize.

underline

If underline is true, the text is underlined. The default is false.

Type: Boolean   *Access: R/W*

The example following superscript (page 603) uses underline.

spell Object

This object allows users to check the spelling of Comments and Form Fields and other spelling domains. To be able to use the `spell` object, the user must have installed the Acrobat Spelling plug-in and the spelling dictionaries.

Note: (Adobe Reader ✖) The `spell` object is not available in versions of Adobe Reader prior to 7.0. In Adobe Reader 7.0, all properties and methods—with the exception of `customDictionaryCreate` (page 613), `customDictionaryDelete` (page 614) and `customDictionaryExport` (page 614)—are accessible.

spell Properties

available

5.0			

`true` if the `spell` object is available.

Note: For Adobe Reader, this property is available only for version 7.0 or later.

Type: Boolean   *Access: R*

Example
```
console.println("Spell checking available: " +
spell.available);
```

dictionaryNames

5.0			

An array of available dictionary names. A subset of this array can be passed to `check` (page 609), `checkText` (page 610), and `checkWord` (page 611), and to `spellDictionaryOrder` (page 206) to force the use of a specific dictionary or dictionaries and the order they should be searched.

A listing of valid dictionary names for the user's installation can be obtained by executing `spell.dictionaryNames` from the console.

Note: For Adobe Reader, this property is available only for version 7.0 or later.

Type: Array   *Access: R*

dictionaryOrder

5.0			

The dictionary array search order specified by the user on the Spelling Preferences panel. The Spelling plug-in will search for words first in the Document Object `spellDictionaryOrder` (page 206) array if it has been set for the document, followed by this array of dictionaries.

Note: For Adobe Reader, this property is available only for version 7.0 or later.

Type: Array   *Access: R*

domainNames

5.0			

The array of spelling domains that have been registered with the Spelling plug-in by other plug-ins. A subset of this array can be passed to `check` (page 609) to limit the scope of the spell check.

Depending on the user's installation, valid domains can include:

```
Everything
Form Field
All Form Fields
Comment
All Comments
```

Note: For Adobe Reader, this property is available only for version 7.0 or later.

Type: Array   *Access: R*

languages

6.0			

This property returns the array of available ISO 639-2/3166-1 language/country codes. A subset of this array can be passed to the `check` (page 609), `checkText` (page 610), `checkWord` (page 611), and `customDictionaryCreate` (page 613) methods, and to the Document Object `spellLanguageOrder` (page 207) property to force the use of a specific language or languages and the order they should be searched.

Note: For Adobe Reader, this property is available only for version 7.0 or later.

Type: Array   *Access: R*

Depending on the user's installation, valid language/country codes can include:

Code	Description	Code	Description
ca_ES	Catalan	el_GR	Greek
cs_CZ	Czech	hu_HU	Hungarian
da_DK	Danish	it_IT	Italian
nl_NL	Dutch	nb_NO	Norwegian – Bokmal
en_CA	English – Canadian	nn_NO	Norwegian – Nynorsk
en_GB	English – UK	pl_PL	Polish
en_US	English – US	pt_BR	Portuguese – Brazil
fi_FI	Finnish	pt_PT	Portuguese
fr_CA	French – Canadian	ru_RU	Russian
fr_FR	French	es_ES	Spanish
de_DE	German	sv_SE	Swedish
de_CH	German – Swiss	tr_TR	Turkish

Note: In Acrobat 7.0, the entries in this array are different from the entries returned in Acrobat 6.0. On input from JavaScript, the Acrobat 6.0 ISO codes are internally mapped onto the new ISO codes in order to not break any JavaScript code developed for Acrobat 6.0. Codes are not translated on output.

Example

List all available language codes.

```
console.println( spell.languages.toSource() );
```

languageOrder

6.0			

The dictionary search order as an array of ISO 639-2, 3166 language codes. It is the order specified by the user on the Spelling Preferences panel. The Spelling plug-in searches for words first in the Document Object `spellLanguageOrder` (page 207) array if it has been set for the document, followed by this array of languages.

Note: For Adobe Reader, this property is available only for version 7.0 or later.

Type: Array   *Access: R*

Example

Get a listing of the dictionary search order.

```
console.println( spell.languageOrder.toSource() );
```

spell Methods

addDictionary

> **Note:** Beginning with Acrobat 6.0, this method is no longer supported and always returns `false`. Use the `customDictionaryOpen` (page 615) method instead.

Adds a dictionary to the list of available dictionaries.

A dictionary actually consists of four files: DDDxxxxx.hyp, DDDxxxxx.lex, DDDxxxxx.clx, and DDDxxxxx.env. The `cFile` parameter must be the device-independent path of the .hyp file, for example, "/c/temp/testdict/TST.hyp". The Spelling plug-in will look in the parent directory of the TST.hyp file for the other three files. All four file names must start with the same unique 3 characters to associate them with each other, and they must end with the dot three extensions listed above, even on a Macintosh.

Parameters

cFile	The device-independent path to the dictionary files.
cName	The dictionary name used in the spelling dialog box. It can be used as the input parameter to the check (page 609), checkText (page 610), and checkWord (page 611) methods.
bShow	(optional) If true (the default), the cName value is combined with "User: " that name is shown in all lists and menus. For example, if cName is "Test", "User: Test" is added to all lists and menus. If false, this custom dictionary is not shown in any lists or menus.

Returns

false

addWord

| 5.0 |  | | |

Adds a new word to a dictionary. See also the removeWord (page 617).

Note: (Security ⊘): Beginning with Acrobat 7.0, this method is allowed only during console or batch events. See "Privileged versus Non-privileged Context" on page 8 for details.

Internally, the spell object scans the user "Not-A-Word" dictionary and removes the word if it is listed there. Otherwise, the word is added to the user dictionary. The actual dictionary is not modified.

Note: For Adobe Reader, this property is available only for version 7.0 or later.

Parameters

cWord	The new word to add.
cName	(optional) The dictionary name or language code. An array of the currently installed dictionaries can be obtained using dictionaryNames (page 605) or languages (page 606).

Returns

true if successful, otherwise, false.

check

| 5.0 | | | |

Presents the Spelling dialog box to allow the user to correct misspelled words in form fields, annotations, or other objects.

Note: For Adobe Reader, this property is available only for version 7.0 or later.

Parameters

`aDomain`	(optional) An array of Document Objects (page 188) that should be checked by the Spelling plug-in, for example, form fields or comments. When you do not supply an array of domains, the "EveryThing" domain will be used. An array of the domains that have been registered can be obtained using the `domainNames` (page 606) property.
`aDictionary`	(optional) The array of dictionary names or language codes that the spell checker should use. The order of the dictionaries in the array is the order the spell checker will use to check for misspelled words. An array of the currently installed dictionaries can be obtained using `spell.dictionaryNames` (page 605) or `spell.languages` (page 606). When this parameter is omitted, the `spellDictionaryOrder` (page 206) list will be searched followed by the `dictionaryOrder` (page 606) list.

Returns

`true` if the user changed or ignored all the flagged words. When the user dismisses the dialog before checking everything, the method returns `false`.

Example

```
var dictionaries = ["de", "French", "en-GB"];
var domains = ["All Form Fields", "All Annotations"];
if (spell.check(domains, dictionaries) )
    console.println("You get an A for spelling.");
else
    console.println("Please spell check this form before \
        you submit.");
```

checkText

5.0			

Presents the spelling dialog box to allow the user to correct misspelled words in the specified string.

Note: For Adobe Reader, this property is available only for version 7.0 or later.

Parameters

cText	The string to check.
aDictionary	(optional) The array of dictionary names or language codes that the spell checker should use. The order of the dictionaries in the array is the order the spell checker will use to check for misspelled words. An array of installed dictionaries can be obtained using spell.dictionaryNames (page 605) or spell.languages (page 606). When this parameter is omitted, the spellDictionaryOrder (page 206) list will be searched followed by the dictionaryOrder (page 606) list.

Returns

The result from the spelling dialog box in a new string.

Example

```
var f = this.getField("Text Box")    // a form text box
f.value = spell.checkText(f.value);
                         // let the user pick the dictionary
```

checkWord

5.0			

Checks the spelling of a specified word.

Note: For Adobe Reader, this property is available only for version 7.0 or later.

Parameters

cWord	The word to check.
aDictionary	(optional) The array of dictionary names or language codes that the spell checker should use , to check for misspelled words. The spell checker uses the dictionaries in the order they appear in the array. An array of installed dictionaries can be obtained using spell.dictionaryNames (page 605) or spell.languages (page 606). If this parameter is omitted, the spellDictionaryOrder (page 206) list is searched, followed by the dictionaryOrder (page 606) list.

Returns

A null object if the word is correct, otherwise an array of alternative spellings for the unknown word.

Example 1

```
var word = "subpinna"; /* misspelling of "subpoena" */
var dictionaries = ["English"];
var f = this.getField("Alternatives") // alternative
spellings list box f.clearItems();
f.setItems(spell.checkWord(word, dictionaries));
```

Example 2

The following script marks misspelled words in the document with a squiggle annotation whose contents are the suggested alternative spellings. The script can be executed from the console, as a mouse-up action within the document, a menu, or as a batch sequence.

```
var ckWord, numWords;
for (var i = 0; i < this.numPages; i++ )
{
    numWords = this.getPageNumWords(i);
    for (var j = 0; j < numWords; j++)
    {
        ckWord = spell.checkWord(this.getPageNthWord(i, j))
        if ( ckWord != null )
        {
            this.addAnnot({
                page: i,
                type: "Squiggly",
                quads: this.getPageNthWordQuads(i, j),
                author: "A. C. Acrobat",
                contents: ckWord.toString()
            });
        }
    }
}
```

customDictionaryClose

6.0			

Closes a custom dictionary that was opened using `customDictionaryOpen` (page 615) or `customDictionaryCreate` (page 613).

Note: For Adobe Reader, this property is available only for version 7.0 or later.

Parameters

cName	Dictionary name used when this dictionary was opened or created.

Returns

`true` if successful, `false` on failure.

---

customDictionaryCreate

6.0		❺	✖

Use this method to create a new custom dictionary file and add it to the list of available dictionaries.

Note: (Security ❺): This method is allowed only during console, menu or batch events. See "Privileged versus Non-privileged Context" on page 8 for details.

Parameters

cName	Dictionary name used in the spelling dialog box. It can be used as the input parameter to check (page 609), checkText (page 610), and checkWord (page 611) methods.
cLanguage	(optional) Use this parameter to associate this dictionary with a language. A list of available languages can be obtained from the spell.languages property.
bShow	(optional) If true (the default), the cName parameter is combined with "User: " and shown that name in all lists and menus. For example, if cName is "Test", "User: Test" is added to all lists and menus. When bShow is false, this custom dictionary is not shown in any lists or menus.

Returns

true if successful, false on failure. This method will fail if the user does not have read and write permission to this directory.

Example

Open this document, the *Acrobat JavaScript Scripting Reference,* in Acrobat and execute the following script in the console. This script extracts the first word of each bookmark. If that word is already in a dictionary, it is discarded. An unknown word—assumed to be the name of an Acrobat JavaScript object, property or method—is added into a newly created dictionary called "JavaScript".

```
spell.customDictionaryCreate("JavaScript", "en", true);
function GetJSTerms(bm, nLevel)
{
    var newWord = bm.name.match(re);
    var ckWord = spell.checkWord( newWord[0] );
    if ( ckWord != null )
    {
        var cWord = spell.addWord( newWord[0], "JavaScript");
        if ( cWord )  console.println( newWord[0] );
    }
```

```
        if (bm.children != null)
        for (var i = 0; i < bm.children.length; i++)
        GetJSTerms(bm.children[i], nLevel + 1);
    }
    console.println("\nAdding New words to the \"JavaScript\" "
        + "dictionary:");
    var re = /^\w+/;
    GetJSTerms(this.bookmarkRoot, 0);
```

customDictionaryDelete

Use this method to close and delete a custom dictionary file that was opened by customDictionaryOpen (page 615) or customDictionaryCreate (page 613).

Note: (Security ): This method is allowed only during console, menu, or batch events. See "Privileged versus Non-privileged Context" on page 8 for details.

Parameters

cName	The name of the dictionary to be deleted. This is the name used when this dictionary was opened or created.

Returns

true if successful, false on failure. This method will fail if the user does not have sufficient file system permission.

Example

Delete a custom dictionary.

```
spell.customDictionaryDelete("JavaScript");
```

customDictionaryExport

6.0   Ⓢ Ⓧ

Exports a custom dictionary to a new file that was opened using the spell methods customDictionaryOpen (page 615) or customDictionaryCreate (page 613).

The user is prompted for an export directory, where the custom dictionary is saved as a .clam file using the dictionary name and language specified in customDictionaryCreate. For example, if the dictionary name is "JavaScript" and the "en" language as specified when it was created, the export file name will be JavaScript-eng.clam.

Exported custom dictionaries can be used in subsequent
`customDictionaryOpen` (page 615) calls.

Note: (Security 🚫): This method is allowed only during console, menu or
batch events. See "Privileged versus Non-privileged Context" on
page 8 for details.

Parameters

cName	The dictionary name used when this dictionary was opened or created.

Returns

`true` if successful, `false` on failure. This method will fail if the user does not
have sufficient file system permission.

Example

Export a custom dictionary, which can then be sent to other users. (See the
example that follows `customDictionaryCreate` (page 613).)

```
spell.customDictionaryExport("JavaScript");
```

customDictionaryOpen

6.0			

Adds a custom export dictionary to the list of available dictionaries. See
`customDictionaryExport` (page 614).

Note: A custom dictionary file can be created using the
`customDictionaryCreate` (page 613) and
`customDictionaryExport` (page 614) methods.

Note: For Adobe Reader, this property is available only for version 7.0 or
later.

Parameters

cDIPath	The device-independent path to the custom dictionary file.
cName	Dictionary name used in the spelling dialog box. It can be used as the input parameter to `check` (page 609), `checkText` (page 610), and `checkWord` (page 611) methods.
bShow	(optional) If `true`, the default, the cName parameter is combined with "User:" and that name is shown in all lists and menus. For example, if cName is "Test", add "User: Test" is added to all lists and menus. When bShow is `false`, this custom dictionary is not shown in any lists or menus.

Returns

`true` if successful, `false` on failure. This method fails if the user does not have read permission for the file.

Example

This example continues the ones following `customDictionaryCreate` (page 613) and `customDictionaryExport` (page 614). It adds a custom export dictionary to the list of available dictionaries.

The user places the custom export dictionary in any folder for which there is read/write permission. A particular choice is the user `dictionaries` folder, whose location of can be obtained from the `app.getPath` method.

```
app.getPath("user", "dictionaries");
```

After the export dictionary has been placed, listing it can be made automatic by adding some folder-level JavaScript. The path to the user `JavaScripts` can be obtained by executing

```
app.getPath("user", "javascript");
```

Finally, create an `.js` file in this folder and add the line

```
var myDictionaries = app.getPath("user", "dictionaries");
spell.customDictionaryOpen( myDictionaries, "JavaScripts",
true);
```

The next time Acrobat is started, the "JavaScript" dictionary will be open and available.

ignoreAll

6.0			

Adds or removes a word from the Spelling ignored-words list of the current document.

Note: For Adobe Reader, this property is available only for version 7.0 or later.

Parameters

cWord	The word to be added or removed from the ignored list.
bIgnore	(optional) If `true` (the default), the word is added to the document ignored word list; if `false`, the word is removed from the ignored list.

Returns

`true` if successful. This method throws an exception if no document is open.

Example

```
var bIgnored = spell.ignoreAll("foo");
if (bIgnored) console.println("\"foo\" will be ignored);
```

removeDictionary

> **Note:** Beginning with Acrobat 6.0, this method is no longer supported. The return value of this method is always `false`. Use the `customDictionaryClose` (page 612) method.

Removes a user dictionary that was added with `addDictionary` (page 608).

Parameters

cName	The name of the dictionary to remove. Must be the same name as was used with `addDictionary`.

Returns

`false`

removeWord

5.0	*P*		

Removes a word from a dictionary. Words cannot be removed from user dictionaries that were created using either `customDictionaryCreate` (page 613) or `customDictionaryExport` (page 614).

See also "addWord" on page 609.

> **Note:** Internally, the `spell` Object (page 605) scans the user dictionary and removes the previously added word if it is there. Otherwise, the word is added to the user's "Not-A-Word" dictionary. The actual dictionary is not modified.

> **Note:** For Adobe Reader, this property is available only for version 7.0 or later.

Parameters

cWord	The word to remove.
cName	(optional) The dictionary name or language code. An array of installed dictionaries can be obtained using `dictionaryNames` (page 605) or `languages` (page 606).

Returns

true if successful, false otherwise

userWords

5.0			

Gets the array of words a user has added to, or removed from, a dictionary. See also addWord (page 609) and checkWord (page 611).

Note: For Adobe Reader, this property is available only for version 7.0 or later.

Parameters

cName	(optional) The dictionary name or language code. An array of installed dictionaries can be obtained using dictionaryNames (page 605) or languages (page 606). If cName is not specified, the default dictionary is used. The default dictionary is the first dictionary specified in the **Spelling** preferences dialog box.
bAdded	(optional) If true, return the user's array of added words. If false, return the user's array of removed words. The default is true.

Returns

The user's array of added or removed words.

Example

List the words added to the "JavaScript" dictionary. (See the example that follows the description of customDictionaryCreate (page 613).)

```
var aUserWords = spell.userWords({cName: "JavaScript"});
aUserWords.toSource();
```

Statement Object

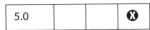

5.0			**✖**

This object is used to execute SQL updates and queries and retrieve the results of these operations. To create a Statement object, use `connection.newStatement` (page 162).

See also:

- Connection Object (page 161)
- ADBC Object (page 10)
- Column Object (page 159), ColumnInfo Object (page 160), Row Object (page 532), TableInfo Object (page 624)

Statement Properties

columnCount

The number of columns in each row of results returned by a query. It is undefined in the case of an update operation.

Type: Number   *Access: R*

rowCount

The number of rows affected by an update. It is *not* the number of rows returned by a query. Its value is undefined in the context of a query.

Type: Number   *Access: R*

Statement Methods

execute

Executes an SQL statement through the context of the Statement object. On failure, `execute` throws an exception.

Note: There is no guarantee that a client can do anything on a statement if an execute has neither failed nor returned all of its data.

Parameters

cSQL	The SQL statement to execute.

Returns

Nothing

Example

```
statement.execute("Select * from ClientData");
```

If the name of the database table or column contains spaces, they must be enclosed in escaped quotes. For example:

```
var execStr1 = "Select firstname, lastname,
    ssn from \"Employee Info\"";
var execStr2 = "Select \"First Name\"  from \"Client Data\"";
statement.execute(execStr1);
statement.execute(execStr2);
```

A cleaner solution is to enclose the whole SQL string with single quotes, so that table and column names can be enclosed with double quotes:

```
var execStr3 = 'Select "First Name","Second Name" from "Client
Data" ';
statement.execute(execStr3);
```

See getRow (page 621) and nextRow (page 622) for extensive examples.

getColumn

Obtains a Column Object (page 159) representing the data in the specified column.

Note: After a column is retrieved with one of these methods, future calls attempting to retrieve the same column may fail.

Parameters

nColumn	The column from which to get the data. It may be a column number or a string containing the name of the column (see "ColumnInfo Object" on page 160).
nDesiredType	(optional) Which of the ADBC JavaScript Types (page 11) best represents the data in the column.

Returns

A Column Object (page 159) representing the data in the specified column, or null on failure.

getColumnArray

Obtains an array of Column Objects (page 159), one for each column in the result set. A best guess is used to decide which of the ADBC JavaScript Types (page 11) best represents the data in the column.

Note: Once a column is retrieved with one of these methods, future calls attempting to retrieve the same column may fail.

Parameters

None

Returns

An array of Column Objects (page 159), or `null` on failure, as well as a zero-length array.

getRow

Obtains a Row Object (page 532) representing the current row. This object contains information from each column. As for `getColumnArray` (page 620), column data is captured in the "best guess" format.

A call to `nextRow` (page 622) should precede a call to `getRow`. Calling `getRow` twice, without an intervening call to `nextRow` (page 622), returns `null` for the second `getRow` call.

Parameters

None

Returns

A Row Object (page 532).

Example 1

Every Row Object (page 532) contains a property for each column in a row of data. Consider the following example:

```
var execStr = "SELECT firstname, lastname, ssn FROM \"Employee
Info\"";
statement.execute(execStr);
statement.nextRow();
row = statement.getRow();
console.println("The first name of the first person retrieved is: "
    + row.firstname.value);
console.println("The last name of the first person retrieved is: "
    + row.lastname.value);
console.println("The ssn of the first person retrieved is: "
    + row.ssn.value);
```

Example 2

If the column name contains spaces, the above syntax for accessing the row properties (for example, `row.firstname.value`) does not work. Alternatively,

```
Connect = ADBC.newConnection("Test Database");
statement = Connect.newStatement();
var execStr = 'Select  "First Name","Second Name"  from
"Client Data" ';
statement.execute(execStr);
statement.nextRow();

// Populate this PDF file
this.getField("name.first").value = row["First Name"].value;
this.getField("name.last").value = row["Second Name"].value;
```

nextRow

Obtains data about the next row of data generated by a previously executed query. This must be called following a call to `execute` (page 619) to acquire the first row of results.

Parameters

None

Returns

Nothing. Throws an exception on `failure` (if, for example, there is no next row).

Example

The following example is a rough outline of how to create a series of buttons and document-level JavaScripts to browse a database and populate a PDF form.

For the `getNextRow` button, defined below, the `nextRow` method is used to retrieve the next row from the database, unless there is an exception thrown (indicating that there is no next row), in which case, we reconnect to the database and use `nextRow` to retrieve the first row of data (again).

```
/* Button Script */
// getConnected button
if (getConnected())
    populateForm(statement.getRow());

// a getNextRow button
try {
    statement.nextRow();
}catch(e){
    getConnected();
}
var row = statement.getRow();
populateForm(row);

/* Document-level JavaScript */
```

```
// getConnected() Doc Level JS
function getConnected()
{
    try {
        ConnectADBCdemo = ADBC.newConnection("ADBCdemo");
        if (ConnectADBCdemo == null)
            throw "Could not connect";
        statement = ConnectADBCdemo.newStatement();
        if (statement == null)
            throw "Could not execute newStatement";
        if (statement.execute("Select * from ClientData"))
            throw "Could not execute the requested SQL";
        if (statement.nextRow())
            throw "Could not obtain next row";
        return true;
    } catch(e) {
        app.alert(e);
        return false;
    }
}
// populateForm()
/* Maps the row data from the database, to a corresponding
text field in the PDF file. */
function populateForm(row)
{
    this.getField("firstname").value = row.FirstName.value;
    this.getField("lastname").value = row.LastName.value;
    this.getField("address").value = row.Address.value;
    this.getField("city").value = row.City.value;
    this.getField("state").value = row.State.value;
    this.getField("zip").value = row.Zipcode.value;
    this.getField("telephone").value = row.Telephone.value;
    this.getField("income").value = row.Income.value;
}
```

TableInfo Object

This generic JavaScript object contains basic information about a table. It is returned by `connection.getTableList` (page 162) and contains the following properties.

Property	Type	Access	Description
name	String	R	The identifying name of a table. This string can be used in SQL statements to identify the table that the TableInfo object is associated with.
description	String	R	A string that contains database-dependent information about the table.

Template Object

Template objects are named pages within the document. These pages may be hidden or visible and can be copied or spawned. They are typically used to dynamically create content (for example, to add pages to an invoice on overflow).

See also the Document Object `templates` (page 207) property, and `createTemplate` (page 227), `getTemplate` (page 259), and `removeTemplate` (page 278) methods.

Template Properties

hidden

Determines whether the template is hidden. Hidden templates cannot be seen by the user until they are spawned or are made visible. When an invisible template is made visible, it is appended to the document.

This property behaves as follows in Adobe Reader:

- Setting this property in versions of Adobe Reader earlier than 5.1 generates an exception.
- For Adobe Reader 5.1 and 6.0, setting this property depends on Advanced Forms Feature document rights.
- For Adobe Reader 7.0, this property cannot be set under any circumstances.

Type: Boolean   *Access: R/W*

name

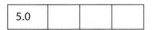

The name of the template that was supplied when the template was created.

Type: String   *Access: R*

Template Methods

spawn

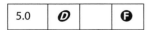

Creates a new page in the document based on the template.

Parameters

nPage	(optional) The 0-based index of the page number after which or on which the new page will be created, depending on the value of bOverlay. The default is 0.
bRename	(optional) Specifies whether form fields on the page should be renamed. The default is true.
bOverlay	(optional) If true (the default), the template is overlaid on the specified page. If false, it is inserted as a new page before the specified page. To append a page to the document, set bOverlay to false and set nPage to the number of pages in the document. **Note:** For certified documents or documents with "Advanced Form Features rights" (**F**), the bOverlay parameter is disabled. A template cannot be overlaid for these types of documents.
oXObject	(optional, Acrobat 6.0) The value of this parameter is the return value of an earlier call to spawn.

Returns

Prior to Acrobat 6.0, this method returned nothing. Now, spawn returns an object representing the page contents of the page spawned. This return object can then be used as the value of the optional parameter oXObject for subsequent calls to spawn.

Note: Repeatedly spawning the same page can cause a large increase in the file size. To avoid this problem, spawn now returns an object that represents the page contents of the spawned page. This return value can be used as the value of the oXObject parameter in subsequent calls to the spawn method to spawn the same page.

Example 1

This example spawns all templates and appends them one by one to the end of the document.

```
var a = this.templates;
for (i = 0; i < a.length; i++)
    a[i].spawn(this.numPages, false, false);
```

Example 2 (Acrobat 6.0)

The following example spawns the same template 31 times using the `oXObject` parameter and return value. Using this technique avoids overly inflating the file size.

```
var t = this.templates;
var T = t[0];
var XO = T.spawn(this.numPages, false, false);
for (var i=0; i<30; i++) T.spawn(this.numPages, false, false,
XO);
```

Thermometer Object

6.0			

This object is a combined status window and progress bar that indicates to the user that a lengthy operation is in progress. To acquire a Thermometer object, use `app.thermometer` (page 57).

Example

This example shows how to use all properties and methods of the Thermometer object.

```
var t = app.thermometer;// acquire a thermometer object
t.duration = this.numPages;
t.begin();
for ( var i = 0; i < this.numPages; i++)
{
   t.value = i;
   t.text = "Processing page " + (i + 1);
   if (t.cancelled) break;// break if operation cancelled
   ... process the page ...
}
t.end();
```

Thermometer Properties

cancelled

Specifies whether the user wants to cancel the current operation. The user can indicate the desire to terminate the operation by pressing the Esc key on the Windows and UNIX platforms and Command-period on the Macintosh platform.

Type: Boolean   *Access: R*

duration

Sets the value that corresponds to a full thermometer display. The thermometer is subsequently filled in by setting its `value` (page 629). The default duration is 100.

Type: Number   *Access: R/W*

text

Sets the text string that is displayed by the thermometer.

Type: String   *Access: R/W*

value

Sets the current value of the thermometer and updates the display. The value can range from 0 (empty) to the value set in `duration` (page 628). For example, if the thermometer's duration is 10, the current value must be between 0 and 10, inclusive. If the value is less than zero, it is set to zero. If the value is greater than `duration`, it is set to `duration` (page 628).

Type: Number   *Access: R/W*

Thermometer Methods

begin

Initializes the thermometer and displays it with the current value as a percentage of the duration.

Parameters

None

Returns

Nothing

Example

Count the words on each page of the current document, report the running total, and use the thermometer to track progress.

```
var t = app.thermometer; // acquire a thermometer object
t.duration = this.numPages;
t.begin();
var cnt=0;
for ( var i = 0; i < this.numPages; i++)
{
    t.value = i;
    t.text = "Processing page " + (i + 1);
    cnt += getPageNumWords(i);
    console.println("There are " + cnt + "words in this doc.");
    if (t.cancelled) break;
}
t.end();
```

end

Draws the thermometer with its current value set to the thermometer's duration (a full thermometer), then removes the thermometer from the display.

Parameters

None

Returns

Nothing

this Object

In JavaScript, the special keyword `this` refers to the current object. In Acrobat, the current object is defined as follows:

- In an object method, it is the object to which the method belongs.
- In a constructor function, it is the object being constructed.
- In a document-level script or field-level script, it is the Document Object (page 188) and therefore can be used to set or get document properties and functions.
- In a function defined in one of the folder-level JavaScripts files, it is undefined. Calling functions should pass the Document Object to any function at this level that needs it.

For example, assume that the following function was defined at the plug-in folder level:

```
function PrintPageNum(doc)
{   /* Print the current page number to the console. */
    console.println("Page = " + doc.pageNum);
}
```

The following script outputs the current page number to the console twice and then prints the page:

```
/* Must pass the document object. */
PrintPageNum(this);
/* Same as the previous call. */
console.println("Page = " + this.pageNum);
/* Prints the current page. */
this.print(false, this.pageNum, this.pageNum);
```

Variable and Function Name Conflicts

Variables and functions that are defined in scripts are parented off of the `this` object. For example:

```
var f = this.getField("Hello");
```

is equivalent to

```
this.f = this.getField("Hello");
```

with the exception that the variable `f` can be garbage collected at any time after the script is run.

Acrobat JavaScript programmers should avoid using property and method names from the Document Object (page 188) as variable names. Using method names after the reserved word `var` will throw an exception, as the following line shows:

```
var getField = 1; // TypeError: redeclaration of function
getField
```

Use of property names will not throw an exception, but the value of the property may not be altered if the property refers to an object:

```
// "title" will return "1", but the document will
// now be named "1".
var title = 1;

// property not altered, info still an object
var info = 1; // "info" will return [object Info]
```

The following is an example of avoiding variable name clash.

```
var f = this.getField("mySignature");
                    // uses the ppklite sig handler

// use "Info" rather than "info" to avoid a clash
var Info = f.signatureInfo();

// some standard signatureInfo properties
console.println("name = " + Info.name);
```

TTS Object

4.05			

The JavaScript `TTS` object allows users to transform text into speech. To be able to use the `TTS` object, the user's computer must have a Text-To-Speech engine installed on it. The Text-To-Speech engine will render text as digital audio and then speak it. It has been implemented mostly with accessibility in mind but can potentially have many other applications.

This object is currently a Windows-only feature and requires that the Microsoft Text to Speech engine be installed in the operating system.

The `TTS` object is present on both the Windows and Macintosh platforms (since it is a JavaScript object). However, it is disabled on Macintosh.

Note: Acrobat 5.0 has taken a very different approach to providing accessibility for disabled users by integrating directly with popular screen readers. Therefore, some of the screen reading features defined in 4.05 using the TTS object have been removed in 5.0 because they conflict with the screen reader. The TTS object remains, however, because it still has useful functionality in its own right that might be popular for multimedia documents.

TTS Properties

available

`true` if the TTS object is available and the Text-To-Speech engine can be used.

Type: Boolean   *Access: R*

Example

```
console.println("Text to speech available: " +
tts.available);
```

numSpeakers

The number of speakers available to the Text-To-Speech engine. See also the `speaker` (page 634) property and the `getNthSpeakerName` (page 634) method.

Type: Integer   *Access: R*

pitch

Sets the baseline pitch for the voice of a speaker. The valid range for pitch is from 0 to 10, with 5 being the default for the mode.

Type: Integer   *Access: R/W*

soundCues

Deprecated. Returns `false`.

Type: Boolean   *Access: R/W*

speaker

Allows users to specify different speakers with different tone qualities when performing text-to-speech. See also the `numSpeakers` (page 633) property and the `getNthSpeakerName` (page 634) method.

Type: String   *Access: R/W*

speechCues

Deprecated. Returns `false`.

Type: Boolean   *Access: R/W*

speechRate

Sets the speed at which text will be spoken by the Text-To-Speech engine. The value for `speechRate` is expressed in number of words per minute.

Type: Integer   *Access: R/W*

volume

Sets the volume for the speech. Valid values are 0 (mute) to 10 (loudest).

Type: Integer   *Access: R/W*

TTS Methods

getNthSpeakerName

Gets the *n*th speaker name in the Text-To-Speech engine. See also the `numSpeakers` (page 633) and `speaker` (page 634) properties.

Parameters

nIndex	The index of the desired speaker name.

Returns

The name of the specified speaker.

Example

Enumerate through all of the speakers available.

```
for (var i = 0; i < tts.numSpeakers; i++) {
    var cSpeaker = tts.getNthSpeakerName(i);
    console.println("Speaker[" + i + "] = " + cSpeaker);
    tts.speaker = cSpeaker;
    tts.qText ("Hello");
    tts.talk();
}
```

pause

Immediately pauses text-to-speech output on a TTS object. Playback of the remaining queued text can be resumed by calling resume (page 636).

Parameters

None

Returns

Nothing

qSilence

Queues a period of silence into the text.

Parameters

nDuration	The amount of silence in milliseconds.

Returns

Nothing

qSound

Puts the specified sound into the queue to be performed by talk (page 637). It accepts one parameter, cSound, from a list of possible sound cue names. These names map directly to sound files stored in the SoundCues folder, if it exists.

```
tts.qSound("DocPrint");// Plays DocPrint.wav
```

The SoundCues folder should exist at the program level for the viewer, for example, `C:\Program Files\Adobe\Acrobat 5.0\SoundCues`.

Note: Windows only—qSound can handle only 22 KHz,16-bit PCM .wav files. These should be at least 1 second long to avoid a queue delay problem in MS SAPI. In case the sound lasts less than 1 second, it should be edited and have a silence added to the end of it.

Parameters

cSound	The sound cue name to use.

Returns

Nothing

qText

Puts text into the queue to be performed by `talk` (page 637).

Parameters

cText	The text to convert to speech.

Returns

Nothing

Example

```
tts.qText("Hello, how are you?");
```

reset

Stops playback of queued text and flushes the queue. Playback of text cannot be resumed with `resume (page 636)`. Additionally, it resets all the properties of the TTS object to their default values.

Parameters

None

Returns

Nothing

resume

Resumes playback of text on a paused TTS object.

Parameters

None

Returns

Nothing

stop

Stops playback of queued text and flushes the queue. Playback of text cannot be resumed with `resume` (page 636).

Parameters

None

Returns

Nothing

talk

Sends whatever is in the queue to be spoken by the Text-To-Speech engine. If text output had been paused, `talk` (page 637) resumes playback of the queued text.

Parameters

None

Returns

Nothing

Example

```
tts.qText("Hello there!");
tts.talk();
```

util Object

A static JavaScript object that defines a number of utility methods and convenience functions for string and date formatting and parsing.

util Methods

crackURL

7.0.5			

Breaks a URL into its component parts.

Parameters

cURL	A string specifying the URL.

Returns

An object containing the following properties:

Property	Description
cScheme	The scheme of the URL. It may be file, http, or https.
cUser	(Optional) The user name specified in the URL.
cPassword	(Optional) The password specified in the URL.
cHost	The hostname of the URL.
nPort	The port number of the URL.
cPath	(Optional) The path portion of the URL.
cParameters	(Optional) The parameter string portion of the URL.
cFragments	(Optional) The fragments of the URL.

This method throws a parameter error if the parameter is missing, the URL is not well-formed, or the URL scheme is not file, http, or https.

Example

The following code

```
util.crackURL("http://example.org/myPath?name0=value0&name1=
value1#frag");
```

would return

```
{
    cScheme: "http",
    cHost: "example.org",
```

```
        nPort: 80,
        cPath: "/myPath",
        cParameters: "?name0=value0&name1=value1",
        cFragments: "frag"
    }
```

iconStreamFromIcon

7.0			

Converts an XObject-based Icon Object (page 434) into an Icon Stream Object (page 435).

Parameters

oIcon	An Icon Object to be converted into an Icon Stream Object (page 435).

Returns

Icon Stream Object

This method allows an icon obtained from the Document Object importIcon (page 263) or getIcon (page 249) methods to be used in a method such as app.addToolButton (page 62), which would otherwise accept only an Icon Stream Object (page 435) as an input parameter.

Example

This example imports an icon into the document-level named icons tree and adds a toolbutton to the application:

```
this.importIcon("myIcon", "/C/temp/myIcon.jpg", 0);
var oIcon = util.iconStreamFromIcon(this.getIcon("myIcon"));
app.addToolButton({
    cName: "myButton",
    oIcon: myIcon,
    cExec: "console.println('My Button!');",
    cTooltext: "My button!",
    nPos: 0
});
```

printd

3.01			

Returns a date using a specified format.

Parameters

cFormat	The date and time format. It can be one of the following types: • A string that is a pattern of supported substrings that are place-holders for date and time data. Recognized date and time strings are shown in the table below. • Beginning with Acrobat 5.0, a number specifying the format. Supported values (along with examples of each format) are: 0: PDF date format. Example: D:20000801145605+07'00' 1: Universal. Example: D:20000801145605+07'00' 2: Localized string. Example: 2000/08/01 14:56:05 • Beginning with Acrobat 7.0, if bXFAPicture is true, this parameter is interpreted using the XFA Picture Clause format.
oDate	A Date object to format. Date objects can be obtained from the Date constructor of core JavaScript or from the util.scand (page 645) method.
bXFAPicture	(optional, Acrobat 7.0) A Boolean specifying whether the value of cFormat is interpreted using the XFA Picture Clause format, which gives extensive support for localized times and dates. See the sections on date and time pictures in *XFA-Picture Clause 2.0 Specification* and *XFA-Picture Clause Version 2.2 – CCJK Addendum* for additional discussion. (See "References" on page 2.) The default is false.

Returns

The formatted date string.

cFormat String Patterns

String	Effect	Example
mmmm	Long month	September
mmm	Abbreviated month	Sep
mm	Numeric month with leading zero	09
m	Numeric month without leading zero	9
dddd	Long day	Wednesday
ddd	Abbreviated day	Wed
dd	Numeric date with leading zero	03
d	Numeric date without leading zero	3
yyyy	Long year	1997
yy	Abbreviated Year	97

String	Effect	Example
HH	24 hour time with leading zero	09
H	24 hour time without leading zero	9
hh	12 hour time with leading zero	09
h	12 hour time without leading zero	9
MM	minutes with leading zero	08
M	minutes without leading zero	8
ss	seconds with leading zero	05
s	seconds without leading zero	5
tt	am/pm indication	am
t	single digit am/pm indication	a
j	Japanese Emperor Year (abbreviated) **Note:** Introduced in Acrobat 6.0. In Acrobat 7.0, this format string has been deprecated in favor of the XFA Picture Clause format.	
jj	Japanese Emperor Year **Note:** Introduced in Acrobat 6.0. In Acrobat 7.0, this format string has been deprecated in favor of the XFA Picture Clause format.	
\	use as an escape character	

Example 1

The following script formats the current date in long format:

```
var d = new Date();
console.println("Today is " + util.printd("mmmm dd, yyyy",
d));
```

Example 2 (Acrobat 5.0)

```
// display date in a local format
console.println(util.printd(2, new Date() ));
```

Example 3 (Acrobat 7.0)

This example uses the XFA-Picture Clause.

```
// execute in console
console.println(
    util.printd("EEE, 'the' D 'of' MMMM, YYYY", new Date(),
true));
// the output on this day is
Tue, the 13 of July, 2004
```

Locale-Sensitive Picture Clauses. Normally processing of picture clauses occurs in the ambient locale. It is possible, however, to indicate that picture processing be done in a specific locale. This is of use when formatting or parsing data that is locale-specific and different from the ambient locale. The syntax for this extension to compound picture clauses is:

```
category-name(locale-name){picture-symbols}
```

The code executed in the console,

```
util.printd("date(fr){DD MMMM, YYYY}", new Date(), true)
```

yields the output on this day,

```
13 juillet, 2004
```

The XFA-Picture Clause gives extensive support for Chinese, Chinese (Taiwan), Japanese, and Korean (CCJK) times and dates. The example below, a custom format script of a text field, gives the current date formatted for a Japanese locale.

```
event.value = util.printd("date(ja){ggYY/M/D}", new Date(),
true)
```

printf

3.01			

Formats one or more values as a string according to a format string. It is similar to the C function of the same name. This method converts and formats incoming arguments into a result string according to a format string (cFormat).

The format string consists of two types of objects:

- Ordinary characters, which are copied to the result string.
- Conversion specifications, each of which causes conversion and formatting of the next successive argument to printf.

Each conversion specification is constructed as follows:

```
%[,nDecSep] [cFlags] [nWidth] [.nPrecision] cConvChar
```

The following table describes the components of a conversion specification.

nDecSep	A comma character (,) followed by a digit that indicates the decimal/separator format:
	• 0: Comma separated, period decimal point
	• 1: No separator, period decimal point
	• 2: Period separated, comma decimal point
	• 3: No separator, comma decimal point
cFlags	Only valid for numeric conversions and consists of a number of characters (in any order), which will modify the specification:
	• +: Specifies that the number will always be formatted with a sign.
	• space: If the first character is not a sign, a space will be prefixed.
	• 0: Specifies padding to the field with leading zeros.
	• #: Specifies an alternate output form. For f, the output will always have a decimal point.
nWidth	A number specifying a minimum field width. The converted argument is formatted to be at least this many characters wide, including the sign and decimal point, and may be wider if necessary. If the converted argument has fewer characters than the field width, it is padded on the left to make up the field width. The padding character is normally a space, but is 0 if the zero padding flag is present (cFlags contains 0).
nPrecision	A period character (.) followed by a number that specifies the number of digits after the decimal point for float conversions.
cConvChar	Indicates how the argument should be interpreted:
	• d: Integer (truncating if necessary)
	• f: Floating-point number
	• s: String
	• x: Integer (truncating if necessary) and formatted in unsigned hexadecimal notation

Parameters

| cFormat | The format string to use. |

Returns

A result string (cResult) formatted as specified.

Example

```
var n = Math.PI * 100;
console.clear();
console.show();
console.println(util.printf("Decimal format: %d", n));
console.println(util.printf("Hex format: %x", n));
console.println(util.printf("Float format: %.2f", n));
console.println(util.printf("String format: %s", n));
```

Output

```
Decimal format: 314
Hex format: 13A
Float format: 314.16
String format: 314.159265358979
```

printx

3.01			

Formats a source string, cSource, according to a formatting string, cFormat. A valid format for cFormat is any string that may contain special masking characters:

Value	Effect
?	Copy next character.
X	Copy next alphanumeric character, skipping any others.
A	Copy next alpha character, skipping any others.
9	Copy next numeric character, skipping any others.
*	Copy the rest of the source string from this point on.
\	Escape character.
>	Uppercase translation until further notice.
<	Lowercase translation until further notice.
=	Preserve case until further notice (default).

Parameters

cFormat	The formatting string to use.
cSource	The source string to use.

Returns

The formatted string.

Example

To format a string as a U.S. telephone number, for example, use the following script:

```
var v = "aaa14159697489zzz";
v = util.printx("9 (999) 999-9999", v);
console.println(v);
```

scand

4.0			

Converts a date into a JavaScript Date object according to rules of a format string. This routine is much more flexible than using the date constructor directly.

Note: Given a two-digit year for input, scand (page 645) uses the *date horizon* heuristic to resolve the ambiguity. If the year is less than 50, it is assumed to be in the 21st century (that is, add 2000). If it is greater than or equal to 50, it is in the 20th century (add 1900).

The supplied date cDate should be in the same format as described by cFormat.

Parameters

cFormat	The rules to use for formatting the date. cFormat uses the same syntax as found in printd (page 639).
cDate	The date to convert.

Returns

The converted Date object, or null if the conversion fails.

Example 1

```
/* Turn the current date into a string. */
var cDate = util.printd("mm/dd/yyyy", new Date());
console.println("Today's date: " + cDate);
/* Parse it back into a date. */
var d = util.scand("mm/dd/yyyy", cDate);
/* Output it in reverse order. */
console.println("Yet again: " + util.printd("yyyy mmm dd",
d));
```

Example 2

The method returns null if the conversions fails, which can occur if the user inputs a data different than what is expected. In this case, test the return value for null.

```
var d= util.scand("mm/dd/yyyy",
this.getField("myDate").value);
   if ( d== null )
       app.alert("Please enter a valid date of the form" +
           " \"mm/dd/yyyy\".")
   else {
       console.println("You entered the date: "
           + util.printd("mmmm dd, yyyy",d));
}
```

spansToXML

6.0			

Converts an array of Span Objects (page 601) into an XML(XFA) String as described in "Rich Text Strings" in section 8.6 of the *PDF Reference*.

Parameters

An array of Span Objects (page 601)	An array of Span objects to be converted into an XML string.

Returns

String

Example

This example gets the value of a rich text field, turns all of the text blue, converts it to an XML string and then prints it to the console.

```
var f = getField("Text1");
var spans = f.richValue;
for(var index = 0; index < spans.length; index++)
    spans[index].textColor = color.blue;
console.println(util.spansToXML(spans));
```

streamFromString

7.0			

This function converts a string to a ReadStream Object (page 519).

Parameters

cString	The string to be converted into a ReadStream Object (page 519).
cCharSet	(optional) The encoding for the string in cString. The options are utf-8, utf-16, Shift-JIS, BigFive, GBK, UHC. The default is utf-8.

Returns

ReadStream Object (page 519)

Example

This example takes the response given in a text field of this document and appends this response to an attached document.

```
var v = this.getField("myTextField").value;
var oFile = this.getDataObjectContents("MyNotes.txt");
var cFile = util.stringFromStream(oFile, "utf-8");
```

```
cFile += "\r\n" + cFile;
oFile = util.streamFromString( cFile, "utf-8");
this.setDataObjectContents("MyNotes.txt", oFile);
```

This example uses the Document Object methods
`getDataObjectContents` (page 247) and `setDataObjectContents`
(page 286) and `util.stringFromStream` (page 647).

stringFromStream

This function converts a ReadStream Object (page 519) to a string.

Parameters

oStream	ReadStream Object (page 519) to be converted into a string.
cCharSet	(optional) The encoding for the string in oStream. The options are utf-8, utf-16, Shift-JIS, BigFive, GBK, UHC. The default is utf-8.

Returns

String

Example

Assume there is a text file embedded in this document. This example reads
the contents of the attachment and displays it in the multiline text field.

```
var oFile = this.getDataObjectContents("MyNotes.txt");
var cFile = util.stringFromStream(oFile, "utf-8");
this.getField("myTextField").value = cFile;
```

This example uses `getDataObjectContents` (page 247) to get the file
stream of the attached document.

xmlToSpans

This function converts an XML (XFA) string as described in "Rich Text Strings" in section
8.6.2 of the *PDF Reference* to an array of Span objects suitable for specifying
as the `richValue` or `richContents` of a field or annotation.

Parameters

a string	An XML (XFA) string to be converted to an array of Span Objects.

Returns

An Array of Span Objects (page 601)

Example

Get the rich text string from "Text1", convert it to XML, then convert it back to an array of Span objects and repopulate the text field.

```
var f = getField("Text1");
var spans = f.richValue;
var str = util.spansToXML(spans);
var spans = util.xmlToSpans(str);
f.richValue = spans;
```

XFA Object

6.0.2			

The XFA object provides access to the XFA `appModel` container. More detailed information is available in the *Acrobat JavaScript Scripting Guide* (see "References" on page 2). Additional XFA documentation is located at http://partners.adobe.com/asn/tech/pdf/xmlformspec.jsp.

An XFA object is returned by the `XMLData.parse` (page 654) and `XMLData.applyXPath (page 650)` methods.

Example

The following code detects whether the PDF document has Acrobat forms or was created by Adobe LiveCycle Designer and has XML forms.

```
if ( typeof xfa == "object" ) {
    if ( this.dynamicXFAForm ) {
        console.println("This is a dynamic XML form.");
    else
        console.println("This is a static XML form.");
}
else  console.println("This is an Acrobat Form.");
```

XMLData Object

XMLData is a static object that allows the creation of a JavaScript object representing an XML document tree and permits the manipulation of arbitrary XML documents through the XFA Data DOM. (In XFA, there are several other DOMs parallel to the Data DOM, but for the purpose of the XMLData object, only the Data DOM is used.)

PDF documents that return true to the Document Object dynamicXFAForm (page 194) property can use the XMLData object but cannot have its form fields manipulated by that object, because the two data DOMs are isolated from each other.

XMLData Methods

applyXPath

7.0			

Enables you to manipulate and query an XML document by using XPath expressions. The XPath language is described in the W3C document *XML Path Language (XPath)*, which is available at http://www.w3.org/TR/xpath.

XPath expressions evaluate to one of the known four types: Boolean, Number, String, Node-set. In JavaScript, they are returned, respectively, as the following types: Boolean, Number, String, and Object.

If an object is returned, it is of type XFA Object (page 649), which represents either a tree started by a single node or a tree started by a list of nodes (a tree list). The type of this object is the same as the one returned by the XMLData.parse (page 654).

Note: XFA provides a query mechanism, SOM expressions, which is similar to that of XPath. Because XPath is widely used in the XML community, the applyXPath method allows users to use XPath expressions if they choose.

Parameters

oXml	An XFAObject object representing an XML document tree.
	Note: An exception is thrown if the value of this parameter is a nodeList XFA object instead of the root of an XML tree.
cXPath	A string parameter with the XPATH query to be performed on the document tree.

Returns

Boolean, Number, String, or XFAObject.

Example

This example shows each of the return types of `XMLData.applyXPath` (Boolean, number, string, or XFAObject). It extracts information from an XML data string, in this case, the family tree of the "Robat" family).

```
var cXMLDoc = "<family name = 'Robat'>\
    <grandad id = 'm1' name = 'A.C.' gender='M'>\
        <child> m2 </child>\
        <personal>\
            <income>100000</income>\
        </personal>\
    </grandad>\
    <dad id = 'm2' name = 'Bob' gender='M'>\
        <parent> m1 </parent>\
        <spouse> m3 </spouse>\
        <child> m4 </child>\
        <child> m5 </child>\
        <child> m6 </child>\
        <personal>\
            <income>75000</income>\
        </personal>\
    </dad>\
    <mom id = 'm3' name = 'Mary' gender='F'>\
        <spouse> m2 </spouse>\
        <personal>\
            <income>25000</income>\
        </personal>\
    </mom>\
    <daughter id = 'm4' name = 'Sue' gender='F'>\
        <parent> m2 </parent>\
        <personal>\
            <income>40000</income>\
        </personal>\
    </daughter>\
    <son id = 'm5' name = 'Jim' gender='M'>\
        <parent> m2 </parent>\
        <personal>\
            <income>35000</income>\
        </personal>\
    </son>\
    <daughter id = 'm6' name = 'Megan' gender='F'>\
        <parent> m2 </parent>\
        <personal>\
            <income>30000</income>\
        </personal>\
    </daughter>\
</family>";
var myXML= XMLData.parse( cXMLDoc, false);
```

The following line returns an XFAObject.

Get mom's data.

```
var a = XMLData.applyXPath(myXML, "//family/mom")
a.saveXML('pretty');
<?xml version="1.0" encoding="UTF-8"?>
<mom id="m3" name="Mary" gender="F">
   <spouse> m2 </spouse>
   <personal>
      <income>25000</income>
   </personal>
</mom>
// get the income element value
a.personal.income.value = "20000"; // change the income
```

Get dad's name, an attribute.

```
var b = XMLData.applyXPath(myXML, "//family/dad/@name");
b.saveXML('pretty');
<?xml version="1.0" encoding="UTF-8"?>
 name="Bob"
// assign to a variable
var dadsName = b.value; // dadsName = "Bob"
```

Get all attributes of dad node.

```
var b = XMLData.applyXPath( myXML,
 "//family/dad/attribute::*" );
for(var i=0; i < b.length; i++)
    console.println(b.item(i).saveXML('pretty'))
```

The loop above outputs the following to the console.

```
<?xml version="1.0" encoding="UTF-8"?>
 id="m2"
<?xml version="1.0" encoding="UTF-8"?>
 name="Bob"
<?xml version="1.0" encoding="UTF-8"?>
 gender="M"
```

Extract particular information from this

```
console.println("For attribute 2, we have "
    + b.item(2).name + " = '"
    + b.item(2).value + "'.");
```

which yields an output of

```
For attribute 2, we have gender = 'M'.
```

Get dad's second child.

```
var c = XMLData.applyXPath(myXML,
 "//family/dad/child[position()=2]");
c.saveXML('pretty')
<?xml version="1.0" encoding="UTF-8"?>
<child> m5 </child>
```

This is the `id` of dad's second child. The examples below get the family data on this child.

The following returns a string.

```
// calculate the value of dadsName using XPath methods.
var dadsName = XMLData.applyXPath(myXML,
    "string(//family/dad/@name)")
// dadsName is assigned a value of "Bob" with this one line.
```

Get the family information on dad's second child. The following line assigns c = "m5". The return value of the call to applyXPath is a string, and he function normalize-space converts its argument to a string and removes any surrounding spaces.

```
var c = XMLData.applyXPath(myXML,
    "normalize-space(//family/dad/child[2])");
var d = "//*[@id = \'" + c + "\']";
            // Note: d= "//*[@id = 'm5']"
XMLData.applyXPath(myXML, d ).saveXML('pretty');
            // show what we have
<son id="m5" name="Jim" gender="M">
  <parent> m2 </parent>
  <personal>
    <income>35000</income>
  </personal>
</son>
```

Now display information about the sixth child node of the family root. The XPath functions name and concat are used.

```
var e = XMLData.applyXPath(myXML,
    "concat(name(//family/child::*[position()=6]), '=',
    //family/child::*[position()=6]/@name)" );
console.println(e); // the output is "daughter=Megan"
```

Get the names of all members of the "Robat" family.

```
e = XMLData.applyXPath(myXML,"//family/child::*" );
for ( var i = 1; i <= e.length; i++ )  {
    var str = "string(//family/child::*["+i+"]/@name)";
    console.println(XMLData.applyXPath(myXML,str));
}
```

The output is

```
A.C.
Bob
Mary
Sue
Jim
Megan
```

The following code shows a Boolean return value.

```
var f = XMLData.applyXPath( myXML, "//family/dad/@id = 'm2'"
);
if ( f == true ) console.println("dad's id is 'm2'");
else console.println("dad's id is not 'm2'");
```

The following code shows a numeric return value.

```
// get dad's income
g = XMLData.applyXPath( myXML,
"number(//family/dad/personal/income)" );
// double dad's salary, implied conversion to a number type
console.println("Dad's double salary is " +
    XMLData.applyXPath( myXML, "//family/dad/personal/income *
2" ) );
```

Now compute the total income of the family "Robat".

```
console.println("Total income of A.C. Robat's family is "
    + XMLData.applyXPath( myXML, "sum(//income)" ) + ".");
```

The above line writes the following to the console.

```
Total income of A.C. Robat's family is 305000.
```

List the individual incomes.

```
var g = XMLData.applyXPath( myXML, "//income")
for ( var i =0; i< g.length; i++)
console.println(g.item(i).value);
```

parse

7.0			

Creates an object representing an XML document tree. Its parameters are the same as those of the `loadXML` method in the XFA Data DOM.

This method returns an object of type XFA Object (page 649) that represents either a tree headed by a single node or a tree started by a list of nodes (a tree list).

Parameters

param1	A string containing the XML document.
param2	(optional) A Boolean specifying whether the root node of the XML document should be ignored. The default value is `true`. If `false`, the root node should not be ignored.

Returns

XFAObject

Example 1

Consider the XML document as first introduced in the example following the `XMLData.applyXPath (page 650)` method.

```
var x = XMLData.parse( cXMLDoc, false );
var y = x.family.name;   // a XFAObject
console.println(y.value); // output to console is "Robat"
```

Get information about dad.

```
y = x.family.dad.id; // a XFAObject
console.println(y.value);       // output to console is "m2"

y = x.family.dad.name.value;      // y = "Bob"
x.family.dad.name.value = "Robert"; // change name to "Robert"
y = x.family.dad.name.value;      // y = "Robert"

y = x.family.dad.personal.income.value; // y = "75000"
x.family.dad.personal.income.value = "80000"; // give dad a
raise
```

Example 2

A create a simple XML document and manipulate it.

```
x = XMLData.parse("<a> <c>A.</c><d>C.</d> </a>", false);
x.saveXML("pretty");
```

The output of the previous line is

```
<?xml version="1.0" encoding="UTF-8"?>
<xfa:data
xmlns:xfa="http://www.xfa.org/schema/xfa-data/1.0/">
   <a>
     <c>A.</c>
     <d>C.</d>
   </a>
</xfa:data>
```

Now create another simple document.

```
y = XMLData.parse("<b>Robat</b>", false);
y.saveXML("pretty");
```

The output of this line is

```
<?xml version="1.0" encoding="UTF-8"?>
<xfa:data
xmlns:xfa="http://www.xfa.org/schema/xfa-data/1.0/">
   <b>Robat</b>
</xfa:data>
```

Append y onto x.

```
x.nodes.append(y.clone(true).nodes.item(0));
x.saveXML("pretty");
```

The result is

```
<?xml version="1.0" encoding="UTF-8"?>
<xfa:data
xmlns:xfa="http://www.xfa.org/schema/xfa-data/1.0/">
   <a>
```

```
        <c>A.</c>
        <d>C.</d>
    </a>
    <b>Robat</b>
</xfa:data>
```

Now execute

```
x.nodes.insert(y.clone(true).nodes.item(0),
x.nodes.item(0));
x.saveXML("pretty")
```

to obtain

```
<?xml version="1.0" encoding="UTF-8"?>
<xfa:data
xmlns:xfa="http://www.xfa.org/schema/xfa-data/1.0/">
    <b>Robat</b>
    <a>
      <c>A.</c>
      <d>C.</d>
    </a>
    <b>Robat</b>
</xfa:data>
```

Now remove these two nodes.

```
x.nodes.remove( x.nodes.namedItem("b") );
x.nodes.remove( x.nodes.namedItem("b") );
```

Now, we are back to the original XML document.

```
<?xml version="1.0" encoding="UTF-8"?>
<xfa:data
xmlns:xfa="http://www.xfa.org/schema/xfa-data/1.0/">
    <a>
      <c>A.</c>
      <d>C.</d>
    </a>
</xfa:data>
```

Executing the following line

```
x.a.nodes.insert( y.clone(true).nodes.item(0),
x.a.nodes.item(0));
x.saveXML("pretty");
```

yields the following output:

```
<?xml version="1.0" encoding="UTF-8"?>
<xfa:data
xmlns:xfa="http://www.xfa.org/schema/xfa-data/1.0/">
    <a>
      <b>Robat</b>
      <c>A.</c>
      <d>C.</d>
    </a>
</xfa:data>
```

Now remove that node just inserted.

```
x.a.nodes.remove( x.a.nodes.namedItem("b"));
```

Now insert y (actually a clone of y) between the first and second children of the element a.

```
x.a.nodes.insert( y.clone(true).nodes.item(0),
x.a.nodes.item(1));
```

This produces the following

```
<?xml version="1.0" encoding="UTF-8"?>
<xfa:data
xmlns:xfa="http://www.xfa.org/schema/xfa-data/1.0/">
   <a>
     <c>A.</c>
     <b>Robat</b>
     <d>C.</d>
   </a>
</xfa:data>
```

Remove that node just inserted:

```
x.a.nodes.remove( x.a.nodes.namedItem("b"));
```

Finally, append y onto a.

```
x.a.nodes.append( y.clone(true).nodes.item(0));
```

yielding

```
<?xml version="1.0" encoding="UTF-8"?>
<xfa:data
xmlns:xfa="http://www.xfa.org/schema/xfa-data/1.0/">
   <a>
     <c>A.</c>
     <d>C.</d>
     <b>Robat</b>
   </a>
</xfa:data>
```

2 | New Features and Changes

This section summarizes the new features and changes introduced in Acrobat 7.0.5 and earlier.

Acrobat 7.0.5 Changes

Columns 5 and 6 of the quick bars have been removed.

The following properties and methods are introduced in Acrobat 7.0.5:

Collab Object (page 153)	methods: 　　`documentToStream` (page 154)
Data Object (page 167)	properties: 　　`description` (page 167)
Document Object (page 188)	properties: 　　`hostContainer` (page 196) 　　`isModal` (page 198) 　　`viewState` (page 208) methods: 　　`addRequirement` (page 215) 　　`removeRequirement` (page 277)
Embedded PDF Object (page 308)	properties: 　　`messageHandler` (page 308) method: 　　`postMessage` (page 309)
HostContainer Object (page 431)	properties: 　　`messageHandler` (page 431) methods: 　　`postMessage` (page 433)
util Object (page 638)	methods: 　　`crackURL` (page 638)

The following properties and methods are modified in Acrobat 7.0.5:

SOAP Object (page 579)	methods: 　　`request` (page 587) (cRequestStyle and cContent parameters added) 　　`response` (page 595) (cRequestStyle and cContent parameters added)

Acrobat 7.0 Changes

The "Acrobat Multimedia JavaScript Reference", which appeared as a separate document in version 6.0.2, has been merged into the "Acrobat JavaScript Scripting Reference". See the section "Introduced in Acrobat 6.0.2" on page 675 for a listing of all Multimedia JavaScript objects, properties and methods.

Execution of JavaScript through a menu event is no longer privileged. There is now support for executing privileged code in a non-privileged context. See "Privileged versus Non-privileged Context" on page 8 for details.

In versions of Acrobat earlier than 7.0, the JavaScript files `AForm.js`, `ADBC.js`, `Annots.js`, `AnWizard.js`, `media.js`, and `SOAP.js` resided in the App JavaScript folder. Beginning with Acrobat 7.0, these files are not shipped with Acrobat Professional, Acrobat Standard or Adobe Reader. In their place, a precompiled bytecode is used to improve performance. The `debugger.js` file in the App folder is not included in the bytecode.

Files in the User JavaScript folder are not included in the precompiled bytecode file.

It is recommended that users put their own `.js` files in the User JavaScript folder, the same place where `glob.js` resides. JavaScript code that sets up menu items (`addMenuItem`, page 59) should be put in `config.js` in the User JavaScript folder. The location of this folder can be found programmatically by executing `app.getPath("user","javascript")` from the console.

Adobe Reader now has a console window. There is a preference under **Edit > Preferences > General > JavaScript** to **Show console on errors and messages**. In addition to errors and exceptions, the console can also be opened programmatically with `console.show()`. See the console Object (page 164) for a few other details.

The debugging capability of the JavaScript Debugging window can be made available for Adobe Reader for Windows and Macintosh platforms. To debug within Adobe Reader, the JavaScript file `debugger.js` needs to be installed, and the windows registry needs to be edited appropriately. See the *Acrobat JavaScript Scripting Guide* for the technical details.

Introduced in Acrobat 7.0

The following properties and methods are introduced in Acrobat 7.0.

Alerter Object (page 14)	methods: `dispatch` (page 14)
Annotation Object (page 19)	properties: `callout` (page 27) `caretSymbol` (page 27)[a] `creationDate` (page 28)[a] `dash` (page 28)[b] `delay` (page 29)[b] `doCaption` (page 29) `intent` (page 31) `leaderExtend` (page 31) `leaderLength` (page 32) `lineEnding` (page 32) `opacity` (page 34)[b] `refType` (page 37) `richDefaults` (page 38)[a] `seqNum` (page 38)[b] `state` (page 39)[a] `stateModel` (page 39)[a] `style` (page 40) `subject` (page 40)[a]
Annot3D Object (page 47)	properties: `activated` (page 47) `context3D` (page 47) `innerRect` (page 47) `name` (page 48) `page` (page 48) `rect` (page 48)

Adobe® Acrobat® Official JavaScript Reference

| XMLData Object (page 650) | methods:
applyXPath (page 650)
parse (page 654) |

a. Present in version 6.0, documented in version 7.0.
b. Present in version 5.0, documented in version 7.0.

Modified in Acrobat 7.0

Changed or Enhanced Objects, Methods, and Properties

The following properties and methods have been changed or enhanced:

app Object (page 49)	methods: addToolButton (page 62) execMenuItem (page 84) getPath (page 86) mailGetAddrs (page 92) openDoc (page 97)
console Object (page 164)	The console window is now available in Adobe Reader.
Document Object (page 188)	methods: createTemplate (page 227) mailDoc (page 268) print (page 273) saveAs (page 282) submitForm (page 295)
Field Object (page 371)	methods: signatureSetSeedValue (page 418)
Index Object (page 437)	methods: build (page 438)
OCG Object (page 485)	properties: name (page 486)
PrintParams Object (page 500)	properties: pageHandling (page 510)
search Object (page 538)	properties: indexes (page 540)

security Object (page 546)	properties: `handlers` (page 547) methods: `getHandler` (page 553)

SecurityHandler Object (page 557)	properties:
	
	`digitalIDs` (page 558)
	
	methods:
	
	    `login` (page 562)
	
	    `newUser` (page 566)

SOAP Object (page 579)	methods:
	
	    `connect` (page 579)
	
	    `request` (page 587)

spell Object (page 605)	The Spell object is not available in Adobe Reader 7.0 or later. methods: `addWord` (page 609)
util Object (page 638)	methods: `printd` (page 639)

Acrobat 6.0 Changes

The notion of a safe path is introduced for this version of Acrobat. See "Safe Path" on page 8 for details.

Introduced in Acrobat 6.0

The following properties and methods are introduced in Acrobat 6:

ADBC Object	`SQL Types` (page 10)

AlternatePresentation Object (page 17)	properties:
	
	    `active` (page 17)
	
	    `type` (page 17)
	
	methods:
	
	    `start` (page 17)
	
	    `stop` (page 18)

Connection Object (page 161)	methods: close (page 161)
dbg Object (page 170)	properties: bps (page 170) methods: c (page 171) cb (page 171) q (page 172) sb (page 172) si (page 173) sn (page 173) so (page 174) sv (page 174)
Directory Object (page 184)	properties: info (page 184) methods: connect (page 187)
DirConnection Object (page 178)	properties: canList (page 178) canDoCustomSearch (page 178) canDoCustomUISearch (page 179) canDoStandardSearch (page 179) groups (page 179) name (page 179) uiName (page 180) methods: search (page 180) setOutputFields (page 182)

Modified in Acrobat 6.0

Changed or Enhanced Objects, Methods, and Properties

The following properties and methods have been changed or enhanced:

app Object (page 49)	methods: addMenuItem (page 59) alert (page 64) listMenuItems (page 90) listToolbarButtons (page 91) response (page 103)
Document Object (page 188)	properties: layout (page 199) zoomType (page 209) methods: createDataObject (page 226) exportAsFDF (page 235) exportAsXFDF (page 237) exportDataObject (page 238) flattenPages (page 243) getField (page 248) (see Extended Methods) getURL (page 259) importDataObject (page 262) importIcon (page 263) print (page 273) saveAs (page 282) spawnPageFromTemplate (page 293) submitForm (page 295)
event Object (page 314)	properties: changeEx (page 327)
Field Object (page 371)	properties: name (page 388) methods: buttonImportIcon (page 401) signatureInfo (page 416) signatureSign (page 421) signatureValidate (page 423)

global Object (page 428)	Persistent global data only applies to variables of type Boolean, Number or String. Acrobat 6.0 has reduced the maximum size of global persistent variables from 32 KB to 2-4 KB. Any data added to the string after this limit is dropped.
search Object (page 538)	methods: query (page 544)
SecurityHandler Object (page 557)	The following were introduced in Acrobat 5.0 as properties and methods of the PPKLite Signature Handler Object. In Acrobat 6.0, they are properties and methods of the SecurityHandler Object. All of these have new descriptions, and some have additional parameters. **Note:** When signing using JavaScript methods, the user's digital signature profile must be a .pfx file, not an .apf, as in earlier versions of Acrobat. To convert an .apf profile to the new .pfx type, use the UI (**Advanced > Manage Digital IDs > My Digital ID Files > Select My Digital ID File**) to import the .apf profile. properties: appearances (page 558) isLoggedIn (page 560) loginName (page 560) loginPath (page 560) name (page 561) signInvisible (page 561) signVisible (page 562) uiName (page 562) methods: login (page 562) logout (page 565) newUser (page 566) setPasswordTimeout (page 568)
Template Object (page 625)t	methods: spawn (page 625)

Extended Methods

The doc.getField (page 248) method has been extended in Acrobat 6.0 so that it retrieves the Field Object (page 371) of individual widgets. See the Field Object for a discussion of widgets and how to work with them.

Deprecated in Acrobat 6.0

search Object	properties:
	`soundex` (page 542)
	`thesaurus` (page 543)
spell Object	methods:
	`addDictionary` (page 608)
	`removeDictionary` (page 617)

Introduced in Acrobat 6.0.2

The following objects, properties and methods are introduced in Acrobat 6.0.2:

XFA Object	

The following table lists the objects, properties and methods of the Multimedia plugin. In Acrobat 6.0.2, multimedia JavaScript was documented in a separate document called the "Acrobat Multimedia JavaScript Reference".

app Object	properties:
	`media` (page 53)
	`monitors` (page 54)
app.media Object (page 115)	properties:
	`align` (page 115)
	`canResize` (page 116)
	`closeReason` (page 116)
	`defaultVisible` (page 116)
	`ifOffScreen` (page 117)
	`layout` (page 117)
	`monitorType` (page 117)
	`openCode` (page 118)
	`over` (page 118)
	`pageEventNames` (page 119)
	`raiseCode` (page 119)
	`raiseSystem` (page 120)
	`renditionType` (page 120)
	`status` (page 120)
	`trace` (page 121)
	`version` (page 121)
	`windowType` (page 121)

app.media Object (continued)	methods:
	`addStockEvents` (page 122)
	`alertFileNotFound` (page 122)
	`alertSelectFailed` (page 123)
	`argsDWIM` (page 124)
	`canPlayOrAlert` (page 124)
	`computeFloatWinRect` (page 125)
	`constrainRectToScreen` (page 126)
	`createPlayer` (page 126)
	`getAltTextData` (page 129)
	`getAltTextSettings` (page 129)
	`getAnnotStockEvents` (page 130)
	`getAnnotTraceEvents` (page 131)
	`getPlayers` (page 131)
	`getPlayerStockEvents` (page 132)
	`getPlayerTraceEvents` (page 133)
	`getRenditionSettings` (page 133)
	`getURLData` (page 133)
	`getURLSettings` (page 134)
	`getWindowBorderSize` (page 136)
	`openPlayer` (page 136)
	`removeStockEvents` (page 138)
	`startPlayer` (page 138)
Document Object (page 188)	properties:
	`innerAppWindowRect` (page 198)
	`innerDocWindowRect` (page 198)
	`media` (page 199)
	`outerAppWindowRect` (page 203)
	`outerDocWindowRect` (page 203)
	`pageWindowRect` (page 204)
Doc.media Object (page 302)	properties:
	`canPlay` (page 302)
	methods:
	`deleteRendition` (page 303)
	`getAnnot` (page 303)
	`getAnnots` (page 304)
	`getRendition` (page 306)
	`newPlayer` (page 306)
event Object (page 314)	A new Screen type used with Multimedia along with associated event names.

Events Object (page 358)	methods:
	add (page 358)
	dispatch (page 359)
	remove (page 361)
EventListener Object (page 338)	methods:
	afterBlur (page 339)
	afterClose (page 340)
	afterDestroy (page 340)
	afterDone (page 341)
	afterError (page 341)
	afterEscape (page 342)
	afterEveryEvent (page 342)
	afterFocus (page 343)
	afterPause (page 344)
	afterPlay (page 344)
	afterReady (page 344)
	afterScript (page 346)
	afterSeek (page 347)
	afterStatus (page 348)
	afterStop (page 348)
	onBlur (page 349)
	onClose (page 349)
	onDestroy (page 350)
	onDone (page 351)
	onError (page 351)
	onEscape (page 352)
	onEveryEvent (page 352)
	onFocus (page 353)
	onGetRect (page 353)
	onPause (page 354)
	onPlay (page 355)
	onReady (page 355)
	onScript (page 355)
	onSeek (page 356)
	onStatus (page 357)
	onStop (page 357)

Adobe® Acrobat® Official JavaScript Reference

Rendition Object (page 520)	properties: `altText` (page 520) `doc` (page 520) `fileName` (page 520) `type` (page 521) `uiName` (page 521) methods: `getPlaySettings` (page 522) `select` (page 523) `testCriteria` (page 524)
ScreenAnnot Object (page 533)	properties: `altText` (page 533) `alwaysShowFocus` (page 533) `display` (page 533) `doc` (page 534) `events` (page 534) `extFocusRect` (page 535) `innerDeviceRect` (page 535) `noTrigger` (page 535) `outerDeviceRect` (page 536) `page` (page 536) `player` (page 536) `rect` (page 536) methods: `hasFocus` (page 537) `setFocus` (page 537)

Acrobat 5.0 Changes

Introduced in Acrobat 5.0

ADBC Object (page 10)	methods:
	    `getDataSourceList` (page 12)
	    `newConnection` (page 12)

Annotation Object (page 19)	properties:
	    `alignment` (page 24)
	    `AP` (page 25)
	    `arrowBegin` (page 25)
	    `arrowEnd` (page 26)
	    `author` (page 27)
	    `contents` (page 28)
	    `doc` (page 29)
	    `fillColor` (page 30)
	    `hidden` (page 30)
	    `modDate` (page 32)
	    `name` (page 33)
	    `noView` (page 34)
	    `page` (page 34)
	    `point` (page 34)
	    `points` (page 35)
	    `popupRect` (page 36)
	    `print` (page 36)
	    `rect` (page 36)
	    `readOnly` (page 37)
	    `rotate` (page 38)
	    `strokeColor` (page 39)
	    `textFont` (page 40)
	    `type` (page 41)
	    `soundIcon` (page 39)
	    `width` (page 42)
	methods:
	    `destroy` (page 42)
	    `getProps` (page 43)
	    `setProps` (page 45)

Adobe® Acrobat® Official JavaScript Reference

PPKLite Signature Handler Object, now listed under the SecurityHandler Object (page 557)	properties:
	appearances (page 558)
	isLoggedIn (page 560)
	loginName (page 560)
	loginPath (page 560)
	name (page 561)
	signInvisible (page 561)
	signVisible (page 562)
	uiName (page 562)
	methods:
	login (page 562)
	logout (page 565)
	newUser (page 566)
	setPasswordTimeout (page 568)
Report Object (page 525)	properties:
	absIndent (page 525)
	color (page 525)
	absIndent (page 525)
	methods:
	breakPage (page 526)
	divide (page 527)
	indent (page 527)
	outdent (page 529)
	open (page 528)
	mail (page 527)
	writeText (page 530)
	save (page 529)
	writeText (page 530)

Statement Object (page 619)	properties:
	columnCount (page 619)
	rowCount (page 619)
	methods:
	execute (page 619)
	getColumn (page 620)
	getColumnArray (page 620)
	getRow (page 621)
	nextRow (page 622)
Template Object (page 625)	properties:
	hidden (page 625)
	name (page 625)
	methods:
	spawn (page 625)

Modified in Acrobat 5.0

The console can act as an editor and can execute JavaScript code.

The following properties and methods have been changed or enhanced:

app Object (page 49)	language (page 53)
	execMenuItem (page 84)
Document Object (page 188)	exportAsFDF (page 235)
	print (page 273)
	submitForm (page 295)
event Object (page 314)	type (page 335)
Field Object (page 371)	textFont (page 396)
	value (page 398)
	buttonImportIcon (page 401)
	getItemAt (page 407)
util Object (page 638)	printd (page 639)

The section related to event Object (page 314) has been greatly enhanced to facilitate better understanding of the Acrobat JavaScript Event model.

Adobe® Acrobat® Official JavaScript Reference

Deprecated in Acrobat 5.0

The following properties and methods have been deprecated:

app Object (page 49)	`fullscreen` (page 52)
	`numPlugIns` (page 54)
	`getNthPlugInName` (page 86)
Document Object (page 188)	`author` (page 190)
	`creationDate` (page 191)
	`creationDate` (page 191)
	`keywords` (page 199)
	`modDate` (page 200)
	`numTemplates` (page 203)
	`producer` (page 205)
	`title` (page 208)
	`getNthTemplate` (page 252)
	`spawnPageFromTemplate` (page 293)
Field Object (page 371)	`hidden` (page 386)
TTS Object (page 633)	`soundCues` (page 634)
	`speechCues` (page 634)

Modified in Acrobat 5.05

- A new symbol has been added to the quick bar denoting which methods are missing from Acrobat™ Approval™.
- In the Document Object (page 188), the property `disclosed` (page 193) has been added.

Modified in Adobe 5.1 Reader

Access to the following properties and methods has changed for the Adobe 5.1 Reader:

Annotation Object (page 19)	properties:		
	alignment (page 24)	modDate (page 32)	readOnly (page 37)
	AP (page 25)	name (page 33)	rotate (page 38)
	arrowBegin (page 25)	noView (page 34)	strokeColor (page 39)
	arrowEnd (page 26)	page (page 34)	textFont (page 40)
	author (page 27)	point (page 34)	type (page 41)
	contents (page 28)	points (page 35)	soundIcon (page 39)
	doc (page 29)	popupRect (page 36)	width (page 42)
	fillColor (page 30)	print (page 36)	
	hidden (page 30)	rect (page 36)	
	methods:		
	destroy (page 42)		
	getProps (page 43)		
	setProps (page 45)		
Document Object (page 188)	properties:		
	selectedAnnots (page 206)		
	methods:		
	addAnnot (page 209)	importAnXFDF (page 261)	
	addField (page 211)	importDataObject (page 262)	
	exportAsFDF (page 235)	mailDoc (page 268)	
	exportAsXFDF (page 237)	mailForm (page 270)	
	getAnnot (page 244)	spawnPageFromTemplate (page 293)	
	getAnnots (page 245)	submitForm (page 295)	
	getNthTemplate (page 252)	syncAnnotScan (page 300)	
	importAnFDF (page 261)		
Template Object (page 625)	methods:		
	spawn (page 625)		

QA
76.9
.F48
A38
2006

Adobe Acrobat 7.0.

$39.99

DATE			